There are many large businesses that understand and value the work PIE carry out in pulling together essential journey planning information to create a high quality, comprehensive and customised mapping guide for disabled drivers.

The following businesses have been supportive of PIE and our main sponsors The Highways Agency and Direct Gov in getting involved with this atlas. PIE would like to offer our thanks for their help.

Balfour Beatty

Balfour Beatty is a world-class engineering, construction services and investment group, well positioned in infrastructure markets which offer significant long-term growth potential. We aim to work in partnership with sophisticated customers for whom infrastructure quality, reliability and efficiency are critical. Our skills are applied in appropriate combinations to meet individual customer needs. We deliver projects that directly improve the lives of people and their communities.

Costain Highways Sector Information

Costain is one of the countries leading construction companies and is recognised for successfully delivering major road schemes throughout the UK. Costain aims to be the No1 provider of highway solution services to all its customers and is committed to working with the Public Information Exchange Group in raising awareness of disabled road users in the UK.

A-one+

A-one+ is a fully integrated highway services joint venture company. In November 2007 A-one+ was appointed as the new Managing Agent Contractor for the Highways Agency's Area 10, which comprises some 500km of motorway and trunk road carriageway and over 2,500 structures throughout Greater Manchester, Cheshire, Merseyside and southern Lancashire. As Managing Agent Contractor, A-one+ is responsible for the day to day operational management and maintenance of the motorway and trunk road network on behalf of the Highways Agency.

Grontmij

Grontmij is a multi-disciplinary engineering consultancy. Our structure, size and strength mean that we can deliver solutions to our clients' challenges on a local, national and international level. We have planned and designed many roads you will find in this Atlas, including the A1(M) in Yorkshire, the M6 in Cumbria and the A1 East of Edinburgh.

AECOM

AECOM is one of the World's most experienced and innovative transportation consultancies. We are not only delivering many of the transport investments needed today but helping to set the agenda for tomorrow. It is our policy to ensure that disability equality is addressed by all those responsible for the organisations major functions and that it is taken account of in policy making and in the day-to day work of employment practice and service delivery.

Carillion

Carillion is the UK's leading support services company with a substantial portfolio of Public Private Partnership projects and an extensive construction business. In the inaugural Sunday Times Best Green Companies Awards in May 2008, Carillion secured first place in the category for large and medium-sized companies with low environmental impact and second place overall.

Skanska

Skanska UK is part of Skanska, one of the world's leading construction groups with expertise in construction, development of commercial and residential projects and public-private partnerships. The Group currently has 60,000 employees in selected home markets in Europe, in the US and Latin America.

Concise Blue Badge UK Road Atlas

Contents

Collins

Specially produced for PIE Enterprises Ltd by Collins, a subsidiary of
HarperCollinsPublishers Ltd.
Mapping © Collins Bartholomew 2008   Tel: 01242 258155

The British city and town population figures are derived from 2001 Census.
Source: National Statistics website: www.statistics.gov.uk
Crown copyright material is reproduced with the permission of the Controller of HMSO.

Information specific to Blue Badge users supplied by PIE Enterprises
© PIE 2008   All rights reserved www.pieguide.com

Accommodation information supplied by Visit Britain / Visit Scotland with caravan
information supplied by Haymarket

PIE would like to give special thanks to Highways Agency, Directgov and VisitBritain for
their support.

General enquires and trade sales: 020 7952 0459   Fax: 020 7952 0451
Email: info@thepieguide.com   www.thepieguide.com

ISBN 978-0-9551711-8-5
Printed in Italy

Be *i*nspired
by Hyundai today

i30

Special Blue Badge savings from your local dealer

- Our wide range of small city cars to 8 seaters
  are all at great prices and brilliantly well equipped

- All models are covered by our Five Year Warranty

- Special terms available for Blue Badge holders. To check special rates
  visit: **www.hyundaiaffinities.co.uk** and enter Affinity code A04 .

fiveyear
w a r r a n t y

Or call on **0845 270 66 84**

HYUNDAI   www.hyundai.co.uk

Models featured: i10, i30, Santa Fe and i800. Discounts vary by model, see terms and conditions for further information.

The Hyundai model range is constantly evolving, and whilst the models shown are all current at the time of publication, please check with your dealer to confirm the availability of these or car models. Offers available for Blue Badge holders only and apply to new cars, subject to availability and may be varied or withdrawn at any time. See your local authorised participating dealer for full terms and conditions of the offers and other purchase terms. Models shown are for illustration purposes only, colour and design details may vary. Metallic paint and any other options are available at an additional cost on all models.

New passenger cars purchased in the UK and sourced through Hyundai Motor UK Limited or its authorised dealers come with Hyundai's 5 year warranty, see your local dealer for full warranty term and conditions. This offer is not to be used in conjunction with any other offer, including but not limited to low or 0% finance offers.

Fuel Consumption in l/100km (mpg) for Hyundai range: Urban 5.5 (51.4) - 15.1 (18.7), Extra urban 3.9 (72.4) - 8.4 (33.6), Combined 4.5 (62.8) - 10.6 (26.6), CO_2 Emissions 118 - 252 g/km.

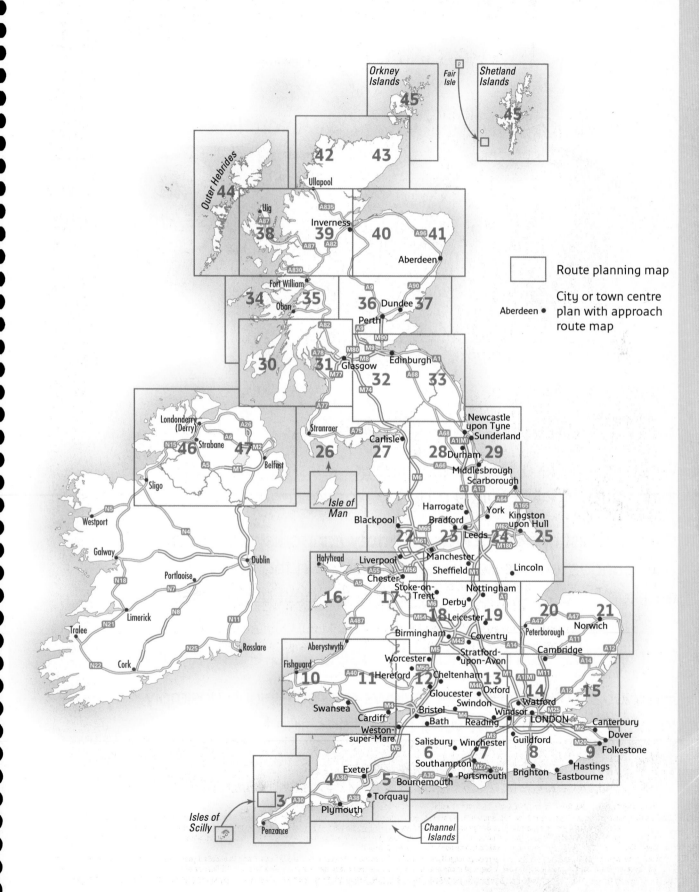

Orkney Islands **45**

Fair Isle

Shetland Islands **45**

Outer Hebrides **44**

42 **43**

Ullapool

Uig

38 Inverness **39** **40** **41**

Aberdeen

Fort William

34 **35** **36** Dundee **37**

Oban Perth

Glasgow **31** **32** **33** Edinburgh

30

Stranraer

Carlisle

Newcastle upon Tyne

26 **27** **28** Durham **29** Sunderland

Londonderry (Derry)

Strabane

46 **47** Belfast

Sligo

Middlesbrough Scarborough

Westport

Isle of Man

Harrogate Bradford York Kingston upon Hull

Blackpool **22** **23** Leeds **24** **25**

Galway

Dublin

Holyhead Liverpool Manchester Sheffield Lincoln

Chester Stoke-on-Trent

Portlaoise **16** **1** Derby Nottingham

Limerick

18 Leicester **19** **20** **21** Norwich

Tralee

Birmingham Coventry Peterborough

Cork Rosslare

Aberystwyth Worcester Stratford-upon-Avon Cambridge

Fishguard Hereford Cheltenham **13** **14** **15**

10 **11** **12** Gloucester Oxford Watford

Swansea Swindon Windsor LONDON

Cardiff Bristol Bath Reading Canterbury Dover

Weston-super-Mare Guildford Folkestone

Salisbury Winchester **8** **9**

6 **7** Brighton Hastings Eastbourne

Southampton Portsmouth

Exeter Bournemouth

4 **5** Torquay

3 Plymouth

Isles of Scilly Penzance

Channel Islands

Route planning map

Aberdeen ● City or town centre plan with approach route map

Airport Parking, Hotels, Lounges & more...

Wherever you're off to, we can help you arrange all the little things that make travelling a better experience.

With a full list of **blue badge friendly** car parks, airport hotels and lounges, our service has won acclaim in the national press and can save you a packet by finding the best deals online.

Our service is impartial, unbiased and easy to use

With 1000's of real customer reviews and our unique gosimply rating system, you know you'll be getting value for money.

That's why smart people gosimply

www.gosimply.com/thepieguide

Welcome to the new PIE guide for Blue Badge drivers. This revised and fully updated edition is a comprehensive UK wide atlas customised for disabled people.

We received a lot of positive encouragement from our first edition with specific advice that we need to 'keep up the good work'. This is most encouraging and thank you for the words of support and encouragement.

There are quite a few differences within this new guide. The principal difference which has been fed back many times is to change the guide to a spiral binding. We have now achieved this whilst keeping the overall cost down which is now priced lower than the first edition guide.

This guide is now much more locally focused to enable you to get a better picture of the facilities in and around these key areas. This includes town plan maps. We have always been asked for more toilet information, which we have added into the town plans, and detailed in the Motorway Service station overview.

Comprehensive journey planning facilities for disabled drivers was a key objective in this revised guide. We specifically sought to work with The Highways Agency who has been most supportive and keen to get journey planning advice to disabled drivers. We asked The Highways Agency to detail out what to do in the case of an emergency and who to call. Also to get more up to date information about journey times, before heading out and while also out on the road. So please look through the Highways Agency section to get familiar with their services.

Parking Rules. We have re-surveyed all the parking bay locations and all the on street parking rules have been updated. We have updated the council table and contact numbers in case you need to speak with council specific experts on the Blue Badge side.

Please note not all car parks are free for blue badge drivers. We have surveyed and customised the icon for each car park to give you advice if the car park is discounted or free for Blue Badge drivers, as well as important things such as height restrictions and accessibility once in the car park.

We have updated the accessible accommodation, partnering with Visit Britain to ensure we have creditable sites. We also have included the 'Exceptional' category whereby a site has met all the standards and is exceptional in terms of accessibility.

Special thanks needs to go to our sponsors in committing their support to this publication along with the various advertisers.

Thank you again to all our existing customers, for users of this guide I hope it makes your life easier and becomes an essential reference for you. Please feel free to send any feedback or comments you have about this guide directly to the email address: info@thepieguide.com

Many thanks

Freddie Talberg
CEO
Public Information Exchange (PIE)
freddie@thepieguide.com

For people with disabilities, travelling by car is the easiest way to get around. The Blue Badge Scheme offers special parking concessions for some people with disabilities e.g. it allows badge holders to park close to their destination. The concessions typically apply only to on street parking but some concessions apply in selected car parks. This fully updated UK atlas illustrates the various concessions throughout the UK from on street city and town centre parking options to concessions close to your destination.

Blue Badge holders are entitled to parking concessions in other EU member states. The latest 'The Blue Badge Scheme: rights and responsibilities in England' leaflet, available from the Department for Transport, explains the concessions and lists all the countries. This leaflet is available from DfT publications 0870 1226 236.

On-street parking concessions

Listed below are the various on-street parking options for Blue Badge holders. You may already be aware that some of the concessions vary across the local authorities with some operating their own local parking concession scheme. You should always check the local street signs to see if such a scheme is in operation. This Guide illustrates where on-street is available and what the concessions are so you can check your destination point before you leave.

The on-street parking options include;

Single & double yellow lines

A Blue Badge holder is usually permitted to park on single or double yellow lines in most areas typically up to 3 hours except where loading restrictions apply. You must ensure

you are not causing an obstruction. Use your clock to indicate your arrival time. Clocks are not required in Scotland where no time limit exists. Blue Badge holders living in Scotland who intend visiting England or Wales should be able to obtain a clock from their local Council.

Red Route box bays

Red Routes mark out important roads identified by the red no-stopping lines or signs along the route. No stopping is permitted on these routes. Red boxes marked on the road indicate that parking, or loading is permitted during the off peak times, normally between 10am and 4 pm. There are specific red route parking box bays which have no time limits and red route loading box bays that typically provide a maximum of 3 hours stay for Blue Badge holders. Ensure you check this time limit and try not to use these during the rush hours.

Pay & Display or metered parking

Badge holders may park free of charge and without time limit at on-street parking meters and on-street pay & display meters unless a local time limit is in force. Payment for parking on Pay & Display or meters (where they still exist) does apply in some areas. Certain Councils provide a period of time free of charge once an initial payment has been made. Please note if your disability prevents you reaching the slot to put your money in, you will need to write to the Council to explain this if you get a ticket

County	Council	
England		
Bedfordshire	Bedford B C	✔
Bedfordshire	Luton B C	✔ Max stay !
Bedfordshire	Mid Bedfordshire D C	✔
Bedfordshire	South Bedfordshire D C	✔ Except when signs display the limit
Berkshire	Bracknell Forest B C	✔
Berkshire	Reading B C	✔ Max stay 4hrs
Berkshire	Slough B C	✔ Max stay !
Berkshire	West Berkshire C	✔

Pay & Display machines often do not give any information on the concessions for Blue Badge holders, however the machines do indicate which Borough they belong to. We have created a table to help you identify the rules for a specific council together with Council telephone details for the Blue Badge scheme. Many authorities, especially coastal authorities, will only offer parking concessions to Blue Badge holders who also display a tax disc indicating their vehicle is taxed in the disabled class and their vehicle is exempt from the road fund licence.

Cashless/Mobile phone payment for Pay & Display (Pay by Phone)

Some Councils are introducing cashless payment for Pay & Display parking. For councils where payment is required by Blue Badge holders you still get the free period of time but the payment needs to be made via mobile phone. You will need to register in advance and set up an account. There are some bays now that are only payable by mobile so be careful if you do not have a mobile or have not pre-registered. Note that until we get a centralised scheme you are likely to need to register with each

Council that operates a Pay by Phone scheme and will still need to display your Blue Badge.

Blue Badge parking bays

You may park without time restriction for free in Blue Badge parking bays which have no maximum stay, unless the signs show a time limit. Be aware in some areas there are signs still appearing in orange. Please note on our map we put the number of hours maximum stay within the symbol. Where it is marked 'U' this means unlimited (no maximum time limit) and where they are marked with a '!' this means check signs locally as times vary.

Residents' parking

You may not park in a residents' parking bay, unless signs to the contrary are displayed. Residents' parking provides a large area of parking spaces in some boroughs. Not all residents' spaces are free for use by Blue Badge holders. See table on page xxix.

Shared use bay

Shared use bays in some Boroughs are a combination of Pay & Display as well as residents parking.

Where NOT to park

Loading bans

Loading bans are shown by a single or double stripe on the kerb. Please ensure you do not park here. You are permitted to pick up or set down a passenger only. Loading bans are typically found on junctions, corners and the entrance or exit of streets. The double stripes indicate no loading at any time while the single stripe should have a post mounted plate indicating the times no loading/unloading is permitted. If there is an arrow on the sign, it indicates the direction in which the prohibition starts.

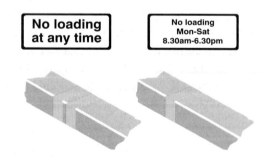

Pedestrian areas

Please note in pedestrian areas, waiting and loading restrictions may be in force even where there are no yellow lines shown on the road or stripes on the kerb. The restrictions in force should be shown on plates displayed at the kerbside.

Red Routes

Red Routes are becoming more widespread appearing in London, the West Midlands and Scotland which prohibit parking for Blue Badge holders within the controlling hours. You can only stop briefly to set down or pick up the badge holder. Stopping to set down other non-disabled passengers is not permitted. Taxis are also permitted to drop down and pick up on Red Routes. There are loading and parking bays available on these routes for parking, please check the signs for times.

Clearways

Some areas are protected by clearway restrictions at certain times (check the plate). On a clearway stopping is not permitted and there is no concession for Blue Badge holders. You must not park where there are double white lines in the centre of the road or even broken white lines.

Others areas NOT permitted to park include;

- Bus lanes and bus stops during the hours of operation. You are allowed to enter a bus lane to pick up and set down. There may be some kerbside restrictions so keep an eye on these. The distance driven in the bus lane needs to be minimal and you cannot enter any bus lane that is 'Bus-only routes'. CCTV is used to enforce these lanes so ensure your Blue Badge is visible.

- Cycle lanes or pavements, footways or verges (except in areas where there are signs showing it is legal).

- On any pedestrian crossing which includes Zebra, Pelican, Toucan (for bicycles) and Puffin crossings.

- Next to any dropped footway either across a driveway or where the kerb has been lowered for pedestrians to cross.

- On zig-zag markings used typically before and after pedestrian crossings or school entrances and on markings where is it is written **KEEP CLEAR**.

- Blue Badge rules do **NOT** often apply at airports.

Other Bay types NOT permitted to park

Do not park in suspended bays (shown by a yellow no parking sign or cones) or business, trader, doctor, police, diplomat, ambulance, motorcycle, or similar bays including taxi ranks. Blue Badge holders are not permitted to use dedicated disabled badge holder bays (indicated by a sign or painted on the street), often with a permit number painted by it.

Local Badge schemes operate in certain Cities in the UK

You may be aware that within Central London the following boroughs have their own registered disabled badge scheme for residents as well as their business residents; Westminster (white badge), Corporation of London (red badge), Kensington and Chelsea (purple badge) and Camden (green badge). Some other cities within the UK also operate their own scheme. Always check the signs to see if a local scheme is in operation.

P **Disabled parking place** Permit DIS. 132 only at any time

Congestion Charging Schemes

London congestion charge

Blue Badge holders are eligible for a 100% discount from congestion charging after registering and making a one-off payment of £10. If your vehicle is exempt from excise duty (road tax) you do not need to register for your discount. For more information contact Transport for London on 0845 900 1234 or visit www.tfl.gov.uk

Durham congestion charge

The Durham Road User Charge applies to vehicles accessing the historic city centre and the approach to Durham's cathedral and castle. A charge of £2 per vehicle applies between 10am and 4pm, Monday to Friday. Disabled people can be issued with an exemption permit by the establishment they are visiting or can reserve a permit in advance provided they have pre-arranged a parking space in advance by contacting NCP Parking Shop on 0191 3846633. Permits are not available where the purpose of the journey is to set down or pick up passengers.

Hazardous places where you should not park

You must ensure you do **NOT** park where it would endanger, obstruct or inconvenience pedestrians or other road users.

For example:

- On a bend in a road
- Near the brow of a hill
- Hump back bridge
- Close to junctions where it would make it difficult for others to see clearly
- By a traffic island, road works etc. where you would make the road much narrower
- Blocking vehicle entrances, particularly emergency vehicles. For further guidance consult **The Highway Code**.

Important to know

Your vehicle cannot legally be wheel clamped on the public highway for parking offences provided a valid Blue Badge is correctly displayed. Be aware that if you park improperly on privately owned land you may risk having your vehicle clamped. If you park where it would cause an obstruction or be a danger to other road users your vehicle could be removed. You could also be prosecuted and your badge withdrawn.

CCTV is being used extensively for bus lanes and parking contraventions enforcement. The cameras may not always pick out the Blue Badge and it is more than likely you will need to appeal these tickets. The cameras also capture moving traffic offences which Blue Badge holders are not exempt from.

What to do if?

- Blue Badge is stolen – report the theft immediately to the Police. The crime reference is likely to be required before a replacement badge can be issued.

- Towed away or clamped – If your Blue Badge is displayed you should not be clamped or towed away even if you park illegally. If the vehicle is causing an obstruction it may be repositioned, but usually to a nearby street.

- Car is missing – If your vehicle is missing call the **TRACE** service 020 7747 4747 (24 hours). They will be able to confirm if it has been towed away and where it has removed to.

- You get a Parking Ticket, Red Route or Bus lane violation (Penalty Charge Notices or PCN) – do not ignore it. You may have to pay more if you do not either pay or contest the ticket promptly. If you want to contest the ticket write to the council concerned.

Fixed Penalty Notices (FPN) are issued by the Police. If you want to contest the ticket you must ask for a court hearing by typically writing to the address on the back of the ticket.

Your duties as a Badge holder

It is your responsibility to ensure that the badge is used properly. It is in your own interest that the badge should retain the respect of other motorists. Please play your part. Do not allow others to use your Blue Badge – this is a criminal offence. To reduce the risk of this happening accidentally, you should remove the badge whenever you are not using the parking concessions.

You must ensure that the details on the front of the badge remain legible. If they become unreadable, the badge must be returned to the local authority to be re-issued.

Ensure you set your clock and display your badge and clock clearly on the dashboard or facia panel where it can be read through the front windscreen.

Abuse of the Blue Badge Scheme

There are several ways in which Blue Badges can be misused. These include:

- Use of the badge when no longer valid.

- Misuse of a valid badge by a friend or relative, with or without the badge holder's knowledge or permission.

- Use by the holder of a badge that has been reported lost or stolen – possibly to obtain another badge for a friend or relative.

- Use of a stolen or copied badge by the thief, forger or someone who has acquired it from them.

Councils are now actively policing Blue Badge abuse.

New Law - Power to inspect

Police officers, traffic wardens, parking attendants and civil enforcement officers NOW have the power to inspect any Blue Badge being used. These people should produce an identity card with a photograph to prove who they are. If they ask to see your badge, you must show it to them; if not, you are breaking the law and could be fined up to £1000.

Only a Police Officer has the power to seize and confiscate lost, stolen, fraudulent, invalid and misused badges.

A gender marker is now being added to the TSO serial number of Blue Badges issued from 15th October 2007. X for male, Y for female to help identify obvious cases of misuse.

Security against Blue Badge theft

Every year thousands of disability parking permits are being stolen that cost Blue Badge holders a replacement broken window and the hassle claiming and waiting for a replacement badge. Ensure your badge is not an easy target to be stolen. When the badge is not required ensure it is kept safely away and out of sight. When you need to use the Badge ensure it is secured within a protective device.

The Blue Badge Protector secures the badge to the car within a metal frame with a lock that feeds through the steering wheel that provides a simple and effective deterrent when parked on the street.

To order the Blue Badge Protector call 0844 847 0875 or order online www.bluebadgeprotector.com. Some local authorities often give these protectors to resident Blue Badge holders.

Finally, ensure you read the signs, set your clock and display your badge and clock clearly.

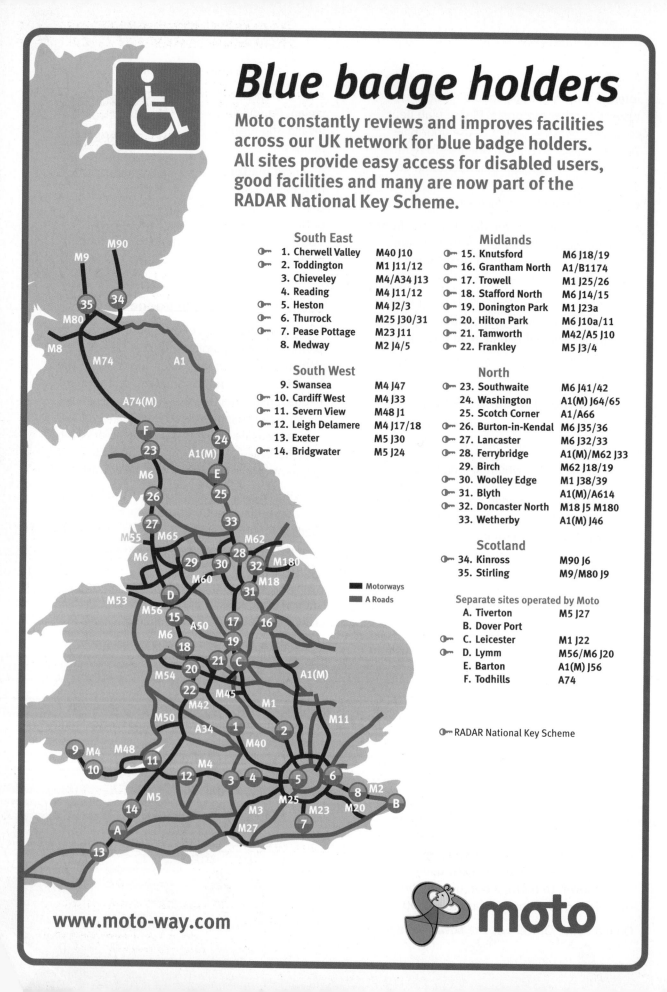

Blue badge holders

Moto constantly reviews and improves facilities across our UK network for blue badge holders. All sites provide easy access for disabled users, good facilities and many are now part of the RADAR National Key Scheme.

South East

☞	1. Cherwell Valley	M40 J10
☞	2. Toddington	M1 J11/12
	3. Chieveley	M4/A34 J13
	4. Reading	M4 J11/12
☞	5. Heston	M4 J2/3
☞	6. Thurrock	M25 J30/31
☞	7. Pease Pottage	M23 J11
	8. Medway	M2 J4/5

South West

	9. Swansea	M4 J47
☞	10. Cardiff West	M4 J33
☞	11. Severn View	M48 J1
☞	12. Leigh Delamere	M4 J17/18
	13. Exeter	M5 J30
☞	14. Bridgwater	M5 J24

Midlands

☞	15. Knutsford	M6 J18/19
☞	16. Grantham North	A1/B1174
☞	17. Trowell	M1 J25/26
☞	18. Stafford North	M6 J14/15
☞	19. Donington Park	M1 J23a
☞	20. Hilton Park	M6 J10a/11
☞	21. Tamworth	M42/A5 J10
☞	22. Frankley	M5 J3/4

North

☞	23. Southwaite	M6 J41/42
	24. Washington	A1(M) J64/65
	25. Scotch Corner	A1/A66
☞	26. Burton-in-Kendal	M6 J35/36
☞	27. Lancaster	M6 J32/33
☞	28. Ferrybridge	A1(M)/M62 J33
	29. Birch	M62 J18/19
☞	30. Woolley Edge	M1 J38/39
☞	31. Blyth	A1(M)/A614
☞	32. Doncaster North	M18 J5 M180
	33. Wetherby	A1(M) J46

Scotland

☞	34. Kinross	M90 J6
	35. Stirling	M9/M80 J9

Separate sites operated by Moto

	A. Tiverton	M5 J27
	B. Dover Port	
☞	C. Leicester	M1 J22
☞	D. Lymm	M56/M6 J20
	E. Barton	A1(M) J56
	F. Todhills	A74

■ Motorways
■ A Roads

☞ RADAR National Key Scheme

www.moto-way.com

moto

There are three major operators of motorway service areas in Britain; RoadChef, Welcome Break and Moto; as well as a small number of independent operators. All motorway service areas are required by law to provide fuel, free toilets and free short term parking 24 hours a day. Details of other facilities provided at each service area are shown opposite, although most of these will not be open 24 hours a day.

As part of its *Think, don't drive tired* road safety campaign the Government has the following tips for drivers:

● If you are feeling tired, opening the window or turning up the radio does not work, instead find a safe place to stop.

● On long journeys take a 15 minute break every 2 hours.

● If feeling tired, a 15 minute nap will help as will drinking 2 cups of coffee or other high caffeine drink. The most effective solution is to have some caffeine and then take a short sleep which gives the caffeine time to kick in.

● Avoid making long trips between midnight and 6am when you are most susceptible to sleepiness.

● Don't begin a journey if you are already feeling tired.

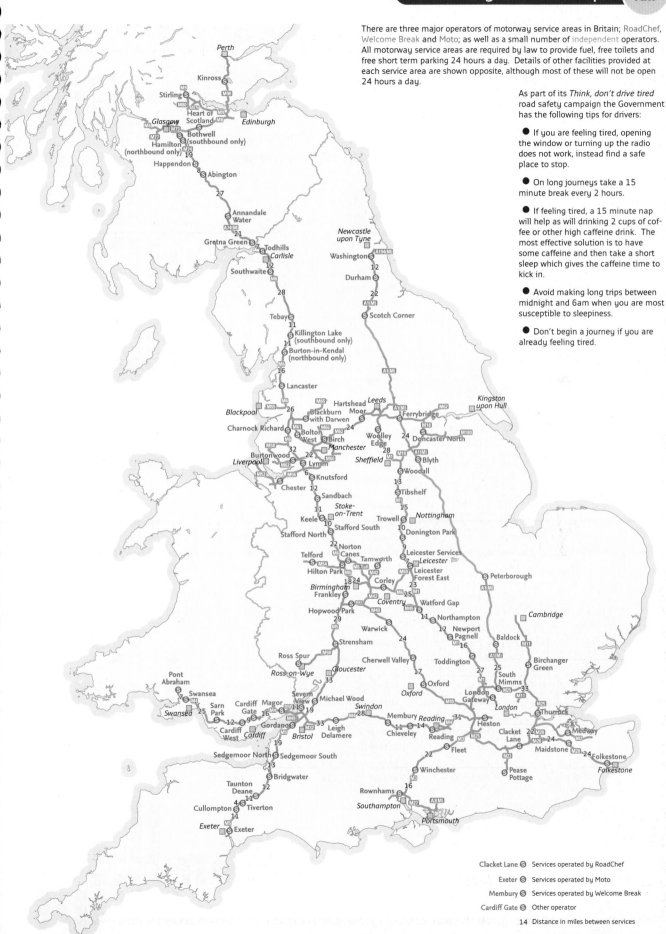

Clacket Lane Ⓢ   Services operated by RoadChef

Exeter Ⓢ   Services operated by Moto

Membury Ⓢ   Services operated by Welcome Break

Cardiff Gate Ⓢ   Other operator

14   Distance in miles between services

Motorway services information

This useful guide indicates where you will find a motorway service station on the main motorways in Great Britain along with information as to the level of service provided. All service areas have fuel, food, toilets, disabled access along with free short term parking, normally two hours. There are three main operators of motorway service areas and if you wish to obtain further information their web sites are listed below.

Moto www.moto-way.com   RoadChef www.roadchef.com   Welcome Break www.welcomebreak.co.uk

Motorway	Junction	Service provider	Service name	Fuel supplier	On-site services
A1(M)	1	Welcome Break	South Mimms	BP	
	10	Extra	Baldock	Shell	
	17	Extra	Peterborough	Shell	
	34	Moto	Blyth	Esso	
	56	Moto	Scotch Corner	Esso	
	61	RoadChef	Durham	Total	
	64	Moto	Washington	Esso	
A74(M)	16	RoadChef	Annandale Water	BP	
	22	Welcome Break	Gretna Green	Shell	
M1	2-4	Welcome Break	London Gateway	Shell	
	11-12	Moto	Toddington	BP	
	14-15	Welcome Break	Newport Pagnell	Shell	
	15A	RoadChef	Northampton	BP	
	16-17	RoadChef	Watford Gap	BP	
	21-21A	Welcome Break	Leicester Forest East	BP	
	22	Moto	Leicester Services	BP	
	23A	Moto	Donington Park	BP	
	25-26	Moto	Trowell	Esso	
	28-29	RoadChef	Tibshelf	Shell	
	30-31	Welcome Break	Woodall	Shell	
	38-39	Moto	Woolley Edge	Esso	
M2	4-5	Moto	Medway	BP	
M3	4A-5	Welcome Break	Fleet	Shell	
	8-9	RoadChef	Winchester	Shell	
M4	3	Moto	Heston	BP	
	11-12	Moto	Reading	BP	
	13	Moto	Chieveley	BP	
	14-15	Welcome Break	Membury	BP	
	17-18	Moto	Leigh Delamere	Esso	
	23A	First Motorway	Magor	Esso	
	30	Welcome Break	Cardiff Gate	Total	
	33	Moto	Cardiff West	Esso	
	36	Welcome Break	Sarn Park	Shell	
	47	Moto	Swansea	BP	
	49	RoadChef	Pont Abraham	BP	
M5	3-4	Moto	Frankley	Esso	
	8	RoadChef	Strensham (South)	BP	
	8	RoadChef	Strensham (North)	Texaco	
	13-14	Welcome Break	Michael Wood	BP	
	19	Welcome Break	Gordano	Shell	
	21-22	RoadChef	Sedgemoor (South)	Esso	
	21-22	Welcome Break	Sedgemoor (North)	Shell	
	24	Moto	Bridgwater	BP	
	25-26	RoadChef	Taunton Deane	Shell	
	27	Moto	Tiverton	Shell	
	28	Extra	Cullompton	Shell	
	29-30	Moto	Exeter	Esso	
M6	3-4	Welcome Break	Corley	Shell	
	10-11	Moto	Hilton Park	BP	
	14-15	RoadChef	Stafford (South)	Esso	
	14-15	Moto	Stafford (North)	BP	

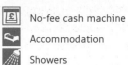

On-site Services:

🔑	National key scheme toilet	💷	Charged cash machine	💷	No-fee cash machine
£	Service shops	i	Information	🛏	Accommodation
££	Other shops	👥	Conference facilities	🚿	Showers

Motorway	Junction	Service provider	Service name	Fuel supplier	On-site services
M6 (continued)	15-16	Welcome Break	Keele	Shell	Charged cash machine, Service shops, Information, Showers
	16-17	RoadChef	Sandbach	Esso	Key toilet, Charged cash machine, Service shops, Accommodation, Showers
	18-19	Moto	Knutsford	BP	Key toilet, Charged cash machine, Service shops, Information, Accommodation, Showers
	20	Moto	Lymm	Total	Key toilet, Charged cash machine, Service shops, Information, Accommodation, Other shops, Showers
	27-28	Welcome Break	Charnock Richard	Shell	Charged cash machine, Service shops
	32-33	Moto	Lancaster	BP	Key toilet, Charged cash machine, Service shops, Information, Accommodation, Other shops, Showers
	35-36	Moto	Burton-in-Kendal (N)	BP	Key toilet, Charged cash machine, Service shops, Information, Showers
	36-37	RoadChef	Killington Lake (S)	BP	Charged cash machine, Service shops, Accommodation
	38-39	Westmorland	Tebay	BP	Key toilet, Charged cash machine, Service shops, Accommodation, Conference facilities, Showers
	41-42	Moto	Southwaite	Esso	Key toilet, Charged cash machine, Service shops, Information, Other shops, Showers
	44-45	Moto	Todhills	BP	Service shops, Accommodation
M6 Toll	T6-T7	RoadChef	Norton Canes	BP	Service shops, Accommodation, Other shops, Conference facilities, Showers
M8	4-5	BP	Heart of Scotland	BP	Service shops, Conference facilities, Showers
M9	9	Moto	Stirling	Esso	Charged cash machine, Service shops, Information, Accommodation, Showers
M11	8	Welcome Break	Birchanger Green	Shell	Charged cash machine, Service shops, Information, Conference facilities, Showers
M18	5	Moto	Doncaster North	BP	Key toilet, Charged cash machine, Service shops, Information, Accommodation, Showers
M20	8	RoadChef	Maidstone	Esso	Key toilet, Service shops, Information, Accommodation, Other shops, Conference facilities, Showers
	11	Stop 24	Folkestone	Shell	Charged cash machine, Service shops, Information, Accommodation, Other shops, Conference facilities, Showers
M23	11	Moto	Pease Pottage	Shell	Key toilet, Charged cash machine, Service shops, Information, Other shops, Showers
M25	5-6	RoadChef	Clacket Lane	Total	Key toilet, Service shops, Information, Accommodation, Other shops, Conference facilities, Showers
	23	Welcome Break	South Mimms	BP	Key toilet, Charged cash machine, Service shops, Information, Accommodation, Other shops, Conference facilities, Showers
	30	Moto	Thurrock	Esso	Key toilet, Charged cash machine, Service shops, Information, Accommodation, Other shops, Showers
M27	3-4	RoadChef	Rownhams	Esso	Charged cash machine, Service shops, Accommodation, Other shops, Conference facilities
M40	8	Welcome Break	Oxford	Shell	Charged cash machine, Service shops, Information, Conference facilities, Showers
	10	Moto	Cherwell Valley	Esso	Charged cash machine, Service shops, Information, Accommodation, Other shops
	12-13	Welcome Break	Warwick	BP	Service shops, Information, Accommodation, Conference facilities, Showers
M42	2	Welcome Break	Hopwood Park	BP	Charged cash machine, Service shops, Information, Other shops, Showers
	10	Moto	Tamworth	Esso	Key toilet, Service shops, Information, Accommodation, Other shops, Showers
M48	1	Moto	Severn View	BP	Key toilet, Charged cash machine, Service shops, Accommodation, Other shops
M50	4	First Motorway	Ross Spur	BP	Service shops, Showers
M54	4	Welcome Break	Telford	Shell	Charged cash machine, Service shops, Information, Accommodation, Conference facilities, Showers
M56	14	RoadChef	Chester	Shell	Key toilet, Charged cash machine, Service shops, Information, Accommodation, Showers
M61	6-7	First Motorway	Bolton West	BP	Charged cash machine, Service shops, Accommodation, Conference facilities, Showers
M62	7-9	Welcome Break	Burtonwood	Shell	Charged cash machine, Service shops, Information, Accommodation, Conference facilities, Showers
	18-19	Moto	Birch	Esso	Charged cash machine, Service shops, Information, Other shops, Conference facilities, Showers
	25-26	Welcome Break	Hartshead Moor	Shell	Charged cash machine, Service shops, Information, Accommodation, Showers
	33	Moto	Ferrybridge	Esso	Charged cash machine, Service shops, Information, Accommodation, Other shops, Showers
M65	4	Extra	Blackburn with Darwen	Shell	Charged cash machine, Service shops, Information, Accommodation, Other shops, Conference facilities, Showers
M74	4-5	RoadChef	Bothwell (South)	BP	Key toilet, Charged cash machine, Service shops, Conference facilities, Showers
	5-6	RoadChef	Hamilton (North)	BP	Key toilet, Service shops, Information, Accommodation, Conference facilities, Showers
	11-12	Cairn Lodge	Happendon	Gulf	Service shops, Conference facilities, Showers
	12-13	Welcome Break	Abington	Shell	Charged cash machine, Service shops, Information, Accommodation, Conference facilities
M90	6	Moto	Kinross Sevices	Esso	Key toilet, Service shops, Information, Accommodation, Showers

HIGHWAYS AGENCY

Helping you plan your journey |

We all want easy journeys but with increasing amounts of traffic on our roads, it's not just about the time in your car, it is also about the time spent planning your journey. We aim to provide helpful information so you can make choices before and during your journey. We've designed these services to give you information when and how you want it.

Highways Agency website
Information online

Our website **www.highways.gov.uk** gives you the latest traffic conditions as well as details of any roadworks or events that may cause congestion. You can see what is being displayed on the variable message signs and even download your own traffic ticker. You can also use the website to view images from the Highways Agency roadside traffic cameras.

Automated telephone service
Phone for the latest information

You can get the latest information on England's motorways and major "A" roads over the phone. Simply call **08700 660 115*** and use the keypad or voice commands to tell us which road or region you are interested in.

Traffic Radio
The latest traffic information over the airwaves

A traffic information station available 24/7 on DAB radio and the internet at **www.trafficradio.org.uk** gives you the latest regional and national traffic information – so you can simply tune in and listen to a continuous broadcast of traffic news.

Highways Agency Information Line
Helping you with your journey

Whether you want to speak to us about traffic conditions, signs, debris on the road, the environment or even recruitment, you can call us 24 hours a day on **08457 50 40 30*** or email us at **ha_info@highways.gsi.gov.uk.**

Variable message signs
Information when you are driving

We use these signs to communicate information and advice to you about roadworks, incidents, emergencies and large events. We have also recently started using them to display travel times, giving you a realistic indication of how long your journey will take.

Transport Direct
Planning your journey using other methods of travel

Transport Direct is an online journey planning and travel information service that covers most modes of transport – including car and public transport. The door-to-door planner shows you various ways of making your journey and includes directions, maps and a CO_2 calculator.

Traffic Broadcast
Traffic information in the media

You can use radio and television broadcasts to receive up-to-date information bulletins about traffic conditions. Operators at our National Traffic Control Centre monitor conditions on the motorway and major 'A' road network 24 hours a day and provide the travel news media with the latest information.

When you are in your car, and if you have an FM RDS radio, simply set the TA/TP (travel announcement) button to receive local travel news.

Information points
The latest information whilst you're on the move

We are gradually installing information points at locations across England, including motorway service areas, shopping centres, ports and airports. These terminals receive up to the minute information from our National Traffic Control Centre and tell you what is happening on the road ahead.

Diversion routes
Where do I go?

We are increasing the number of signed diversion routes to help you find your way if you are diverted off our road because of a serious incident. The signs will help to direct you back to the road that you were originally travelling on so that you can continue your journey.

Regional leaflets

We publish a set of six regional leaflets every quarter to help you plan your journey. These contain details of any large events or roadworks that may cause delays in your area. You can subscribe to receive them quarterly by calling **08457 50 40 30***.

 Mobile phone - switch off before you drive off

Traffic Officers |

Traffic Officer Paul Williams based in the East Midlands region explains how the service works to help our customers, whether you are a passenger or a driver with a disability.

If your vehicle develops a problem on the motorway, the Highway Code states that you should pull onto the hard shoulder, leave the vehicle via the passenger door and call for help using an emergency phone.

But if you have a disability this can be difficult. You may not be able to leave your vehicle, get to the nearest emergency phone or wait away from the hard shoulder.

As Traffic Officers, it is our job to ensure your safety and we are specially trained to deal with all kinds of emergency situations.

If you break down and have a disability which limits your mobility, our advice is to stay in your vehicle, switch on hazard warning lights, and dial 999 using a mobile telephone.

To assist you in calling for help, there are large blue driver location signs at the side of many motorways which allow you to tell the emergency services or Highways Agency where you are. Alternatively, all motorways have marker posts on the hard shoulder to help us find you quickly.

If you can get to the emergency roadside telephone, we have improved access to the phones for wheelchair users at a number of sites, and are continuing to do so. A text facility is also available for you to communicate with our operators.

When we arrive, if you are unable to get out of your car we can cone off the lane behind the vehicle, use our Traffic Officer vehicle to protect against oncoming traffic, and help you arrange for your vehicle to be recovered. We will even stay with you, if this is needed to keep you safe, until you are able to safely leave the motorway.

And while you are on the hard shoulder, our colleagues based in seven regional control centres across England will be using motorway cameras to ensure you and other motorists are safe, set electronic signs warning drivers of problems ahead and also take emergency calls from customers in trouble both from mobile phones and via the emergency roadside telephones.

We patrol 24/7 to provide reassurance to vulnerable customers, stopping behind broken down vehicles on the hard shoulder to check if the driver needs help. We also carry out welfare checks to ensure anyone stuck in traffic behind an accident or broken down in the hard shoulder isn't at risk to help everyone make their journeys safely and reliably.

Active Traffic Management |

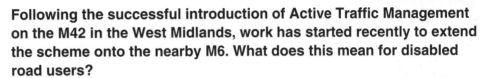

Following the successful introduction of Active Traffic Management on the M42 in the West Midlands, work has started recently to extend the scheme onto the nearby M6. What does this mean for disabled road users?

The results from the M42 have been impressive – reduced journey times, improved reliability of journeys, better information to drivers and, crucially, fewer accidents.

How does it work?

Variable speed limits, determined by detectors in the road surface, are displayed on overhead gantries. When the red 'X' over the hard shoulder changes to a speed limit, the hard shoulder is available to drivers as an extra lane. Before this can happen, on-road staff and control room colleagues with CCTV cameras check the hard shoulder for debris or vehicles. This system is popular, with 93% of drivers surveyed saying they felt it was clear when they should and shouldn't use the hard shoulder.

Safety

Safety is paramount to the design of the scheme and additional features have been added to make it as safe as possible. Large lay-bys have been built at regular intervals for broken down vehicles. They contain the latest emergency roadside telephones, all behind safety barriers and with full wheelchair access, linking you to the nearby control centre.

Traffic Officer Paul Williams explains what to do in an emergency on the previous page, but if this were to happen when hard shoulder running is in place, additional safety mechanisms are in place. Control centre operators have over 190 CCTV cameras, allowing them to spot you immediately if you are involved in an accident or breakdown. They can close any affected lane(s) straight away by displaying a red 'X' on the digital signs. This flexible approach means that you are protected from traffic approaching from behind and emergency vehicles can use the empty lane for access in the event of a major incident.

For more information on the Highways Agency or Active Traffic Management please call **08457 50 40 30*** or visit **www.highways.gov.uk.**

Think Ahead Move Ahead
Your guide to easier journeys

BEFORE YOU GO
Check your route using.....

- A road atlas
- Transport Direct at **www.transportdirect.info**

Check the traffic conditions

- Our live web updates at **www.highways.gov.uk/trafficinfo**
- Our automated telephone line updates on **08700 660 115***
- Traffic Radio on DAB digital radio and at **www.highways.gov.uk/radio**
- Ceefax, BBCi and **www.bbc.co.uk/travelnews.**

Check the weather forecast

- Met Office at **www.metoffice.gov.uk**

AS YOU TRAVEL
Check for changing travel conditions

- Our variable message signs
- BBC and local radio travel news
- Our automated telephone line updates on **08700 660 115***
- Our information points available at some motorway service areas.

Report any problems you see

- Highways Agency Information Line **08457 50 40 30***.

And remember

- Plan your journey to allow for a 15 minute break every two hours.

*Calls from BT landlines to 0845 numbers will cost no more than 4p per minute and to 0870 numbers no more than 8p per minute, mobile calls usually cost more. Please check with your service provider.

 Mobile phone - switch off before you drive off

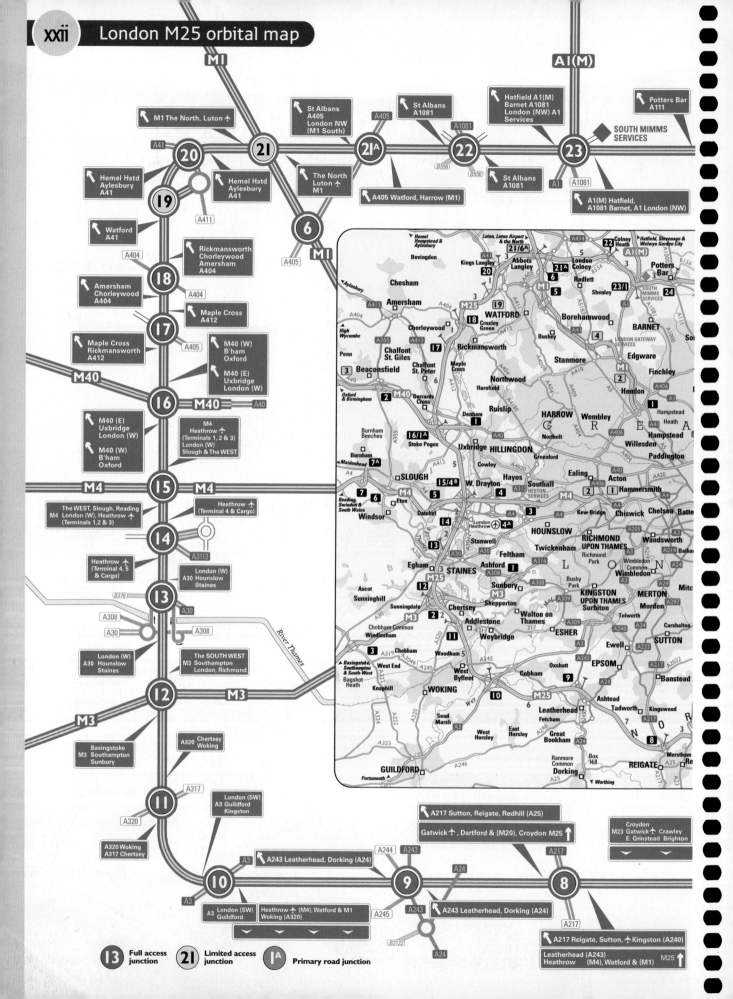

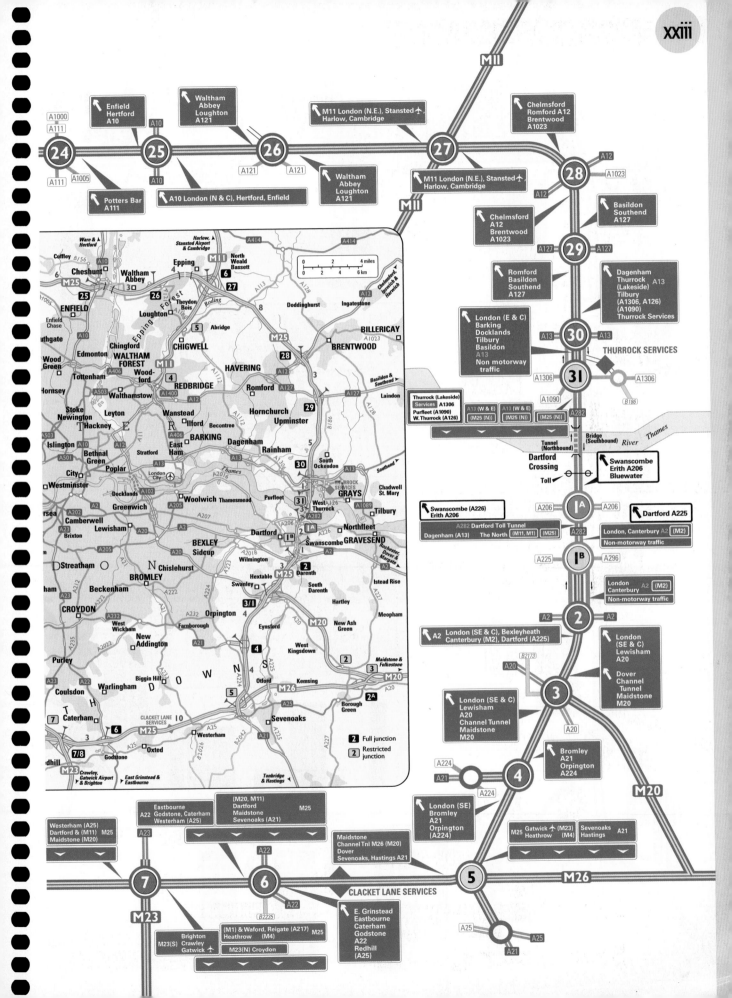

M11

Enfield
Hertford
A10

Waltham
Abbey
Loughton
A121

M11 London (N.E.), Stansted ✈,
Harlow, Cambridge

Chelmsford
Romford A12
Brentwood
A1023

24 **25** **26** **27**

A1000
A111

A111 A1005

A121 A121

A10

A12

28 A1023

A12

A12

Potters Bar
A111

A10 London (N & C), Hertford, Enfield

Waltham
Abbey
Loughton
A121

M11 London (N.E.), Stansted ✈,
Harlow, Cambridge

M11

Chelmsford
A12
Brentwood
A1023

Basildon
Southend
A127

A127 **29** A127

Romford
Basildon
Southend
A127

Dagenham
Thurrock
(Lakeside)
Tilbury
(A1306, A126)
(A1090)
Thurrock Services

London (E & C)
Barking
Docklands
Tilbury
Basildon
A13
Non motorway
traffic

A13 **30** A13

THURROCK SERVICES

A1306 **31** A1306

B186

Thurrock (Lakeside)
Services A1306
Purfleet (A1090)
W. Thurrock (A126)

A13 (W & E)
(M25 (N))

A13 (W & E)
(M25 (N))

A1090

A13 (W & E)
(M25 (N))

A282

River Thames

Tunnel
(Northbound)

Bridge
(Southbound)

Dartford
Crossing

Toll

Swanscombe
Erith A206
Bluewater

Swanscombe (A226)
Erith A206

A206 **IA** A206

Dartford A225

A282 Dartford Toll Tunnel
Dagenham (A13)   The North   (M11, M1) (M25)

London, Canterbury A2 (M2)
Non-motorway traffic

A225 **IB** A296

London
Canterbury A2 (M2)
Non-motorway traffic

A2 London (SE & C), Bexleyheath
Canterbury (M2), Dartford (A225)

A2 **2** A2

London
(SE & C)
Lewisham
A20

Dover
Channel
Tunnel
Maidstone
M20

B2173

A20

London (SE & C)
Lewisham
A20
Channel Tunnel
Maidstone
M20

3

A20

Bromley
A21
Orpington
A224

M20

A224 **4**

A21

A21

London (SE)
Bromley
A21
Orpington
(A224)

M25 Gatwick ✈ (M23)   Sevenoaks   A21
Heathrow (M4)   Hastings

5 **M26**

A25 A25

A21

Map detail

Ware &
Hertford

Cuffley B156

Cheshunt

Harlow,
Stansted Airport
& Cambridge

Epping

North Weald
Bassett

A414

A414

Chelmsford,
Ipswich &
Harwich

Waltham
Abbey

M11

M25

ENFIELD

25

6

A10

4

26

Theydon
Bois

Loughton

Epping Forest

Doddinghurst

Ingatestone

A128

A12

BILLERICAY

Enfield
Chase

A10

Abridge

5

A113

Roding

8

BRENTWOOD

Southgate

Edmonton

Chingford

M11

CHIGWELL

A1023

28

Wood
Green

WALTHAM
FOREST

Woodford

4

REDBRIDGE

HAVERING

A12

3

Basildon &
Southend

Hornsey

Tottenham

Walthamstow

Leyton

Wanstead

Ilford

Becontree

A12

Romford

A127

Laindon

B186

Stoke
Newington

Hackney

Ilford

BARKING

Dagenham

Hornchurch

Upminster

A178

Islington

Bethnal
Green

Stratford

East
Ham

A13

Rainham

5

30

South
Ockendon

A13

Southend

City

Poplar

Thames

A13

THURROCK
SERVICES

GRAYS

Chadwell
St. Mary

Westminster

London
City

A102

Docklands

Woolwich

Thamesmead

Purfleet

31

West
Thurrock

A126

A1089

Tilbury

Camberwell

Greenwich

A205

A207

A2

A282

Northfleet

Swanscombe

GRAVESEND

Rochester,
Dover &
Margate

Lewisham

Brixton

A20

Dartford

IA

A226

A2

Streatham

BEXLEY

Sidcup

A2018

Wilmington

3

IB

Istead Rise

BROMLEY

Chislehurst

A224

Hextable

Swanley

2

Darenth

South
Darenth

Hartley

Meopham

A227

Beckenham

A222

3/1

4

M20

New Ash
Green

CROYDON

A232

Orpington

Farnborough

A21

West
Kingsdown

A20

New
Addington

A21

4

West
Kingsdown

A25

Maidstone &
Folkestone

Purley

Eynsford

2

M20

Biggin Hill

D O W N **5** S

Otford

Kemsing

A20

Coulsdon

A22

Warlingham

CLACKET LANE
SERVICES

6

M25

Westerham

Sevenoaks

2A

Borough
Green

Caterham

7

7/8

Godstone

Oxted

B2026

A25

Westerham

A21

A25

A227

Tonbridge
& Hastings

2 Full junction

2 Restricted
junction

M23

Crawley,
Gatwick Airport
& Brighton

East Grinstead &
Eastbourne

Scale

0   2   4 miles
0   2   4   6 km

Westerham (A25)
Dartford & (M11) M25
Maidstone (M20)

Eastbourne
A22 Godstone, Caterham
Westerham (A25)

(M20, M11)
Dartford
Maidstone
Sevenoaks (A21)

M25

Maidstone
Channel Tnl M26 (M20)
Dover
Sevenoaks, Hastings A21

E. Grinstead
Eastbourne
Caterham
Godstone
A22
Redhill
(A25)

7 **6**

CLACKET LANE SERVICES

M23

A23

A22

A22

B2235

Brighton
M23(S) Crawley
Gatwick ✈

(M1) & Waford, Reigate (A217) M25
Heathrow (M4)

M23(N) Croydon

A25

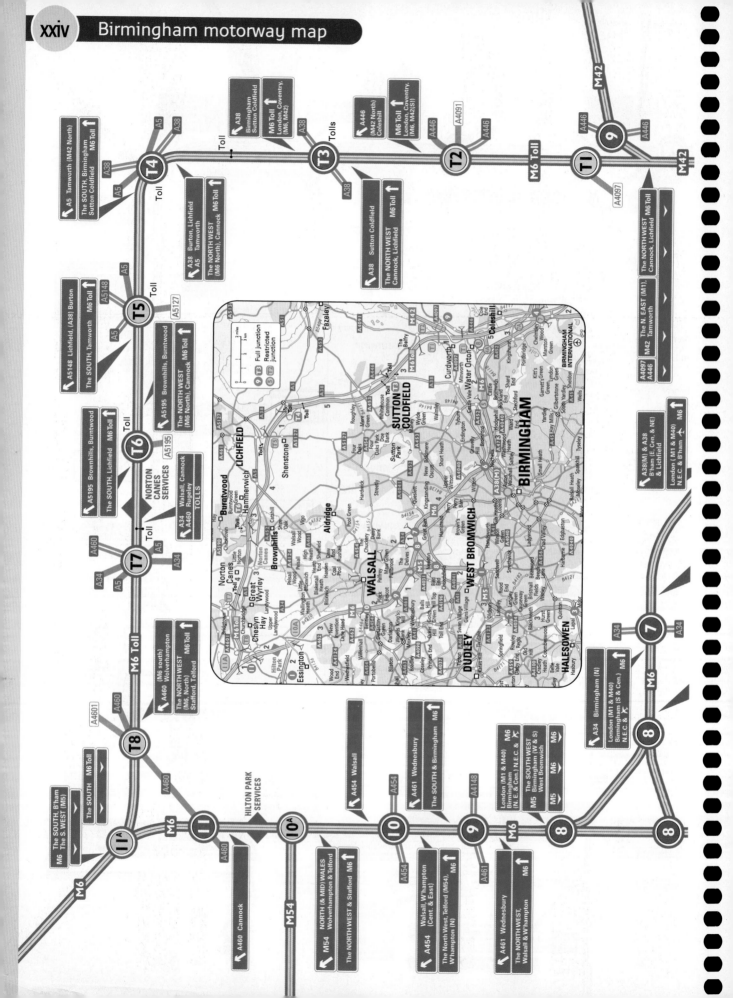

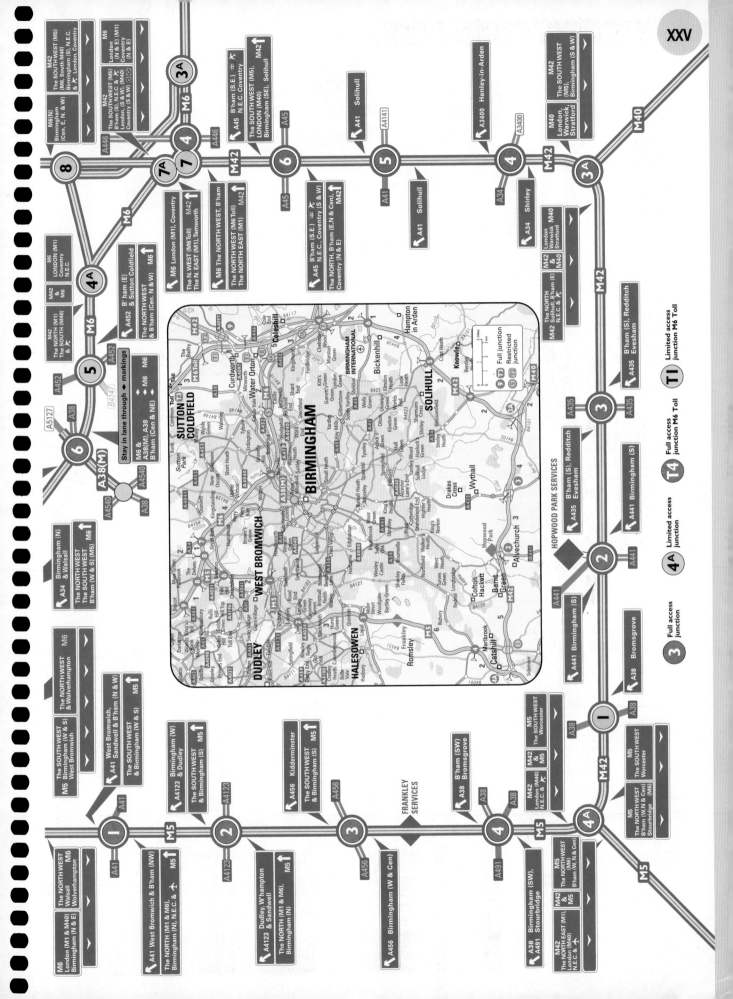

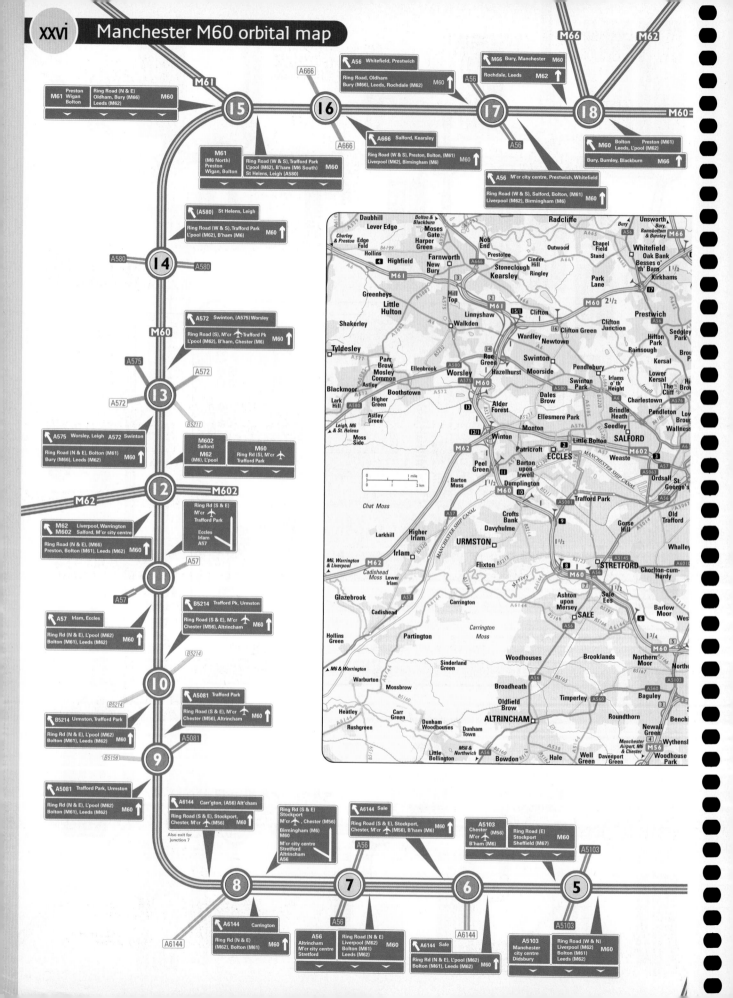

M61 → **M60**
Preston, Wigan, Bolton | Ring Road (N & E), Oldham, Bury (M66), Leeds (M62)

15

16

↑ A56 Whitefield, Prestwich
Ring Road, Oldham, Bury (M66), Leeds, Rochdale (M62) **M60** ↑

↖ M66 Bury, Manchester **M60**
Rochdale, Leeds **M62**

17

18

↗ M60 Bolton, Preston (M61), Leeds, L'pool (M62)
Bury, Burnley, Blackburn **M66** ↑

A666

↑ A666 Salford, Kearsley
Ring Road (W & S), Preston, Bolton, (M61), Liverpool (M62), Birmingham (M6) **M60** ↑

↑ A56 M'cr city centre, Prestwich, Whitefield
Ring Road (W & S), Salford, Bolton, (M61), Liverpool (M62), Birmingham (M6) **M60** ↑

M61
(M6 North), Preston, Wigan, Bolton | Ring Road (W & S), Trafford Park, L'pool (M62), B'ham (M6 South), St Helens, Leigh (A580) **M60**

↑ (A580) St Helens, Leigh
Ring Road (W & S), Trafford Park, L'pool (M62), B'ham (M6) **M60** ↑

A580 **14** **A580**

↑ A572 Swinton, (A575) Worsley
Ring Road (S), M'cr ✈ Trafford Pk, L'pool (M62), B'ham (M6), Chester (M6) **M60** ↑

M60

A575

A572

13

A572

↑ A575 Worsley, Leigh **A572** Swinton
Ring Road (N & E), Bolton (M61), Bury (M66), Leeds (M62) **M60** ↑

M602
Salford
M62 (M6), L'pool | **M60** Ring Rd (S), M'cr ✈ Trafford Park

12 **M602**

M62

↑ M62 Liverpool, Warrington
M602 Salford, M'cr city centre
Ring Road (N & E), (M66), Preston, Bolton (M61), Leeds (M62) **M60** ↑

Ring Rd (S & E)
M'cr ✈ Trafford Park
Eccles, Irlam, A57

11

A57

A57

↑ A57 Irlam, Eccles
Ring Rd (N & E), L'pool (M62), Bolton (M61), Leeds (M62) **M60** ↑

↑ B5214 Trafford Pk, Urmston
Ring Road (S & E), M'cr ✈ Chester (M56), Altrincham **M60** ↑

B5214

10

↑ B5214 Urmston, Trafford Park
Ring Rd (N & E), L'pool (M62), Bolton (M61), Leeds (M62) **M60** ↑

↑ A5081 Trafford Park
Ring Road (S & E), M'cr ✈ Chester (M56), Altrincham **M60** ↑

B5214

A5081

B5158

9

↑ A5081 Trafford Park, Urmston
Ring Rd (N & E), L'pool (M62), Bolton (M61), Leeds (M62) **M60**

↑ A6144 Carr'gton, (A56) Alt'cham
Ring Road (S & E), Stockport, Chester, M'cr ✈ (M56) **M60** ↑

Also exit for junction 7

Ring Rd (S & E)
Stockport
M'cr ✈, Chester (M56)
Birmingham (M6)
M60
M'cr city centre
Stretford
Altrincham
A56

↑ A6144 Sale
Ring Road (S & E), Stockport, Chester, M'cr ✈ (M56), B'ham (M6) **M60** ↑

A56

A5103
Chester
M'cr ✈ (M56)
B'ham (M6) | Ring Road (E)
Stockport
Sheffield (M67) **M60**

A5103

8 **7** **6** **5**

A6144

↑ A6144 Carrington
Ring Rd (N & E) (M62), Bolton (M61) **M60** ↑

A6144

A56
Altrincham
M'cr city centre
Stretford | Ring Road (N & E)
Liverpool (M62)
Bolton (M61)
Leeds (M62) **M60** ↑

A56

A6144

↑ A6144 Sale
Ring Rd (N & E), L'pool (M62), Bolton (M61), Leeds (M62) **M60** ↑

A6144

A5103
Manchester city centre
Didsbury | Ring Road (W & N)
Liverpool (M62)
Bolton (M61)
Leeds (M62) **M60**

A5103

Map place names

Daubhill, Lever Edge, Chorley & Preston, Edge Fold, Hollins, Highfield, Greenheys, Little Hulton, Shakerley, Tyldesley, Parr Brow, Mosley Common, Ellenbrook, Blackmoor, Astley, Boothstown, Lark Hill, Higher Green, Astley Green, Leigh, M6 & St Helens, Moss Side, Chat Moss, Larkhill, Irlam, Cadishead Moss, Lower Irlam, M6, Warrington & Liverpool, Glazebrook, Cadishead, Hollins Green, Partington, Heatley, Rushgreen, Warburton, Mossbrow, Carr Green, Dunham Woodhouses, Dunham Town, Little Bollington, M56 & Northwich, Bowdon, Hale, Well Green, Davenport Green, Manchester Airport, M6 & Chester, Woodhouse Park, Wythensh, Newall Green, Benchi, Roundthorn, Baguley, Timperley, Oldfield Brow, Broadheath, Altrincham, Woodhouses, Brooklands, Northern Moor, Barlow Moor, Sale, Sale Eees, Ashton upon Mersey, Carrington, Sinderland Green, Carrington Moss, Flixton, Stretford, Chorlton-cum-Hardy, Whalley, Old Trafford, Gorse Hill, Urmston, Davyhulme, Crofts Bank, Trafford Park, Barton Moss, Peel Green, Dumplington, Barton upon Irwell, Eccles, Weaste, Ordsall, St George's, Salford, Little Bolton, Patricroft, Winton, Monton, Seedley, Pendleton, Wallness, Brindle Heath, Charlestown, Ellesmere Park, Alder Forest, Dales Brow, Swinton Park, The Cliff, Lower Kersal, Irlams o' th' Height, Kersal, Sedgley Park, Hilton Park, Rainsough, Prestwich, Clifton Junction, Clifton Green, Newtown, Wardley, Swinton, Hazelhurst, Moorside, Pendlebury, Roe Green, Hill Top, Clifton, Linnyshaw, Walkden, Kearsley, Stoneclough, Ringley, Cinder Hill, Prestolee, Outwood, Park Lane, Besses o' th' Barn, Oak Bank, Kirkhams, Whitefield, Chapel Field, Stand, Unsworth, Bury, Ramsbottom & Burnley, Radcliffe, Bolton & Blackburn, Moses Gate, Harper Green, Nob End, Farnworth, New Bury, Daubhill

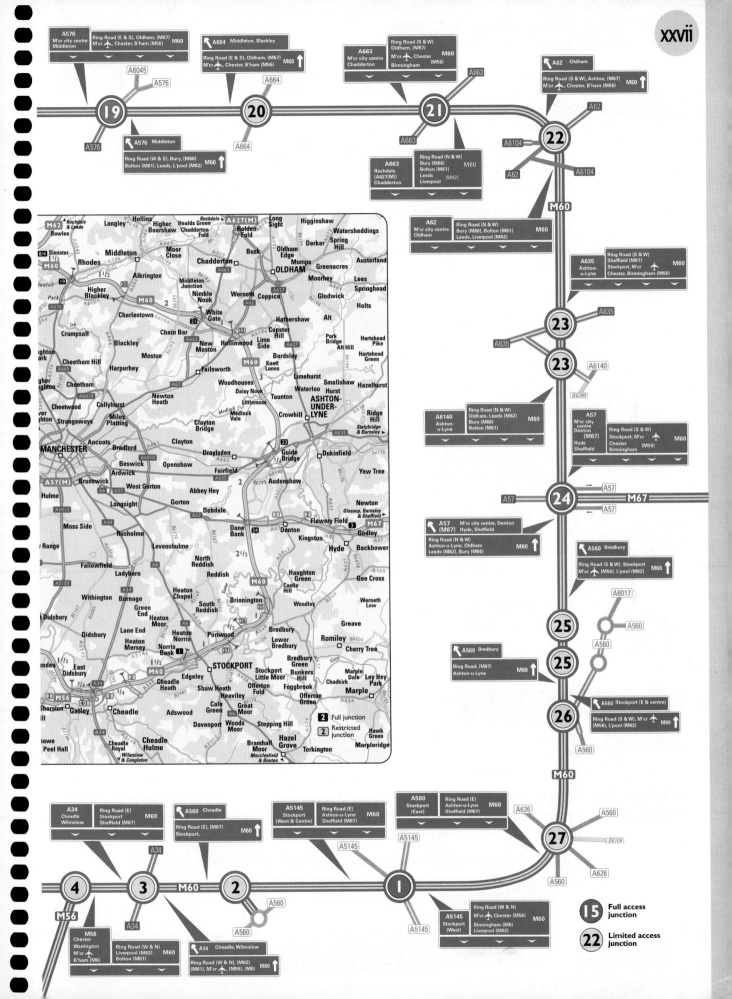

19

A576
M'cr city centre
Middleton

Ring Road (E & S), Oldham, (M67)
M'cr ✈, Chester, B'ham (M56) | M60

A6045
A576

A576 Middleton

Ring Road (W & S), Bury, (M66)
Bolton (M61), Leeds, L'pool (M62) | M60

20

A664 Middleton, Blackley

Ring Road (E & S), Oldham, (M67)
M'cr ✈, Chester, B'ham (M56) | M60

A664

21

A663
M'cr city centre
Chadderton

Ring Road (S & W)
Oldham, (M67)
M'cr ✈, Chester
Birmingham | M60

A663

A663
Rochdale
(A627(M))
Chadderton

Ring Road (N & W)
Bury (M66)
Bolton (M61)
Leeds
Liverpool | M60

22

A62 Oldham

Ring Road (S & W), Ashton, (M67)
M'cr ✈, Chester, B'ham (M56) | M60

A62

A6104

A62

A6104

M60

A62
M'cr city centre
Oldham

Ring Road (N & W)
Bury (M66), Bolton (M61)
Leeds, Liverpool (M62) | M60

A635
Ashton-
u-Lyne

Ring Road (S & W)
Sheffield (M67)
Stockport, M'cr ✈
Chester, Birmingham (M56) | M60

23

A635

A635

23

A6140

B6390

A6140
Ashton-
u-Lyne

Ring Road (N & W)
Oldham, Leeds (M62)
Bury (M66)
Bolton (M61) | M60

A57
M'cr city
centre
Denton
(M67)
Hyde
Sheffield

Ring Road (S & W)
Stockport, M'cr ✈
Chester
Birmingham (M56) | M60

24

A57

M67

A57

A57
(M67)
M'cr city centre, Denton
Hyde, Sheffield

Ring Road (N & W)
Ashton-u-Lyne, Oldham
Leeds (M62), Bury (M66) | M60

A560 Bredbury

Ring Road (S & W), Stockport
M'cr ✈ (M56), L'pool (M62) | M60

A6017

25

A560

A560

A560 Bredbury

Ring Road, (M67)
Ashton-u-Lyne | M60

25

A560

A560 Stockport (E & centre)

Ring Road (S & W), M'cr ✈
(M56), L'pool (M62) | M60

26

A560

M60

A626

A560

A560
Stockport
(East)

Ring Road (E)
Ashton-u-Lyne (M60)
Sheffield (M67) | M60

27

A560

A626

B6104

MAP (enclosed area):

Rochdale & Leeds · M62 · Bowlee · Langley · Hollins · Higher Boarshaw · Heals Green · Chadderton Fold · Holden Fold · Long Sight · Higginshaw · Watersheddings · Spring Hill · Derker · Oldham Edge · Mumps · Greenacres · Austerland · 8/4 Simister · Middleton · Moor Close · Chadderton · OLDHAM · Moorhey · Lees · Springhead · Rhodes · Alkrington · Middleton Junction · Nimble Nook · Werneth · Coppice · Glodwick · Holts · Higher Blackley · White Gate · Hathershaw · Copster Hill · Park Bridge · Hartshead Pike · Charlestown · Chain Bar · New Moston · Hollinwood · Lime Side · Alt Hill · Hartshead Green · Crumpsall · Blackley · Moston · Bardsley · Knott Lanes · Smallshaw · Hurst · Hazelhurst · Cheetham Hill · Harpurhey · Failsworth · Woodhouses · Daisy Nook · Waterloo · Limehurst · ASHTON-UNDER-LYNE · Ridge Hill · Cheetham · Collyhurst · Newton Heath · Littlemoss · Taunton · Stalybridge & Barnsley · Cheetwood · Strangeways · Miles Platting · Clayton Bridge · Medlock Vale · Crowhill · MANCHESTER · Ancoats · Bradford · Clayton · Droylsden · Guide Bridge · Dukinfield · Yew Tree · Brunswick · Beswick · Openshaw · Fairfield · Audenshaw · Newton · Hulme · West Gorton · Abbey Hey · Glossop, Barnsley & Sheffield · Longsight · Gorton · Debdale · Flowery Field · Godley · Moss Side · Dane Bank · Denton · Kingston · Hyde · Backbower · Fallowfield · North Reddish · Reddish · Haughton Green · Gee Cross · Werneth Low · Withington · Burnage · Green End · Heaton Chapel · South Reddish · Brinnington · Woodley · Greave · Didsbury · Lane End · Heaton Moor · Bredbury · Romiley · Cherry Tree · East Didsbury · Heaton Mersey · Heaton Norris · Portwood · Lower Bredbury · Bredbury Green · Marple Dale · Chadkirk · Ley Hey Park · Norris Bank · STOCKPORT · Bunkers Hill · Marple · M56 · Gatley · Cheadle Heath · Edgeley · Stockport Little Moor · Offerton Fold · Foggbrook · Offerton Green · Cheadle · Shaw Heath · Heaviley · Adswood · Cale Green · Great Moor · Marple · Davenport · Woods Moor · Stepping Hill · Hawk Green · Cheadle Royal · Cheadle Hulme · Bramhall Moor · Hazel Grove · Torkington · Marpleridge · Sharston · Peel Hall · Wilmslow & Congleton · Macclesfield & Buxton

2 Full junction
2 Restricted junction

4

M56

M56
Chester
Warrington
M'cr ✈
B'ham (M6)

Ring Road (W & N), (M62)
(M61), M'cr ✈ (M56), (M6)
Bolton (M61) | M60

3

A34

A34 Cheadle, Wilmslow

Ring Road (W & N), (M62)
(M61), M'cr ✈ (M56), (M6)
Bolton (M61) | M60

M60

2

A560

A560

1

A5145

A5145
Stockport
(West)

Ring Road (W & N)
M'cr ✈, Chester (M56)
Birmingham (M6)
Liverpool (M62) | M60

A34
Cheadle
Wilmslow

Ring Road (E)
Stockport
Sheffield (M67) | M60

A34

A560 Cheadle

Ring Road (E), (M67)
Stockport, | M60

A5145

A5145
Stockport
(West & Centre)

Ring Road (E)
(M67)
Stockport, | M60

A5145

A560
Stockport
(East)

Ring Road (E)
Ashton-u-Lyne (M60)
Sheffield (M67) | M60

A5145

15 Full access junction

22 Limited access junction

TRANSPORT SCOTLAND

Transport Scotland

Transport Scotland is the national transport agency for Scotland. Our purpose is to help deliver the Scottish Government's vision for transport, making a real difference for people and businesses using the national rail and road networks.

Transport Scotland is responsible for helping to deliver the Government's £3 billion capital investment programme over the next decade, overseeing the safe and efficient running of Scotland's trunk roads and rail networks and establishing and running a national scheme for concessionary travel in Scotland.

Visit www.transportscotland.gov.uk

Traffic Scotland

'Traffic Scotland' is Transport Scotland's web-based information service for road users on Scotland's motorway and trunk road network. Its purpose is to help drivers make informed choices about the timing, routing and travel mode for current or future journeys.

Traffic Scotland currently provides up to date information on the Scottish motorways and trunk road network in relation to:

- current and planned road works;
- accidents and current incidents;
- levels of congestion;
- severe weather warnings;
- significant planned events that impact on the network e.g. concerts;
- park and ride facilities;
- signposting to alternative public transport provision; and
- links to other useful travel related websites

For more information visit www.trafficscotland.org

Roads For All – making your journey easier

The Trunk Road Disability Equality Scheme and Action Plan, Roads for All, was published in December 2006 and sets out objectives for improved accessibility on Scotland's Trunk Road Network.

Preparation for this began in July 2006 and was overseen by a Working Group with membership drawn from various stakeholders – including representatives of disability groups and public transport operators.

This year Transport Scotland is building on work taken forward in 2007 which included an audit of the network by beginning to prioritise the audit findings and producing a Guide to Good Practice in Inclusive Design to enhance our ability to deliver on our accessibility objectives.

For more details visit:
www.transportscotland.gov.uk/files/documents/roads/Roads-for-All-revised.pdf

We hope that the table below will help to simplify the Blue Badge Parking Rules in all of the council boroughs and districts in England, Scotland, Wales and Northern Ireland.

The authorities that administers the regulations is not always clear. The highways are often administered by the county councils or unitary authorities, however many councils have opted to decriminalise the parking regulations in populated areas or areas with a high number of visitors. This causes confusion on the Blue Badge Parking concessions.

We have contacted all the authorities in the U.K. and this table shows all the council areas with the rules that apply. We have detailed within the table the authority responsible for each area.

More and more councils are opting to decriminalise the parking

in their area, several are looking to simplify their parking regulations for Blue Badge holders and abolish older schemes that have been unpopular.

The Blue Badge Scheme provides a national arrangement that councils provide free parking in blue badge bays, on-street meters, pay-and-display meters and yellow lines (where its safe to do so). Councils are not required by the scheme to provide free parking in residents bays and off street car parks, however many do so. See the table below for variations.

If you are aware of any changes please let us know at **info@thepieguide.com**. We hope that with the councils continued co-operation and feedback from Blue Badge holders we can keep this rules table updated on **www.bluebadge.direct.gov.uk**

Key
! The rules may vary locally
B C Borough Council
D C District Council
– Not applicable

County	Council	Blue Badge Park FREE with no time restrictions	Pay & Display (On street only) Park FREE with No time restrictions during the enforced time period	Shared Use Bays (Pay & Display and Resident) Park FREE with No time restrictions during the enforced time period	Resident Bays Park with no time restrictions during the enforced time period	Single & Double Yellow Lines Park for a maximum 3 hrs on a Single or Double Yellow Line	Council Owned Car Parks Free or Discounted parking for the Blue Badge Holders	Council Specific Contact Number For the Blue Badge Scheme
England								
Bedfordshire	Bedford B C	✔	✔	✔	✔	✔	✔ Unlimited	01234 228557
Bedfordshire	Luton B C	✔ Max stay !	✔	–	✘	✔	✔ Unlimited	01582 547516
Bedfordshire	Mid Bedfordshire D C	✔	✔	✔	✘	✔	✘	01234 228557
Bedfordshire	South Bedfordshire D C	✔ Except when signs display the limit	–	–	✔	✔	✔	01582 472222
Berkshire	Bracknell Forest B C	✔	✔	–	–	✔	✔ in P&D Car Parks only	01344 351465
Berkshire	Reading B C	✔ Max stay 4hrs	–	–	✘	✔	✔ Unlimited	
Berkshire	Slough B C	✔ Max stay !	✔	–	✘	✔	✔ Unlimited	01753 690400
Berkshire	West Berkshire C	✔			✘	✔	✔ Unlimited	01635 503090
Berkshire	Windsor & Maidenhead Royal B C	✔	✔	–	✘	✔	✔ Unlimited	01628 683711
Berkshire	Wokingham D C	✔	✔	–	✘	✔	✔ Unlimited	0118 974 6800
Bristol	Bristol City C	✔ Max stay !	✔	–	–	✔	✔ Unlimited	0117 922 2198
Buckinghamshire	Aylesbury Vale D C	✔	✔	–	✔	✔	✔ Unlimited	01296 382902
Buckinghamshire	Chiltern D C	✔	✔	–	✔	✔	✔ Unlimited	01296 382902
Buckinghamshire	Milton Keynes B C	✔	✔	✘	✘	✔	✔ Unlimited	01908 253449
Buckinghamshire	South Bucks D C	✔	✔	–	✘	✔	✔ Unlimited	01296 382902
Buckinghamshire	Wycombe D C	✔	✔ Max stay 2hrs	✔	✔	✔	✔ Unlimited	01296 382902
Cambridgeshire	Cambridge City C	✔	✔	–	✘	✔	✔ Max stay 3hrs	0845 045 5204
Cambridgeshire	East Cambridgeshire D C	✔	–	–	✘	✔	✔ Unlimited	0845 045 5204
Cambridgeshire	Fenland D C	✔	–	–	✔	✔	✔ Unlimited	0845 045 5204
Cambridgeshire	Huntingdonshire D C	✔	✔	–	✘	✔	✔ Unlimited	0845 045 5204
Cambridgeshire	Peterborough City C	✔	✔	–	✘	✔	✔ Unlimited	0845 045 5204
Cambridgeshire	South Cambridgeshire D C	✔ Max stay !	✔ Max stay 3hrs	–	✘	✔	✔ Unlimited	0845 045 5204
Cheshire	Chester City C	✔ Max stay 4hrs	✔ Max stay 4hrs	–	✔ Max stay 24hrs	✔	✔ !	0845 1131133
Cheshire	Congleton B C	✔	✔	–	–	✔	✔ Unlimited	0845 1131133
Cheshire	Crewe & Nantwich B C	✔	✔	–	✘	✔	✔ Unlimited	0845 1131133
Cheshire	Ellesmere Port & Neston B C	✔ Max stay 4hrs	✔ Max stay 4hrs	–	✘	✔	✔ Max stay 4hrs	0845 1131133
Cheshire	Halton B C	✔	✔	–	–	✔	✔ Unlimited	0151 907 8309
Cheshire	Macclesfield B C	✔	✔	–	–	✔	✘	0845 1131133
Cheshire	Vale Royal B C	✔ Max stay 4hrs	✔ Max stay 4hrs	–	✘	✔	✔ Unlimited	0845 1131133
Cheshire	Warrington B C	✔	✔	–	✘	✔	✔ Unlimited !	01925 444239
Cornwall	Caradon D C	✔	✔	–	✘	✔	✘	01579 342919
Cornwall	Carrick D C	✔ (Require Vehicle Exeption Tax)	✔ (Tax)	–	✘	✔	✘	01872 278533
Cornwall	Kerrier D C	✔	✔	–	✘	✔	✔ Max stay rules apply	01209 614000
Cornwall	North Cornwall D C	✔	✔	–	✘	✔	✔ If Tax Exempt	01208 262800
Cornwall	Penwith D C	✔ Max stay 3hrs	✔ Max stay 3hrs	–	✘	✔	✔ Unlimited	
Cornwall	Restormel B C	✔	–	–	–	✔	✘	01872 323658

Free parking on Single & Double Yellow lines (3hrs max) except where loading and unloading restrictions apply, Pay & Display, Shared Use, Residents and Blue Badge Bays

Free parking in most places (Single & Double Yellow lines (3hrs max) & Pay & Display) except Residents Bays

Free parking in most places (Single & Double Yellow lines (3hrs max) & Pay & Display) except Shared Use and Residents Bays

Free parking in Blue badge bays and Single & Double Yellow lines (3hrs max) only

Free parking in Blue badge bays with limited concessions on Pay & Display

Free parking in Blue badge bays only

XXX

Key		Blue Badge Park FREE with no time restrictions	Pay & Display (On street only) Park FREE with No time restrictions during the enforced time period	Shared Use Bays (Pay & Display and Resident) Park FREE with No time restrictions during the enforced time period	Resident Bays Park with no time restrictions during the enforced time period	Single & Double Yellow Lines Park for a maximum 3 hrs on a Single or Double Yellow Line	Council Owned Car Parks Free or Discounted parking for the Blue Badge Holders	Council Specific Contact Number For the Blue Badge Scheme
! The rules may vary locally **B C** Borough Council **D C** District Council **–** Not applicable								
County	**Council**							
Cumbria	Carlisle City C	✔ Except when signs display the limit	–	–	✔	✔	✔ Unlimited Unless specified	01228 607080
Cumbria	Allerdale B C	✔ Max stay !	✔	–	✘	✔	✔ Unlimited	01900 325348
Cumbria	Barrow-in-Furness B C	✔	–	–	✔	✔	✔ Unlimited	01229 894894
Cumbria	Copeland B C	✔	✔ Max stay 4 hrs	✔	✔	✔	✔ Unlimited	01228 607000
Cumbria	Eden D C	✔	✔ !	–	✘	✔	✔ Unlimited	
Cumbria	South Lakeland D C	✔	–	–	✘	✔	✔ Max stay 3hrs	01539 773377
Derbyshire	Derby City C	✔ Max stay 3hrs	✔ Max stay 3hrs	–	✔	✔	✔ Unlimited if Tax Exempt	01332 716715
Derbyshire	Amber Valley B C	✔ Max stay 3hrs	✔ Max stay 3hrs	–	✘	✔	✔ Unlimited	
Derbyshire	Bolsover D C	✔	–	–	✘	✔	✘	01629 772220
Derbyshire	Chesterfield B C	✔	✔	–	✔	✔	✔ Unlimited	
Derbyshire	Derbyshire Dales D C	✔	✔	–	✘	✔	✔ Unlimited	01629 772233
Derbyshire	Erewash B C	✔	✔	–	✘	✔	✔ Unlimited	01159 072244
Derbyshire	High Peak B C	✔	✔	–	✘	✔	✔ Unlimited	08456 058058
Derbyshire	North East Derbyshire D C	✔ Max stay !	✔	–	✘	✔	✔ Unlimited	01629 580000 ext 2222
Derbyshire	South Derbyshire D C	✔	–	–	✘	✔	✔ Unlimited	
Devon	Torbay C	✔	–	–	✘	✔	✔ 1 hr free once payment made	0800 444000
Devon	East Devon D C	✔ Except when signs display the limit	✔	–	✘	✔	✘	01392 381300
Devon	Exeter City C	✔	✔	–	✔	✔	✔ Unlimited	01392 382000
Devon	Mid Devon D C	✔ Max stay 3hrs	–	–	✘	✔	✘	01884 255255
Devon	North Devon D C	✔	–	–	–	✔	✘	0800 444000
Devon	Plymouth City C	✔	✔	–	✔ Max stay 3 hrs	✔	✔ Unlimited	01752 308686
Devon	South Hams D C	✔ Max stay !	✔	✔	✔	✔	✘	0800 444000
Devon	Teignbridge D C	✔ Max stay 3hrs	✔	✔	✘	✔	✘	0800 444000
Devon	Torridge D C	P	–	–	–	✔	✘	0800 444000
Devon	West Devon B C	✔	–	–	–	✔	✔ 1 hrs free once payment made	0800 444000
Dorset	Borough of Poole	✔ Max stay !	✔ Max stay 3hrs!	–	✔	✔	✔ If Tax Exempt	01202 633605
Dorset	Bournemouth B C	✔ Max stay !	✔ Max stay 3hrs	✔	✘	✔	✘	01202 458774
Dorset	Christchurch B C	✔ Max stay !	✔ (Tax)	–	✘	✔	✔ If Tax Exempt	01305 251000
Dorset	East Dorset D C	✔ Max stay !	✔	–	✔ Max stay 3 hrs	✔	✔ !	01305 224321
Dorset	North Dorset D C	✔ Max stay !	✔	–	✔ Max stay 3 hrs	✔	✘	01305 224321
Dorset	Purbeck D C	✔	–	–	✘	✔	–	01305 224321
Dorset	West Dorset D C	✔	✔	✔	✘	✔	✔ If Tax Exempt Max 3hrs	01305 224321
Dorset	Weymouth & Portland B C	✔	✔	✔	✘	✔	✘	01305 224321
Durham	Darlington B C	✔ Max stay !	✔ Max stay 3hrs	–	✘	✔	✔ Max stay 3hrs	01325 346200
Durham	Chester-le-Street D C	✔ !	✔	–	–	✔	✘	0191 383 6001
Durham	Derwentside D C	✔ Except when signs display the limit	–	✔	✔	✔	✔ Unlimited	0191 383 6001
Durham	Durham City C	✔	✔	–	✘	✔	✘	0191 383 6001
Durham	Easington D C	P	P	P	P	✔	✔ Except Automated Car parks	0845 850 5010
Durham	Hartlepool B C	✔	✔ Max stay 3hrs	–	✔ Max stay 3 hrs	✔	✔ Max stay 3hrs	01429 523369
Durham	Sedgefield B C	✔	✔	–	✔	✔	✔ Unlimited	0845 850 5010
Durham	Stockton-on-Tees B C	✔	✔	–	✘	✔	✔ Unlimited	01642 528499
Durham	Teesdale D C	✔ Max stay 3hrs	✔ !	–	✔	✔	✔ Unlimited	0191 383 6001
Durham	Wear Valley D C	✔	✔	–	✔	✔	✔ Unlimited	0191 383 6001
East Sussex	Brighton & Hove City C	✔	✔	–	✘	✔	✔ Unlimited	01273 296270
East Sussex	Eastbourne B C	✔	✔	✔	✘	✔	✔	01323 466680
East Sussex	Hastings B C	✔	✔ Max stay 3hrs	✔	✘	✔	✔ 3hrs Max (Disabled Bay Only)	0845 608 0191
East Sussex	Lewes D C	✔ Max stay 3hrs	✔	–	–	✔	✔ Unlimited	0845 608 0191
East Sussex	Rother D C	✔	✔	–	✘	✔	✔ Permit required	01424 787507
East Sussex	Wealden D C	✔ Max stay 3hrs	✔ Max stay 3hrs!	✔ Max stay 3hrs	✘	✔	✔ Unlimited	01323 443322
East Yorkshire	East Riding of Yorkshire C	✔	!	–	✔	✔	✘	01482 393939
East Yorkshire	Kingston upon Hull City C	✔	✔	✔	✔	✔	✔ Unlimited	01482 300300

Free parking on Single & Double Yellow lines (3hrs max) except where loading and unloading restrictions apply, Pay & Display, Shared Use, Residents and Blue Badge Bays

Free parking in most places (Single & Double Yellow lines (3hrs max) & Pay & Display) except Residents Bays

Free parking in most places (Single & Double Yellow lines (3hrs max) & Pay & Display) except Shared Use and Residents Bays

Free parking in Blue badge bays and Single & Double Yellow lines (3hrs max) only

Free parking in Blue badge bays with limited concessions on Pay & Display

Free parking in Blue badge bays only

Users should be aware that this information may change at any time. This information was correct as of October 2008. Compiled by PIE Enterprises Ltd © 2008. All rights reserved.

Key
- **!** The rules may vary locally
- **B C** Borough Council
- **D C** District Council
- **−** Not applicable

County	Council	Blue Badge Park FREE with no time restrictions	Pay & Display (On street only) Park FREE with No time restrictions during the enforced time period	Shared Use Bays (Pay & Display and Resident) Park FREE with No time restrictions during the enforced time period	Resident Bays Park with no time restrictions during the enforced time period	Single & Double Yellow Lines Park for a maximum 3 hrs on a Single or Double Yellow Line	Council Owned Car Parks Free or Discounted parking for the Blue Badge Holders	Council Specific Contact Number For the Blue Badge Scheme
Essex	Basildon D C	✔	✔	✔ Max stay 3hrs	✔ Max stay 3 hrs	✔	✔ Unlimited	01268 643333
Essex	Braintree D C	✔	✔	−	✗	✔	✔ Unlimited	020 8227 2334
Essex	Brentwood B C	✔	✔	✔	✔	✔	✔ Unlimited	0845 603 7630
Essex	Castle Point B C	✔	−	−	✔	✔	✔ Unlimited	
Essex	Chelmsford B C	✔ Max stay !	✔ Max stay 3hrs !	✔ Max stay 3hrs	✔ Max stay 3 hrs	✔	✔ Unlimited	01245 434090
Essex	Colchester B C	✔ Max stay !	✔ Max stay 3hrs	−	✗	✔	✔ Except Automated Car parks	01255 253423
Essex	Epping Forest D C	✔	✔	✗	✗	✔	✔ Unlimited	
Essex	Harlow D C	✔	✔	✗	✗	✔	✔ Unlimited	
Essex	Maldon D C	✔	✔	−	✗	✔	✔ Unlimited	
Essex	Rochford D C	✔ Max stay 3hrs	−	−	−	✔	✔ If Tax Exempt	
Essex	Southend-on-Sea B C	✔	✔	✔	✔	✔	✔ Unlimited	01702 534261
Essex	Tendring D C	✔	−	−	✗	✔	✔ Max stay 3hrs Pay for extra time	0845 603 7630
Essex	Thurrock C	✔	✔ Max stay Displayed by Plate	−	✔	✔	✔ Max stay Displayed by Car Park	01375 652652
Essex	Uttlesford D C	✔	✔	−	✔	✔	✔ Unlimited	01799 510510
Gloucestershire	Cheltenham B C	✔ Max stay !	✔ Max stay 2hrs	✔ Max stay 3hrs	✔ Max stay 2hrs	✔ Max 2 hrs	✔ Max stay 2hrs	01242 5325000
Gloucestershire	Cotswold D C	✔	✔ !	−	−	✔	✔ Unlimited	01452 426000
Gloucestershire	Forest of Dean D C	✔	−	−	−	✔	✔ Unlimited	01594 820500
Gloucestershire	Gloucester City C	✔ Max stay !	✔ Max stay 3hrs	✔ Max stay 3hrs	✔	✔	✔ Max stay 3hrs	01452 426868
Gloucestershire	South Gloucestershire C	✔	−	−	−	✔	✔ Unlimited !	01454 865994
Gloucestershire	Stroud D C	✔	✔	✔	✗	✔	✔ Unlimited	01453 760500
Gloucestershire	Tewkesbury B C	✔	✔	−	✗	✔	✔ Unlimited	01453 760500
Greater London	Hillingdon London B C	✔	✔	✔	✔	✔	!	01453 760500
Greater London	Barking & Dagenham London B C	✔ Max stay 4hrs	✔ Max stay 4hrs	−	✔ Max stay 4hrs	✔	✔ Unlimited	020 8227 2334
Greater London	Barnet London B C	✔ Max stay !	✔	✔	✔	✔	✔ Max stay 3hrs	020 8359 4131
Greater London	Bexley London B C	✔	✔	✔	✔	✔	✔ Unlimited	01322 344823
Greater London	Brent London B C	✔	✔	✔	✔	✔	✔ Unlimited	020 8937 4097
Greater London	Bromley London B C	✔ !	✔ !	✔ !	✗	✔	✔ Unlimited	020 8461 7629
Greater London	Camden London B C	✔	✗ 1 hr free once payment made	✗	✗	✗	✗	020 7974 4646 *1
Greater London	Camden London B C	✔	✔	✔	✔	✔	✗	020 7974 4646 *2
Greater London	Corporation of London	✔ Max stay 3hrs	✗ 1 hr free once payment made	−	✗	✗	✗	020 7332 1548 *3
Greater London	Croydon London B C	✔	✔	✔	✔	✔	✔	020 8726 7100
Greater London	Ealing London B C	✔	✔ Max stay 3hrs!	✔ Max stay 3hrs	✔	✔	✔ Unlimited	020 8825 6677
Greater London	Enfield London B C	✔	✔	✔	✔	✔	✔ Unlimited	020 8379 1000
Greater London	wich London B C	✔	✔	✔	✗	✔	✗	020 8921 2388
Greater London	Hackney London B C	✔	✔	✔	✗	✔	✔ Unlimited	020 8356 8370
Greater London	Hammersmith & Fulham London B C	✔	✔	✔	✔	✔	✔ Unlimited	020 8753 5133/4
Greater London	Haringey London B C	✔	✔	✔	✔	✔	✔ Unlimited	020 8489 1865
Greater London	Harrow London B C	✔	✔	✔	✔	✔	✔ Unlimited	020 8863 5611
Greater London	Havering London B C	✔	✔	✔	✔	✔	✗	01708 432 797
Greater London	Hounslow London B C	✔ Max stay 3hrs	✔	✔	✗	✔	✗	020 8583 3073
Greater London	Islington London B C	✔	✔	✔	✔	✔	✗	020 7527 6108
Greater London	Kensington & Chelsea Royal B C	✔ Max stay 4hrs Mon–Fri	✗ 1 hr free once payment made	✗	✗	✗ 20 mins to unload/load	✗	020 7361 3108 *4
Greater London	Lambeth London B C	✔ Max stay 3hrs	✔	✔	✔	✔	✗	020 7926 9000
Greater London	Lewisham London B C	✔	✔	✔	✗	✔	✗	020 8314 8129
Greater London	Merton London B C	✔	✔	✔	✔	✔	✔ Unlimited	020 8545 4661
Greater London	Newham London B C	✔ !	✔	✔	✔	✔	✔ Unlimited	020 8430 2000
Greater London	Redbridge London B C	✔	✔	✔	✗	✔	✔ Unlimited	020 8708 3636
Greater London	Richmond upon Thames London B C	✔	✔	✔	✔	✔	✔ Pass Required	020 8831 6096 / 6312
Greater London	Royal Borough of Kingston upon Thames	✔ Max stay 3hrs	✔ Max stay 3hrs	−	✔	✔	✔ Unlimited	020 8547 6600
Greater London	Southwark London B C	✔ Except when signs display the limit	✔	✔	✗	✔	✔	0870 600 6768
Greater London	Sutton London B C	✔	✔	✔	✗	✔	✗	020 8770 5341

*1 Part of Camden Borough Council is exempt from the Blue Badge Scheme and they operate their own GREEN Badge Scheme

*2 An area of Camden Borough Council that operates the Blue Badge Scheme

*3 Corporation of London is exempt from the Blue Badge Scheme and they operate their own RED Badge Scheme

*4 The Royal Borough of Kensington & Chelsea is exempt from the Blue Badge Scheme and they operate their own PURPLE Badge Scheme

Key
- **!** The rules may vary locally
- **B C** Borough Council
- **D C** District Council
- **–** Not applicable

County	Council	Blue Badge Park FREE with no time restrictions	Pay & Display (On street only) Park FREE with No time restrictions during the enforced time period	Shared Use Bays (Pay & Display and Resident) Park FREE with No time restrictions during the enforced time period	Resident Bays Park with no time restrictions during the enforced time period	Single & Double Yellow Lines Park for a maximum 3 hrs on a Single or Double Yellow Line	Council Owned Car Parks Free or Discounted parking for the Blue Badge Holders	Council Specific Contact Number For the Blue Badge Scheme
Greater London	Tower Hamlets London B C	✔ Max stay 3hrs !	✔	✔	✗	✔	✔ In Blue Badge Bays Only	020 7364 3788
Greater London	Waltham Forest London Borough	✔ Max stay 3hrs	✔	✔	✔	✔	✔ Unlimited	020 8496 1659
Greater London	Wandsworth B C	✔	✔	✔	✔	✔	✗	020 8871 7709
Greater London	Westminster City C	✔ Max stay 4hrs	✗ 1 hr free once payment made	✔ 1 hr free once payment made	✗	✗	✗	020 7823 4567
Greater Manchester	Salford City C	✔	✔	–	✗	✔	✔ Unlimited	0161 909 6508
Greater Manchester	Trafford Metropolitan Borough	✔ Max stay 3hrs !	✔	✔	✗	✔	✔ !	0161 912 1388
Greater Manchester	Wigan Metropolitan B C	✔	✔	–	✗	✔	✔ Unlimited	01942 244991
Greater Manchester	Bolton Metropolitan B C	✔	✔	–	✗	✔	✔ Unlimited	01204 337266
Greater Manchester	Bury Metropolitan B C	✔	✔ Max 3 hrs unless signs displays otherwise		✗	✔	✔ In Blue Badge Bays Only	0161 253 6855
Greater Manchester	Manchester City C	✔	✔	✔	✔	✔	✔ Unlimited	0161 819 1993
Greater Manchester	Oldham Metropolitan B C	✔	✔ Max stay 3hrs !	–	✗	✔	✔ Unlimited	0161 911 3000
Greater Manchester	Rochdale Metropolitan B C	✔ !	✔ Max stay 3hrs	✔	✗	✔	✗	01706 644106
Greater Manchester	Stockport Metropolitan B C	✔ Max stay 3hrs	✔ Max stay 3hrs	–	✗	✔	✔ Max stay 3hrs	0161 427 7011
Greater Manchester	Tameside Metropolitan B C	✔	–	–	–	✔	✔ Unlimited	0161 342 2462
Hampshire	Basingstoke & Deane B C	✔ Max stay 3hrs	✔	✔	✔	✔	✔ Unlimited	01962 845117
Hampshire	East Hampshire D C	✔	✔	–	✗	✔	✔ Unlimited	01962 841841
Hampshire	Eastleigh B C	✔	✔	–	✔	✔	✔ Unlimited	01962 841841
Hampshire	Fareham B C	✔	✔	–	✔	✔	✔ Unlimited	01962 841841
Hampshire	Gosport B C	✔	✔	–	✗	✔	✔ Unlimited	01962 841841
Hampshire	Hart D C	✔	✔	✔	✔	✔	✔ Unlimited	01962 847747
Hampshire	Havant B C	✔	✔	–	–	✔	✔ Unlimited	01962 841841
Hampshire	New Forest D C	✔	✔	–	✗	✔	✔ Unlimited	01962 847747
Hampshire	Portsmouth City C	✔	✔	✔ Max stay 3hrs	✔	✔	✔ Unlimited!	02392 841176
Hampshire	Rushmoor B C	✔	✔ Max stay 3hrs	–	✗	✔	✔ Unlimited !	01962 847650
Hampshire	Southampton City C	✔	✔	✔	✔	✔	✔ Except Automated Car parks	023 8022 3855
Hampshire	Test Valley B C	✔ Max stay 3hrs	✔ Max stay 3hrs	–	✔	✔	✔ Unlimited	01962 847650
Hampshire	Winchester City C	✔	✔	✔	✔	✔	✔ in P&D Car Parks only	01962 840222
Hertfordshire	Broxbourne B C	✔	✔	–	✗	✔	✔ Unlimited	01992 555555
Hertfordshire	Dacorum B C	✔	✔	–	✗	✔	✗	01923 471400
Hertfordshire	East Hertfordshire D C	✔	✗	–	✗	✔	✔ Unlimited	01438 737400
Hertfordshire	Hertsmere B C	✔ Max stay !	✔	–	✗	✔	✔ Unlimited	01438 737400
Hertfordshire	North Hertfordshire D C	✔ Max stay 3hrs	✔	–	✔	✔	✔ Unlimited	
Hertfordshire	St Albans D C	✔	✔ Max stay 3hrs	✔ Max stay 3hrs	✔	✔	✔ Unlimited	01438 737400
Hertfordshire	Stevenage B C	✔ Max stay 3hrs !	–	–	✗	✔	✔ With Season Discount Card	
Hertfordshire	Three Rivers D C	✔	✔	–	✗	✔	✗	
Hertfordshire	Watford B C	✔	✔	✔	✗	✔	✗	01923 471400
Hertfordshire	Welwyn Hatfield D C	✔ Max stay 3hrs !	–	–	✗	✔	!	
Isle of Man	Isle of Man Government	✔	–	–	✗	✔	✔ Unlimited	01624 686325
Isle of Wight	Isle of Wight C	✔	✔	–	✗	✔	✔ Unlimited	01983 821000
Isles of Scilly	Isle of Scilly C	✔	–	–	–	✔	✔	01720 422148
Kent	Ashford B C	✔	✔	–	✗	✔	✔ Max stay 3hrs Pay for extra time	01622 605020
Kent	Canterbury City C	✔ Max stay 3hrs	✔	✔ Max stay 3hrs	✔	✔	✔ Unlimited	01622 605020
Kent	Dartford B C	✔ Max stay 3hrs	✔ Max stay 3hrs	–	✗	✔	✗	01622 605020
Kent	Dover D C	✔	✔	–	✔	✔	✔ Max stay 3hrs	01622 605020
Kent	Gravesham B C	✔	✔	✔ !	✔	✔	✔ Unlimited	01622 605020
Kent	Maidstone B C	✔	✔	–	✗	✔	✔ Unlimited	01622 605020
Kent	Medway C	✔ Max stay 3hrs	–	–	✔	✔	✔ Except Automated Car parks	01634 306000
Kent	Sevenoaks D C	✔	✔	–	✔	✔	✔ Unlimited	01622 605020
Kent	Shepway D C	✔	✔ Max stay 3hrs	–	✔	✔	✔ Unlimited	01622 605020
Kent	Swale B C	✔	✔ Max stay 3hrs	✔ Max stay 3hrs	✔	✔	✔ Max stay 4hrs	01622 605020
Kent	Thanet D C	✔	✔	–	✔	✔	✔ Unlimited	01622 605020

*5 Greater London — Westminster City C

*5 City of Westminster is exempt from the Blue Badge Scheme and they operate their own WHITE Badge Scheme

- Free parking on Single & Double Yellow lines (3hrs max) except where loading and unloading restrictions apply, Pay & Display, Shared Use, Residents and Blue Badge Bays
- Free parking in most places (Single & Double Yellow lines (3hrs max) & Pay & Display) except Residents Bays
- Free parking in most places (Single & Double Yellow lines (3hrs max) & Pay & Display) except Shared Use and Residents Bays
- Free parking in Blue badge bays and Single & Double Yellow lines (3hrs max) only
- Free parking in Blue badge bays with limited concessions on Pay & Display
- Free parking in Blue badge bays only

	Key ! The rules may vary locally B C Borough Council D C District Council – Not applicable	Blue Badge Park FREE with no time restrictions	Pay & Display (On street only) Park FREE with No time restrictions during the enforced time period	Shared Use Bays (Pay & Display and Resident) Park FREE with No time restrictions during the enforced time period	Resident Bays Park with no time restrictions during the enforced time period	Single & Double Yellow Lines Park for a maximum 3 hrs on a Single or Double Yellow Line	Council Owned Car Parks Free or Discounted parking for the Blue Badge Holders	Council Specific Contact Number For the Blue Badge Scheme
County	Council							
Kent	Tonbridge & Malling B C	✔	✔ Max 3hrs	–	✔	✔	✔ Unlimited in BB Bay Max stay 3hrs if not BB Bay	01622 605020
Kent	Tunbridge Wells B C	✔	✔	✔	✘	✔	✔ Unlimited	01622 605020
Lancashire	Blackburn with Darwen BC	✔	✔	–	✘	✔	✔ Unlimited	01254 585381
Lancashire	Blackpool B C	✔ Max stay !	✔	–	✘	✔	✔ Max stay 3hrs in BB bay only	01253 477752
Lancashire	Burnley B C	✔ Max stay 12hrs	✔ Max stay 3hrs	–	✘	✔	✔ Max stay 3hrs Pay for extra time	0845 053 0049
Lancashire	Chorley B C	✔ Max stay 3hrs	✔ Max stay 3hrs	–	✘	✔	✔ Unlimited	0845 053 0049
Lancashire	Fylde B C	✔	✔ Max stay 3hrs	–	✔	✔	✔ Max stay 3hrs Pay for extra time	0845 053 0049
Lancashire	Hyndburn B C	✔ Max stay 3hrs	✔	–	✔	✔	✔ Unlimited	0845 053 0049
Lancashire	Lancaster City C	✔	✔	✔	✘	✔	✔ Unlimited	01524 66246
Lancashire	Pendle B C	✔	–	–	✔	✔	✔ Unlimited in BB Bay Limited if not BB Bay	01772 533689
Lancashire	Preston City C	✔	✔	–	✘	✔	✔ Unlimited	01772 533689
Lancashire	Ribble Valley B C	✔	✔	–	✘	✔	✔ Unlimited	01772 533689
Lancashire	Rossendale B C	✔	–	–	✘	✔	✔ Unlimited	01706 211221
Lancashire	South Ribble B C	✔	✔	–	✔	✔	✔ Unlimited	01772 533689
Lancashire	West Lancashire D C	✔	✔	–	✘	✔	✔ Unlimited	01695 577177
Lancashire	Wyre B C	✔ Max stay 3hrs	–	–	✔	✔	✘	0845 053 0049
Leicestershire	Leicester City C	✔ Max stay 3hrs	✔	–	✔	✔	✔ Unlimited	0116 2527000
Leicestershire	Blaby D C	✔	–	–	–	✔	✔ Unlimited	0116 2657584
Leicestershire	Charnwood B C	✔	–	–	✔	✔	✔	0116 2657584
Leicestershire	Harborough D C	✔	–	–	–	✔	✔ Unlimited	0116 2657584
Leicestershire	Hinckley & Bosworth B C	✔	–	–	–	✔	✔ Unlimited	0116 2657584
Leicestershire	Melton B C	✔ Max stay !	✔ Max stay 3hrs	✔ Max stay 3hrs	✔	✔	✘	0116 2657523
Leicestershire	North West Leicestershire D C	✔	–	–	–	✔	✔ Unlimited	0116 2657523
Leicestershire	Oadby & Wigston B C	✔ Max stay 3hrs	✔ Max stay 3hrs	–	✘	✔	✔ Unlimited	0116 2657523
Lincolnshire	Boston B C	✔	✔	–	–	✔	✔ Unlimited	0845 603 0536
Lincolnshire	East Lindsey D C	✔	✔	–	✘	✔	✘	0845 603 0536
Lincolnshire	Lincoln City C	✔ Max stay 3hrs	✔	–	–	✔	✔	01522 782155
Lincolnshire	North Kesteven D C	✔	–	–	–	✔	✔ Unlimited	01529 414155 01522 699699
Lincolnshire	South Holland D C	✔	✔	–	✘	✔	✘	0845 603 0536
Lincolnshire	South Kesteven D C	✔	✔	–	–	✔	✘	01522 550711
Lincolnshire	West Lindsey D C	✔	✔	–	✘	✔	✔ Unlimited	0845 603 0536
Lincolnshire (part of)	North East Lincolnshire C	✔	✔ !	–	✘	✔	✔ Unlimited	01472 325289
Lincolnshire (part of)	North Lincolnshire C	✔	✔ !	–	✔	✔	✔ Unlimited	01724 297979
Merseyside	Wirral Metropolitan B C	✔	✔	✔	✔	✔	✔ Unlimited	0151 666 5099
Merseyside	Knowsley Metropolitan B C	✔	✔	–	✘	✔	✔ Unlimited	0151 443 3841
Merseyside	Liverpool City C	✔	✔	✔	✘	✔	✔ Unlimited	0151 233 3000
Merseyside	Sefton C	✔	–	–	✘	✔	✔ Unlimited	0845 140 0845
Merseyside	St Helens Metropolitan B C	✔ Max stay 2hrs	–	–	✘	✔	✘	01744 456000
Norfolk	Norwich City C	✔ !	✔	✔	✘	✔	✔ Unlimited !	0844 800 8014
Norfolk	Breckland D C	✔	✔	–	✘	✔	✔ Unlimited	0844 800 8014
Norfolk	Broadland D C	✔	–	–	✘	✔	✔ Unlimited	0844 800 8014
Norfolk	Great Yarmouth B C	✔	✔	–	✘	✔	✔ Unlimited	0844 800 8020
Norfolk	King's Lynn & West Norfolk B C	✔	✔	✔	✘	✔	✔ Unlimited	0844 800 8020
Norfolk	North Norfolk D C	✔	✔ !	–	–	✔	✘	0844 800 8014
Norfolk	South Norfolk C	✔	–	–	✘	✔	✔	01508 533853
North Yorkshire	York City C	✔	✔	✔	✔	✔	✔ Max stay rules apply	01609 779999 *6
North Yorkshire	Craven D C	✔ Max stay 3hrs !	✔	–	–	✔	✔ Unlimited	01609 779999
North Yorkshire	Hambleton D C	✔	✔	✔	✘	✔	✘	01609 779999
North Yorkshire	Harrogate B C	✔	✔	–	✔ !	✔	✔ Unlimited	01609 779999
North Yorkshire	Richmondshire D C	✔ Max stay 3hrs	✔	–	✘	✔	✔ !	01609 779999
North Yorkshire	Ryedale D C	✔	✔	–	✘	✔	✘ but allowed an additional hour free	01609 779999

Free parking on Single & Double Yellow lines (3hrs max) except where loading and unloading restrictions apply, Pay & Display, Shared Use, Residents and Blue Badge Bays

Free parking in most places (Single & Double Yellow lines (3hrs max) & Pay & Display) except Residents Bays

Free parking in most places (Single & Double Yellow lines (3hrs max) & Pay & Display) except Shared Use and Residents Bays

Free parking in Blue badge bays and Single & Double Yellow lines (3hrs max) only

Free parking in Blue badge bays with limited concessions on Pay & Display

Free parking in Blue badge bays only

*6 Blue badge holders can obtain a permit to enter and park in the pedestrian zone for a 2hr Max Stay

North Yorkshire - Staffordshire

xxxiv

Key

!	The rules may vary locally
B C	Borough Council
D C	District Council
–	Not applicable

County	Council	Blue Badge Park FREE with no time restrictions	Pay & Display (On street only) Park FREE with No time restrictions during the enforced time period	Shared Use Bays (Pay & Display and Resident) Park FREE with No time restrictions during the enforced time period	Resident Bays Park with no time restrictions during the enforced time period	Single & Double Yellow Lines Park for a maximum 3 hrs on a Single or Double Yellow Line	Council Owned Car Parks Free or Discounted parking for the Blue Badge Holders	Council Specific Contact Number For the Blue Badge Scheme
North Yorkshire	Scarborough B C	✔ Max stay 3hrs	✔	–	✘	✔	✘	01609 779999
North Yorkshire	Selby D C	✔	✔	–	✘	✔	✔ Unlimited	01609 779999
Northamptonshire	Corby B C	✔	–	–	–	✔	✘	01604 236236
Northamptonshire	Daventry D C	✔	✔	–	–	✔	✔ Unlimited	01604 654364
Northamptonshire	East Northamptonshire D C	✔	–	–	–	✔	✔ Unlimited	01604 654364
Northamptonshire	Kettering B C	✔	✔	–	✔	✔	✔ Unlimited	01604 654365
Northamptonshire	Northampton B C	✔ Max stay 3hrs	✔	–	✔	✔	✔ Unlimited	01604 654364
Northamptonshire	South Northamptonshire C	✔ Max stay 3hrs	✔ Max stay 3hrs	–	✘	✔	✔ Unlimited	01604 654363
Northamptonshire	Wellingborough B C	✔	✔	–	–	✔	✔ Unlimited	01604 654364
Northumberland	Alnwick D C	✔ !	✔ !	–	✘	✔	✔ Unlimited	01665 510505
Northumberland	Berwick–upon–Tweed B C	✔	✔	–	✘	✔	✔ Unlimited	01670 533000
Northumberland	Blyth Valley B C	✔	✔	–	✘	✔	✔ Unlimited	01670 354316
Northumberland	Castle Morpeth B C	✔	✔	–	✔	✔	✔ In Blue Badge Bays Only	01670 533000
Northumberland	Tynedale C	✔ Max stay !	✔ Max stay 2hrs !	–	✘	✔	✔ Unlimited	01434 603582
Northumberland	Wansbeck D C	✔	✔	–	✘	✔	✔ Unlimited	01670 533000
Nottinghamshire	Ashfield D C	✔	✔	✔	✘	✔	✔ Unlimited	01623 405300
Nottinghamshire	Bassetlaw D C	✔	✔	–	✘	✔	✔ only in BB Bays, With Car Park's Time Limit	01909 535602
Nottinghamshire	Broxtowe B C	✔	–	–	✔	✔	✔ Unlimited	0115 917 5800
Nottinghamshire	Gedling B C	✔	✔	–	✘	✔	✔ In Blue Badge Bays Only: max 3hrs otherwise	0115 901 2957
Nottinghamshire	Mansfield D C	✔ Max stay 3hrs	✔	–	✘	✔	✔ Except Automated Car parks	01623 433433
Nottinghamshire	Newark & Sherwood D C	✔ !	✔	–	✘	✔	✔ Unlimited	01636 682700
Nottinghamshire	Nottingham City C	✔	✔	–	✘	✔	✔ Unlimited	0115 915 9835
Nottinghamshire	Rushcliffe B C	✔ Max stay 3hrs	✔	–	✘	✔	✔ Except Automated Car parks	0115 914 1500
Oxfordshire	Cherwell D C	✔	✔	–	–	✔	✔ Unlimited	01865 854409
Oxfordshire	Oxford City C	✔	✔	✔	✔	✔	✘	0845 050 7666
Oxfordshire	South Oxfordshire D C	✔	✔	–	–	✔	✔ Unlimited	01865 854409
Oxfordshire	Vale of White Horse D C	✔	✔	–	✔	✔	✔ Unlimited	01235 520202
Oxfordshire	West Oxfordshire D C	✔	✔	–	–	✔	✔ Unlimited	01865 854409
Rutland	Rutland C C	✔	–	✔	✔	✔	✔ in P&D Car Parks only	01572 758375
Shropshire	Telford & Wrekin B C	✔ Max stay 3hrs	✘ Double Time once payment made	–	✘	✔	✘	01952 202016
Shropshire	Bridgnorth D C	✔	–	–	✘	✔	✔ Max stay 3hrs	01743 450920
Shropshire	North Shropshire D C	✔	✔ Max stay 3hrs	–	✔	✔	✔ Unlimited	01743 450920
Shropshire	Oswestry B C	✔	✔	–	✘	✔	✘	01743 450920
Shropshire	Shrewsbury & Atcham B C	✔	✔ Max 3hrs	–	✘	✔	✘ discounted by car parks	01743 450920
Shropshire	South Shropshire D C	✔ Max stay 3hrs	✔ Max stay 3hrs	–	✘	✔	✔ Max stay 3hrs	01743 450920
Somerset	North Somerset D C	✔ Max stay 2hrs	✔	–	✘	✔	✘	01934 634725
Somerset	Bath & North East Somerset C	✔	✔	–	✔	✔	✔ Unlimited	01225 394147
Somerset	Mendip D C	✔	✔	✔	✔	✔	✔ Unlimited	0845 345 9133
Somerset	Sedgemoor D C	✔	✔	–	–	✔	✔ Unlimited	0845 345 9133
Somerset	South Somerset D C	✔	✔	–	✘	✔	✔ Unlimited	0845 345 9133
Somerset	Taunton Deane D C	✔	✔ Max stay 3hrs	–	✘	✔	✔ Unlimited	0845 345 9133
Somerset	West Somerset D C	✔ Max stay 3hrs	✔ Max stay 3hrs	✔	✘	✔	✘	0845 345 9133
South Yorkshire	Barnsley Metropolitan B C	✔ Max stay !	✔	–	✘	✔	✔ Unlimited	01226 772163
South Yorkshire	Doncaster Metropolitan B C	✔	✔	✔ Max 3 hrs	✔ Max 3hrs	✔	✔ In Blue Badge Bays Only	01302 737711
South Yorkshire	Rotherham Metropolitan B C	✔ Max stay !	✔	✔	✘	✔	✔ Unlimited !	01709 382121
South Yorkshire	Sheffield City C	✔ Max stay 4hrs	✔	✔	✘	✔	✔ Unlimited	01142 734897
Staffordshire	Cannock Chase D C	✔	✔	–	✔	✔	✔ Unlimited	01543 510300
Staffordshire	East Staffordshire B C	✔	✔	–	✘	✔	✔ Unlimited	01283 239888
Staffordshire	Lichfield D C	✔	✔	–	–	✔	✔ Unlimited	01543 510800
Staffordshire	Newcastle under Lyme B C	✔ Max stay 3hrs	–	–	–	✔	✔ Unlimited	01785 276950

*7 Special Permit to access City Centre pedestrian zones

Free parking on Single & Double Yellow lines (3hrs max) except where loading and unloading restrictions apply, Pay & Display, Shared Use, Residents and Blue Badge Bays

Free parking in most places (Single & Double Yellow lines (3hrs max) & Pay & Display) except Residents Bays

Free parking in most places (Single & Double Yellow lines (3hrs max) & Pay & Display) except Shared Use and Residents Bays

Free parking in Blue badge bays and Single & Double Yellow lines (3hrs max) only

Free parking in Blue badge bays with limited concessions on Pay & Display

Free parking in Blue badge bays only

Key		Blue Badge Park FREE with no time restrictions	Pay & Display (On street only) Park FREE with No time restrictions during the enforced time period	Shared Use Bays (Pay & Display and Resident) Park FREE with No time restrictions during the enforced time period	Resident Bays Park with no time restrictions during the enforced time period	Single & Double Yellow Lines Park for a maximum 3 hrs on a Single or Double Yellow Line	Council Owned Car Parks Free or Discounted parking for the Blue Badge Holders	Council Specific Contact Number For the Blue Badge Scheme
County	**Council**							
Staffordshire	South Staffordshire C	✔	✔	–	–	✔	✔ Unlimited	01785 276950
Staffordshire	Stafford B C	✔	✔	–	✘	✔	✔ Unlimited	01785 276950
Staffordshire	Staffordshire Moorlands D C	✔	✔	–	✘	✔	✔ !	01785 276950
Staffordshire	Stoke on Trent City C	✔ Max stay 3hrs	✔ Max stay 3hrs	–	✘	✔	✔ Unlimited	01782 234567
Staffordshire	Tamworth B C	✔	✔	–	✔	✔	✘	01827 709709
Suffolk	Babergh D C	✔	–	–	✘	✔	✔ Unlimited! Max 3hrs in very few	0845 602 3023
Suffolk	Forest Heath D C	✔	–	–	–	✔	✔ Unlimited	0845 023 023
Suffolk	Ipswich B C	✔ !	✔	–	✔	✔	✔ Unlimited !	01773 583000
Suffolk	Mid Suffolk D C	✔ Max stay 3hrs	✔ Max stay 3hrs	–	✘	✔	✔ Unlimited	0845 602 3023
Suffolk	St Edmundsbury B C	✔ !	✔	✔	✘	✔	✔ Unlimited	01284 763233
Suffolk	Suffolk Coastal D C	✔	✔	–	✘	✔	✔ Unlimited !	0845 602 3023
Suffolk	Waveney D C	✔ Max stay 3hrs	–	–	✔	✔	✔ Unlimited	08456 023 023
Surrey	Elmbridge B C	✔ Max stay 3hrs	✔	–	✔	✔	✔ Unlimited	0208 541 8981
Surrey	Epsom & Ewell B C	✔	✔	–	✔	✔	✔ Unlimited	08456 009 009
Surrey	Guildford B C	✔ !	✔	✔	✔	✔	✔ in P&D Car Parks only	08456 009 009
Surrey	Mole Valley D C	✔	✔	–	–	✔	✔ Unlimited	0845 600 9009
Surrey	Reigate & Banstead B C	✔	–	–	✘	✔	✔ Unlimited	01737 276000
Surrey	Runnymede B C	✔	–	–	–	✔	✔ Unlimited	01932 838383
Surrey	Spelthorne B C	✔	✔	–	✘	✔	✘	08456 009 009
Surrey	Surrey Heath B C	✔	✔	–	–	✔	✔ in P&D Car Parks only	08456 009 009
Surrey	Tandridge D C	✔ Max stay 3hrs	✔ !	–	–	✔	✔ After 9.30am	08456 009 009
Surrey	Waverley B C	✔ Max stay 3hrs	✔ !	–	✘	✔	✔ Unlimited	01483 523333
Surrey	Woking B C	✔	✔	✔	✔	✔	✔ Unlimited	None Supplied
Tyne & Wear	Gateshead Metropolitan B C	✔	✔	–	✘	✔	✔ Unlimited	0191 433 2429
Tyne & Wear	Newcastle upon Tyne City C	✔	✔	✔	✔	✔	✔ Unlimited	0191 211 6111
Tyne & Wear	North Tyneside Metropolitan B C	✔	✔	–	✘	✔	✔ Unlimited	0191 200 5308
Tyne & Wear	South Tyneside Metropolitan B C	✔ Max stay 3hrs	✔ Max stay 3hrs	✔	✔	✔	✔ Unlimited	0191 423 0200
Tyne & Wear	Sunderland City C	✔	✔	–	✘	✔	✔ in P&D Car Parks only	0191 520510
Warwickshire	North Warwickshire B C	✔ Max stay 3hrs !	✔ Max stay 3hrs	–	✘	✔	✘	01926 410410
Warwickshire	Nuneaton & Bedworth B C	✔	✔	–	✘	✔	✔ Unlimited	01926 410410
Warwickshire	Rugby B C	✔ Max stay 3hrs	✔ !	✔	✔	✔	✔ Unlimited	01926 410410
Warwickshire	Stratford on Avon D C	✔	✔	–	✔	✔	✔ Unlimited	01926 410410
Warwickshire	Warwick D C	✔	✔	–	✔	✔	✔ Unlimited	01926 410410
West Midlands	Birmingham City C	✔	✔	✔	✘	✔	✔ Unlimited	0121 303 6644
West Midlands	well Metropolitan B C	✔ Max stay !	✔	✔	✔ Max stay 3 hrs	✔	✔ Unlimited	0121 520 0201
West Midlands	Coventry City C	✔	✔	–	✘	✔	✔ Unlimited	0276 785210
West Midlands	Dudley Metropolitan B C	✔	✔	–	✘	✔	✔ Unlimited	01384 815822
West Midlands	Solihull Metropolitan B C	✔ Max stay 3hrs	–	–	–	✔	✔ Unlimited	01217 046000
West Midlands	Walsall Metropolitan B C	✔ Max stay 3hrs	✔	–	✘	✔	✔ Unlimited !	01922 653560
West Midlands	Wolverhampton City C	✔ Max stay 3hrs	✔	–	✔	✔	✘	
West Sussex	Adur D C	✔	✔	–	✘	✔	✔ Unlimited	01243 756759
West Sussex	Arun D C	✔	✔	–	✘	✔	✔ Unlimited	01243 756759
West Sussex	Chichester D C	✔	✔ (Voucher Parking)	–	✘	✔	✔ Unlimited	01243 756759
West Sussex	Crawley B C	✔	✔	–	✘	✔	✔ Unlimited	01243 756759
West Sussex	Horsham D C	✔ Max stay !	✔	✔	✘	✔	✔ Unlimited !	01243 777653
West Sussex	Mid Sussex D C	✔	✔	–	✘	✔	✔ Unlimited	01243 756759
West Sussex	Worthing B C	✔	✔	–	✘	✔	✔ Unlimited	01243 756759
West Yorkshire	City of Bradford Metropolitan D C	✔ Max stay !	✔	–	✘	✔	✔ Unlimited	
West Yorkshire	Calderdale Metropolitan B C	✔	✔	–	✘	✔	✘	01422 363561
West Yorkshire	City of Wakefield Metropolitan D C	✔	✔	–	✘	✔	✔ Unlimited	0800 1696520
West Yorkshire	Kirklees Metropolitan B C	✔	✔	–	✘	✔	✔ Unlimited	01924 325070
West Yorkshire	Leeds City C	✔	✔	–	✘	✔	✔ Unlimited	0113 398 4700
Wiltshire	Swindon B C	✔ Max stay 3hrs	✔	–	✔	✔	✔ in P&D Car Parks only	01793 463725
Wiltshire	Kennet D C	✔ Max stay !	✔	–	–	✔	✔ Max stay 3hrs Pay for extra time	01225 713000

Key

!	The rules may vary locally
B C	Borough Council
D C	District Council
–	Not applicable

Free parking on Single & Double Yellow lines (3hrs max) except where loading and unloading restrictions apply, Pay & Display, Shared Use, Residents and Blue Badge Bays

Free parking in most places (Single & Double Yellow lines (3hrs max) & Pay & Display) except Residents Bays

Free parking in most places (Single & Double Yellow lines (3hrs max) & Pay & Display) except Shared Use and Residents Bays

Free parking in Blue badge bays and Single & Double Yellow lines (3hrs max) only

Free parking in Blue badge bays with limited concessions on Pay & Display

Free parking in Blue badge bays only

XXXVI

Wiltshire - Northern Ireland - Scotland

Key			Blue Badge Park FREE with no time restrictions	Pay & Display (On street only) Park FREE with No time restrictions during the enforced time period	Shared Use Bays (Pay & Display and Resident) Park FREE with No time restrictions during the enforced time period	Resident Bays Park with no time restrictions during the enforced time period	Single & Double Yellow Lines Park for a maximum 3 hrs on a Single or Double Yellow Line	Council Owned Car Parks Free or Discounted parking for the Blue Badge Holders	Council Specific Contact Number For the Blue Badge Scheme

Key:
! The rules may vary locally
B C Borough Council
D C District Council
– Not applicable

County	Council	Blue Badge	Pay & Display	Shared Use Bays	Resident Bays	Single & Double Yellow Lines	Council Owned Car Parks	Council Specific Contact Number
Wiltshire	North Wiltshire D C	✔ Max stay !	–	–	–	✔	✔ Unlimited	01225 713000
Wiltshire	Salisbury D C	✔ Max stay 3hrs	✔	–	✔	✔	✔ Max stay rules apply	01225 713000
Wiltshire	West Wiltshire D C	✔ Max stay !	✔	–	✘	✔	✔ Max stay 3hrs	01225 713 000
Worcestershire	Bromsgrove D C	✔	✔	–	✘	✔	✘	01527 881288
Worcestershire	Malvern Hills D C	✔	–	–	✘	✔	✔ Unlimited !	01684 862 151
Worcestershire	Redditch B C	✔	✔	–	✘	✔	✔ Unlimited	01527 534123
Worcestershire	Worcester City C	✔ Max stay 3hrs	✔ Max stay 3hrs	–	✘	✔	✔ Max stay 3hrs in Short stay Unlimited in Long stay!	01905 722233
Worcestershire	Wychavon D C	✔	✔	–	✘	✔	✔ Unlimited	01386 565000
Worcestershire	Wyre Forest D C	✔	✔	–	✘	✔	✔ Unlimited	01562 732 928
Yorkshire (parts of)	Middlesbrough C	✔	✔	✔	✘	✔	✔ Unlimited	01642 726004
Yorkshire (parts of)	Redcar & Cleveland B C	✔ Max stay 3hrs	✔ Max stay 3hrs!	✔	✘	✔	✔ Max stay 3hrs!	01642 771500
Northern Ireland								
	Antrim B C	✔ Max stay 3hrs	–	–	✔	✔	✘	028 6634 3700
	Ards B C	✔ Max stay 3hrs	–	–	–	✔	✘	028 6634 3700
	Armagh City & D C	✔ Max stay 3hrs	✔	–	✔	✔	✘	028 6634 3700
	Ballymena B C	✔ Max stay 3hrs	✔	–	✔	✔	✘	028 6634 3700
	Ballymoney B C	✔ Max stay 3hrs	✔	✔	✔	✔	✘	028 2766 1810
	Banbridge B C	✔ Max stay 3hrs	✔	–	✔	✔	✘	028 6634 3700
	Belfast City C	✔ Max stay 3hrs	✔	–	✔	✔	✘	028 6634 3730
	Carrickfergus B C	✔ Max stay 3hrs	✔	–	✔	✔	✘	028 6634 3700
	Castlereagh B C	✔ Max stay 3hrs	✔	–	✔	✔	✔ Unlimited	028 6634 3700
	Coleraine B C	✔ Max stay 3hrs Unless signs says otherwise	✔	✔	✔	✔	✘	028 6634 3700
	Cookstown D C	✔ Max stay 3hrs	✔ Max stay 3hrs	✔	✔	✔	✔ Max stay 3hrs Pay for extra time	028 6634 3700
	Craigavon B C	✔ Max stay 3hrs	✔	–	✔	✔	✘	028 6634 3700
	Derry City C	✔ Max stay 3hrs	✔	–	✔	✔	✘	028 6634 3700
	Down D C	✔ Max stay 3hrs Unless signs says otherwise	✔	–	–	✔	✘	028 6634 3700
	Dungannon & South Tyrone B C	✔ Max stay 3hrs	✔	–	✔	✔	✘	028 6634 3700
	Fermanagh D C	✔ Max stay 3hrs	✔	–	✔	✔	✘	028 6634 3700
	Larne B C	✔ Max stay 3hrs	✔	–	✔	✔	✘	028 6634 3700
	Limavady B C	✔ Max stay 3hrs	✔	–	✔	✔	✘	028 6634 3700
	Lisburn City C	✔ Max stay 3hrs	✔	–	✔	✔	✘	028 6634 3700
	Londonderry City C	✔ Max stay 3hrs	✔	–	✔	✔	✘	028 6634 3700
	Magherafelt D C	✔ Max stay 3hrs	✔	–	✔	✔	✘	028 6634 3700
	Moyle D C	✔ Max stay 3hrs	✔	–	✔	✔	✘	028 6634 3700
	Newry & Mourne D C	✔ Max stay 3hrs	✔	–	✔	✔	✘	028 6634 3700
	Newtownabbey B C	✔ Max stay 3hrs	✔	–	✔	✔	✘	028 6634 3700
	North Down B C	✔ Max stay 3hrs	✔	–	✔	✔	✘	028 6634 3700
	Omagh D C	✔ Max stay 3hrs	✔	–	✔	✔	✘	028 6634 3700
	Strabane D C	✔ Max stay 3hrs	✔	–	✔	✔	✘	028 6634 3700
Scotland								
*8	Aberdeen City C	✔	✔	✔	✔ !	✔ Unlimited	✔ Unlimited	01224 522659
	Aberdeenshire C	✔	✔	✔	✔	✔ Unlimited	✘	
	Angus C	✔	✔	✔	✔	✔ Unlimited	✔ Unlimited	01307 474664
	Argyll & Bute C	✔	✔	–	✔	✔ Unlimited	✔ Unlimited	
	Clackmannanshire C	✔	–	–	✘	✔ Unlimited	✔ Unlimited	01529 452542
	Dumfries & Galloway C	✔	–	–	–	✔ Unlimited	✔ Unlimited	01387 26 0000
	Dundee City C	✔	✔	–	✔	✔ Unlimited	✔ Unlimited	01382 438310
	East Ayrshire C	✔ Max stay !	✔	–	–	✔ Unlimited	✔ Unlimited	01563 576000

*8 The council operates Blue Badge scheme and operates their own GREEN Badge Policy

Free parking on Single & Double Yellow lines (3hrs max) except where loading and unloading restrictions apply, Pay & Display, Shared Use, Residents and Blue Badge Bays

Free parking in most places (Single & Double Yellow lines (3hrs max) & Pay & Display) except Residents Bays

Free parking in most places (Single & Double Yellow lines (3hrs max) & Pay & Display) except Shared Use and Residents Bays

Free parking in Blue badge bays and Single & Double Yellow lines (3hrs max) only

Free parking in Blue badge bays with limited concessions on Pay & Display

Free parking in Blue badge bays only

Users should be aware that this information may change at any time. This information was correct as of October 2008. Compiled by PIE Enterprises Ltd © 2008. All rights reserved.

Key
! The rules may vary locally
B C Borough Council
D C District Council
– Not applicable

County	Council	Blue Badge Park FREE with no time restrictions	Pay & Display (On street only) Park FREE with No time restrictions during the enforced time period	Shared Use Bays (Pay & Display and Resident) Park FREE with No time restrictions during the enforced time period	Resident Bays Park with no time restrictions during the enforced time period	Single & Double Yellow Lines Park for a maximum 3 hrs on a Single or Double Yellow Line	Council Owned Car Parks Free or Discounted parking for the Blue Badge Holders	Council Specific Contact Number For the Blue Badge Scheme
	East Dunbartonshire C	✔	✔	–	–	✔ Unlimited	✔ Unlimited	0141 7751311
	East Lothian D C	✔	✔	–	–	✔ Unlimited	✔ Unlimited	0162 082 7367
	East Renfrewshire C	✔	✔	–	✘	✔ Unlimited	✔ Unlimited	0141 5773001
	Edinburgh City C	✔	✔	–	✘	✔ Unlimited	✘	0131 469 3840
	Falkirk C	✔	✔	–	✘	✔ Unlimited	✔ Unlimited	01324 504725
	Fife C	✔	✔	✔	✘	✔ Unlimited	✔ Unlimited	
	Glasgow City C	✔	✔	✔ !	✘	✔ Unlimited	✔ Unlimited (P & D Only)	
	Highland C	✔	✔	–	✘	✔ Unlimited	!	01463 702142
	Inverclyde C	✔	–	–	–	✔ Unlimited	✔ Unlimited	01475 714100
	Midlothian C	✔	–	–	–	✔ Unlimited	✔ Unlimited	0131 271 3522
	Moray C	✔ Max stay 3hrs	✔	–	✘	✔ Unlimited	✘	01343551339
	North Ayrshire C	✔	–	–	✘	✔ Unlimited	✘	01294 317700
	North Lanarkshire C	✔	–	–	–	✔ Unlimited	✔	01698 332000
	Orkney Islands C	✔	✔	–	–	✔ Unlimited	✔ Unlimited	01856 873535
	Perth & Kinross C	✔	✔	–	–	✔ Unlimited	✔ Unlimited	01738 476868
	Renfrewshire C	✔	✔	✔	✔	✔ Unlimited	✔ Unlimited	0141 842 5000
	Scottish Borders C	✔	✔	–	✔	✔ Unlimited	✔ Unlimited	
	Shetland Islands C	✔	–	–	–	✔ Unlimited	✔ Unlimited	01595 74 4319
	South Ayrshire C	✔	✔	–	✘	✔ Unlimited	✔ Unlimited	
	South Lanarkshire C	✔	✔	✔	✔	✔ Unlimited	✔ If Not automated	01698 454444
	Stirling C	✔	✔	✔	✘	✔ Unlimited	✔ Unlimited	0845 277 7000
	West Dunbartonshire C	✔	–	–	–	✔ Unlimited	✔ Unlimited	01389 737000
	West Lothian C	✔ Max stay !	–	–	–	✔ Unlimited	✔ Unlimited	01506 775287
	Western Isles / Comhairle nan Eilean Siar	✔	–	–	–	✔ Unlimited	✔ Unlimited	01851 709611
Wales								
	Blaenau Gwent C C B C	✔ Max stay 3hrs	✔	–	✘	✔	✔ Unlimited	
	Bridgend County B C	✔ Max stay !	–	–	✘	✔ Unlimited	✔ Unlimited	01656 642200
	Caerphilly County B C	✔	–	–	–	✔	–	0808 100 2500
	Cardiff C C	✔	✔	–	✔ Max stay 3 hrs	✔ Unlimited	!	02920 521855
	Carmarthenshire C C	✔ Max stay !	✔ Max stay 3hrs	–	✔	✔	✔ Max stay 3 hrs Pay for extra time	01267 224401
	Ceredigion C C	✔	–	–	–	✔	✘	01545 574000
	Conwy County B C	✔	✔	✔	✘	✔ Unlimited	✔ In Blue Badge Bays Only	01492 574000
	Denbighshire C C	✔	✔	–	✘	✔ Unlimited	!	
	Flintshire C C	✔	✔	–	✘	✔ Unlimited	!	01352 701304
	Isle of Anglesey C C	✔	–	–	✘	✔	✔ Unlimited	01248 750157
	Merthyr Tydfil County B C	✔	✔	✔	✘	✔ Unlimited	✘	01685 724500
	Monmouthshire C C	✔	✔	✘	✔	✔ Unlimited	!	01873 735394
	Neath Port Talbot County B C	✔	✔	–	✘	✔ Unlimited	!	
	Newport City C	✔	✔	✔	✘	✔	✔ Unlimited if surface Car Park	01633 656656
	Pembrokeshire C C	✔ Max stay !	–	–	✘	✔ Unlimited	✔ Max stay 3hrs	01437 760999
	Powys C C	✔	✔	✔	✘	✔ Unlimited	!	01597 826000
	Rhondda Cynon Taff County B C	✔	–	–	✔	✔	✔ Unlimited	01443 431513
	Swansea City & B C	✔ Max stay !	–	–	✘	✔ Unlimited	!	
	Torfaen County B C	✔	✔	–	✔	✔	✔ Unlimited	01495 762200
	Vale of Glamorgan C	✔	✔	–	✘	✔	✔ Unlimited	01446 730 402
Channel Islands								
	The States of Guernsey	✔	✔	✔	✘	✔ Unlimited	✘	01481 243400
	The States of Jersey	✔ Max stay !	✔	–	✔	✔ Unlimited	✔ Max stay 12hrs	01534 603000

Free parking on Single & Double Yellow lines (3hrs max) except where loading and unloading restrictions apply, Pay & Display, Shared Use, Residents and Blue Badge Bays

Free parking in most places (Single & Double Yellow lines (3hrs max) & Pay & Display) except Residents Bays

Free parking in most places (Single & Double Yellow lines (3hrs max) & Pay & Display) except Shared Use and Residents Bays

Free parking in Blue badge bays and Single & Double Yellow lines (3hrs max) only

Free parking in Blue badge bays with limited concessions on Pay & Display

Free parking in Blue badge bays only

(See page 174 for general abbreviations and page 177 for administrative area abbreviations)

ROUTE PLANNING MAPS Pages 3-47

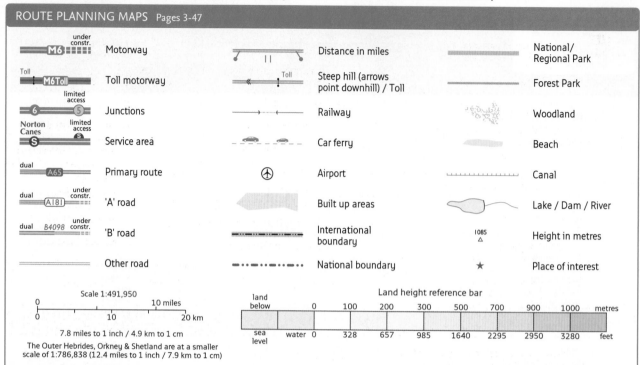

Motorway (under constr.)	Distance in miles	National / Regional Park
Toll motorway (M6Toll)	Steep hill (arrows point downhill) / Toll	Forest Park
Junctions (limited access)	Railway	Woodland
Service area (Norton Canes, limited access)	Car ferry	Beach
Primary route (dual A65)	Airport	Canal
'A' road (dual A181, under constr.)	Built up areas	Lake / Dam / River
'B' road (dual B4098, under constr.)	International boundary	Height in metres (1085)
Other road	National boundary	Place of interest

Scale 1:491,950

0 ———— 10 miles
0 ——— 10 ——— 20 km

7.8 miles to 1 inch / 4.9 km to 1 cm

The Outer Hebrides, Orkney & Shetland are at a smaller scale of 1:786,838 (12.4 miles to 1 inch / 7.9 km to 1 cm)

Land height reference bar

land below	0	100	200	300	500	700	900	1000	metres
sea level	water 0	328	657	985	1640	2295	2950	3280	feet

APPROACH ROUTE MAPS Pages 48 to 172 (even numbers)

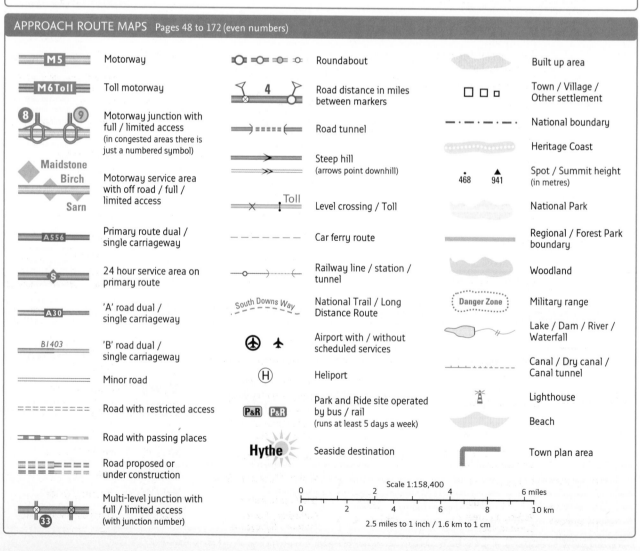

Motorway (M5)	Roundabout	Built up area
Toll motorway (M6Toll)	Road distance in miles between markers	Town / Village / Other settlement
Motorway junction with full / limited access (in congested areas there is just a numbered symbol)	Road tunnel	National boundary
Motorway service area with off road / full / limited access (Maidstone, Birch, Sarn)	Steep hill (arrows point downhill)	Heritage Coast
Primary route dual / single carriageway (A556)	Level crossing / Toll	Spot / Summit height (in metres) (468, 941)
24 hour service area on primary route	Car ferry route	National Park
'A' road dual / single carriageway (A30)	Railway line / station / tunnel	Regional / Forest Park boundary
'B' road dual / single carriageway (B1403)	National Trail / Long Distance Route (South Downs Way)	Woodland
Minor road	Airport with / without scheduled services	Military range (Danger Zone)
Road with restricted access	Heliport	Lake / Dam / River / Waterfall
Road with passing places	Park and Ride site operated by bus / rail (runs at least 5 days a week) (P&R)	Canal / Dry canal / Canal tunnel
Road proposed or under construction	Seaside destination (Hythe)	Lighthouse
Multi-level junction with full / limited access (with junction number) (33)		Beach
		Town plan area

Scale 1:158,400

0 ———— 2 ———— 4 ———— 6 miles
0 —— 2 —— 4 —— 6 —— 8 —— 10 km

2.5 miles to 1 inch / 1.6 km to 1 cm

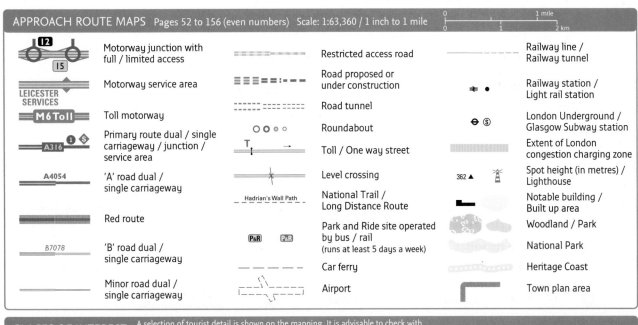

APPROACH ROUTE MAPS Pages 52 to 156 (even numbers) Scale: 1:63,360 / 1 inch to 1 mile

	Motorway junction with full / limited access
LEICESTER SERVICES	Motorway service area
M6 Toll	Toll motorway
A316	Primary route dual / single carriageway / junction / service area
A4054	'A' road dual / single carriageway
	Red route
B7078	'B' road dual / single carriageway
	Minor road dual / single carriageway

	Restricted access road
	Road proposed or under construction
	Road tunnel
○○○○	Roundabout
T	Toll / One way street
	Level crossing
Hadrian's Wall Path	National Trail / Long Distance Route
P&R P&R	Park and Ride site operated by bus / rail (runs at least 5 days a week)
	Car ferry
	Airport

	Railway line / Railway tunnel
	Railway station / Light rail station
	London Underground / Glasgow Subway station
	Extent of London congestion charging zone
362 ▲	Spot height (in metres) / Lighthouse
	Notable building / Built up area
	Woodland / Park
	National Park
	Heritage Coast
	Town plan area

PLACES OF INTEREST
A selection of tourist detail is shown on the mapping. It is advisable to check with the local tourist information centre regarding opening times and facilities available.

Any of the following symbols may appear on the map in maroon ★ which indicates that the site has World Heritage status.

i	Tourist information centre (open all year)
i	Tourist information centre (open seasonally)
m	Ancient monument
	Aquarium
	Aqueduct / Viaduct
	Arboretum
1643	Battlefield
	Blue flag beach
Å	Camp site / Caravan site
	Castle
	Cave
	Country park
	County cricket ground

	Distillery
	Ecclesiastical building
	Event venue
	Farm park
	Garden
	Golf course
	Historic house
	Historic ship
	Major football club
£	Major shopping centre / Outlet village
	Major sports venue
	Motor racing circuit
	Mountain bike trail
	Museum / Art gallery

	Nature reserve (NNR indicates a National Nature Reserve)
	Racecourse
	Rail Freight Terminal
	Ski slope (artificial / natural)
	Spotlight nature reserve (Best sites for access to nature)
	Steam railway centre / Preserved railway
	Surfing beach
	Theme park
	University
	Vineyard
	Wildlife park / Zoo
★	Other interesting feature
(NT) (NTS)	National Trust / National Trust for Scotland property

CITY AND TOWN CENTRE MAPS Pages 49 to 173 (odd numbers) Scale: All at different scales, see individual plans for scale bars

M8	Motorway
A4	Primary route dual / single carriageway / Junction
A40	'A' road dual / single carriageway
B507	'B' road dual / single carriageway
Toll	Other road dual / single carriageway / Toll
	Red route
	Access restriction
	Pedestrian street / Street market

	Minor road / Track
	One way street / Orbital route
FB	Footpath / Footbridge
	Main / other National Rail station
	London Underground / Overground station
	Light Rail / Station
	Vehicle / Pedestrian ferry
	Bus / coach station
	Cathedral / Church / Mosque / Synagogue

	Park / Garden / Sports ground
↑↑↑↑	Cemetery
	Leisure & tourism
	Shopping
	Administration & law
	Health & welfare
	Education
	Industry / Office
	Other notable building

Symbols appear on all scales of mapping

   Accessible accommodation   Accessible beach

   Disabled friendly caravan site   Forum of Mobility Centres

   Shopmobility   Toll with discount for Blue Badge holders

   Site with wheelchair accessible boat

Symbols appear on urban maps and town plans

Petrol stations

Petrol station   Petrol station with service call

Petrol station with accessible toilet for the disabled   Petrol station with service call and accessible toilet for the disabled

Symbols appear on town plans

Toilets

Public toilet   Wheelchair accessible public toilet

Public toilet with National Key Scheme toilet   Changing place toilet

On Street Parking

Blue Badge parking bay

Red Route box bay

Character within circle refers to parking duration e.g.

❶ 1 hour   ❷ 2 hours
❸ 3 hours   ❹ 4 hours
❻ 6 hours
Ⓤ unlimited   ❗ check signs locally

Off Street Parking

Car park   Car park with height restriction of **2.20m** or less

Car park free or discounted for Blue Badge holders   Car park with height restrictions free or discounted for Blue Badge holders

Number within square refers to the accessibility of the car park as defined by the accessibility grading below eg: **D1** is a car park discounted for Blue Badge holder, accessible to a wheelchair-user travelling independently

Definition of accessibility grading used for car parks

1 - Accessible to a wheelchair-user travelling independently

 2 - Accessible to a wheelchair-user travelling with assistance

 3 - Accessible to a wheelchair-user or someone with limited mobility, able to walk a few paces and up a maximum of three steps

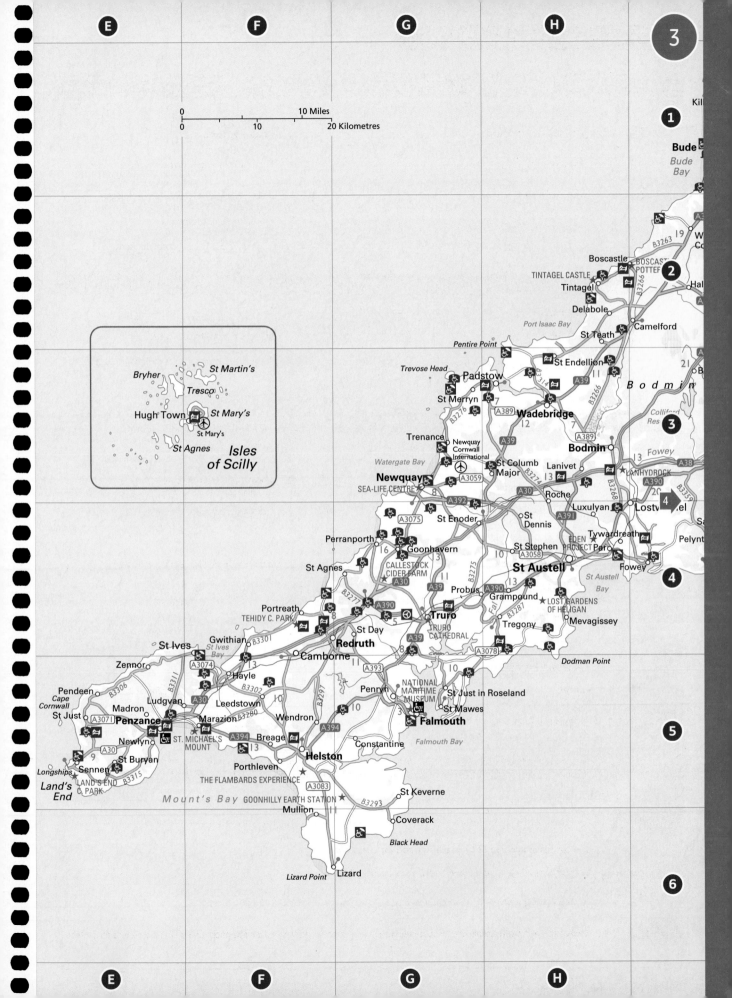

E   **F**   **G**   **H**

1

0   10 Miles
0   10   20 Kilometres

Kil

Bude
*Bude
Bay*

B3263 19   W
Co

Boscastle
TINTAGEL CASTLE   BOSCAST
POTTEF
Tintagel
Delabole   Hal

Port Isaac Bay   Camelford
St Teath
2

21

Pentire Point
St Endellion
Trevose Head   *B o d m i n*
Padstow
St Merryn   7   11
B3276   **Wadebridge**   *Colliford
Res*
Trenance   12   **A389**
Newquay   **Bodmin**   13   *Fowey*   **3**
Cornwall
International   St Columb   Lanivet   13   A38
Watergate Bay   Major   13   LANHYDROCK   A390
Isles   **Newquay**   **A3059**   Roche   Luxulyan   B3359
of Scilly   SEA-LIFE CENTRE   8   A392   A391   Lostw el   **4**
A3075   St   A30   Tywardreath
St Enoder   Dennis   EDEN   Pelynt
Perranporth   PROJECT Paro
Goonhavern   St Stephen   Fowey
16   10   A3058
CALLESTOCK   11   B3275   St Austell   **4**
St Agnes   CIDER FARM   A30   **St Austell**   *St Austell
A39   Probus   A390   13   Bay*
Portreath   B3277   Grampound   B3287   LOST GARDENS
TEHIDY C. PARK   8   A390   OF HELIGAN
St Ives   St Day   5   **Truro**   Tregony   Mevagissey
Zennor   *St Ives   B3301*   TRURO   A39
Bay   **Redruth**   CATHEDRAL   8   *Dodman Point*
Gwithian   **Camborne**   11   10
Pendeen   Hayle   A393   Penryn   NATIONAL
Cape   B3306   13   B3302   MARITIME
Cornwall   Madron   Ludgvan   10   MUSEUM   St Just in Roseland
St Just   A3071   Leedstown   B3280   3   St Mawes
Penzance   Marazion   Wendron   **Falmouth**
Newlyn   A30   ST. MICHAEL'S   A394   Breage   A394   *Falmouth Bay*
9   A30   MOUNT   13   Constantine
Longships   Sennen   St Buryan   **Helston**   St Keverne   **5**
LAND'S END   B3315   Porthleven
Land's   C. PARK   THE FLAMBARDS EXPERIENCE   A3083
End   *Mount's Bay* GOONHILLY EARTH STATION   B3293
Mullion   Coverack

Black Head
6

Lizard Point   Lizard

E   **F**   **G**   **H**

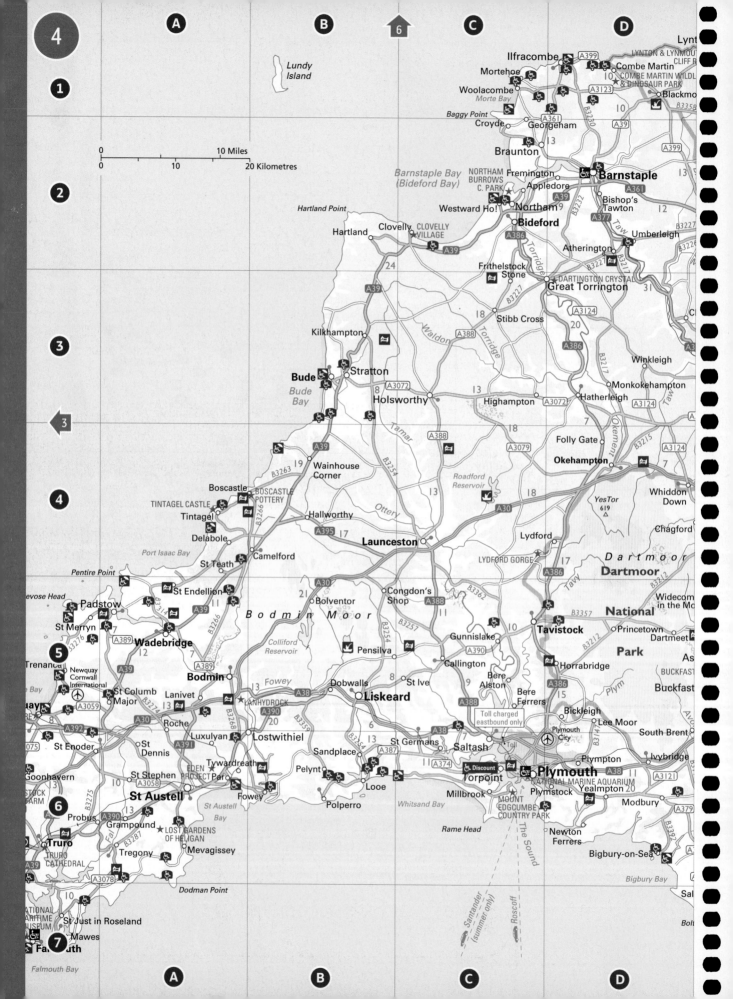

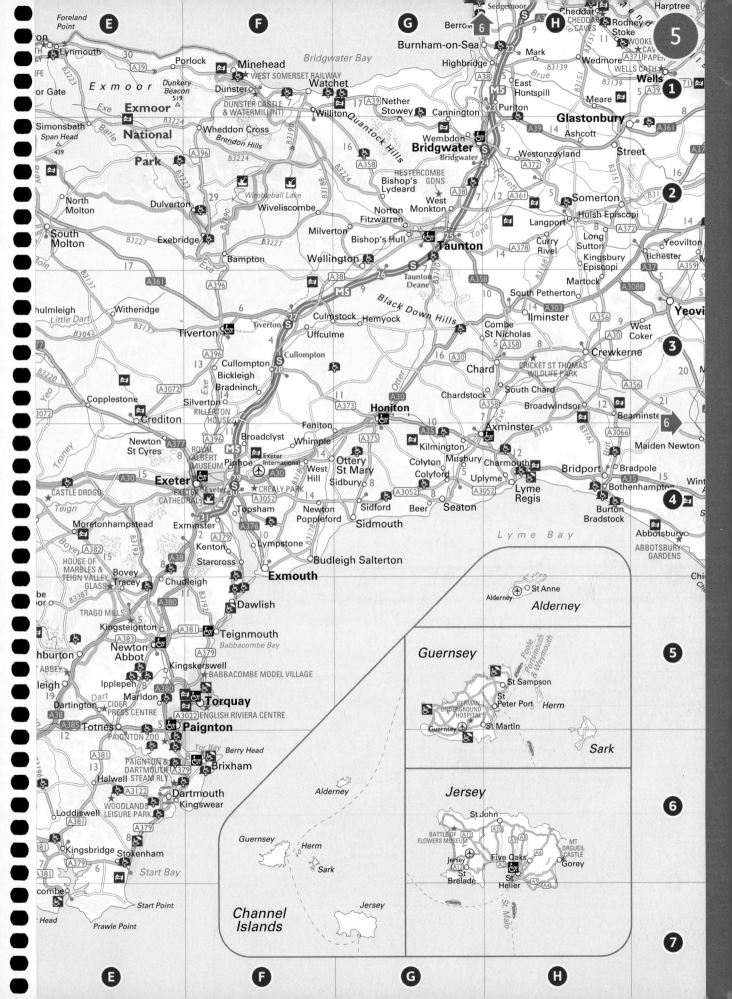

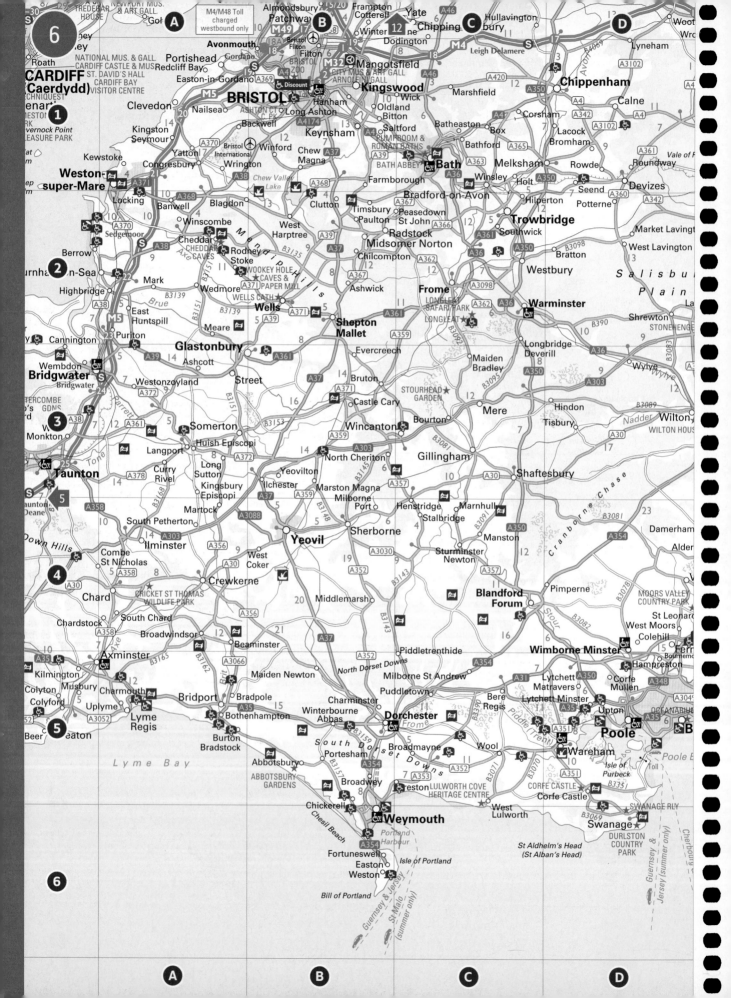

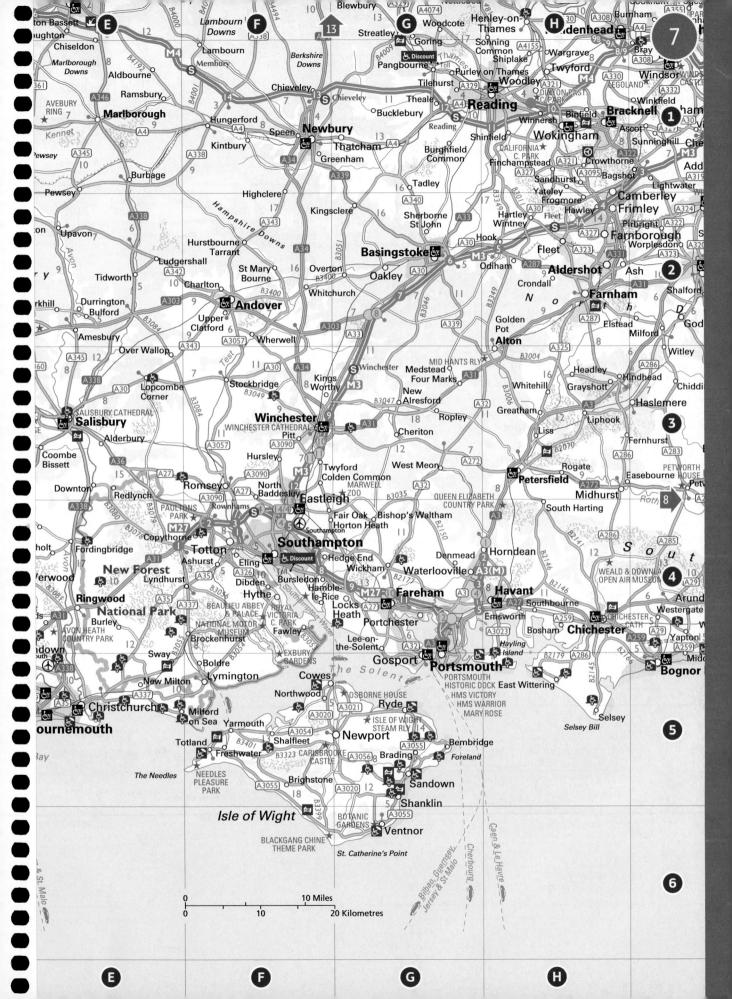

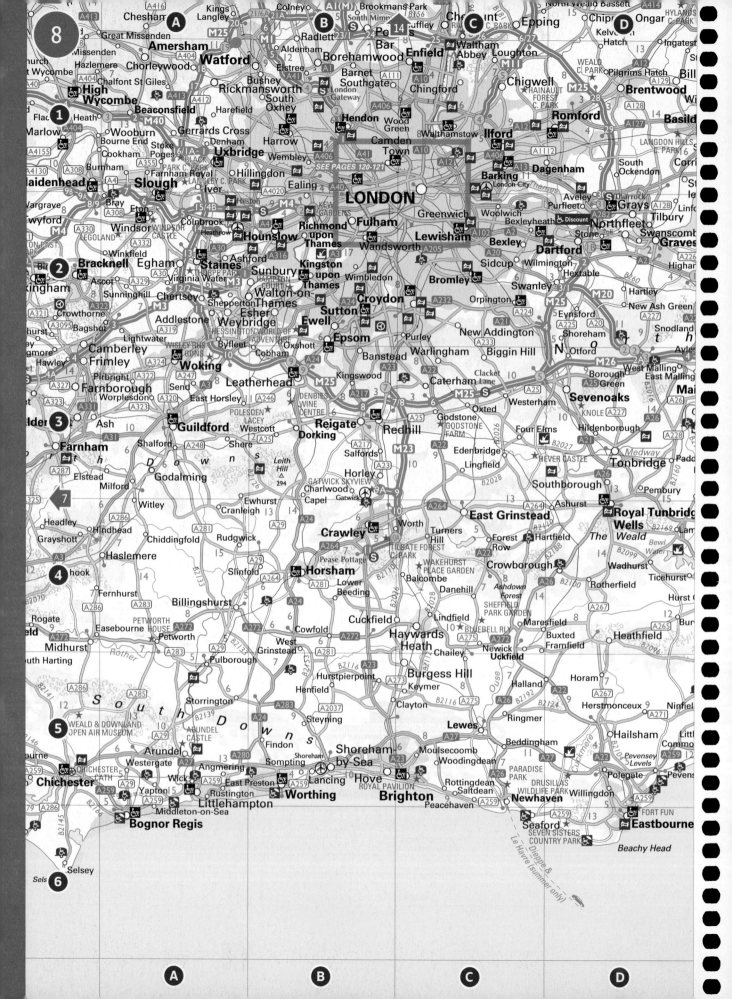

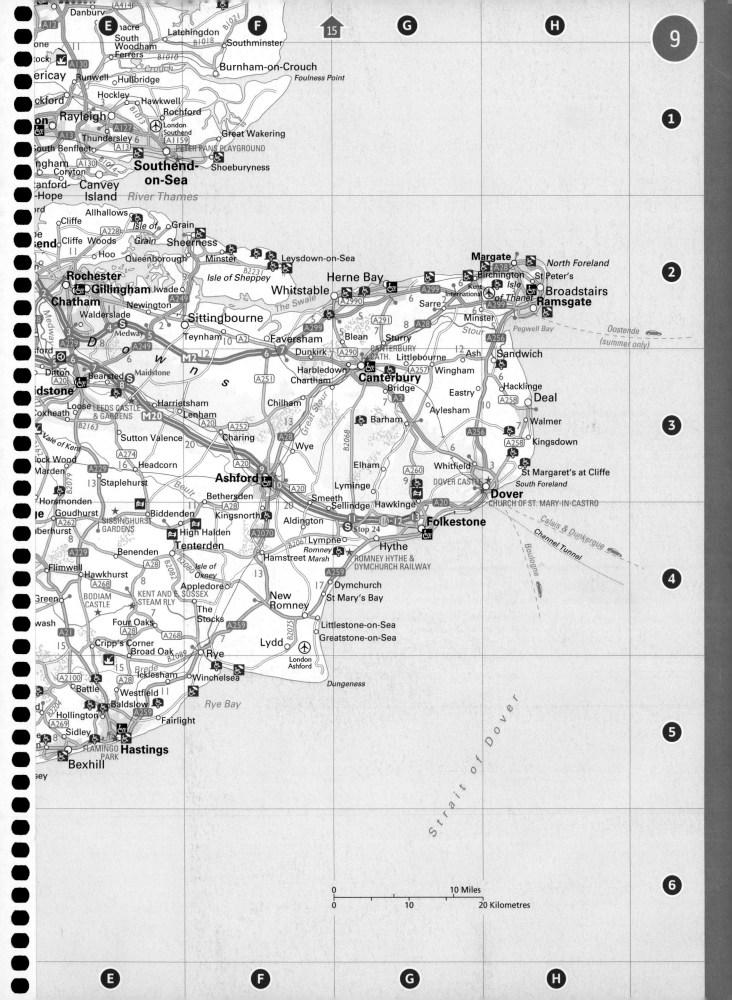

A414 Danbury
A12
South
Woodham
Latchingdon
B1018
Southminster
Ferrers
B1010
Burnham-on-Crouch
Crouch
Foulness Point
Runwell
Hullbridge
Hockley
Hawkwell
Rochford
Rayleigh
Thundersley
London
Southend
Great Wakering
A127
South Benfleet
A13
PETER PAN'S PLAYGROUND
Coryton
Canvey
Southend-
Shoeburyness
Island
on-Sea
River Thames

Allhallows
Cliffe
Isle of
Grain
Cliffe
Woods
Grain
Sheerness
Hoo
Queenborough
Minster
Leysdown-on-Sea
Margate
North Foreland
Rochester
Isle of Sheppey
Birchington
St Peter's
Gillingham
Wade
The Swale
Herne Bay
Kent
Isle
Broadstairs
Chatham
Whitstable
International
of Thanet
Walderslade
Newington
A299
Sarre
Ramsgate
Sittingbourne
A2990
Minster
Oostende
Medway
Teynham
A291
Blean
Sturry
Stour
Pegwell Bay
(summer only)
Ditton
Faversham
CANTERBURY
Littlebourne
Ash
Sandwich
Bearsted
Maidstone
Dunkirk
A290
CATH.
Hacklinge
Maidstone
Harbledown
Canterbury
Wingham
Loose
LEEDS CASTLE
Chartham
Bridge
Eastry
A258
Deal
Coxheath
& GARDENS
A2
Aylesham
M20
Harrietsham
Chilham
Barham
Walmer
Sutton Valence
Lenham
Charing
Wye
A258
Kingsdown
Vale of Kent
A274
Headcorn
A20
A28
Elham
Whitfield
St Margaret's at Cliffe
Marden
Staplehurst
Ashford
Lyminge
A260
DOVER CASTLE
South Foreland
Horsmonden
Bethersden
Smeeth
Whitfield
Dover
Goudhurst
Biddenden
Kingsnorth
Sellindge
Hawkinge
CHURCH OF ST. MARY-IN-CASTRO
High Halden
Aldington
Stop 24
A20
Folkestone
Calais & Dunkergue
Tenterden
Lympne
Hythe
Channel Tunnel
Benenden
Hamstreet
Romney
Flimwell
Isle
ROMNEY HYTHE &
Marsh
Hawkhurst
of Oxney
DYMCHURCH RAILWAY
BODIAM
KENT AND E. SUSSEX
Appledore
CASTLE
STEAM RLY
A259
Dymchurch
Four Oaks
The
St Mary's Bay
Cripp's Corner
Stocks
A259
Littlestone-on-Sea
Broad Oak
Rye
Lydd
Greatstone-on-Sea
London
Icklesham
Ashford
SISSINGHURST
GARDENS
Battle
Westfield
Winchelsea
Dungeness
Baldslow
Rye Bay
Hollington
Sidley
Fairlight
FLAMINGO
Hastings
PARK
Bexhill

Strait of Dover

0   10 Miles
0   10   20 Kilometres

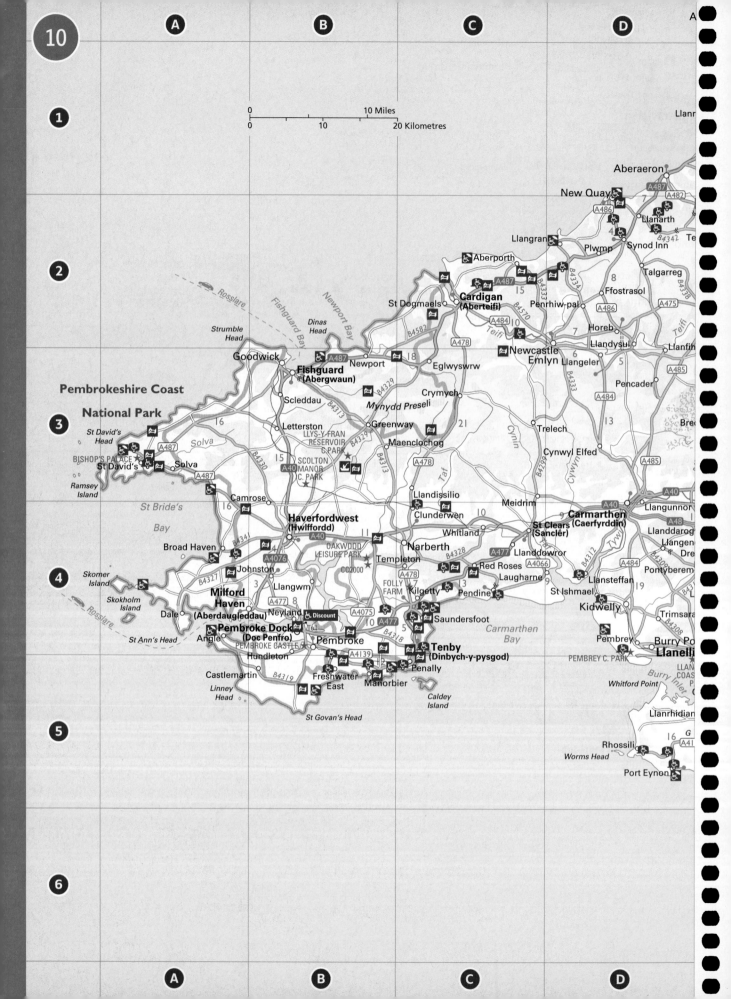

Pembrokeshire Coast

National Park

0 | 10 Miles
0 | 10 | 20 Kilometres

St David's Head
BISHOP'S PALACE
St David's
Ramsey Island
St Bride's Bay

Skomer Island
Skokholm Island
Rosslare

Dale
St Ann's Head
Angle
Hundleton
Castlemartin
Linney Head
St Govan's Head

Goodwick
Fishguard
(Abergwaun)
Scleddau
Letterston
Camrose
Broad Haven
Johnston
Milford Haven
(Aberdaugleddau)
Neyland
Pembroke Dock
(Doc Penfro)
PEMBROKE CASTLE
Pembroke
Freshwater East
Manorbier

Strumble Head
Dinas Head
Newport Bay
Rosslare
Fishguard Bay

Newport
Mynydd Preseli
Greenway
Maenclochog
Llandissilio
Clunderwen
Whitland
Narberth
Templeton
OAKWOOD LEISURE PARK
CC2000
FOLLY FARM
Kilgetty
Saundersfoot
Tenby
(Dinbych-y-pysgod)
Penally
Caldey Island

St Dogmaels
Aberporth
Cardigan
(Aberteifi)
Eglwyswrw
Crymych
Trelech
Cynwyl Elfed
Meidrim
St Clears
(Sanclêr)
Llanddowror
Red Roses
Laugharne
Pendine
Carmarthen Bay

New Quay
Llangran
Plwmp
Synod Inn
Penrhiw-pal
Newcastle Emlyn
Llangeler
Horeb
Llandysul
Pencader

Aberaeron
Llanarth
Talgarreg
Ffostrasol

Carmarthen
(Caerfyrddin)
Llangunnor
Llanddarog
Llangen
Pontyberem
Llansteffan
St Ishmael
Kidwelly
Trimsaran
Pembrey
PEMBREY C. PARK
Burry Po
Llanelli

Rhossili
Worms Head
Port Eynon
Whitford Point
Llanrhidian

Bro

St Bride's Bay
Solva
A487
B4330
A4076
B4327
B4341
A477
A4075
A4139
B4318
A4319
A40
A478
B4329
B4313
B4582
LLYS-Y-FRAN RESERVOIR C. PARK
SCOLTON MANOR C. PARK
Haverfordwest
(Hwlffordd)
Llangwm
Taf
Cynin
Teifi
Tywi
Cywyn
B4313
A487
A486
A475
A485
A48
A484
A40
A4066
A477
B4328
B4312
B4308
A484

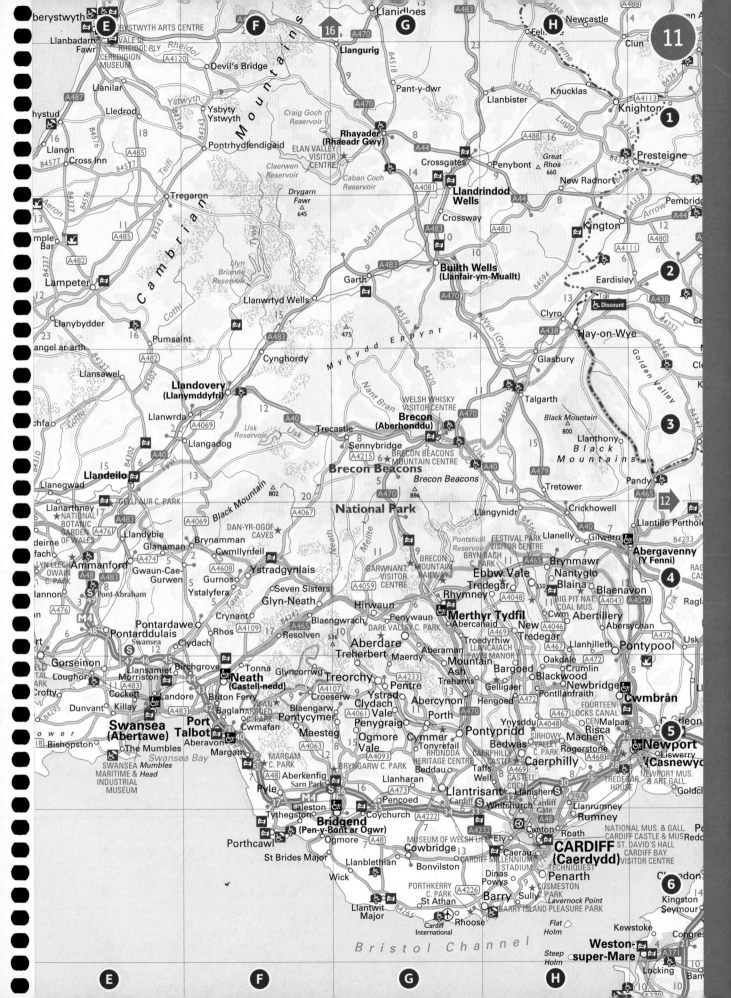

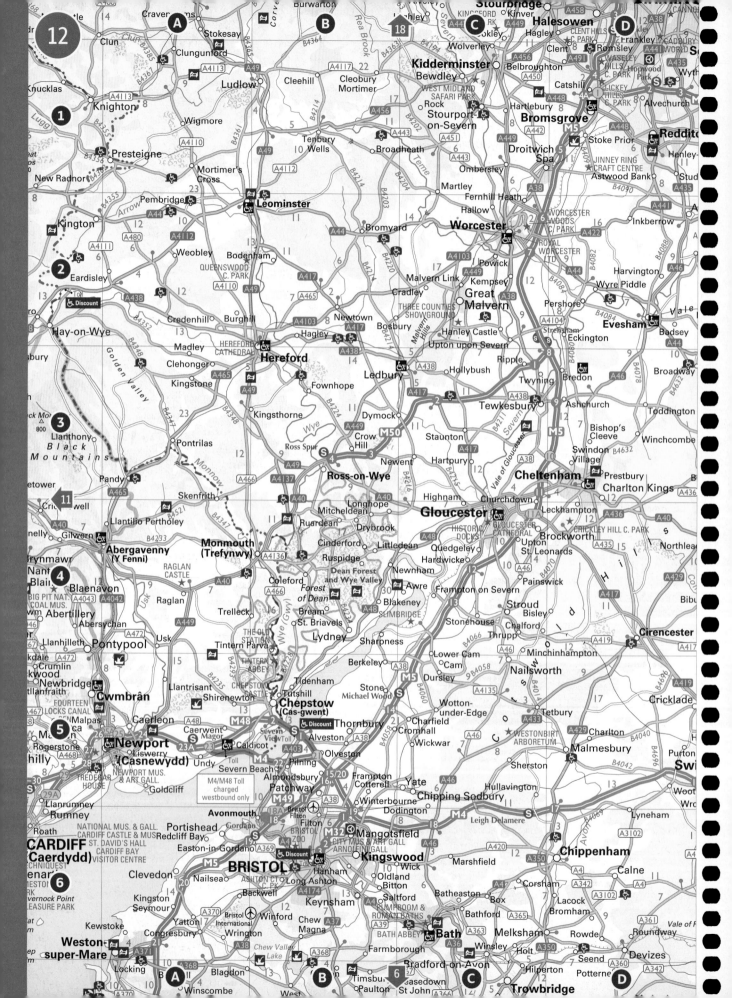

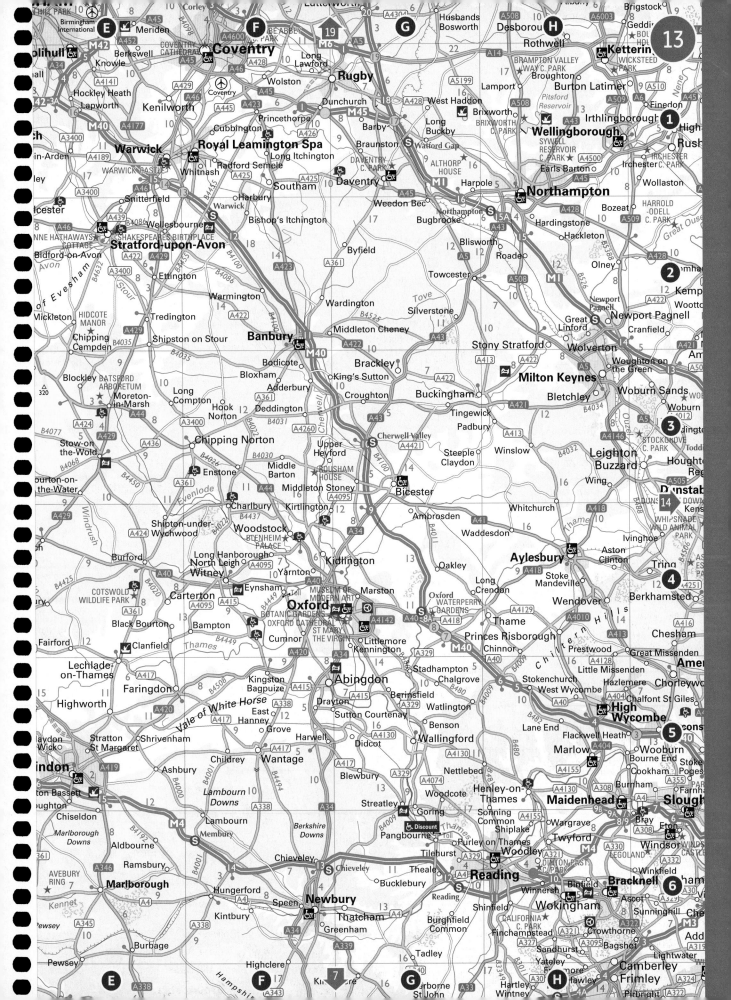

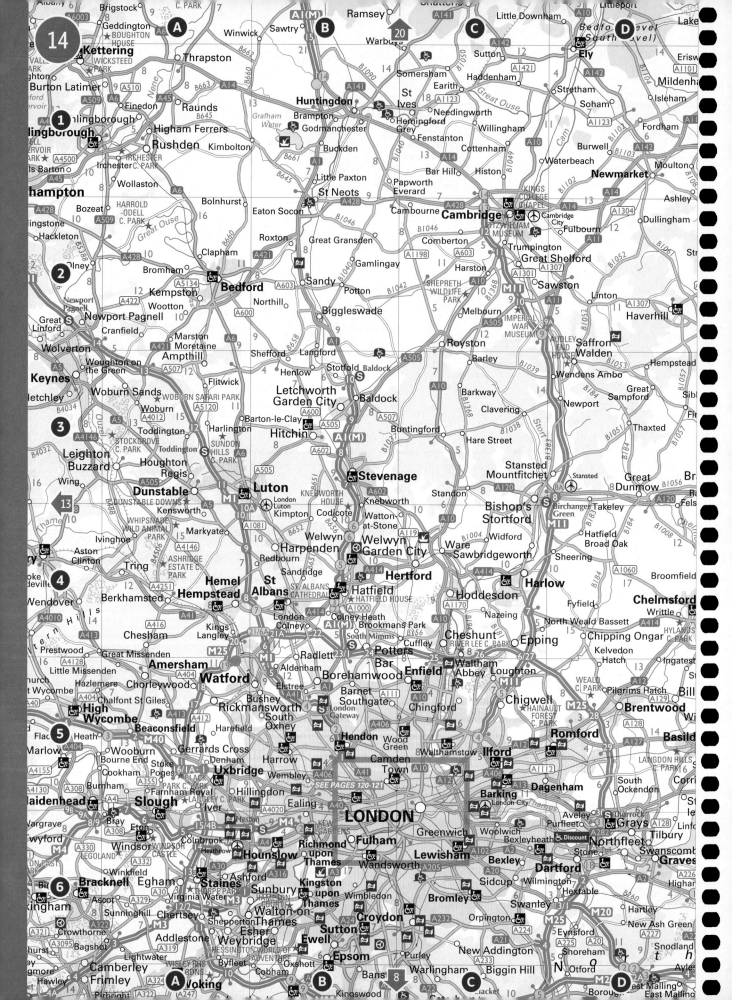

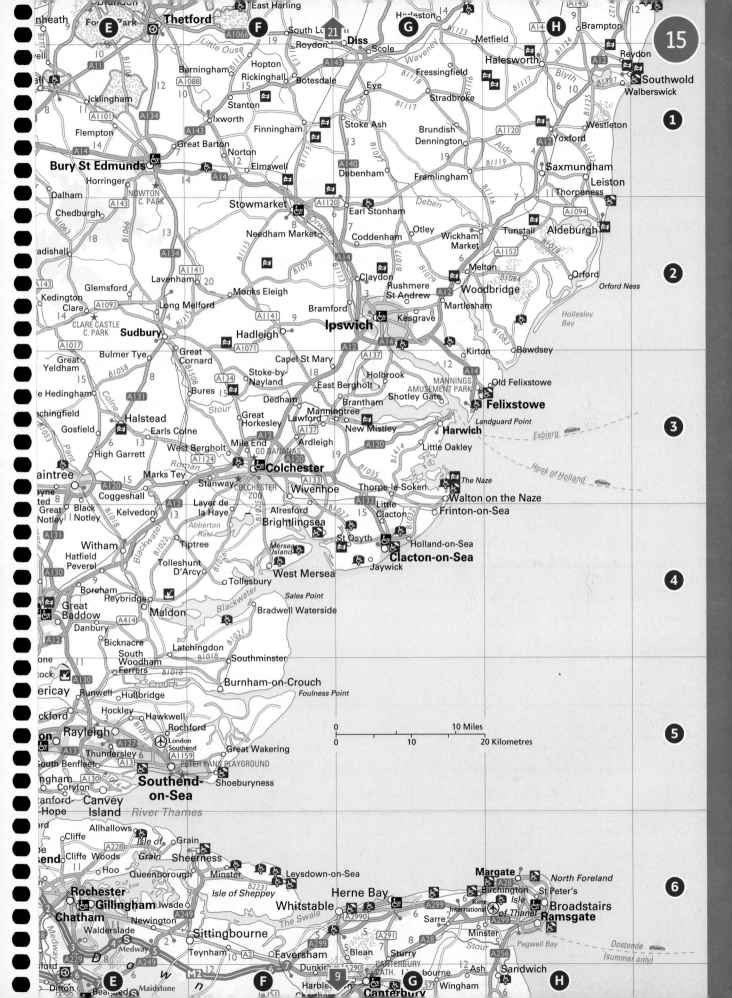

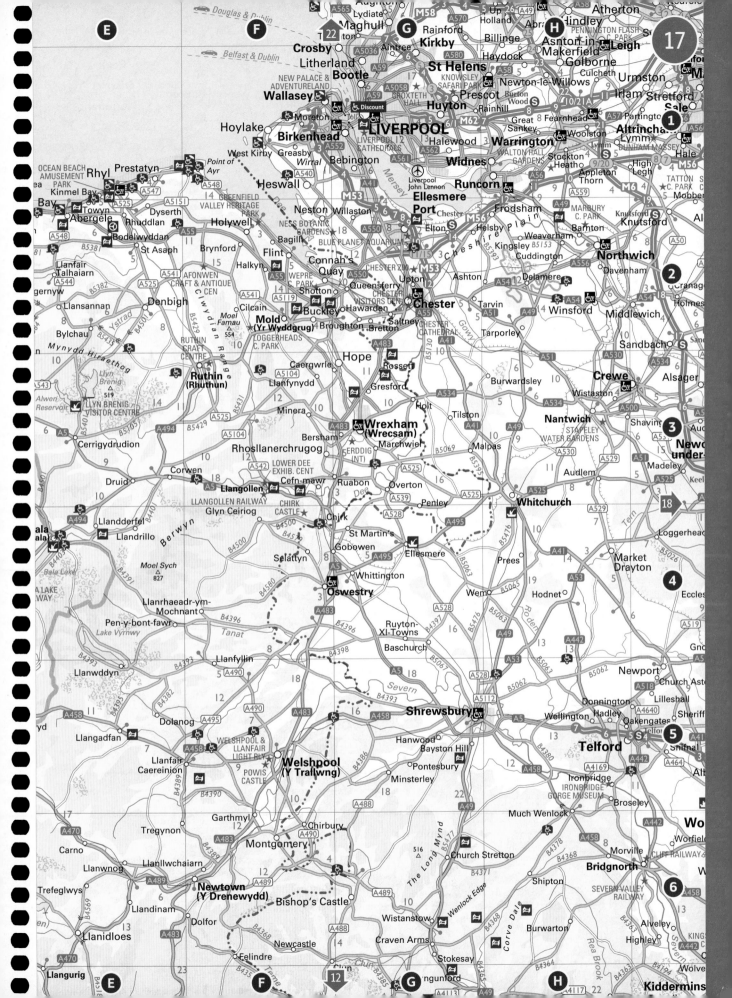

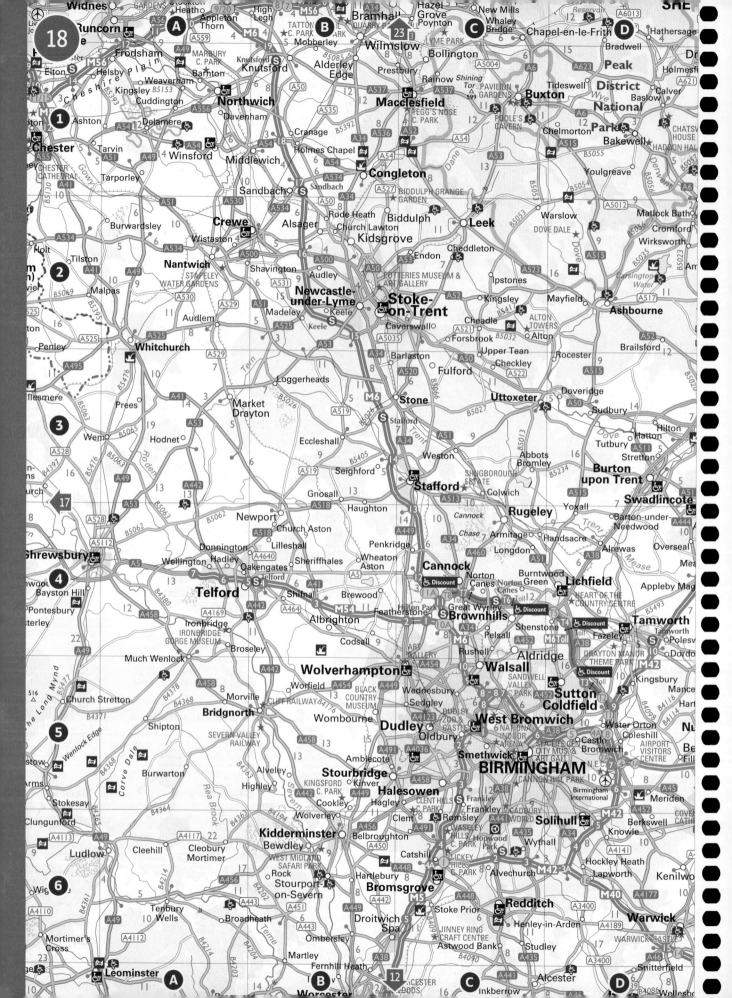

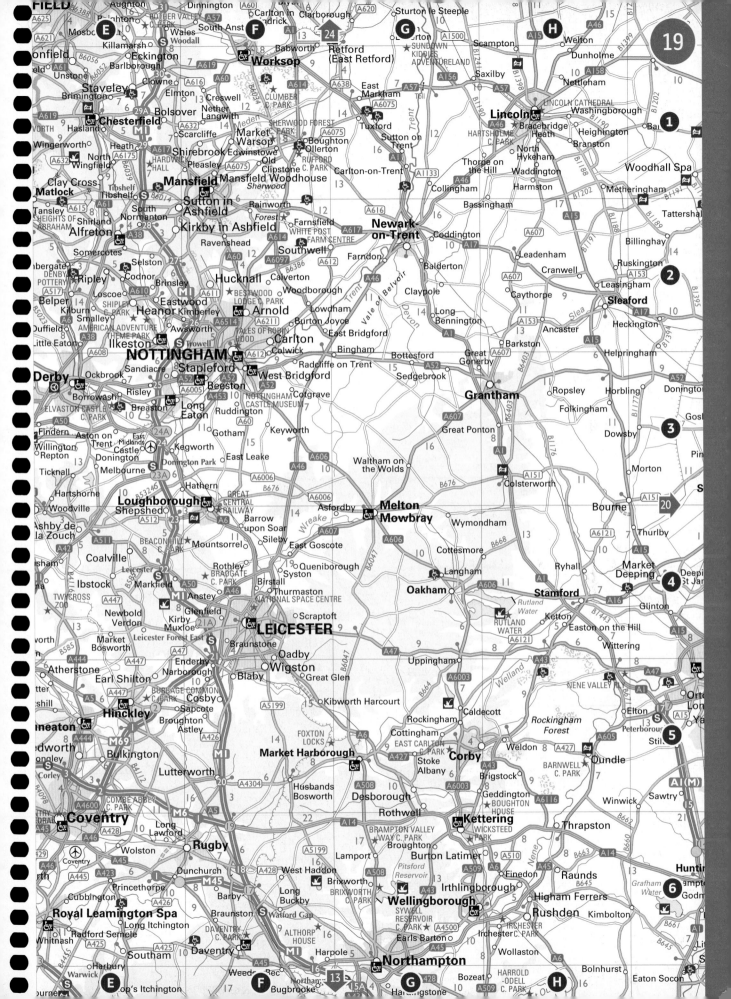

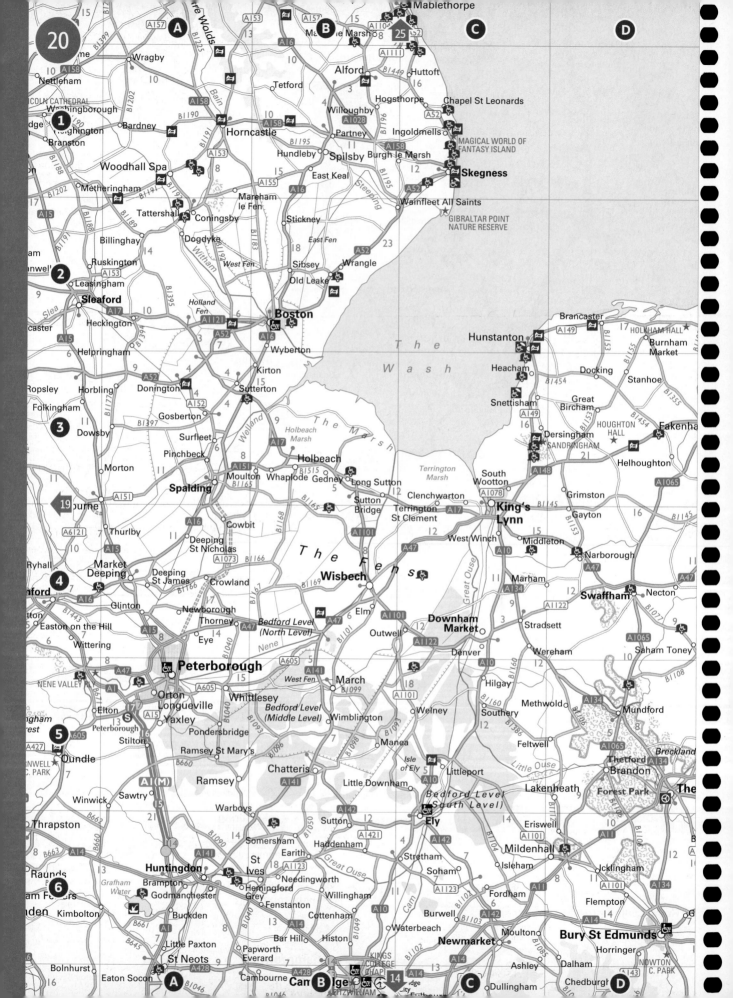

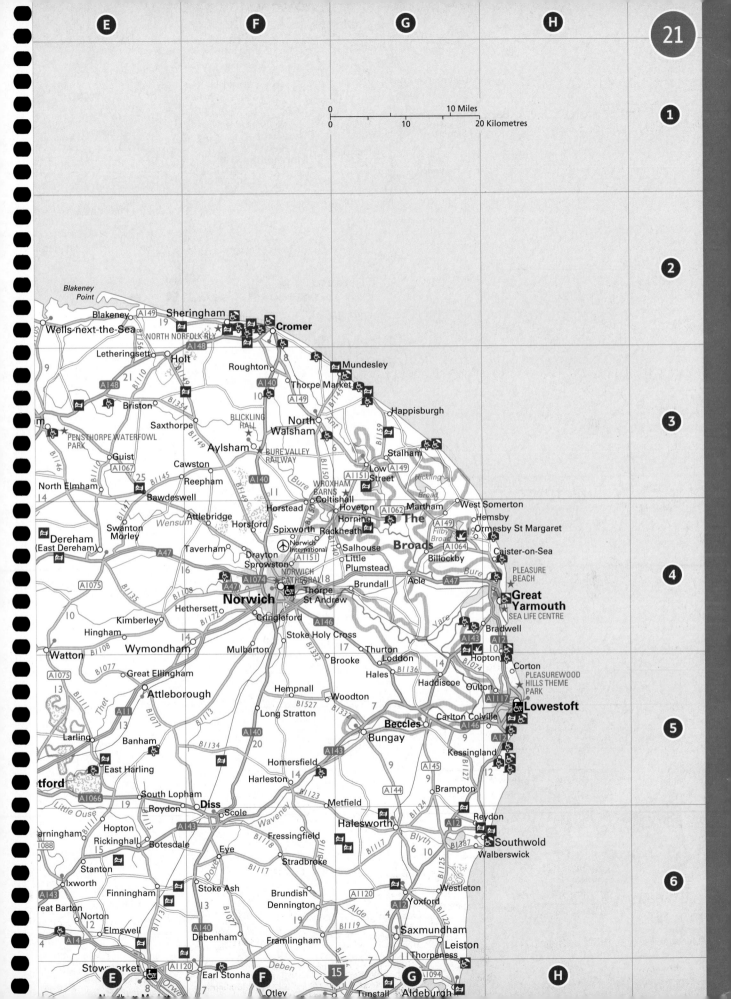

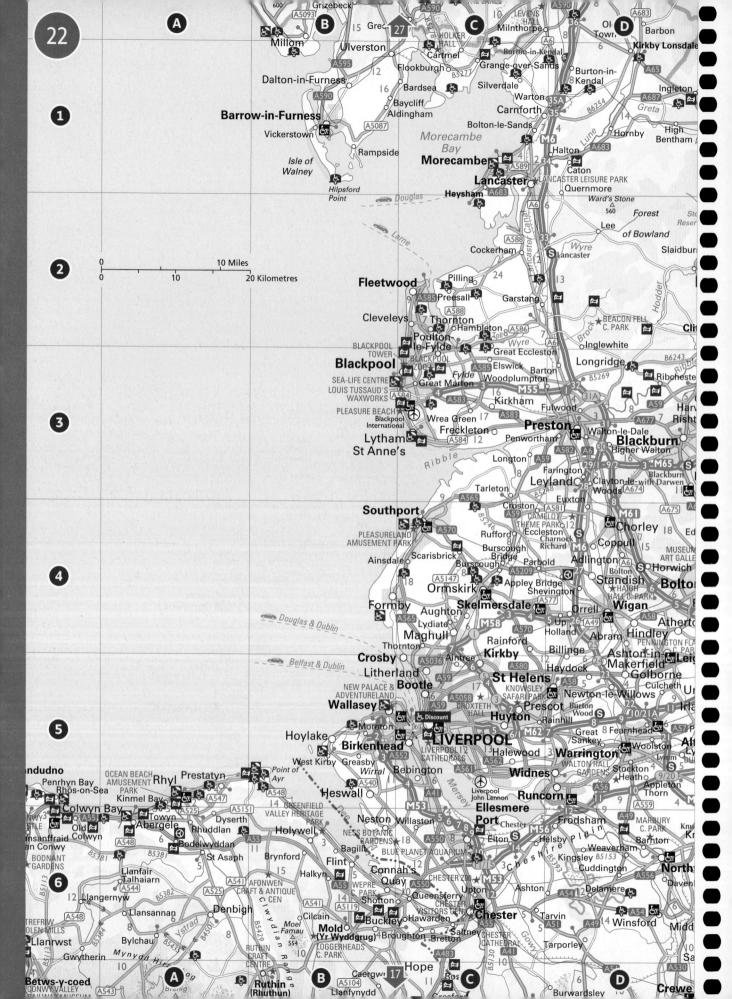

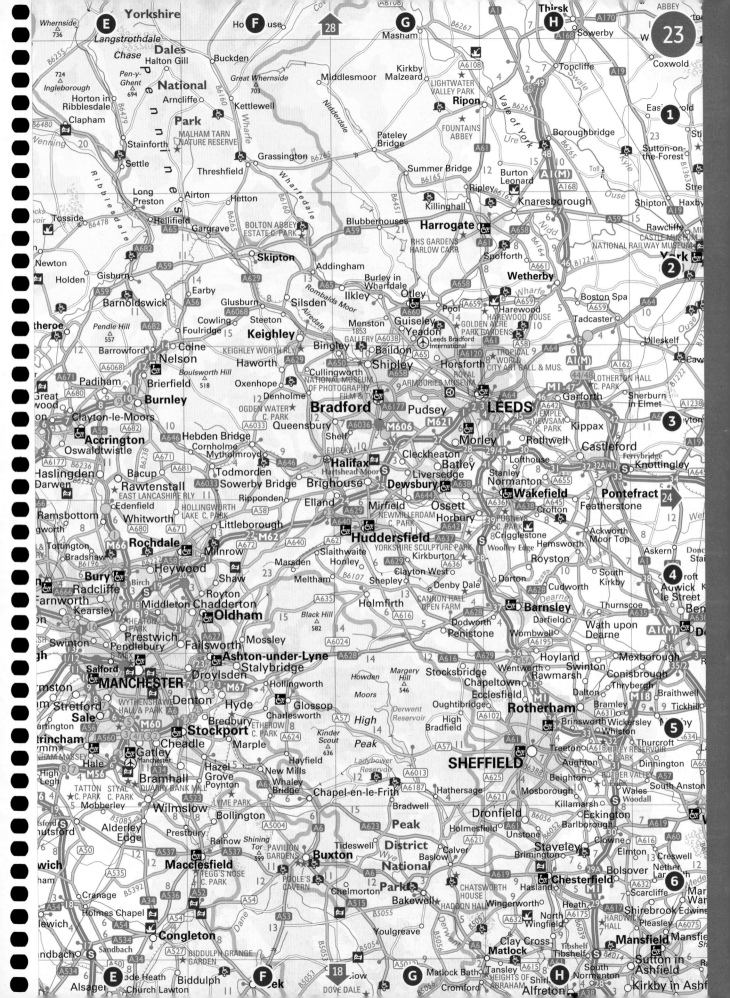

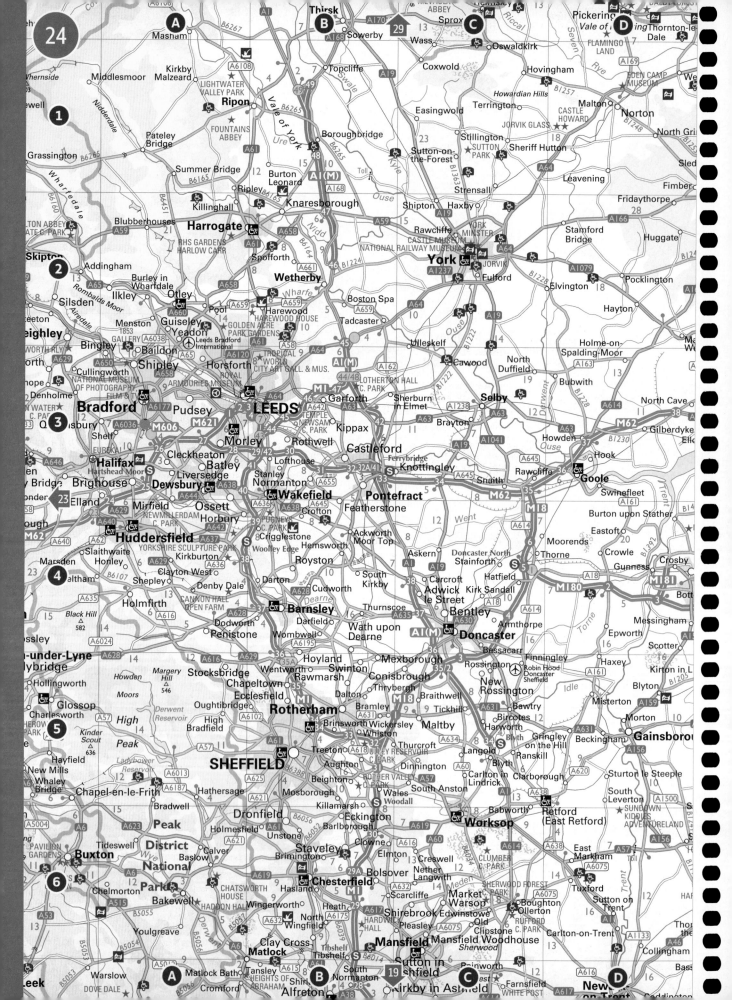

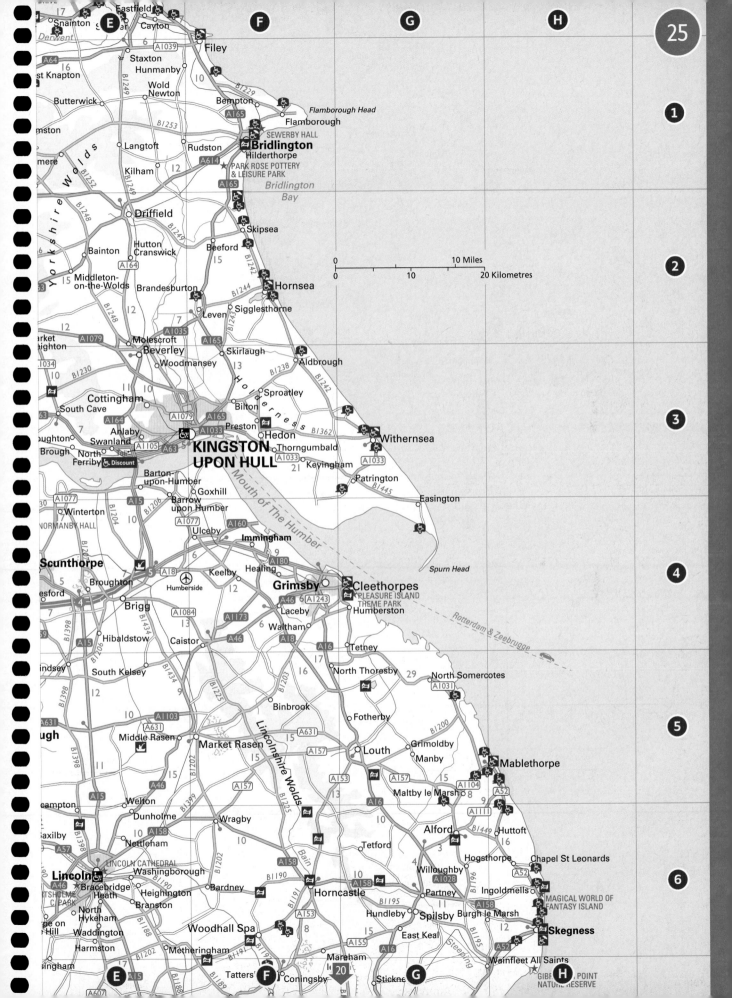

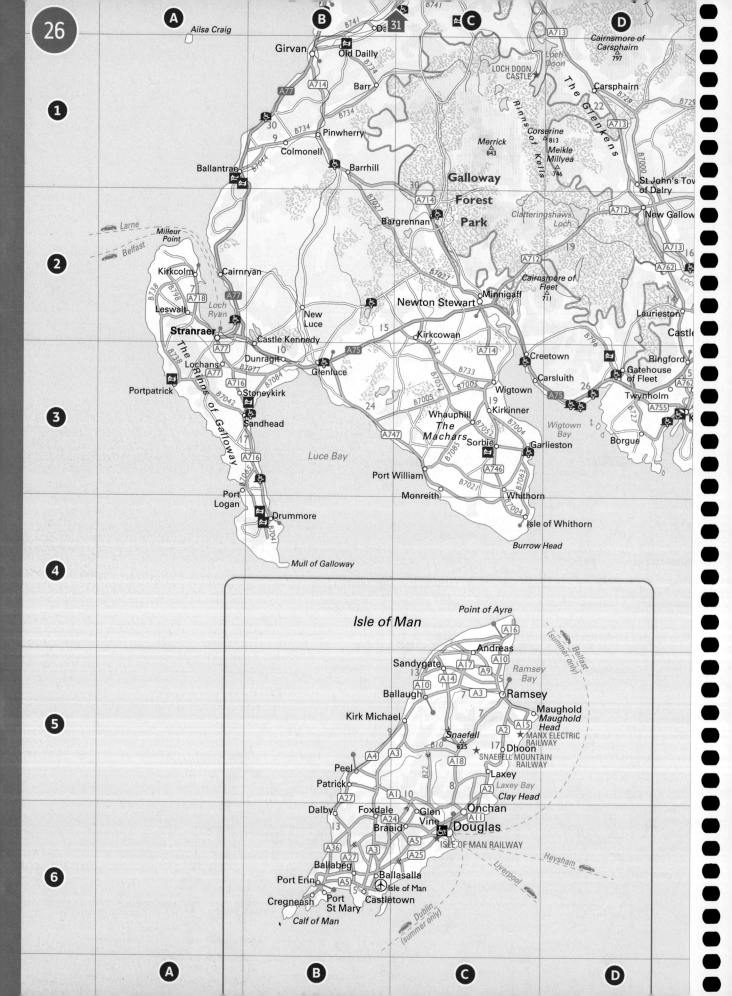

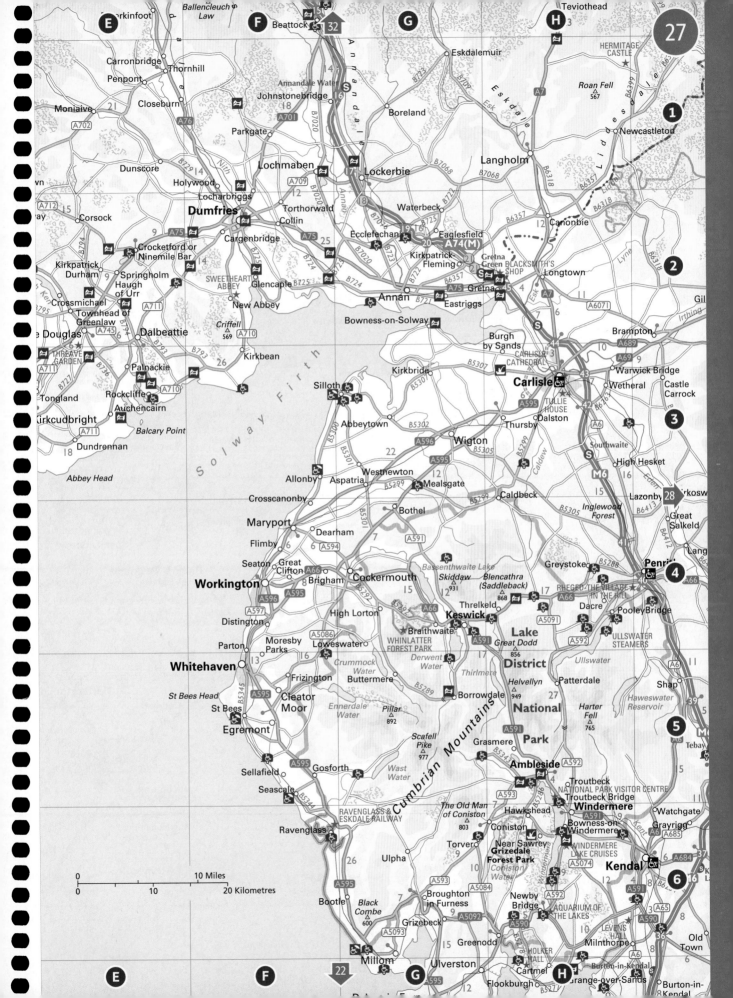

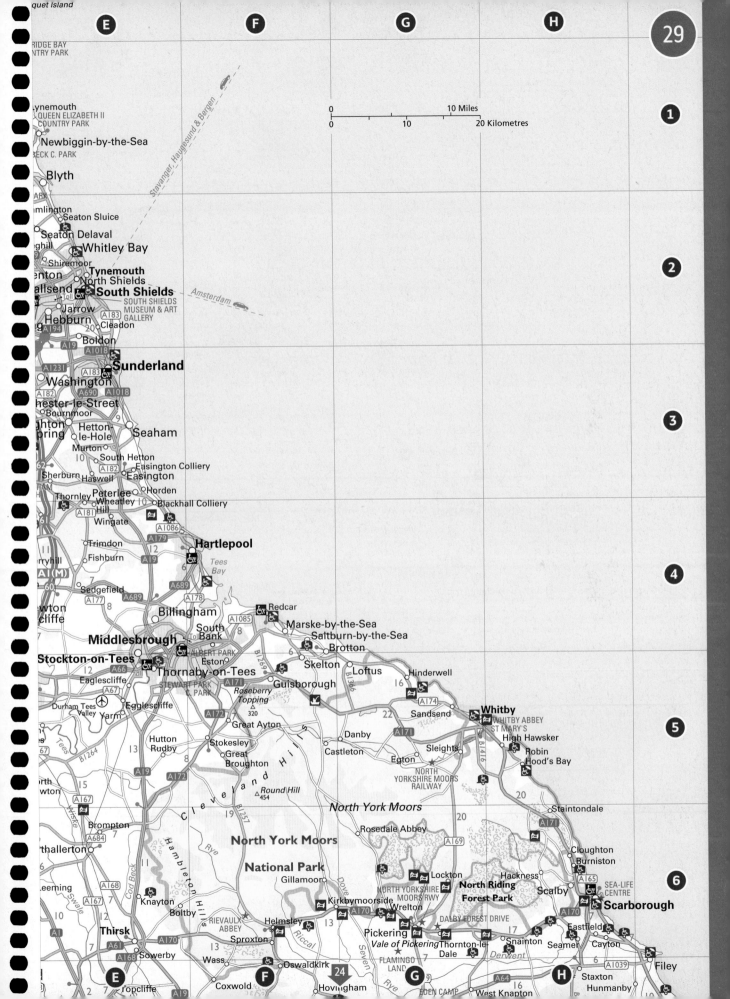

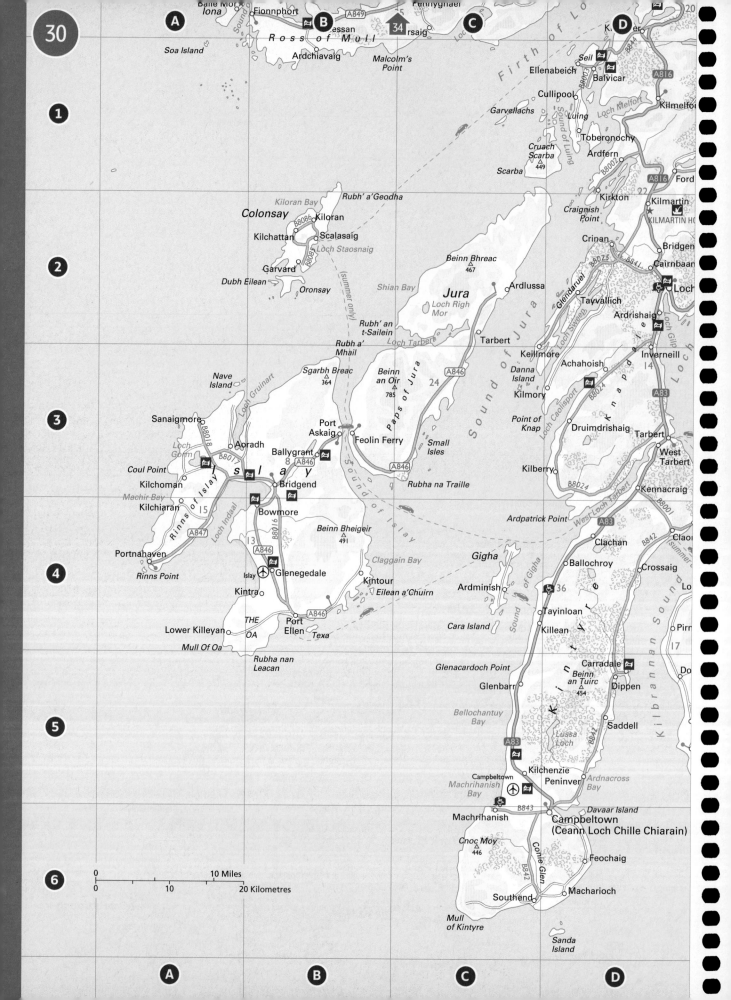

Iona
Baile Mor
Fionnphort
A849
essan
Ross of Mull
34
rsaig
Pennyghael
Firth of Lo
K   er
B841
Soa Island
Ardchiavaig
Malcolm's
Point
Seil
Ellenabeich
Balvicar
A816
Cullipool
Kilmelfor
Garvellachs
Luing
Loch Melfort
Sound of Luing
Toberonochy
Ardfern
B8002
Cruach
Scarba
Scarba
449
A816
Ford

Kiloran Bay
Rubh' a'Geodha
Kirkton
22
Kilmartin
Colonsay
B8086
Kiloran
KILMARTIN HO
Craignish
Point
Kilchattan
Scalasaig
Crinan
Bridgen
Garvard
Lòch Staosnaig
B8085
Beinn Bhreac
467
Cairnbaan
Loch
Dubh Eilean
Ardlussa
A846
B8025
Oronsay
Shian Bay
Jura
Tayvallich
Glendaruel
Loch Righ
Mor
Ardrishaig
Rubh' an
t-Sailein
Tarbert
Keillmore
Inverneill
Rubh a'
Mhail
Loch Tarbert
Loch Sweep
A83
Nave
Island
Sgarbh Breac
364
Beinn
an Oir
785
Paps of Jura
A846
24
Danna
Island
Achahoish
Knapd
Loch Caolisport
B8024
Sanaigmore
Kilmory
Point of
Knap
Druimdrishaig
Tarbert
B8018
Aoradh
Port
Askaig
Feolin Ferry
West
Tarbert
Loch
Gorm
B8017
Ballygrant
8   A846
Small
Isles
Kilberry
Coul Point
I s l a y
Bridgend
Kennacraig
Rubha na Traille
B8024
Kilchoman
Machir Bay
Bowmore
Ardpatrick Point
West Loch Tarbert
A83
Clao
Kilchiaran
15
B8016
Beinn Bheigeir
491
Clachan
Portnahaven
A847
A846
13
Claggain Bay
Gigha
Ballochroy
Crossaig
Lo
Rinns Point
Islay
Glenegedale
Kintour
Eilean a'Chuirn
Ardminish
36
Sound of Gigha
Tayinloan
Pirn
Kintra
Cara Island
Killean
17
THE
OA
Port
Ellen
Texa
Lower Killeyan
Mull Of Oa
Carradale
Do
Rubha nan
Leacan
Glenacardoch Point
Beinn
an Tuirc
454
Dippen
Glenbarr
Bellochantuy
Bay
Saddell
Lussa
Loch
Kilchenzie
Campbeltown
Machrihanish
Bay
Peninver
Ardnacross
Bay
Davaar Island
Machrihanish
Campbeltown
(Ceann Loch Chille Chiarain)
Cnoc Moy
446
Feochaig
Conie Glen
Southend
Macharioch
0   10 Miles
0   10   20 Kilometres
Mull
of Kintyre
Sanda
Island

A   B   C   D

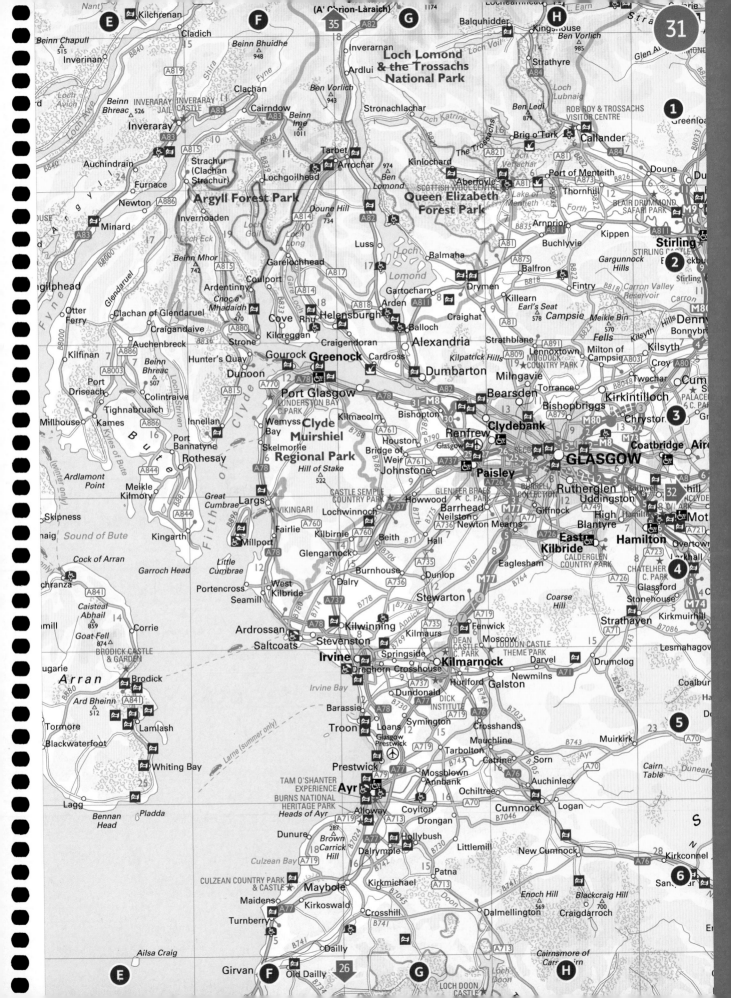

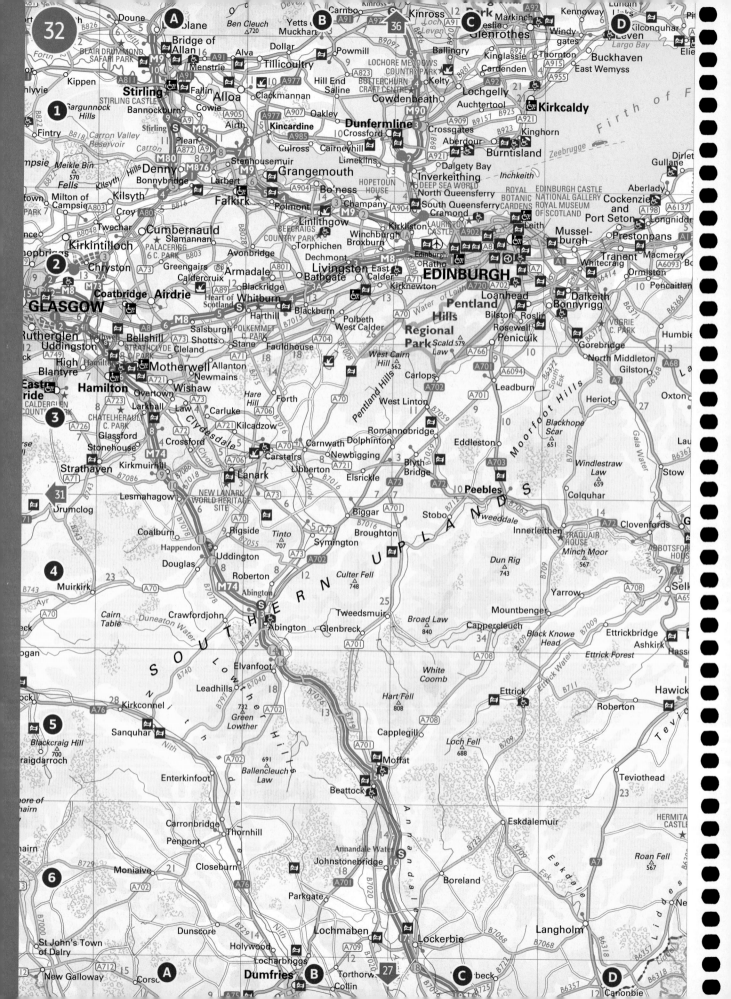

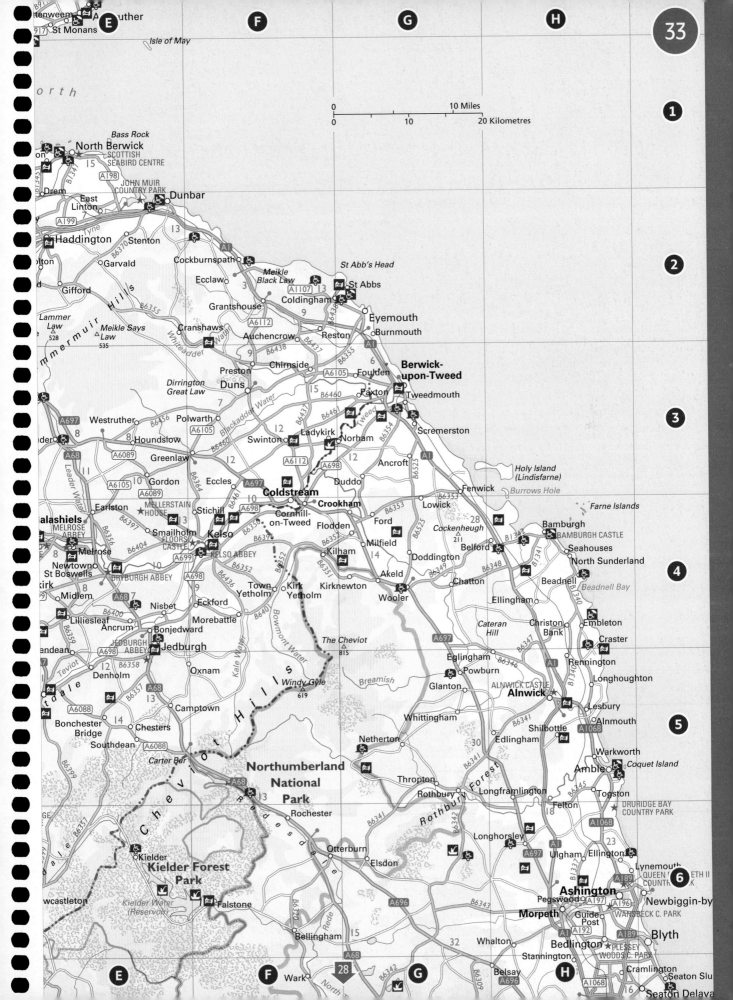

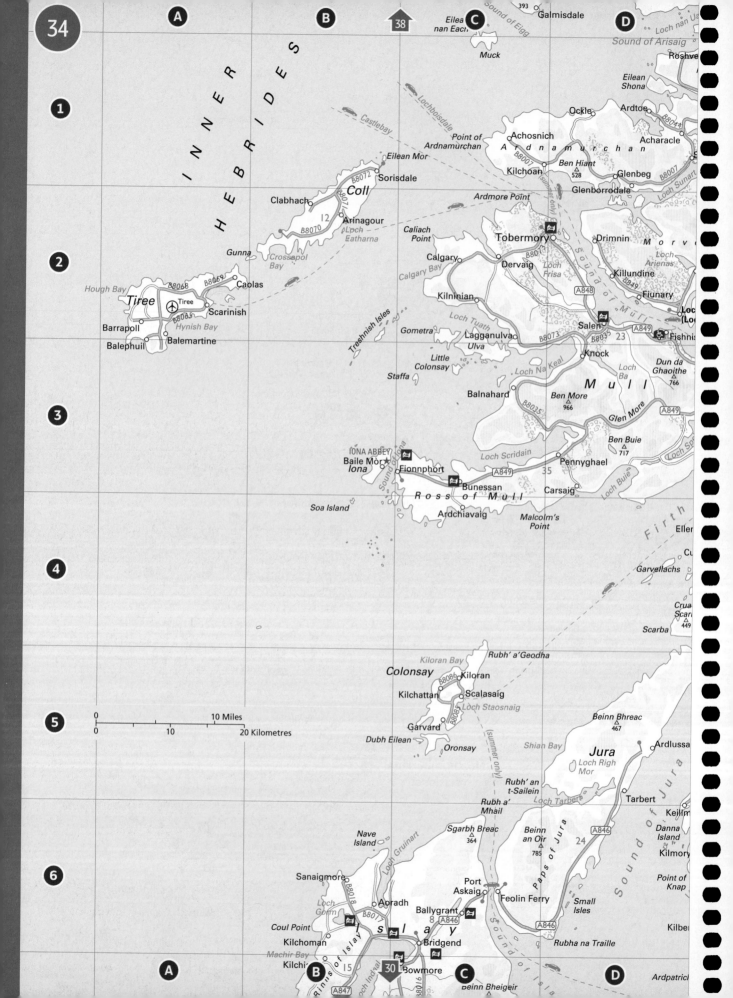

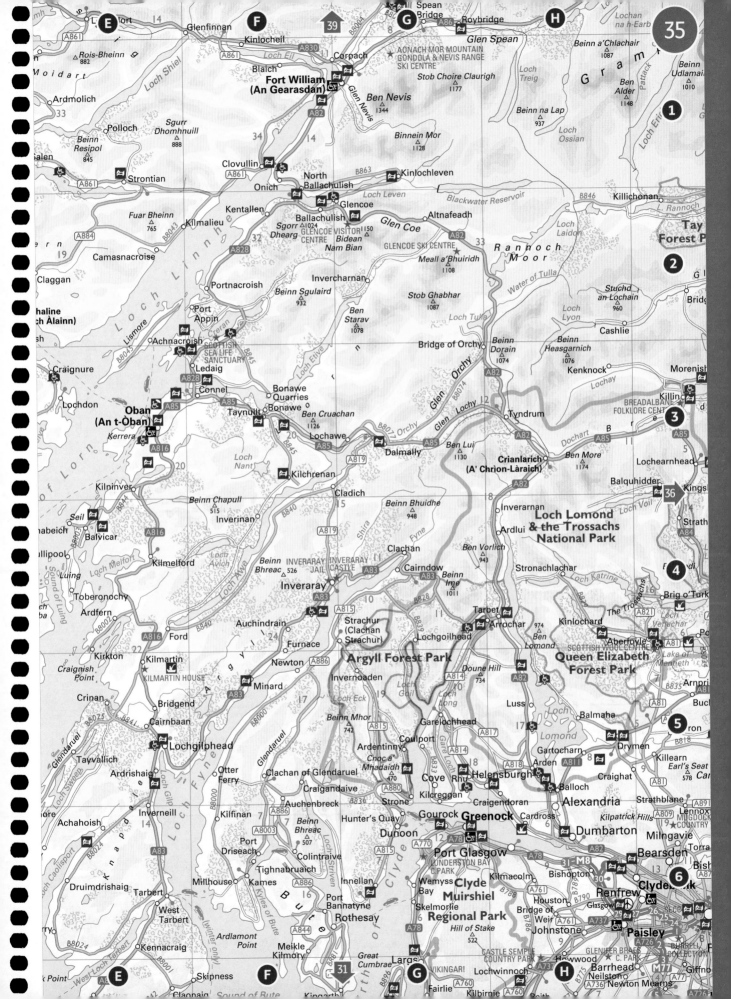

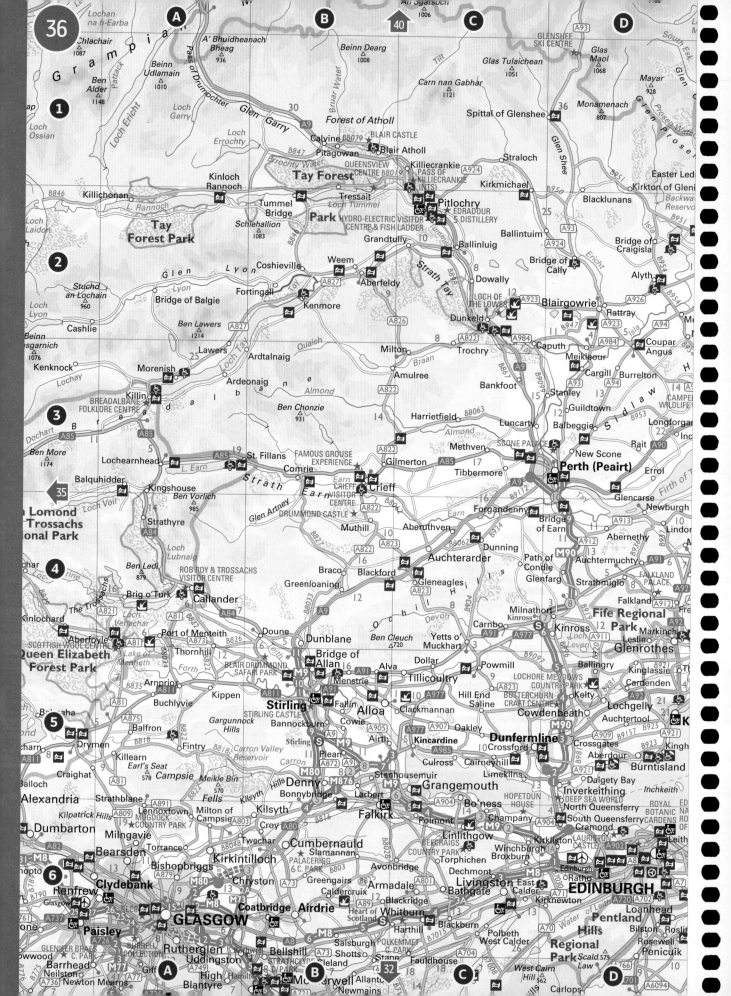

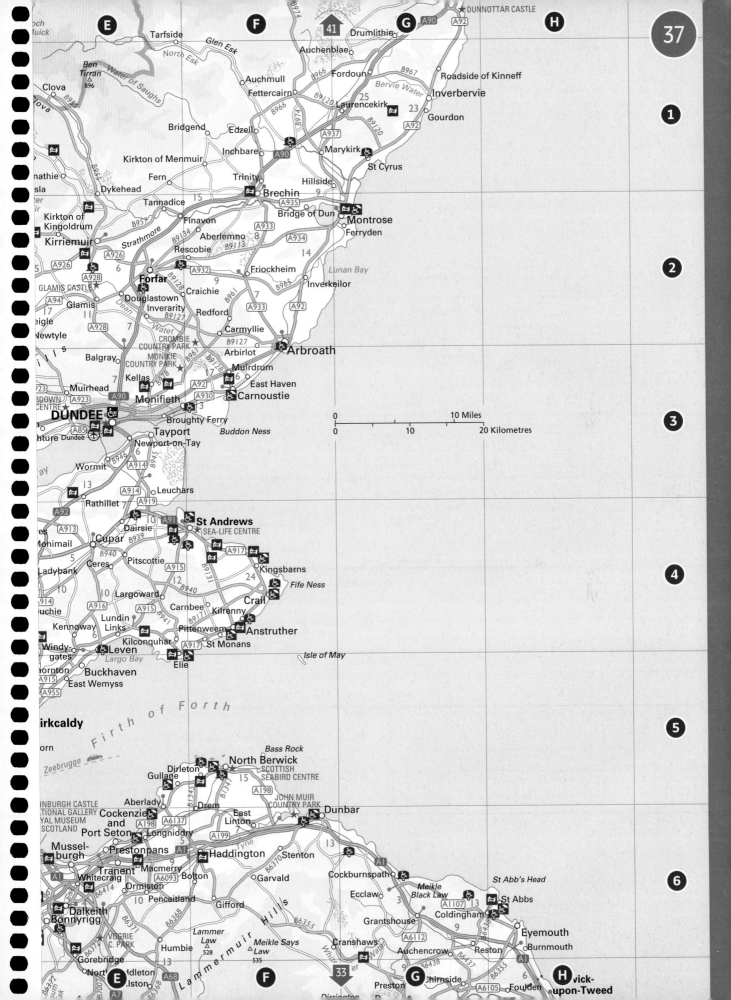

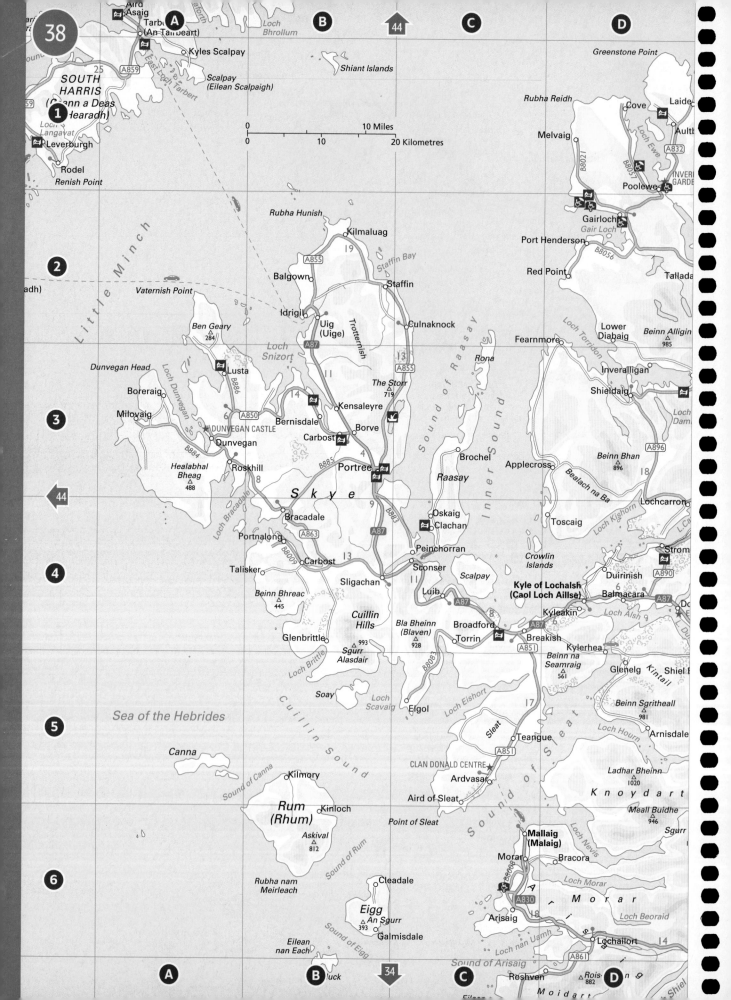

A B 44 C D

SOUTH HARRIS (Ceann a Deas na Hearadh)

Aird of Asaig
Tarbert (An Tairbeart)
Kyles Scalpay
Scalpay (Eilean Scalpaigh)
Shiant Islands
Greenstone Point
Rubha Reidh
Cove
Laide
Melvaig
Aultb
Loch Langavat
Leverburgh
Rodel
Renish Point
Poolewe
INVER GARDE
Gairloch
Gair Loch
Port Henderson
Red Point
Tallada
Rubha Hunish
Kilmaluag
Staffin Bay
Balgown
Staffin
Idrigil
Uig (Uige)
Culnaknock
Fearnmore
Lower Diabaig
Beinn Alligin 985
Little Minch
Vaternish Point
Ben Geary 284
Loch Snizort
Trotternish
Rona
Loch Torridon
Inveralligan
Shieldaig
Loch Dam
Dunvegan Head
Lusta
The Storr 719
Boreraig
Kensaleyre
Brochel
Applecross
Beinn Bhan 896
Beinn Bheac
Miloyaig
DUNVEGAN CASTLE
Bernisdale
Borve
Raasay
Bealach na Ba
Dunvegan
Carbost
Healabhal Bheag 488
Roskhill
Portree
Lochcarron
Skye
Oskaig
Clachan
Toscaig
Loch Kishorn
L. Car
Strom
Bracadale
Peinchorran
Crowlin Islands
Duirinish
Portnalong
Sconser
Scalpay
A890
Carbost
Talisker
Sligachan
Luib
Kyle of Lochalsh (Caol Loch Aillse)
Balmacara
Beinn Bhreac 445
Cuillin Hills
Kyleakin
Loch Alsh
Do
Broadford
Kylerhea
Glenelg
Shiel
Glenbrittle
Bla Bheinn (Blaven) 928
Torrin
Breakish
Kintail
Sgurr Alasdair 993
Beinn na Seamraig 561
Beinn Sgritheall 981
Soay
Loch Brittle
Loch Scavaig
Elgol
Loch Eishort
Cuillin Sound
Sea of the Hebrides
Sleat
Teangue
Loch Hourn
Arnisdale
Sound of Sleat
Canna
CLAN DONALD CENTRE
Ladhar Bheinn 1020
Sound of Canna
Kilmory
Ardvasar
Aird of Sleat
Knoydart
Rum (Rhum)
Kinloch
Point of Sleat
Meall Buidhe 946
Sgurr
Askival 812
Mallaig (Malaig)
Sound of Rum
Morar
Bracora
Rubha nam Meirleach
Cleadale
Loch Nevis
Loch Morar
Morar
Arisaig
Loch Beoraid
Eigg
An Sgurr 393
Galmisdale
Loch nan Uamh
Lochailort
Eilean nan Each
Sound of Eigg
Sound of Arisaig
Roshven
Rois 882
Moidart
A Buck B 34 C D

0 ... 10 Miles
0 ... 10 ... 20 Kilometres

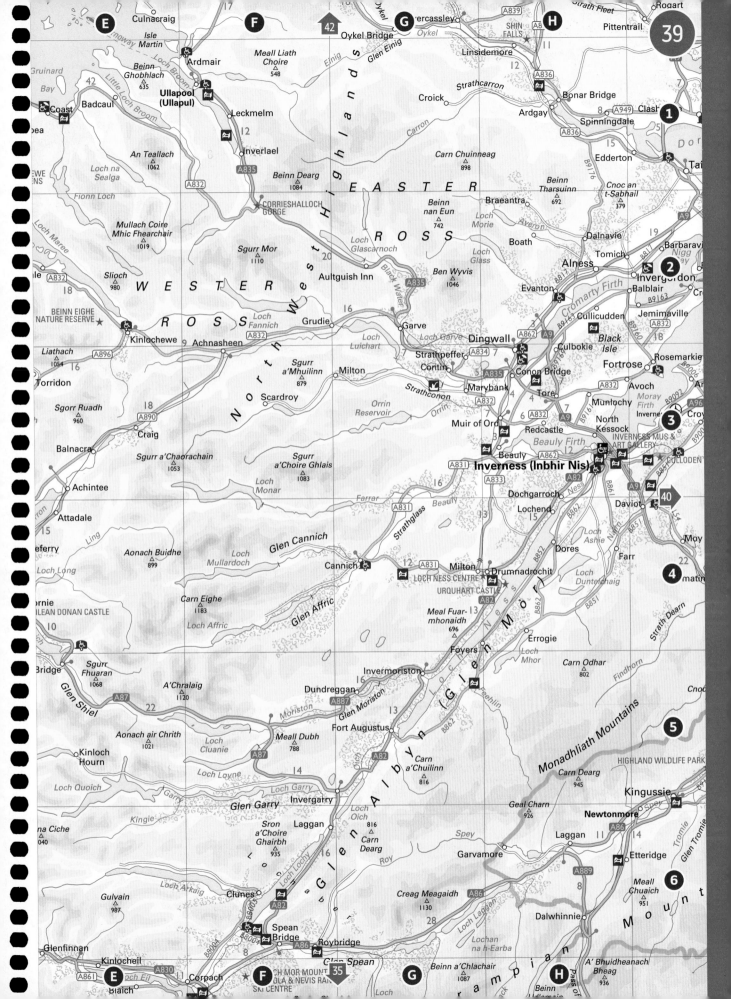

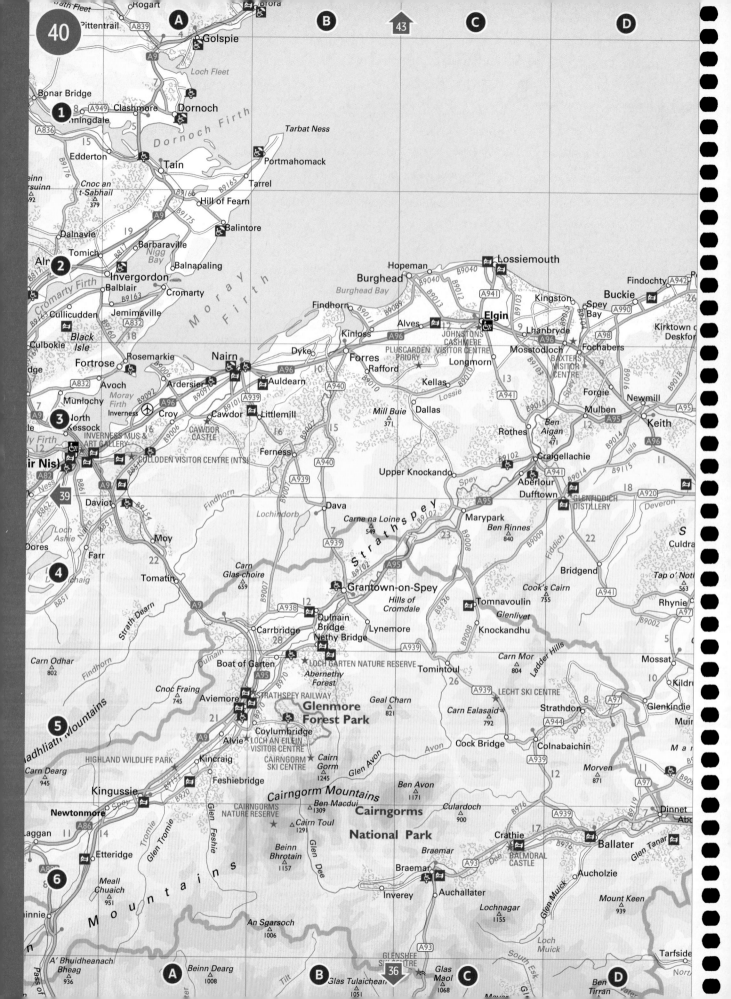

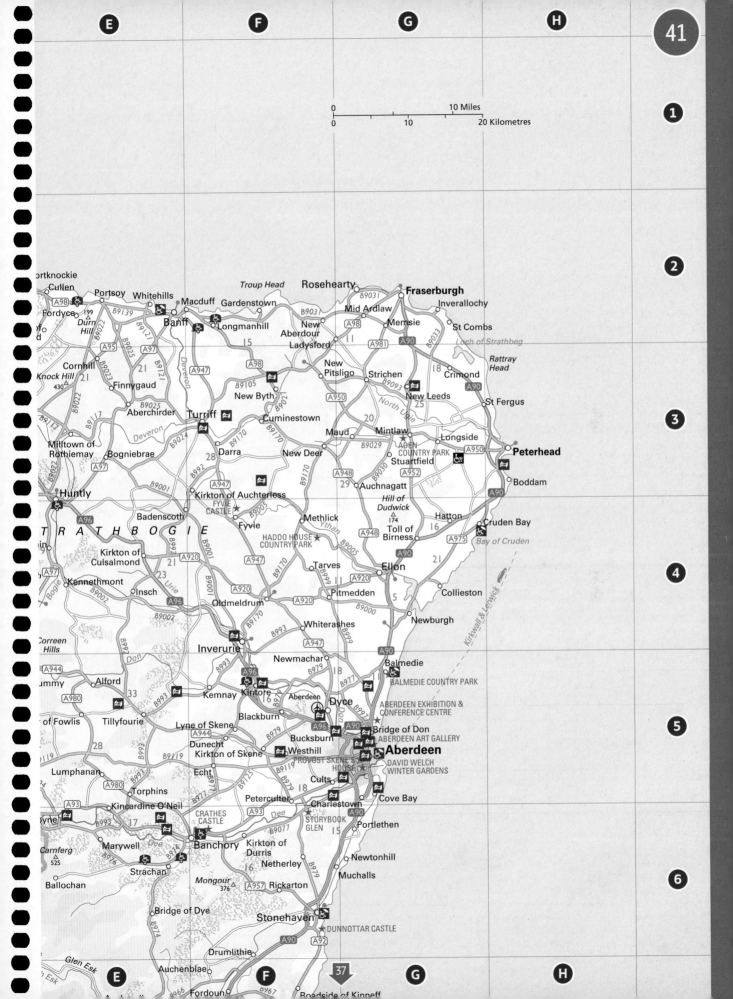

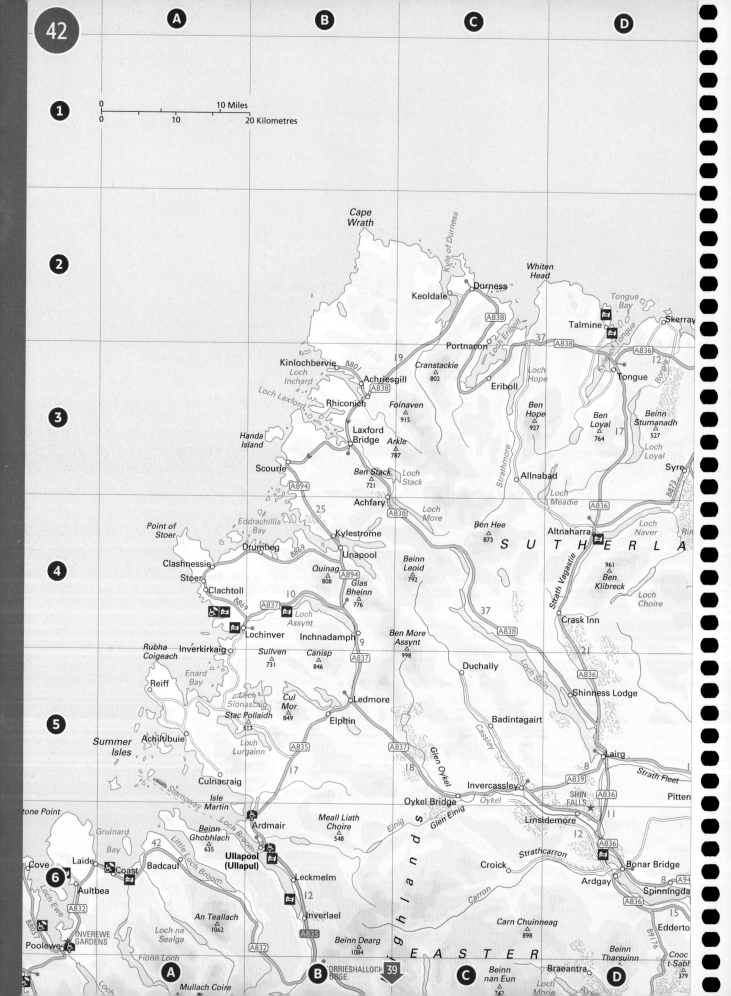

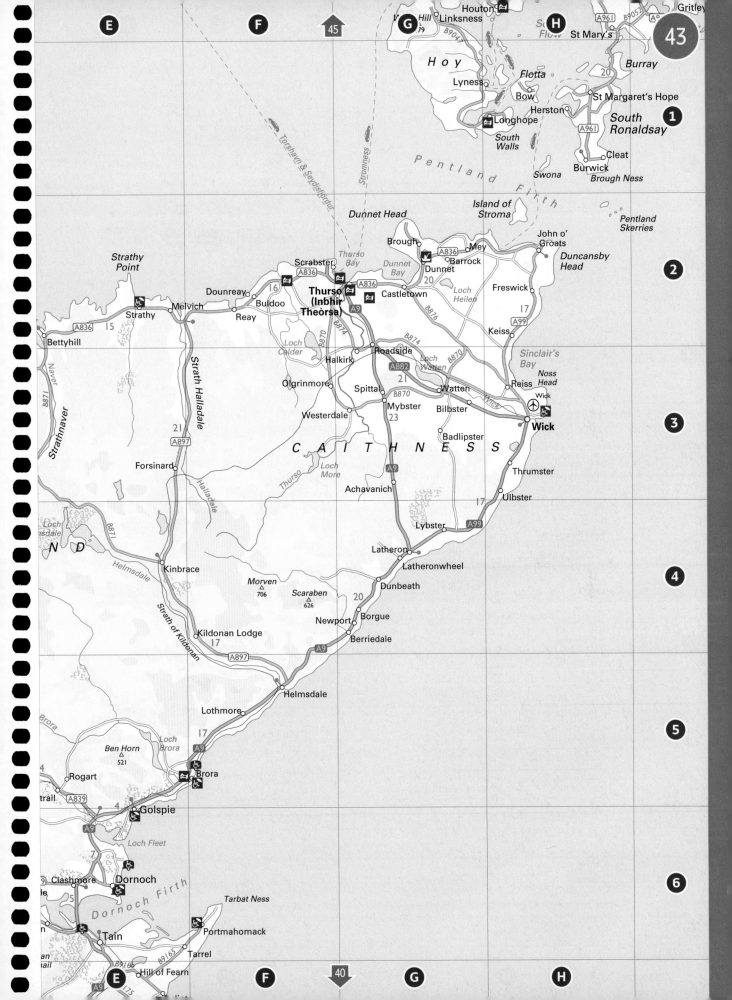

E F 45 G H

1
Houton
Hill · Linksness
79
B9047
A961
B9052
Gritley
S. · Flow
St Mary's
H o y
Burray
Lyness
Flotta
Bow
St Margaret's Hope
Herston
20
A961
South
Ronaldsay
Longhope
South
Walls
Cleat
Burwick
Brough Ness

S t r o m n e s s

P e n t l a n d   F i r t h
Swona
Pentland
Skerries

Tórshavn & Seyðisfjörður

2
Dunnet Head
Island of
Stroma
Brough
A836
Mey
John o'
Groats
Duncansby
Head
Scrabster
A836
Barrock
Thurso
Bay
Dunnet
Bay
Dunnet
Dounreay
16
A836
Castletown
Freswick
Strathy
Point
Thurso
(Inbhir
Theòrsa)
A9
20
Loch
Heilen
17
A99
Keiss
Buldoo
Melvich
Reay
B876
Strathy
15
A836
B874
Loch
Calder
B874
Roadside
Sinclair's
Bay
Bettyhill
Halkirk
Loch
Watten
B870
Noss
Head
Reiss

3
Olgrinmore
A882
21
Watten
Strathnaver
Strath Halladale
Spittal
Mybster
Bilbster
Wick
Wick
21
A897
Westerdale
23
Badlipster
Forsinard
C A I T H N E S S
Thrumster
A9
Halladale
17
Achavanich
Ulbster

4
N D
Loch
...sdale
B871
Lybster
A99
Helmsdale
Latheron
Kinbrace
Latheronwheel
Morven
△
706
Scaraben
△
626
20
Dunbeath
Strath of Kildonan
Kildonan Lodge
17
Newport
Borgue
A897
A9
Berriedale

5
Brora
Lothmore
Helmsdale
Loch
Brora
17
A9
Ben Horn
△
521
Brora

6
4
Rogart
A839
Golspie
A9
Loch Fleet
7
...trail
Clashmore
5
Dornoch
Tarbat Ness
...le
D o r n o c h   F i r t h
Tain
Portmahomack
B9165
Tarrel
A9
B9166
Hill of Fearn
175

E F 40 G H

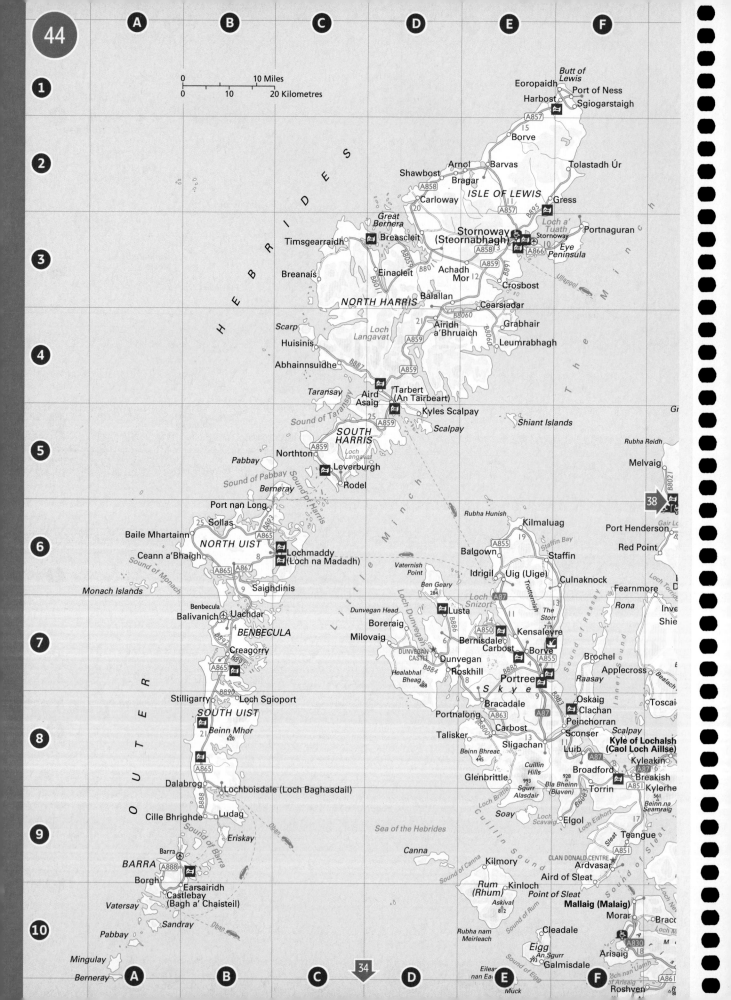

A B C D E F

1

0   10 Miles
0   10   20 Kilometres

Butt of Lewis
Eoropaidh
Port of Ness
Harbost
Sgiogarstaigh
A857
15
Borve

2

Arnol   Barvas
Shawbost
Bragar   Tolastadh Úr
A858
Carloway   *ISLE OF LEWIS*
A857   B895   Gress
20
Great
Bernera   Loch a'
Tuath
Timsgearraidh   Breascleit   Stornoway   Stornoway
(Steornabhagh)   Portnaguran
A866   Eye
Peninsula
Breanais   Einacleit   A859   10
880   Achadh   Crosbost
Mor   12

3

HEBRIDES   *NORTH HARRIS*   Balallan   Cearsiadar
Scarp   Loch   21   Airidh   Grabhair
Langavat   a'Bhruaich   B8060
Huisinis   B8064   Leumrabhagh
A859
Abhainnsuidhe   B887   A859

4

Taransay   Aird
Asaig   Tarbert   Shiant Islands
(An Tairbeart)
Sound of Taransay   25   Kyles Scalpay
A859   Scalpay   Gr

5

SOUTH HARRIS   Rubha Reidh
Pabbay   Northton   Loch   Melvaig
Langavat
Sound of Pabbay   Leverburgh
Berneray   Rodel   B8021
Sound of Harris   38

6

Port nan Long   Rubha Hunish
25   Sollas   Kilmaluag
Baile Mhartainn   A855   19   Port Henderson
NORTH UIST   Staffin Bay   Red Point
Ceann a'Bhaigh   8   Lochmaddy   Staffin
A865   A867   (Loch na Madadh)   Vaternish   Balgown   Culnaknock   Fearnmore
Point
Monach Islands   Saighdinis   Ben Geary   Idrigil   Uig (Uige)   Rona   Inve
284   Loch   Troternish   Shie
Sound of Monach   Snizort   A87   13
Benbecula   Dunvegan Head   Lusta   11   The
Balivanich   Uachdar   B886   Storr   Sound of Raasay
Benbecula   Boreraig   A850   719   Brochel
Balivanich   Milovaig   6   Bernisdale   Kensaleyre   Applecross

7

Uachdar   DUNVEGAN   Carbost   Borve   Raasay   Toscai
BENBECULA   CASTLE   Dunvegan   A855   Bealach
4   Healabhal   Roskhill   4   Oskaig
Creagorry   Bheag   8   Portree   Clachan
488   *Skye*   9   Peinchorran   Scalpay
Stilligarry   Bracadale   A87   Sconser   Kyle of Lochalsh
A865   Loch Sgioport   Portnalong   A863   13   Luib   (Caol Loch Aillse)
SOUTH UIST   B8009   Carbost   Sligachan   Kyleakin

8

Talisker   Beinn Bhreac   A87   16
21   Beinn Mhor   445   Broadford   Breakish
620   Cuillin   928   A851
Hills   Bla Bheinn   Torrin   Kylerhe
A865   Glenbrittle   993   (Blaven)   561
Sgurr   Beinn na
Dalabrog   Alasdair   Seamraig
Lochboisdale (Loch Baghasdail)   Loch   Soay   Loch Eishort   17
Cille Bhrighde   Ludag   Brittle   Elgol   Teangue
OUTER   Oban   Sea of the Hebrides   Loch   Sleat   A851

9

Eriskay   Canna   Scavaig   CLAN DONALD CENTRE
Sound of Barra   Kilmory   Ardvasar
Barra   Kinloch   Aird of Sleat
BARRA   A888   Rum   Point of Sleat
Borgh   Earsairidh   (Rhum)   **Mallaig (Malaig)**
Castlebay   Askival   Morar   Brac

10

Vatersay   (Bagh a' Chaisteil)   812   Cleadale
Sandray   Rubha nam   Eigg   Arisaig   A830
Pabbay   Meirleach   An Sgurr   18
393   Galmisdale
Mingulay   Eilean   Sound of Eigg   A861
Berneray   nan Eag   Muck   Roshven

34

A B C D E F

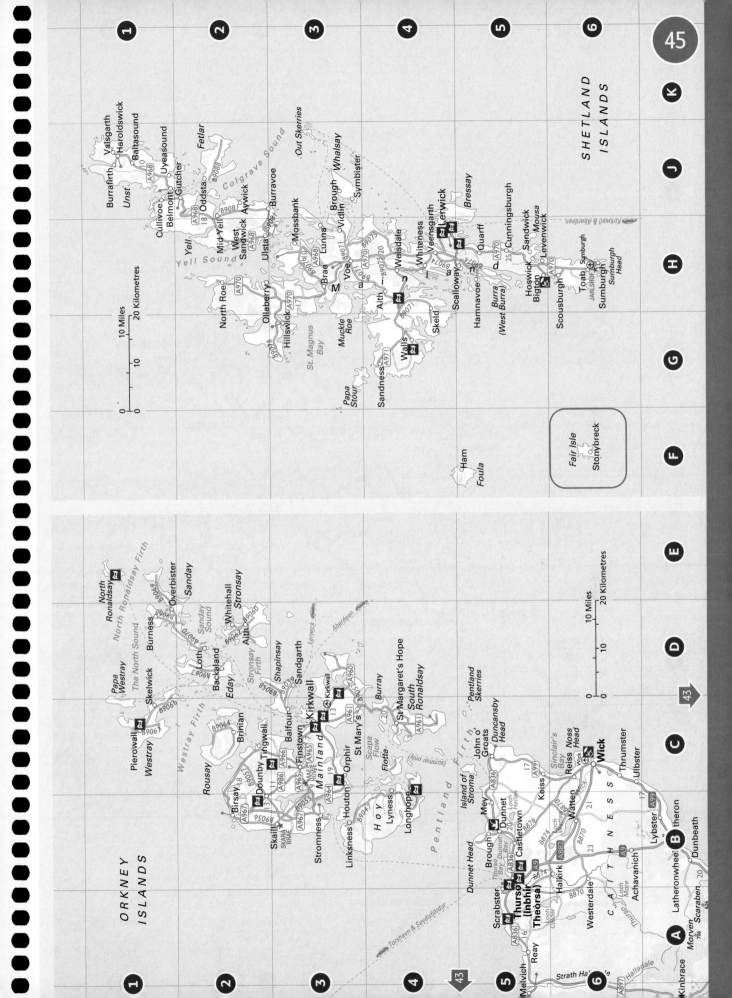

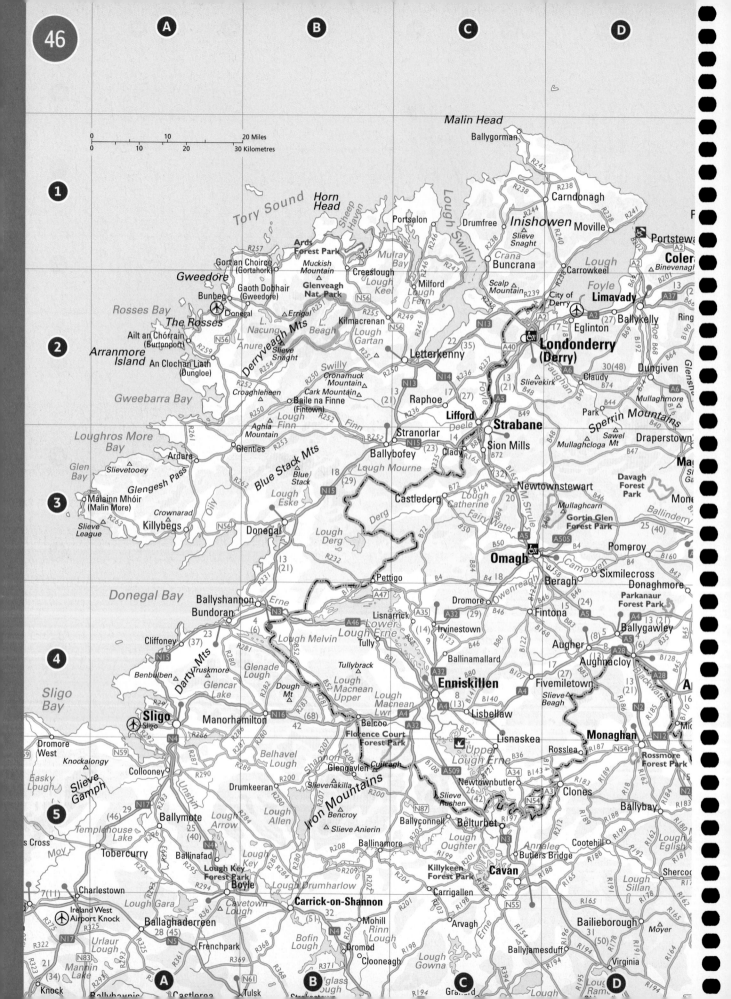

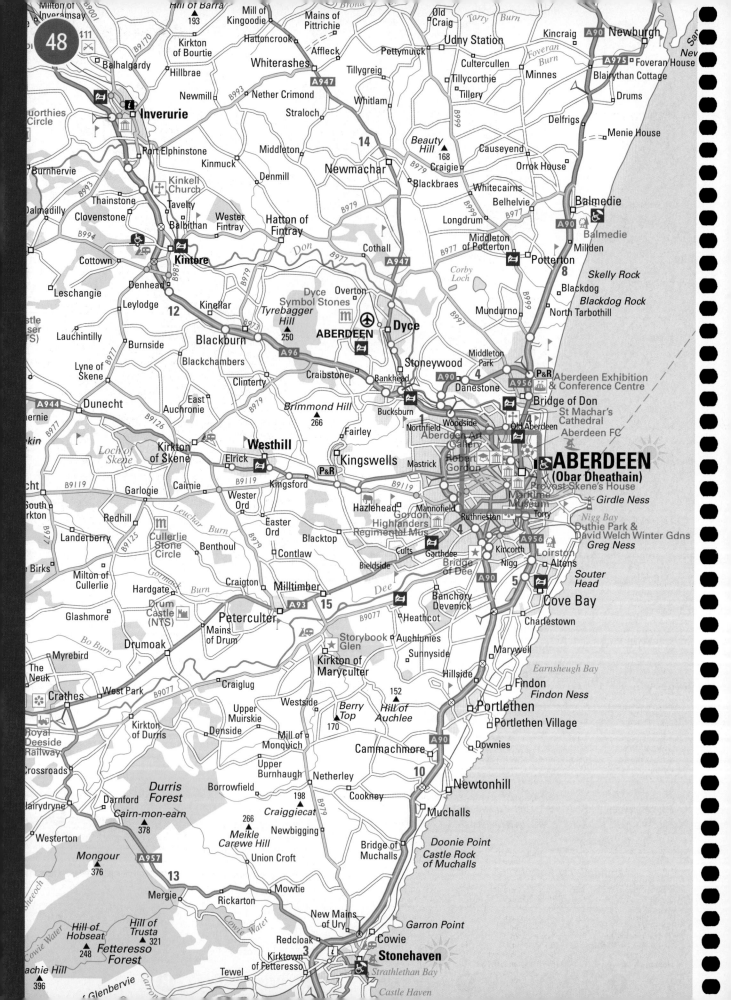

INDEX TO STREET NAMES

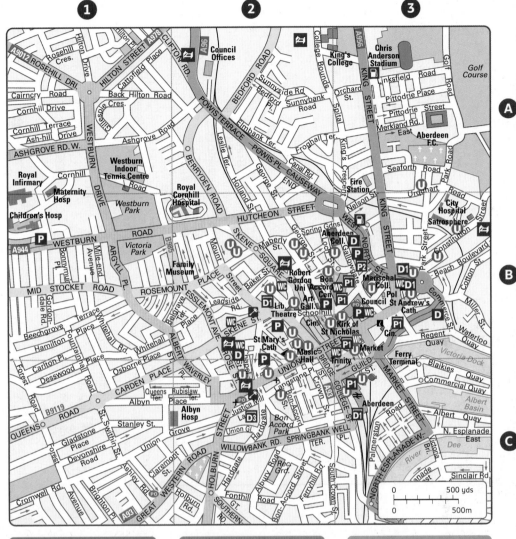

ADMINISTRATION

ABERDEEN CITY COUNCIL,
ST NICHOLAS HOUSE,
BROAD STREET,
ABERDEEN,
AB10 1AR

www.aberdeencity.gov.uk
☎ 01224 522000

HOSPITAL

ABERDEEN ROYAL
INFIRMARY,
FORESTERHILL,
ABERDEEN,
AB25 2ZN

☎ 0845 456 6000

VISITOR INFORMATION

23 UNION STREET,
ABERDEEN,
AB11 5BP

☎ 01224 288828

Aberdeen
Population: 184,788.

Cathedral and university city and commercial centre on E coast 57m/92km NE of Dundee. Known as 'The Granite City', local stone having been used in many of its buildings. By 13c, Aberdeen had become an important centre for trade and fishing and remains a major port and commercial base. In 19c shipbuilding brought great prosperity to the city. These industries had receded by mid 20c but the city's prospects were transformed when North Sea oil was discovered in 1970, turning it into a city of great wealth. St. Machar's Cathedral at Old Aberdeen. Many museums and art galleries. Extensive flower gardens. Airport at Dyce, 6m/9km NW of Aberdeen.

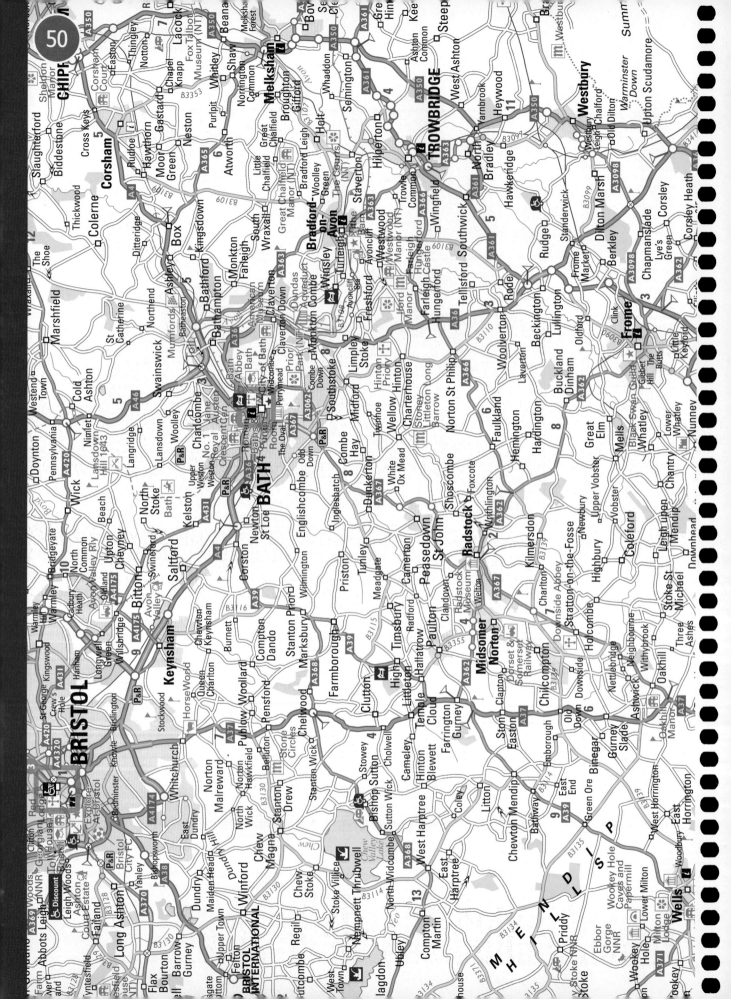

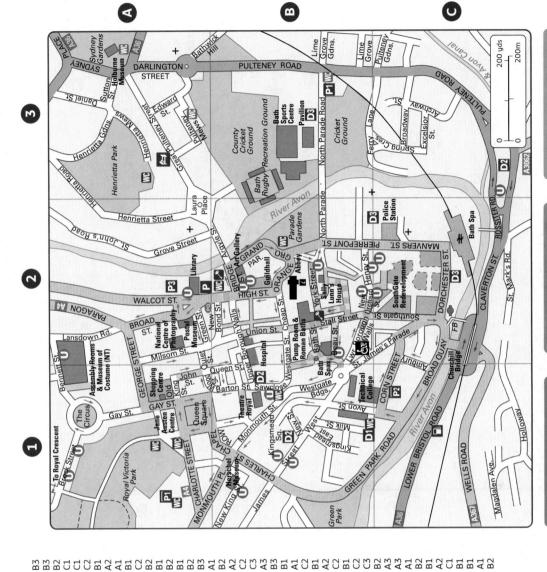

Bath *B. & N.E.Som.*
Population: 90,144.

City, spa on River Avon, World Heritage Site, 11m/18km SE of Bristol. Abbey church rebuilt 1501. Natural hot springs unique in Britain drew Romans to Bath, which they named 'Aquae Sulis'. Roman baths and 18c Pump Room are open to visitors. In 18c it was most fashionable resort in country. Many Georgian buildings and elegant crescents remain, including The Circus and Royal Crescent. Museum of Costume in restored Assembly Rooms. Holds annual summer music festival. American Museum housed in Claverton Manor 3m/4km SE. University.

VISITOR INFORMATION

ABBEY CHAMBERS,
ABBEY CHURCHYARD,
BATH,
BA1 1LY
☎ 0906 711 2000

HOSPITAL

ROYAL UNITED HOSPITAL,
COMBE PARK,
BATH,
BA1 3NG
☎ 01225 428331

ADMINISTRATION

BATH & NORTH EAST
SOMERSET COUNCIL
THE GUILDHALL,
HIGH STREET,
BATH, BA1 5AW
www.bathnes.gov.uk
☎ 01225 477000

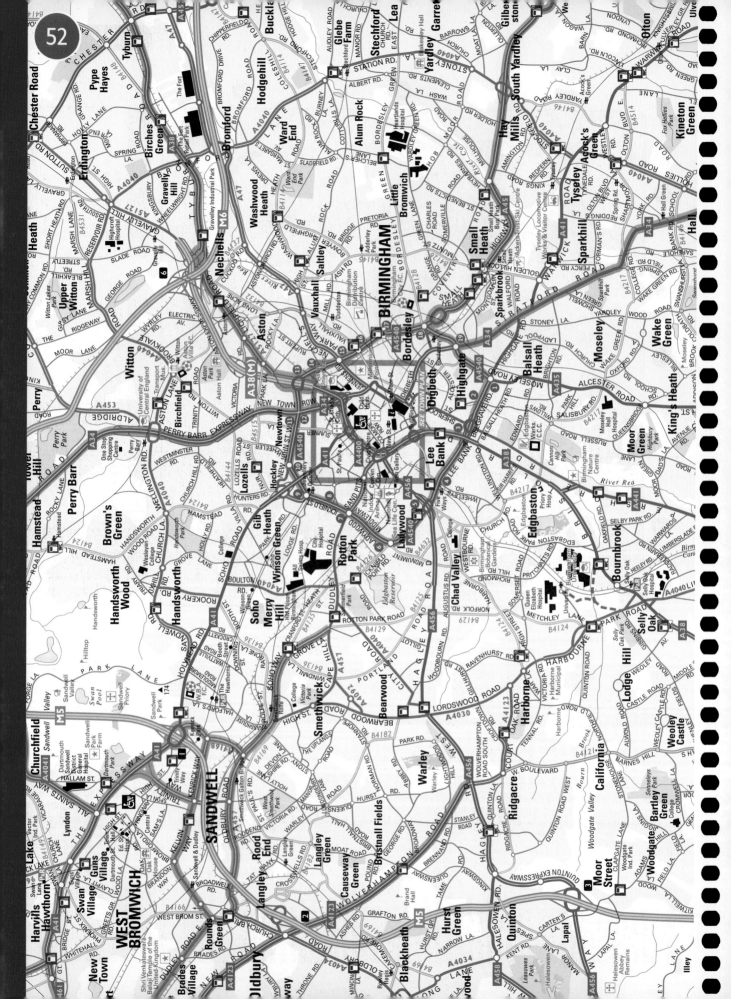

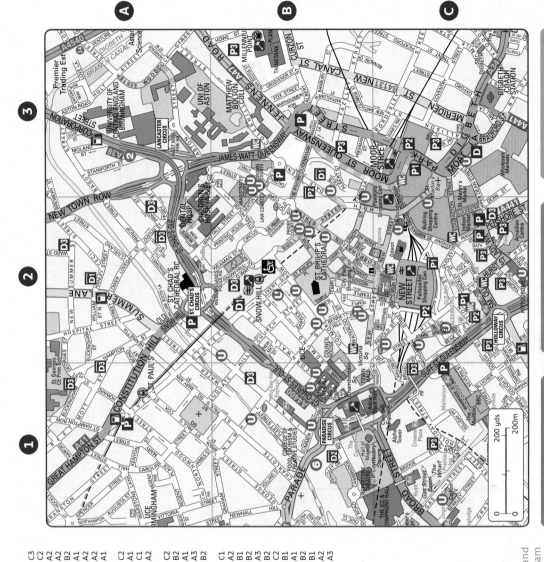

VISITOR INFORMATION

THE ROTUNDA,
150 NEW STREET,
BIRMINGHAM,
B2 4PA

☎ 0870 225 0127

HOSPITAL

CITY HOSPITAL,
DUDLEY ROAD,
BIRMINGHAM,
B18 7QH

☎ 0121 554 3801

ADMINISTRATION

BIRMINGHAM CITY COUNCIL,
COUNCIL HOUSE,
VICTORIA SQUARE,
BIRMINGHAM,
B1 1BB

www.birmingham.gov.uk
☎ 0121 303 9944

INDEX TO SELECTIVE STREET NAMES

Birmingham *W.Mid.*
Population: 970,892.

England's second city and manufacturing, commercial and communications centre, 100m/160km NW of London. Birmingham was home to many pioneers of Industrial Revolution. Current economic trend is towards post-industrial activities, concentrating on convention and exhibition trades and tourism. To S of city is planned village of Bournville, established by Quaker chocolate magnates George and Richard Cadbury in 1879, influenced by utopian ideas of William Morris. Universities. City has many galleries and museums, particularly around 19c Victoria and Chamberlain Squares. Anglican and Catholic cathedrals. Birmingham International Airport 7m/11km E of city centre.

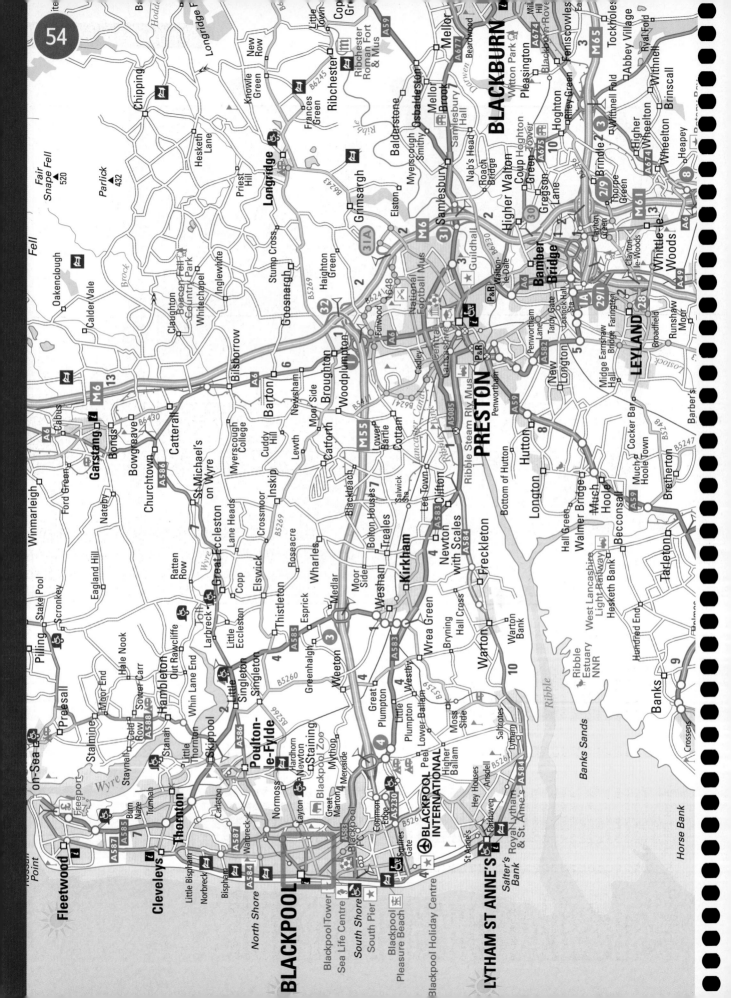

Blackpool B'pool.
Population: 142,283.

Town, large coastal resort and conference centre on Irish Sea, 15m/24km W of Preston. Became fashionable resort in 19c, still very popular today. 7m/11km long 'Golden Mile' of tram route, beach, piers and amusement arcades. Blackpool Pleasure Beach funfair park, 518ft/158m high Tower entertainment complex, annual autumn Illuminations along 5m/8km of Promenade, Zoo, Sea Life Centre, The Sandcastle indoor pool complex and Winter Gardens. Airport 3m/5km S of town.

VISITOR INFORMATION

1 CLIFTON STREET,
BLACKPOOL,
FY1 1LY

☎ 01253 478222

HOSPITAL

VICTORIA HOSPITAL,
WHINNEY HEYS ROAD,
BLACKPOOL,
FY3 8NR

☎ 01253 300000

ADMINISTRATION

BLACKPOOL COUNCIL,
TOWN HALL,
BLACKPOOL,
FY1 1AD

www.blackpool.gov.uk
☎ 01253 477477

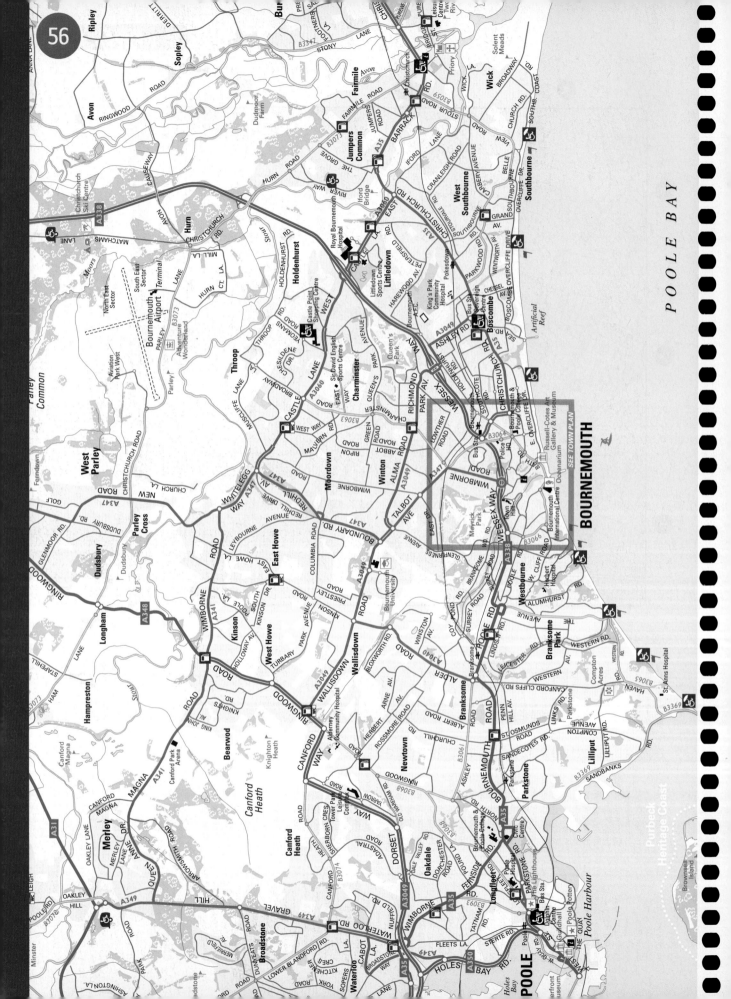

POOLE BAY

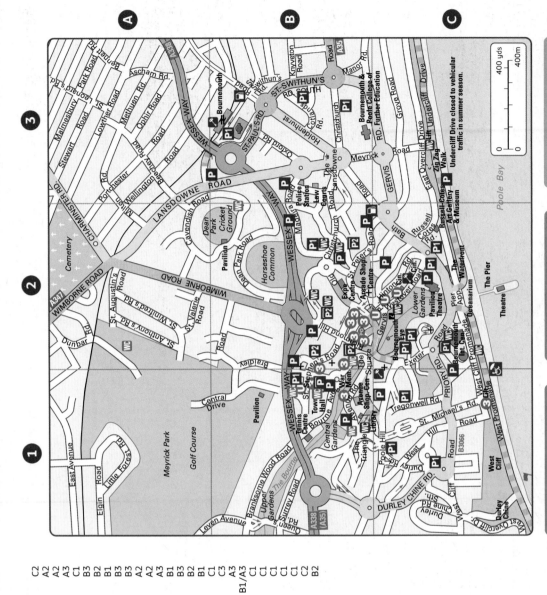

Bournemouth *Bourne.*
Population: 167,527.

Town, large seaside resort with mild climate, 24m/39km SW of Southampton. Town developed from a few cottages in 1810 to present conurbation. Sandy beach and pier. Extensive parks and gardens including Compton Acres, a display of international garden styles. Russell-Cotes Art Gallery and Museum houses Victorian and oriental collection. University. Conference, business and shopping centre. Bournemouth International Airport, 5m/8km NE of town centre.

VISITOR INFORMATION

WESTOVER ROAD,
BOURNEMOUTH,
BH1 2BU

☎ 0845 05 11 700

HOSPITAL

ROYAL BOURNEMOUTH
HOSPITAL,
CASTLE LANE EAST,
BOURNEMOUTH,
BH7 7DW

☎ 01202 303626

ADMINISTRATION

BOURNEMOUTH BOROUGH
COUNCIL,
TOWN HALL,
BOURNE AVENUE,
BOURNEMOUTH, BH2 6DY
☎ 01202 451451

www.bournemouth.gov.uk

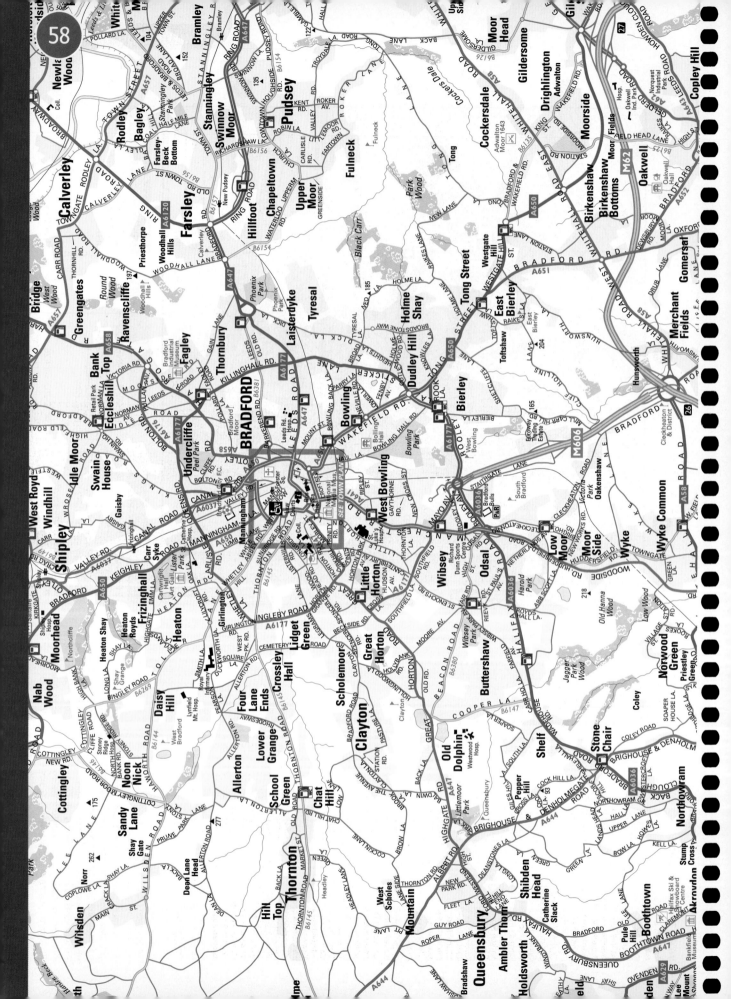

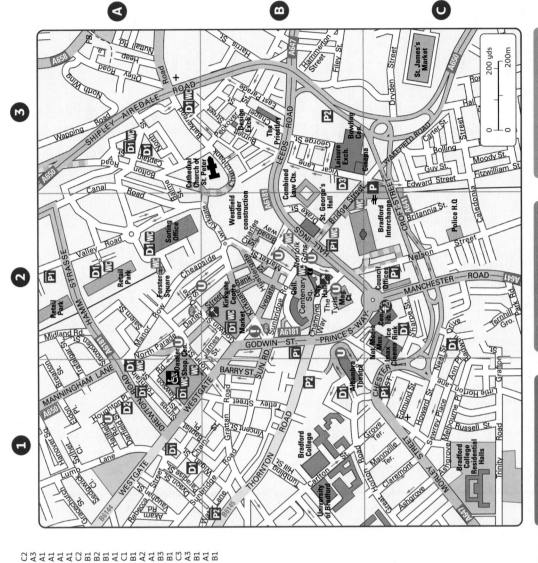

VISITOR INFORMATION

CITY HALL,
CENTENARY SQUARE,
BRADFORD,
BD1 1HY

☎ 01274 433678

HOSPITAL

BRADFORD ROYAL
INFIRMARY,
DUCKWORTH LANE,
BRADFORD,
BD9 6RJ

☎ 01274 542200

ADMINISTRATION

CITY OF BRADFORD
METROPOLITAN
DISTRICT COUNCIL,
CITY HALL, CENTENARY SQ,
BRADFORD, BD1 1HY

www.bradford.gov.uk
☎ 01274 432111

INDEX TO STREET NAMES

Bradford *W.Yorks.*
Population: 293,717.

Industrial city, 8m/13km W of Leeds. Cathedral is former parish church. Previously known as wool capital of the world, Bradford is now less dependent upon the textile industry. Impressions Gallery and Gallery 1 exhibits innovative photography, art and craft with some historic pieces. University. Home to National Media Museum with IMAX cinema screen. Titus Salt built Saltaire 3m/5km N, which is a model industrial village and a World Heritage Site. Salt's Mill, originally for textiles, now houses David Hockney art in the 1853 gallery. Leeds Bradford International Airport at Yeadon, 6m/10km NE.

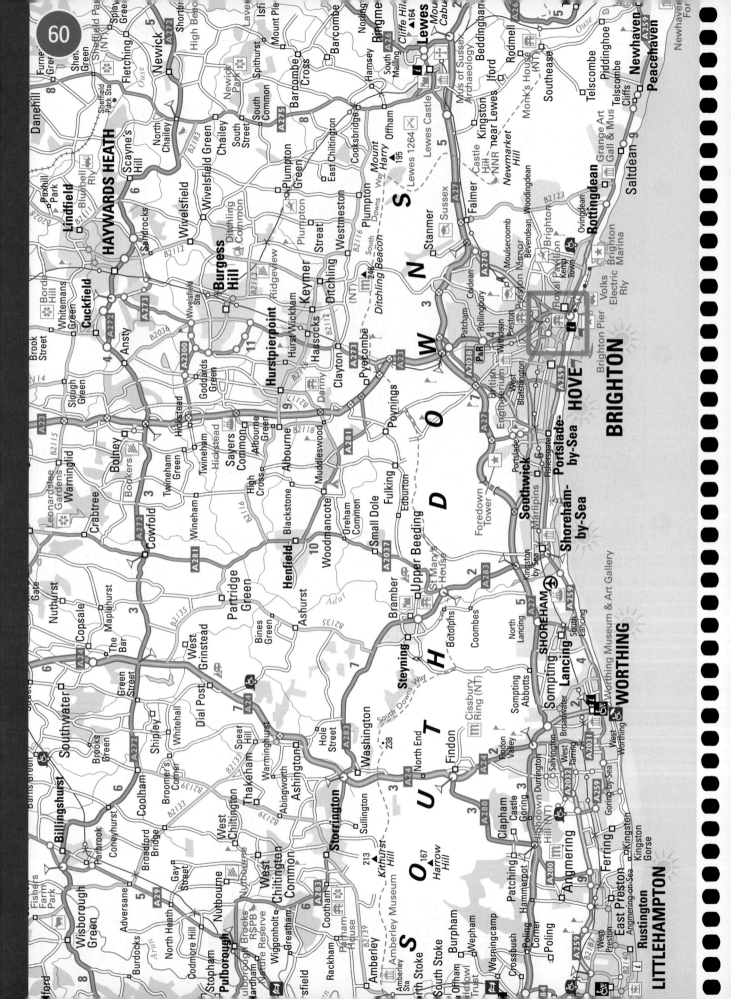

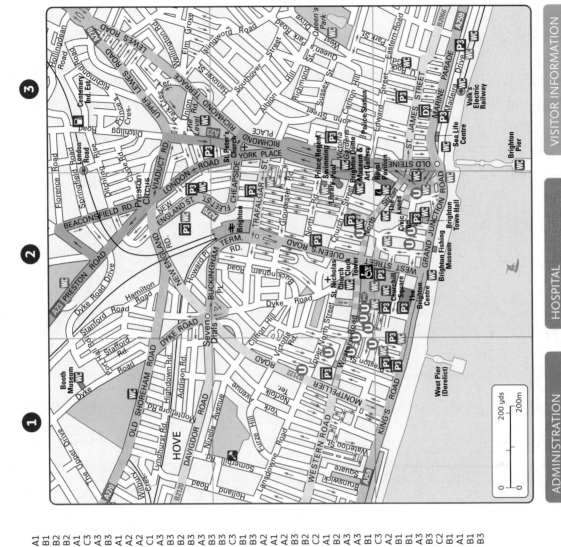

Brighton *B. & H.*
Population: 134,293.

City (with Hove), seaside resort, sailing and conference centre, 48m/77km S of London. Previously a fishing village known as Brighthelmstone, centred on current Lanes area. Brighton became fashionable as a sea-bathing resort in the 18c. Patronized by the Prince Regent in 1780s who built the Royal Pavilion in Oriental style as a summer palace. Regency squares at Kemp Town. Amusement arcades on 1899 Palace Pier. Annual festivals. Language schools. Universities.

VISITOR INFORMATION

ROYAL PAVILION SHOP,
4–5 PAVILION BUILDINGS,
BRIGHTON,
BN1 1EE

☎ 0906 711 2255

HOSPITAL

ROYAL SUSSEX COUNTY
HOSPITAL,
EASTERN ROAD,
BRIGHTON,
BN2 5BE

☎ 01273 696955

ADMINISTRATION

BRIGHTON & HOVE
CITY COUNCIL,
KING'S HOUSE,
GRAND AVENUE,
HOVE, BN3 2LS
☎ 01273 290000
www.brighton-hove.gov.uk

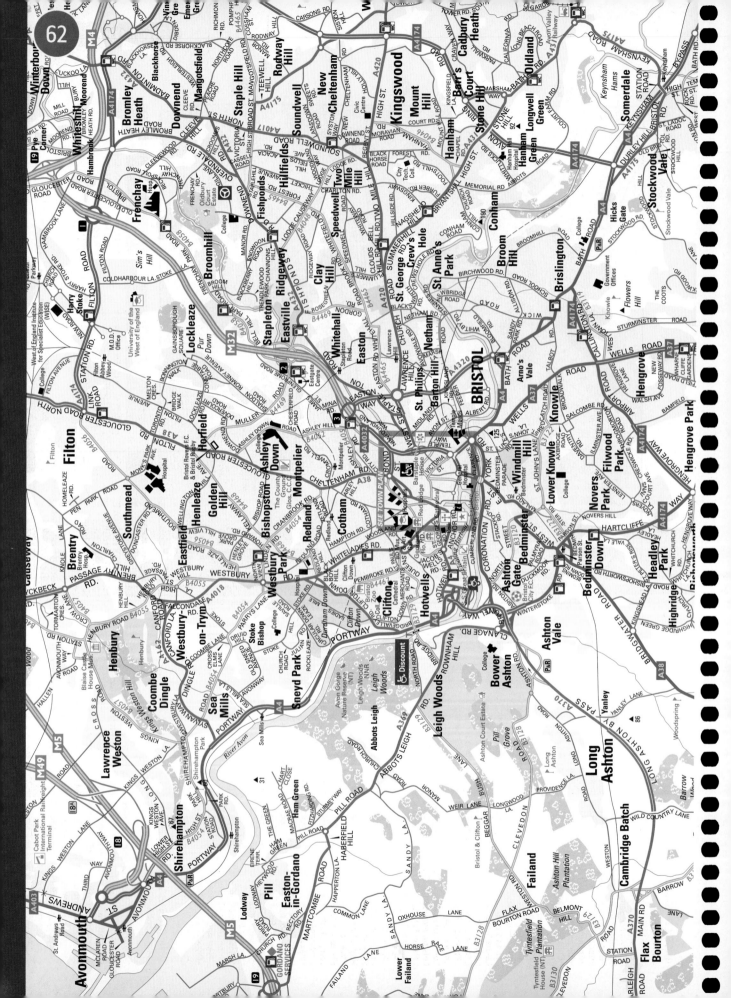

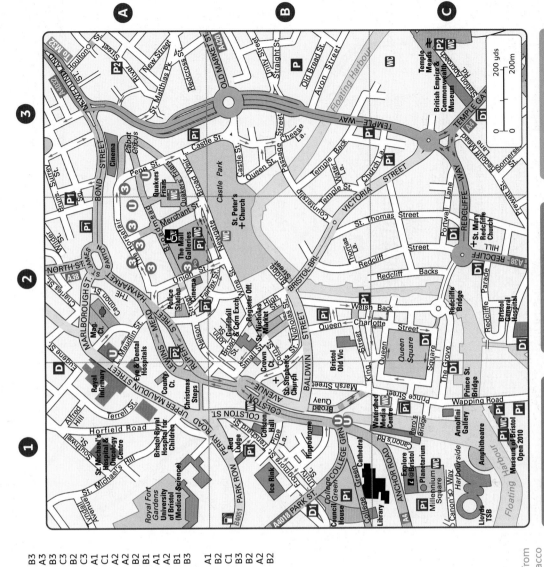

Bristol

Population: 420,556.

City, 106m/171km W of London. Port on River Avon dates from medieval times. Bristol grew from transatlantic trade in rum, tobacco and slaves. In Georgian times, Bristol's population was second only to London and many Georgian buildings still stand, including the Theatre Royal, the oldest working theatre in the country. Bristol is now a commercial and industrial centre. Cathedral dates from 12c and was originally an abbey. 15c Temple Church tower and walls (English Heritage). Restored iron ship SS Great Britain and Museum of Bristol (open 2010) in city docks area. Universities. 245ft/75m high Clifton Suspension Bridge completed in 1864 across the Avon Gorge NW of the city. Bristol International Airport at Lulsgate 7m/11km SW.

VISITOR INFORMATION

EXPLORE@BRISTOL,
ANCHOR ROAD,
HARBOURSIDE,
BRISTOL,
BS1 5DB
☎ 0906 711 2191

HOSPITAL

BRISTOL ROYAL INFIRMARY,
MARLBOROUGH STREET,
BRISTOL,
BS2 8HW
☎ 0117 923 0000

ADMINISTRATION

BRISTOL CITY COUNCIL,
THE COUNCIL HOUSE,
COLLEGE GREEN,
BRISTOL,
BS1 5TR
www.bristol-city.gov.uk
☎ 0117 922 2000

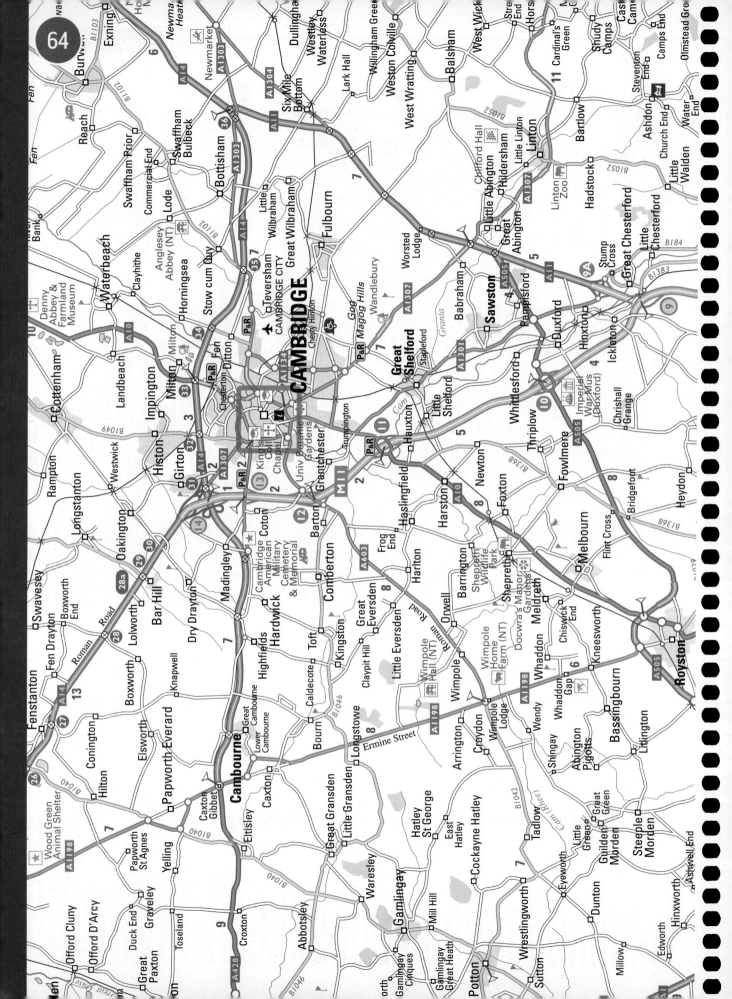

Cambridge *Cambs.*
Population: 117,717.

University city on River Cam 49m/79km N of London. First college founded here in 1284. Historic tensions existed between students and townspeople since 14c, and came to a head during Peasants' Revolt of 1381 in which five townsfolk were hanged. Oliver Cromwell was a graduate of Sidney Sussex College and local MP at a time when the University was chiefly Royalist. 1870s saw foundation of first women's colleges, but women were not awarded degrees until after 1947. University's notable graduates include prime ministers, foreign heads of state, literary giants, philosophers and spies. Cambridge Footlights regularly provide a platform for future stars of stage, screen and television. Cambridge boasts many fine museums, art galleries and buildings of interest, including King's College Chapel and Fitzwilliam Museum. Airport at Teversham 3m/4km E.

VISITOR INFORMATION

WHEELER STREET,
CAMBRIDGE,
CB2 3QB

☎ 0871 226 8006

HOSPITAL

ADDENBROOKE'S HOSPITAL,
HILLS ROAD,
CAMBRIDGE,
CB2 2QQ

☎ 01223 245151

ADMINISTRATION

CAMBRIDGE CITY COUNCIL,
THE GUILDHALL,
MARKET SQUARE,
CAMBRIDGE,
CB2 3Q

🖥 www.cambridge.gov.uk
☎ 01223 457000

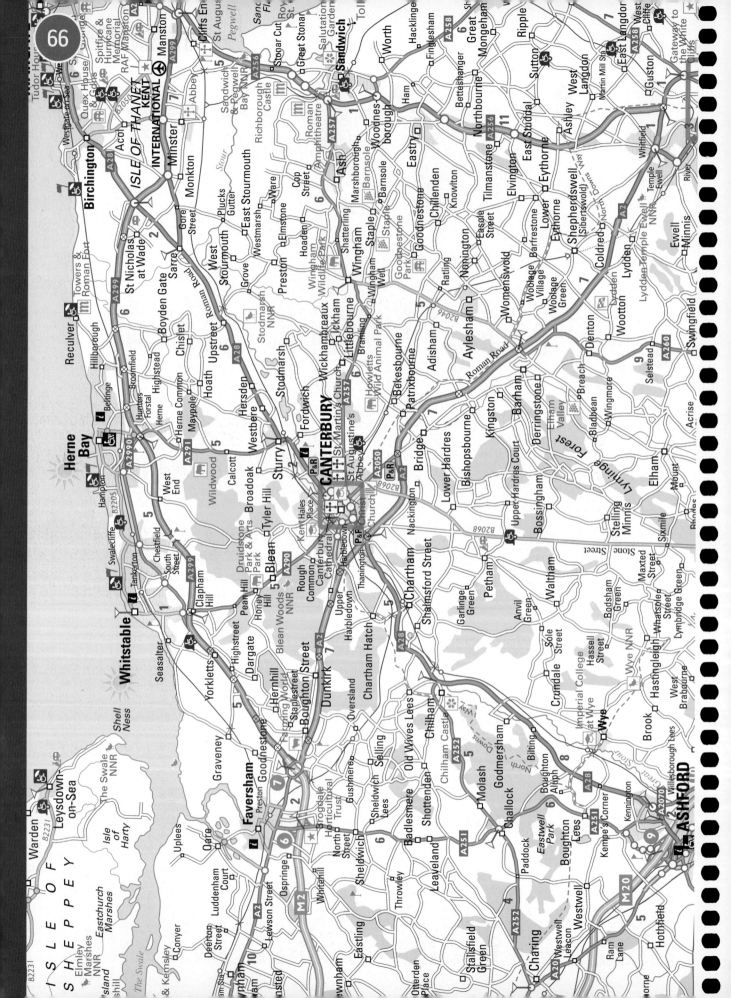

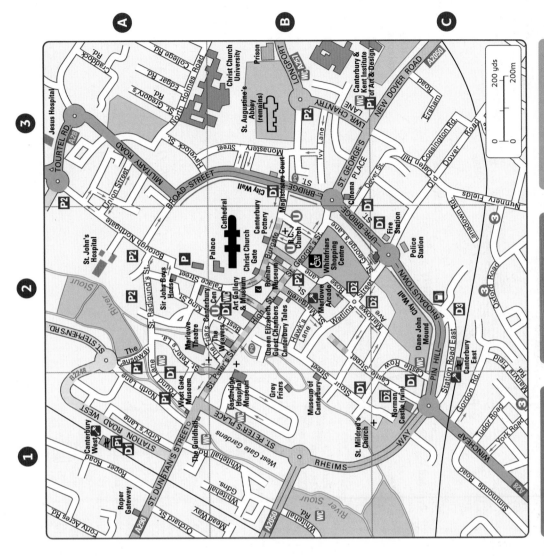

VISITOR INFORMATION

12-13 SUN STREET,
THE BUTTERMARKET,
CANTERBURY,
CT1 2HX

☎ 01227 378100

HOSPITAL

KENT & CANTERBURY
HOSPITAL,
ETHELBERT ROAD,
CANTERBURY,
CT1 3NG

☎ 01227 766877

ADMINISTRATION

CANTERBURY CITY COUNCIL,
COUNCIL OFFICES,
MILITARY ROAD,
CANTERBURY,
CT1 1YW
www.canterbury.gov.uk
☎ 01227 862000

INDEX TO STREET NAMES

Canterbury *Kent*
Population: 43,552.

Premier cathedral city and seat of Primate of Church of England on Great Stour River, 54m/88km E of London. University. Site of Roman settlement Durovernum. After Romans left, Saxons renamed town Cantwaraburig. First cathedral in England built on site of current Christ Church Cathedral in AD 602. Thomas à Becket assassinated in Canterbury in 1170, turning Cathedral into great Christian shrine and destination of many pilgrimages, such as those detailed in Geoffrey Chaucer's Canterbury Tales. Becket's tomb destroyed on orders of Henry VIII. Cathedral was backdrop for premiere of T.S. Eliot's play 'Murder in the Cathedral' in 1935 and is now part of a World Heritage Site. City suffered extensive damage during World War II. Many museums and galleries explaining city's rich heritage. Roman and medieval remains, including city walls. Industrial development on outskirts. University of Kent on hill to N.

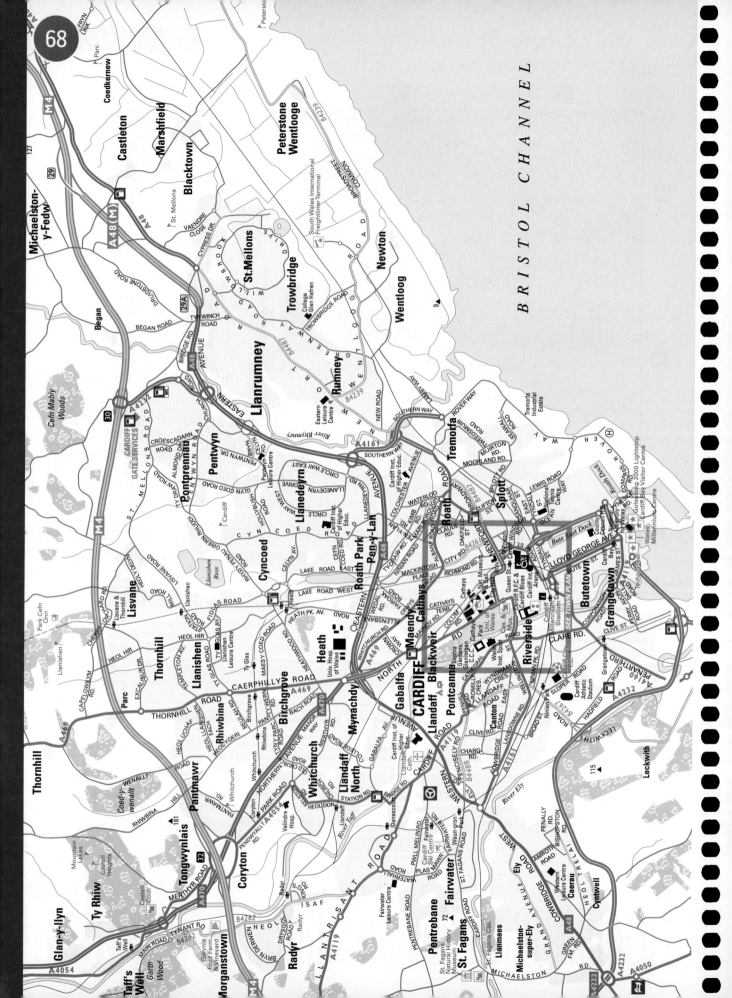

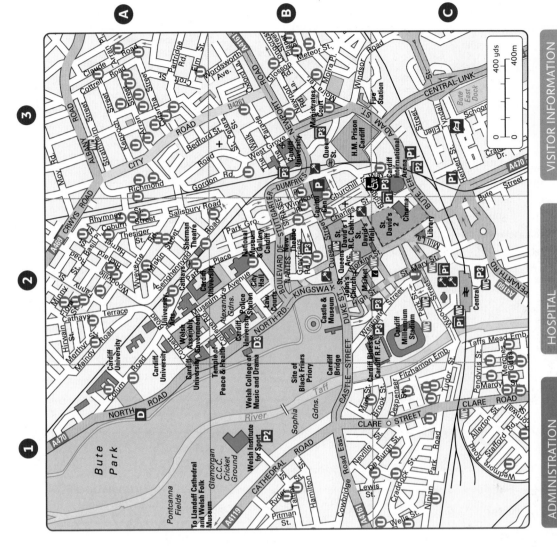

VISITOR INFORMATION

THE OLD LIBRARY,
TRINITY STREET,
CARDIFF,
CF10 1BH

☎ 0870 1211 258

HOSPITAL

UNIVERSITY HOSPITAL OF
WALES,
HEATH PARK,
CARDIFF,
CF14 4XW

☎ 029 2074 7747

ADMINISTRATION

CARDIFF COUNCIL,
C2C HELP CENTRE,
MARLAND HOUSE,
CENTRAL SQUARE,
CARDIFF, CF10 1EP

www.cardiff.gov.uk
☎ 029 2087 2087

INDEX TO STREET NAMES

Cardiff (Caerdydd).
Population: 292,150.

City, capital of Wales since 1955. Romans founded military fort and small settlement on site of present day Cardiff. Uninhabited between departure of Romans and Norman conquest centuries later. Fishing village until development of coal mining in 19c. Population rose from 1000 in 1801 to 170,000 a century later, with city becoming one of busiest ports in the world. Dock trade collapsed in 1930s. Since establishment as Welsh capital, many governmental, administrative and media organisations have moved to city. Major refurbishment and development programme still under way. Cardiff Bay area now major tourist centre and includes Techniquest, a science discovery centre, and is the location of the new Welsh Assembly building. Millennium Stadium Cardiff Arms Park is the home of Welsh Rugby Union and also hosts other sporting and entertainment events. Many museums including National Museum of Wales. Universities.

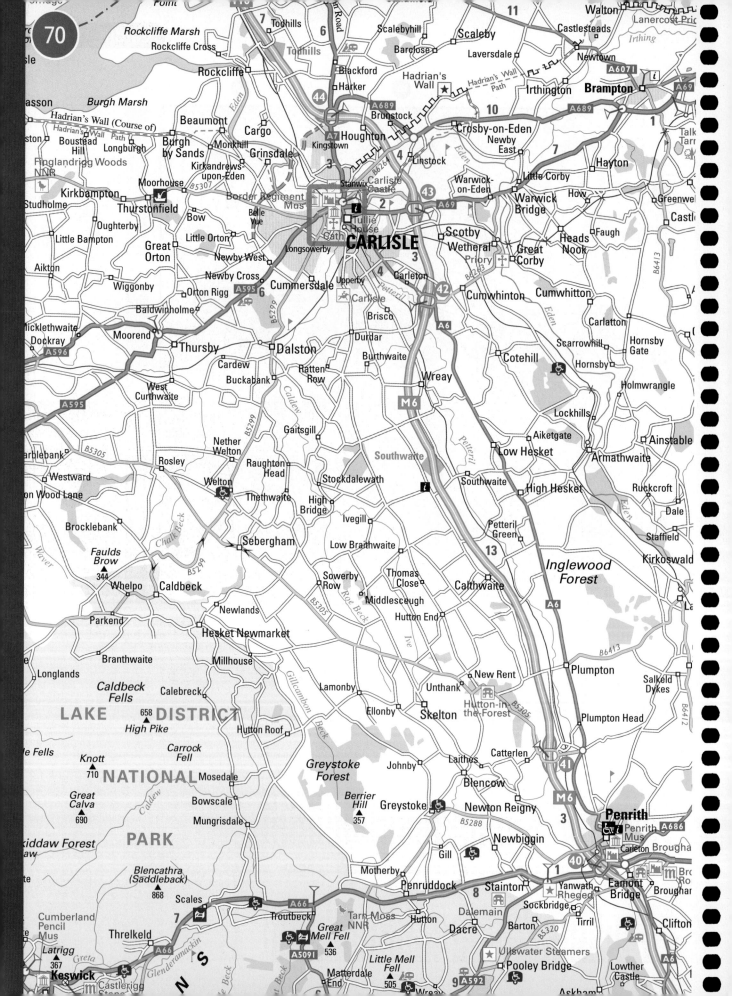

ADMINISTRATION

CARLISLE CITY COUNCIL,
THE CIVIC CENTRE,
CARLISLE,
CA3 8QG

www.carlisle-city.gov.uk
☎ 01228 817000

HOSPITAL

CUMBERLAND INFIRMARY,
NEWTOWN ROAD,
CARLISLE,
CA2 7HY

☎ 01228 523444

VISITOR INFORMATION

OLD TOWN HALL,
GREEN MARKET,
CARLISLE,
CA3 8JE

☎ 01228 625600

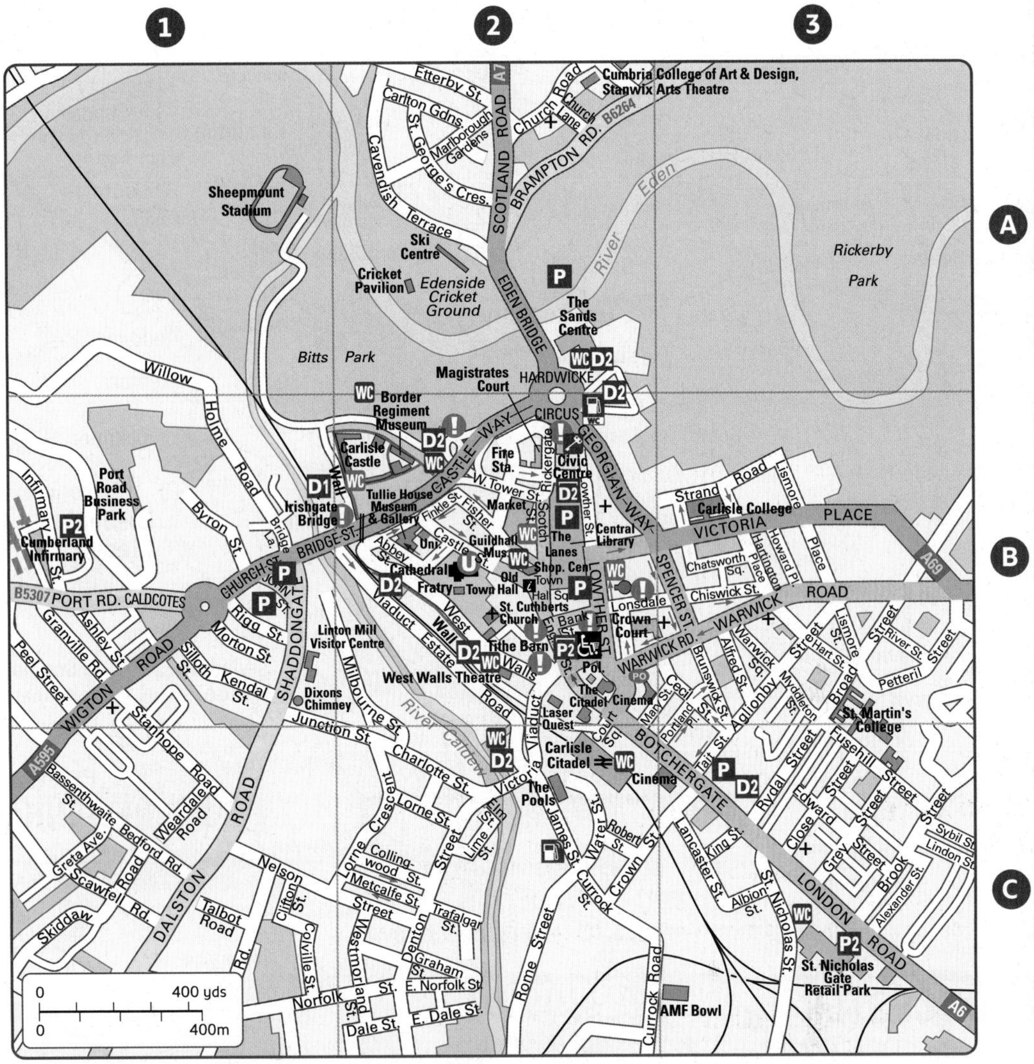

INDEX TO STREET NAMES

Abbey Street	B2
Aglionby Street	B3
Albion Street	C3
Alexander Street	C3
Alfred Street	B3
Ashley Street	B1
Bank Street	B2
Bassenthwaite Street	C1
Bedford Road	C1
Botchergate	C2
Brampton Road	A2
Bridge Lane	B1
Bridge Street	B1
Broad Street	B3
Brook Street	C3
Brunswick Street	B3
Byron Street	B1
Caldcotes	B1
Carlton Gardens	A2
Castle Street	B2
Castle Way	B2
Cavendish Terrace	A2
Cecil Street	B3
Charlotte Street	C2
Chatsworth Square	B3
Chiswick Street	B3
Church Lane	A2
Church Road	A2
Church Street	B1
Clifton Street	C1
Close Street	C3
Collingwood Street	C2
Colville Street	C1
Crown Street	C2
Currock Road	C2
Currock Street	C2
Dale Street	C2
Denton Street	C2
Dunmail Drive	C1
East Dale Street	C2
East Norfolk Street	C2
Eden Bridge	A2
Edward Street	C3
Elm Street	C2
English Street	B2
Etterby Street	A2
Finkle Street	B2
Fisher Street	B2
Fusehill Street	C3
Georgian Way	B2
Goschen Road	C1
Graham Street	C2
Granville Road	B1
Greta Avenue	C1
Grey Street	C3
Hardwicke Circus	A2
Hart Street	B3
Hartington Place	B3
Howard Place	B3
Infirmary Street	B1
James Street	C2
John Street	B1
Junction Street	B1
Kendal Street	B1
King Street	C3
Lancaster Street	C3
Lime Street	C2
Lindon Street	C3
Lismore Place	B3
Lismore Street	B3
London Road	C3
Lonsdale	B2
Lorne Crescent	C2
Lorne Street	C2
Lowther Street	B2
Marlborough Gardens	A2
Mary Street	B2
Metcalfe Street	C2
Milbourne Street	B2
Morton Street	B1
Myddleton Street	B3
Nelson Street	C1
Norfolk Road	C1
Norfolk Street	C1
Peel Street	B1
Petteril Street	B3
Port Road	B1
Portland Place	C3
Rickergate	B2
Rigg Street	B1
River Street	B3
Robert Street	C2
Rome Street	C2
Rydal Street	C3
St. George's Crescent	A2
St. James Road	C1
St. Nicholas Street	C3
Scawfell Road	C1
Scotch Street	B2
Scotland Road	A2
Shaddongate	B1
Silloth Street	B1
Skiddaw Road	C1
Spencer Street	B3
Stanhope Road	B1
Strand Road	B3
Sybil Street	C3
Tait Street	C3
Talbot Road	C1
Trafalgar Street	C2
Viaduct Estate Road	B2
Victoria Place	B3
Victoria Viaduct	C2
Warwick Road	B2
Warwick Square	B3
Water Street	C2
Weardale Road	C1
West Tower Street	B2
West Walls	B2
Westmorland Street	C2
Wigton Road	B1
Willow Holme Road	A1

Carlisle *Cumb.*
Population: 71,773.

Cathedral city at confluence of River Eden and River Caldew, 54m/87km W of Newcastle upon Tyne. Once a Roman military base and later fought over by Scots and English, line of Hadrian's wall (a World Heritage Site) runs through the northern suburbs. Castle above the River Eden, completed in 12c, houses a military museum. Cathedral partially destroyed by fire in 17c has two surviving bays of 12c and a magnificent East window. Tullie House Museum imaginatively tells of the city's turbulent past. University of Northumbria. Racecourse 2m/4km S. Airport 6m/9km NE.

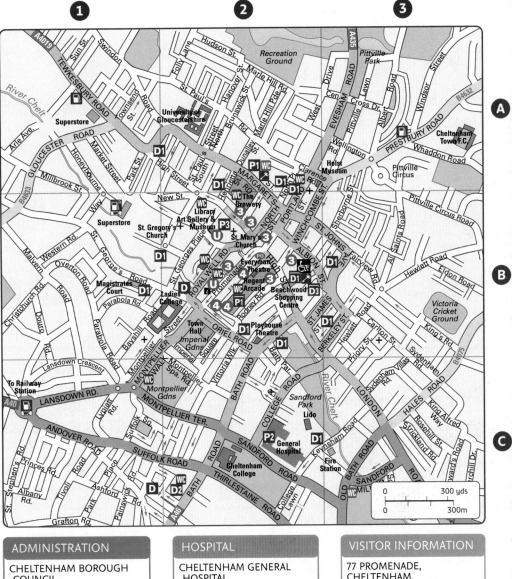

ADMINISTRATION

CHELTENHAM BOROUGH COUNCIL, MUNICIPAL OFFICES, PROMENADE, CHELTENHAM, GL50 9SA

www.cheltenham.gov.uk
☎ 01242 262626

HOSPITAL

CHELTENHAM GENERAL HOSPITAL, SANDFORD ROAD, CHELTENHAM, GL53 7AN

☎ 08454 222222

VISITOR INFORMATION

77 PROMENADE, CHELTENHAM, GL50 1PJ

☎ 01242 522878

Cheltenham *Glos.*
Population: 98,875.

Largest town in The Cotswolds, 8m/12km NE of Gloucester. Shopping and tourist centre, with some light industry. Mainly residential, with many Regency and Victorian buildings and public gardens. Formerly a spa town, Pittville Pump Room built between 1825 and 1830 overlooks Pittville Park and is now used for concerts. Art Gallery and Museum. Ladies' College founded 1853. Racecourse to the N hosts Cheltenham Gold Cup race meeting. Other events include Cheltenham International Music Festival and Festival of Literature. Birthplace of composer Gustav Holst. University of Gloucestershire. Airport 4m/7km W at Staverton.

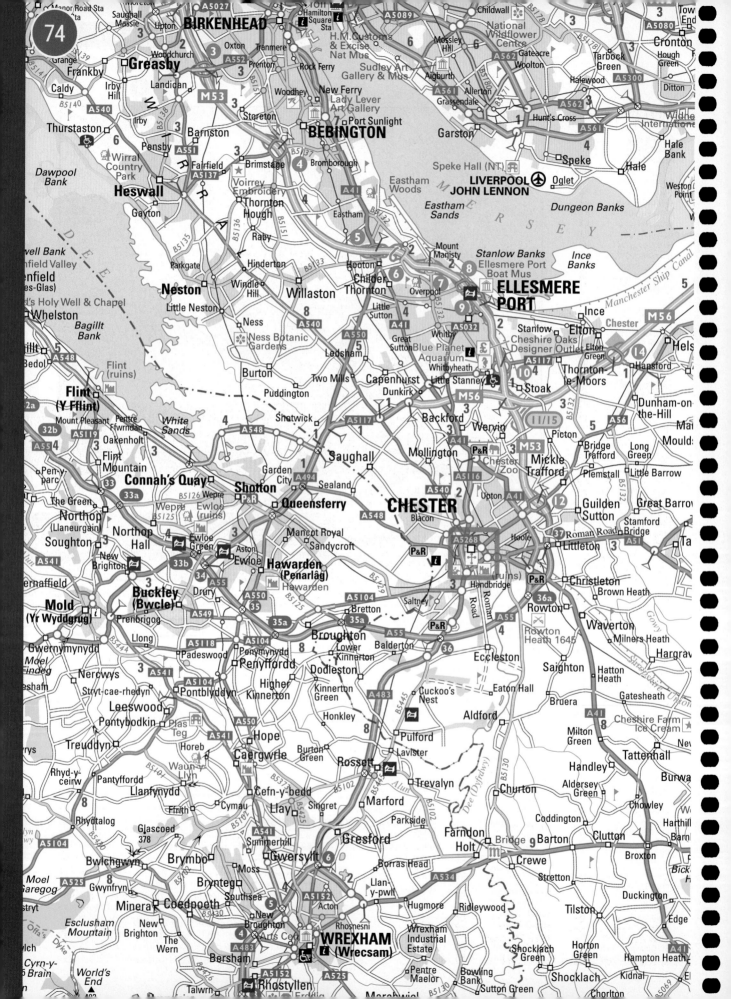

INDEX TO STREET NAMES

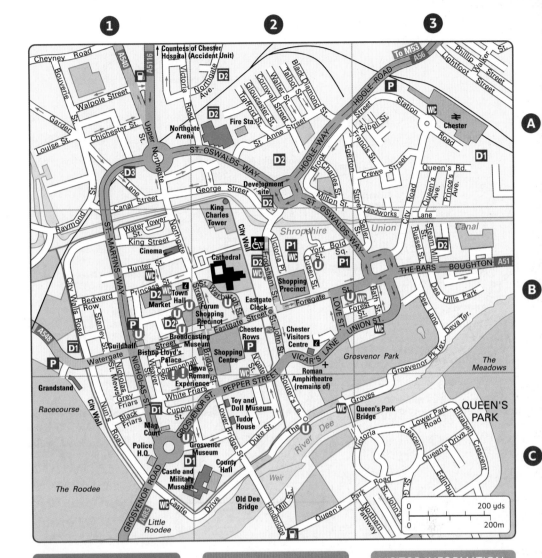

ADMINISTRATION

CHESTER CITY COUNCIL,
THE FORUM,
CHESTER,
CH1 2HS

www.chester.gov.uk
☎ 01244 324324

HOSPITAL

COUNTESS OF CHESTER
HOSPITAL,
HEALTH PARK,
LIVERPOOL ROAD,
CHESTER,
CH2 1UL

☎ 01244 365000

VISITOR INFORMATION

TOWN HALL,
NORTHGATE STREET,
CHESTER,
CH1 2HJ

☎ 01244 402111

Chester *Ches.*
Population: 80,121.

County town and cathedral city on River Dee, 34m/54km SW of Manchester and 15m/24km SE of Birkenhead. Commercial, financial and tourist centre built on Roman town of Deva. Includes biggest Roman amphitheatre in Britain (English Heritage) and well preserved medieval walls (English Heritage). Castle, now county hall, includes 12c Agricola Tower (English Heritage). Cathedral with remains of original Norman abbey. Famed for Tudor timber-framed buildings which include Chester Rows, two-tier galleried shops and Bishop Lloyd's House, with ornate 16c carved façade. Eastgate clock built to commemorate Queen Victoria's diamond jubilee in 1897. Racecourse 1m/2km SW of city centre; zoo 3m/4km N of city centre.

INDEX TO STREET NAMES

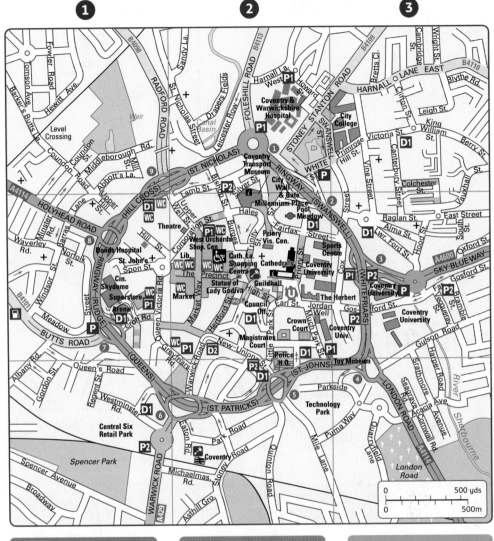

ADMINISTRATION

COVENTRY CITY COUNCIL,
COUNCIL HOUSE,
EARL STREET,
COVENTRY,
CV1 5RR

www.coventry.gov.uk
☎ 024 7683 3333

HOSPITAL

UNIVERSITY HOSPITAL,
CLIFFORD BRIDGE ROAD,
COVENTRY,
CV2 2DX

☎ 024 7696 4000

VISITOR INFORMATION

ST. MICHAEL'S TOWER
4 PRIORY STREET,
COVENTRY,
CV1 5AB

☎ 024 7622 7264

Coventry *W.Mid.*
Population: 303,475.

City, 17m/27km E of Birmingham. St. Michael's cathedral built 1954-62 beside ruins of medieval cathedral destroyed in air raid in 1940. The centre of the city was rebuilt in the 1950s and 1960s following WW II bombing, but some old buildings remain, including Bonds Hospital and the medieval Guildhall. A town rich from textile industry in middle ages, and for its motor car industry in the 20c; other important industries are manufacturing and engineering. Coventry Transport Museum. The Herbert is an Arts, Media, Museum and History Centre. Universities. Civil airport at Baginton to S. Coventry Canal runs N to Trent and Mersey Canal at Fradley Junction near Lichfield.

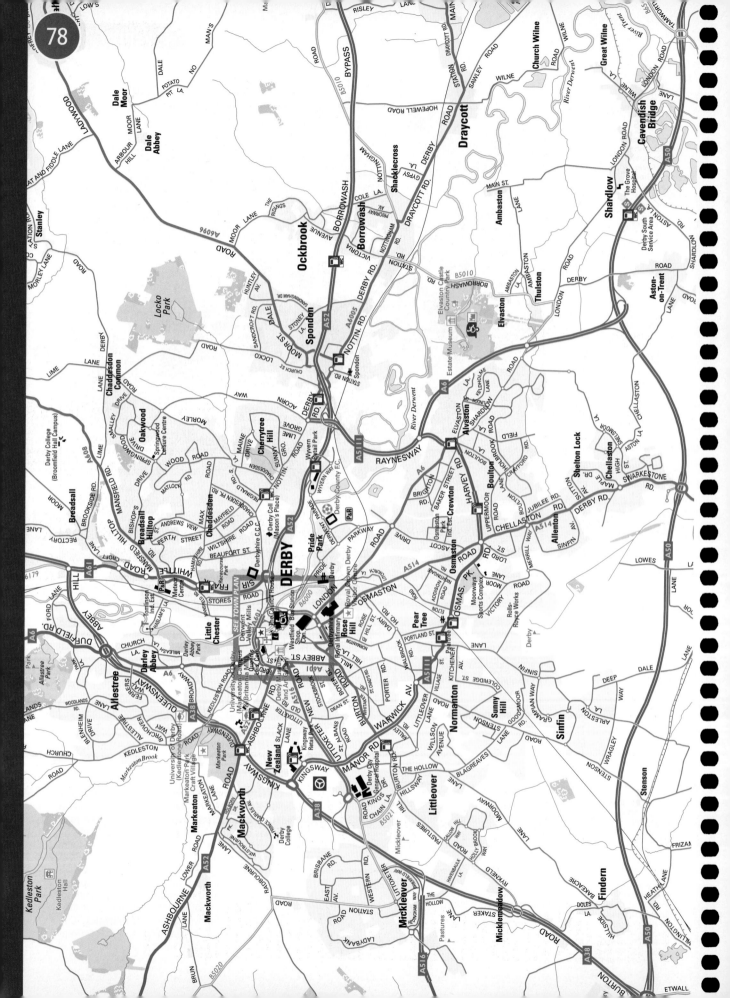

INDEX TO STREET NAMES

Derby
Population: 229,407.

Industrial city and county town on River Derwent, southern extent of Derwent Valley World Heritage Site, 35m/56km NE of Birmingham. Shopping and entertainment centre. Cathedral mainly by James Gibbs, 1725. Both manufacturing and engineering are important to local economy. Derby Industrial Museum charts city's industrial history with emphasis on Rolls Royce aircraft engineering, railways and textiles. Tours at Royal Crown Derby porcelain factory. University.

VISITOR INFORMATION
ASSEMBLY ROOMS,
MARKET PLACE,
DERBY,
DE1 3AH
☎ 01332 255802

HOSPITAL
DERBYSHIRE ROYAL
INFIRMARY,
LONDON ROAD,
DERBY,
DE1 2QY
☎ 01332 347141

ADMINISTRATION
DERBY CITY COUNCIL,
THE COUNCIL HOUSE,
CORPORATION STREET,
DERBY,
DE1 2FE
☎ 01332 293111
www.derby.gov.uk

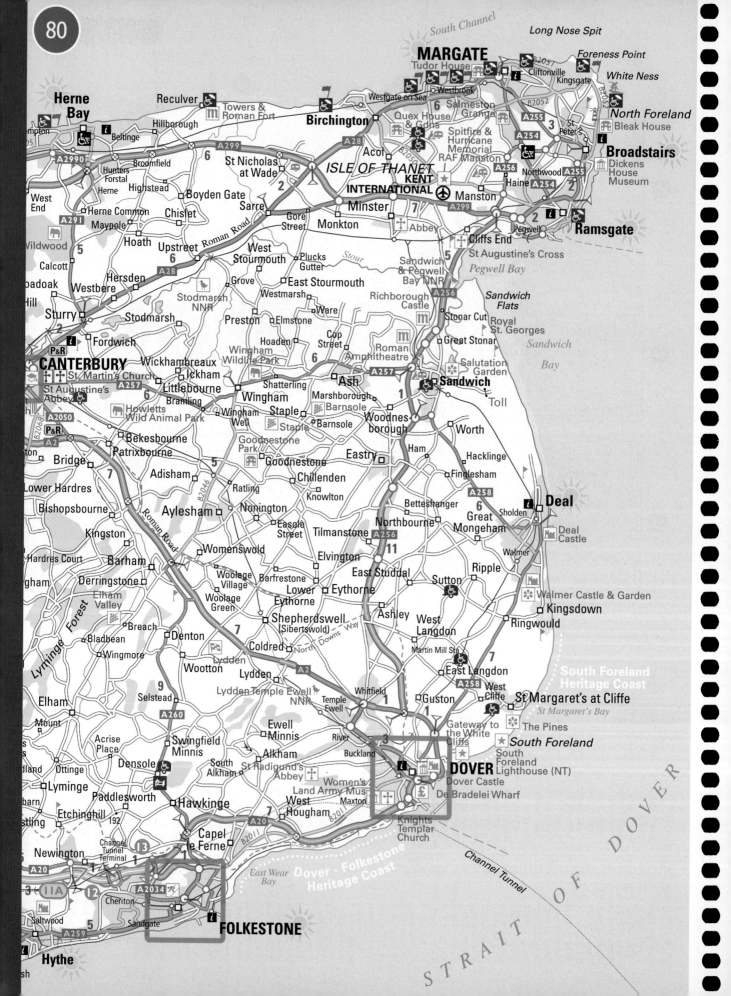

MARGATE

South Channel
Long Nose Spit
Foreness Point
White Ness
North Foreland

Herne Bay
Reculver
Tudor House
Cliftonville
Kingsgate
Westgate on Sea
Westbrook
Salmeston Grange
Bleak House

Hillborough
Beltinge
Towers & Roman Fort
Birchington
Quex House & Gdns
Spitfire & Hurricane Memorial
RAF Manston
St Peter's
Broadstairs
Dickens House Museum

West End
Hunters Forstal
Herne
Broomfield
Highstead
St Nicholas at Wade
Acol
ISLE OF THANET
KENT INTERNATIONAL
Manston
Northwood
Haine
Minster

Herne Common
Maypole
Boyden Gate
Sarre
Gore Street
Monkton
Abbey
Cliffs End
Pegwell
Ramsgate

Wildwood
Calcott
Hoath
Upstreet
Roman Road
West Stourmouth
Plucks Gutter
Stour
St Augustine's Cross
Pegwell Bay

Hersden
Grove
East Stourmouth
Westmarsh
Sandwich & Pegwell Bay NNR
Sandwich Flats

adoak Hill
Westbere
Stodmarsh
Ware
Richborough Castle
Stonar Cut
Royal St. Georges
Sandwich Bay

Sturry
Stodmarsh NNR
Preston
Elmstone
Roman Amphitheatre
Great Stonar

Fordwich
Hoaden
Cop Street
Roman Amphitheatre
Stonar Cut

CANTERBURY
St Martin's Church
Wickhambreaux
Ickham
Wingham Wildlife Park
Shatterling
Ash
Marshborough
Barnsole
Sandwich
Toll

St Augustine's Abbey
Littlebourne
Bramling
Wingham
Staple
Barnsole
Woodnesborough
Worth

Howletts Wild Animal Park
Wingham Well
Staple
Goodnestone Park
Eastry
Ham
Hacklinge

Bekesbourne
Patrixbourne
Goodnestone
Chillenden
Knowlton
Betteshanger
Finglesham

Bridge
Adisham
Ratling
Nonington
Northbourne
Great Mongeham
Deal
Sholden
Deal Castle

Lower Hardres
Bishopsbourne
Kingston
Aylesham
Easole Street
Tilmanstone
Elvington
Walmer

Hardres Court
Barham
Womenswold
Barfrestone
Lower Eythorne
East Studdal
Sutton
Ripple
Walmer Castle & Garden

gham
Derringstone
Woolage Village
Woolage Green
Shepherdswell (Sibertswold)
Eythorne
Ashley
West Langdon
Kingsdown
Ringwould

Elham Valley
Breach
Bladbean
Wingmore
Denton
Coldred
North Downs Way
West Langdon
East Langdon
South Foreland Heritage Coast

Elham
Selsted
Wootton
Lydden
Lydden
Whitfield
Guston
West Cliffe
St Margaret's at Cliffe
St Margaret's Bay

Mount
Acrise Place
Swingfield Minnis
Lydden Temple Ewell NNR
Temple Ewell
The Pines

Ottinge
Densole
South Alkham
St Radigund's Abbey
River
Gateway to the White Cliffs
South Foreland
South Foreland Lighthouse (NT)

Lyminge
Paddlesworth
Hawkinge
Alkham
Buckland
Women's Land Army Mus
DOVER
Dover Castle
De Bradelei Wharf

barn
Etchinghill
192
West Hougham
Maxton
Knights Templar Church

Newington
Channel Tunnel Terminal
Capel le Ferne
East Wear Bay
Dover - Folkestone Heritage Coast
Channel Tunnel

Saltwood
Cheriton
Sandgate
FOLKESTONE

Hythe
STRAIT OF DOVER

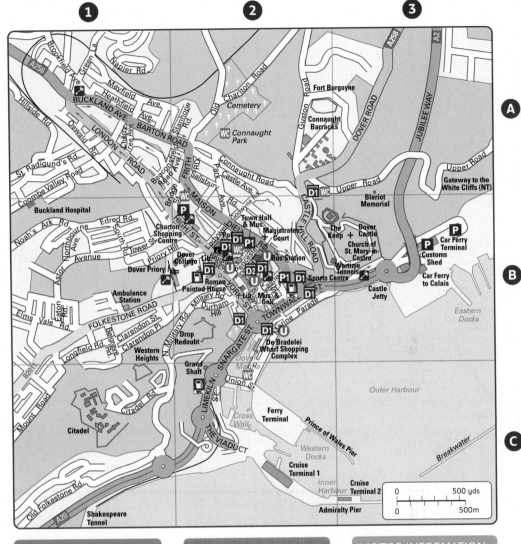

ADMINISTRATION

DOVER DISTRICT COUNCIL,
WHITE CLIFFS BUSINESS PARK,
DOVER,
CT16 3PJ

www.dover.gov.uk
☎ 01304 821199

HOSPITAL

KENT & CANTERBURY
HOSPITAL,
ETHELBERT ROAD,
CANTERBURY,
CT1 3NG

☎ 01227 766877

VISITOR INFORMATION

OLD TOWN GAOL,
BIGGIN STREET,
DOVER,
CT16 1DL

☎ 01304 205108

Dover *Kent*
Population: 34,087.

Town, cinque port, resort and Channel port on Strait of
Dover, 15m/24km SE of Canterbury, with large modern
docks for freight and passengers. Dominated by high
white cliffs and medieval castle (English Heritage)
enclosing the Pharos, AD 50 remains of Roman
lighthouse. Remains of 12c Knights Templar Church
(English Heritage) across valley from castle. Sections of
moat of 19c fort at Western Heights (English Heritage),
above town on W side of harbour. White Cliffs
Experience re-creates Roman and wartime Dover.

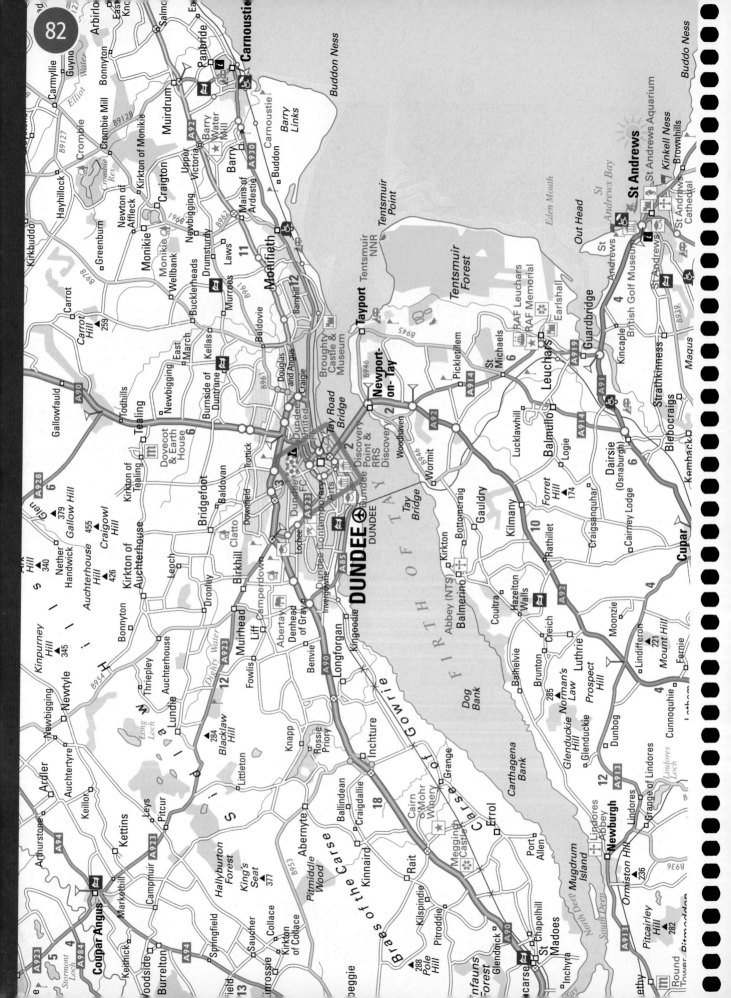

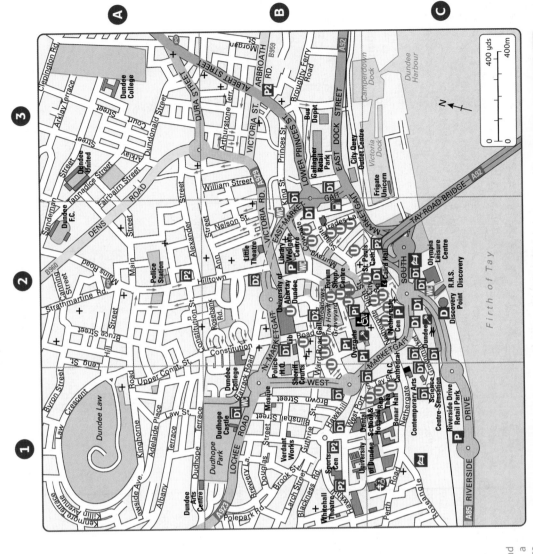

Dundee
Population: 154,674.

Scotland's fourth largest city, commercial and industrial centre and port, 18m/29km E of Perth on N side of Firth of Tay, crossed here by a 1m/2km road bridge and a 2m/3km railway bridge. Robert the Bruce declared King of the Scots in Dundee in 1309. Sustained severe damage during Civil War and again prior to Jacobite uprising. City recovered in early 19c and became Britain's main processor of jute. One of largest employers in Dundee today is D.C. Thomson, publisher of The Beano and The Dandy. Many museums and art galleries. Cultural centre, occasionally playing host to overflow from Edinburgh Festival. Episcopal cathedral on site of former castle. Universities. Ship 'Discovery' in which Captain Scott travelled to Antarctic has returned to Victoria dock, where she was built.

VISITOR INFORMATION

21 CASTLE STREET,
DUNDEE,
DD1 3AA

☎ 01382 527527

HOSPITAL

NINEWELLS HOSPITAL,
NINEWELLS ROAD,
DUNDEE,
DD1 9SY

☎ 01382 660111

ADMINISTRATION

DUNDEE CITY COUNCIL,
CITY CHAMBERS,
21 CITY SQUARE,
DUNDEE,
DD1 3BD
www.dundeecity.gov.uk
☎ 01382 434000

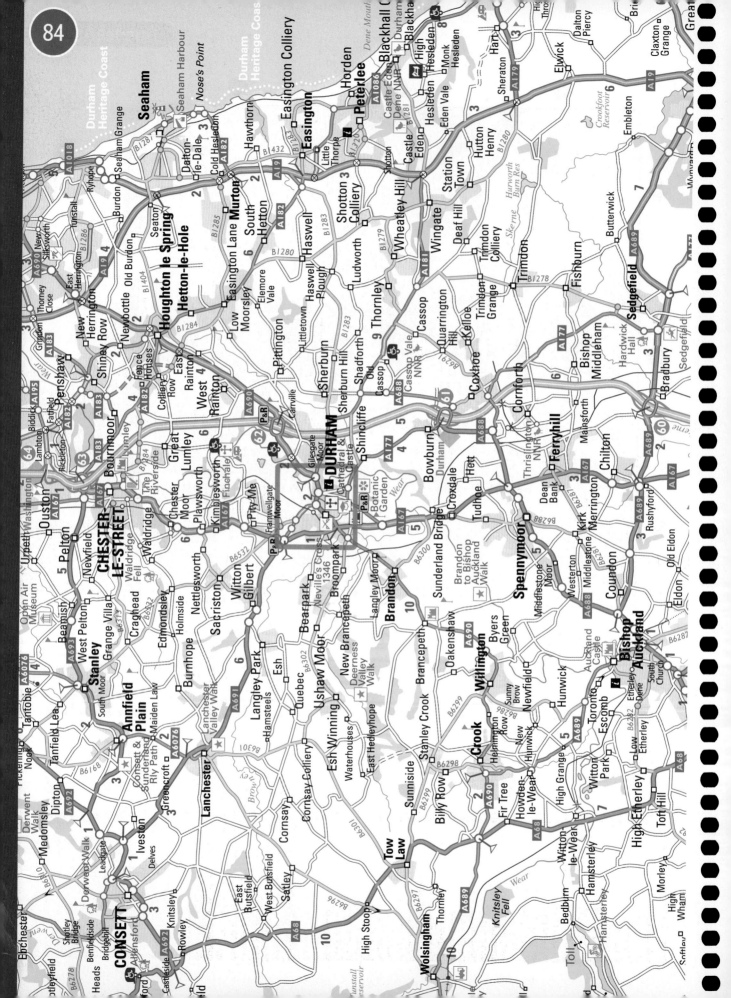

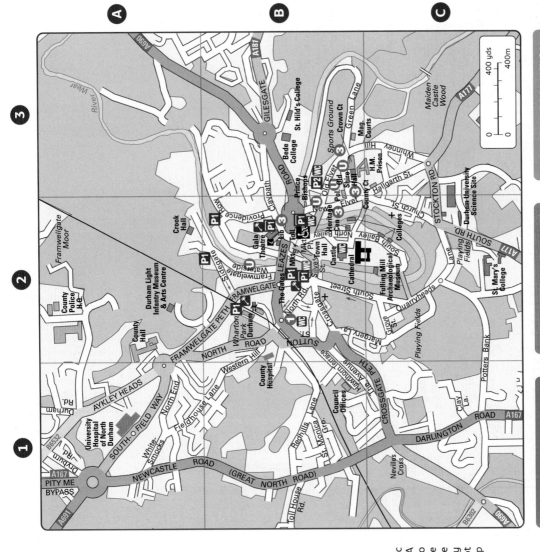

Durham congestion charge

The Durham Road User Charge applies to vehicles accessing the historic city centre and the approach to Durham's cathedral and castle. A charge of £2 per vehicle applies between 10am and 4pm, Monday to Friday. Disabled people can be issued with an exemption permit by the establishment they are visiting or can reserve a permit in advance provided they have pre-arranged a parking space in advance by contacting NCP Parking Shop on 0191 386633. Permits are not available where the purpose of the journey is to set down or pick up passengers.

Durham *Dur.*
Population: 42,939.

Cathedral city on narrow bend in River Wear, 14m/22km S of Newcastle upon Tyne. Norman-Romanesque cathedral founded in 1093 on site of shrine of St. Cuthbert is World Heritage Site along with the Motte-and-bailey castle dating from 1072 (now part of the University). England's third oldest University founded in 1832. Collection in Fulling Mill Museum of Archaelogy illustrates history of city. Museum of Oriental Art. Light Infantry Museum. Art Gallery. University Botanic Garden S of city.

VISITOR INFORMATION

2 MILLENNIUM PLACE,
DURHAM,
DH1 1WA

☎ 0191 384 3720

HOSPITAL

UNIVERSITY HOSPITAL OF
NORTH DURHAM,
NORTH ROAD,
DURHAM,
DH1 5TW

☎ 0191 333 2333

ADMINISTRATION

CITY OF DURHAM COUNCIL,
17 CLAYPATH,
DURHAM,
DH1 1RH

www.durhamcity.gov.uk
☎ 0191 301 8499

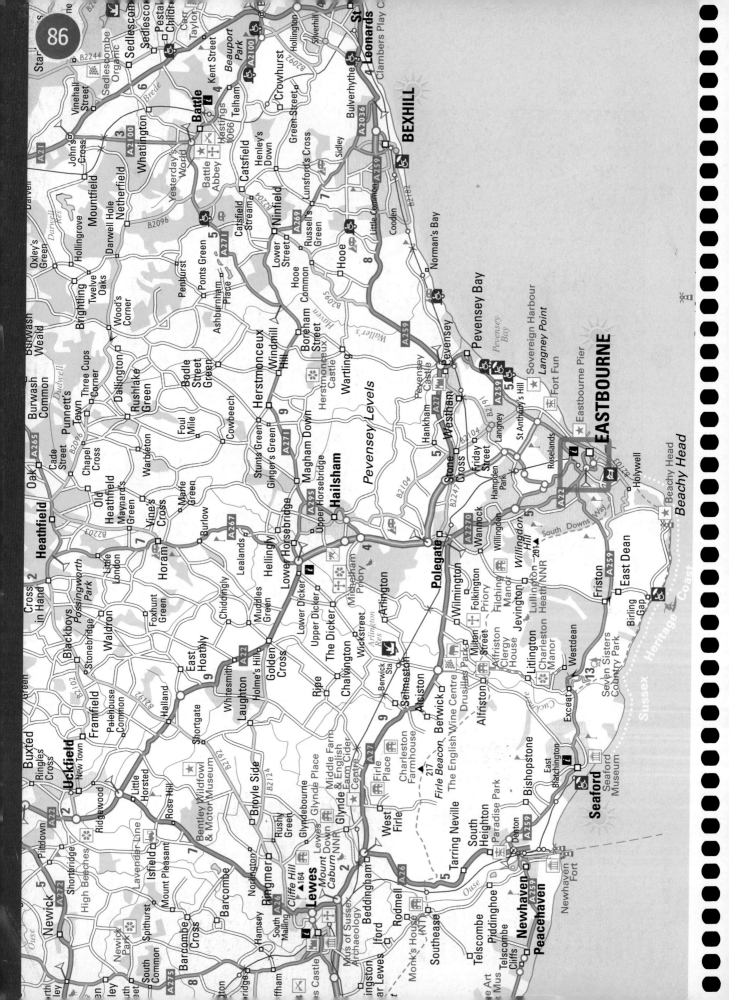

VISITOR INFORMATION

3 CORNFIELD ROAD,
EASTBOURNE,
BN21 4QL

☎ 0871 663 0031

HOSPITAL

EASTBOURNE DISTRICT
GENERAL HOSPITAL,
KING'S DRIVE,
EASTBOURNE,
BN21 2UD

☎ 01323 417400

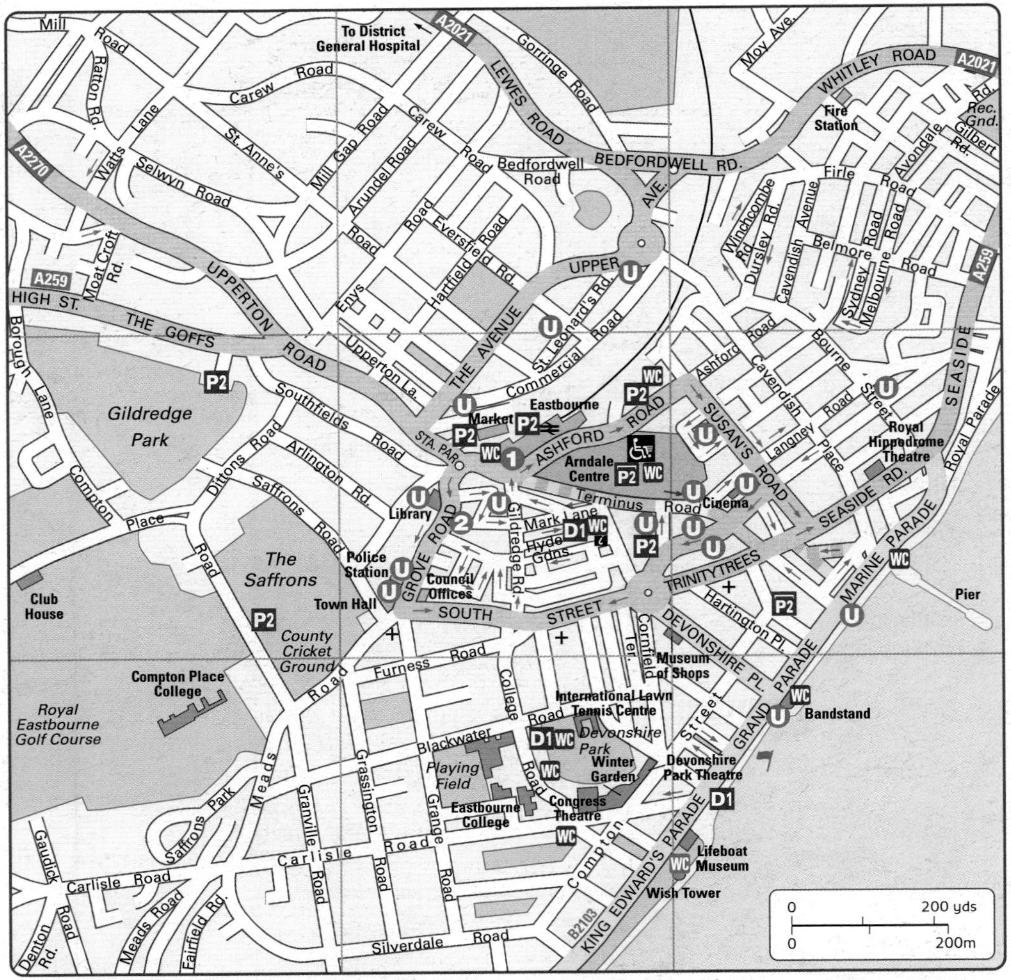

ADMINISTRATION

EASTBOURNE BOROUGH
COUNCIL,
TOWN HALL,
GROVE ROAD,
EASTBOURNE, BN21 4UG
www.eastbourne.gov.uk
☎ 01323 410000

Eastbourne *E.Suss.*
Population: 106,592.

Town, coastal resort and conference centre, 19m/31km E of Brighton. South Downs Way begins at Beachy Head, the 163m/536ft chalk cliff on the outskirts of the town. Eastbourne hosts an International Folk Festival and international tennis at Devonshire Park.

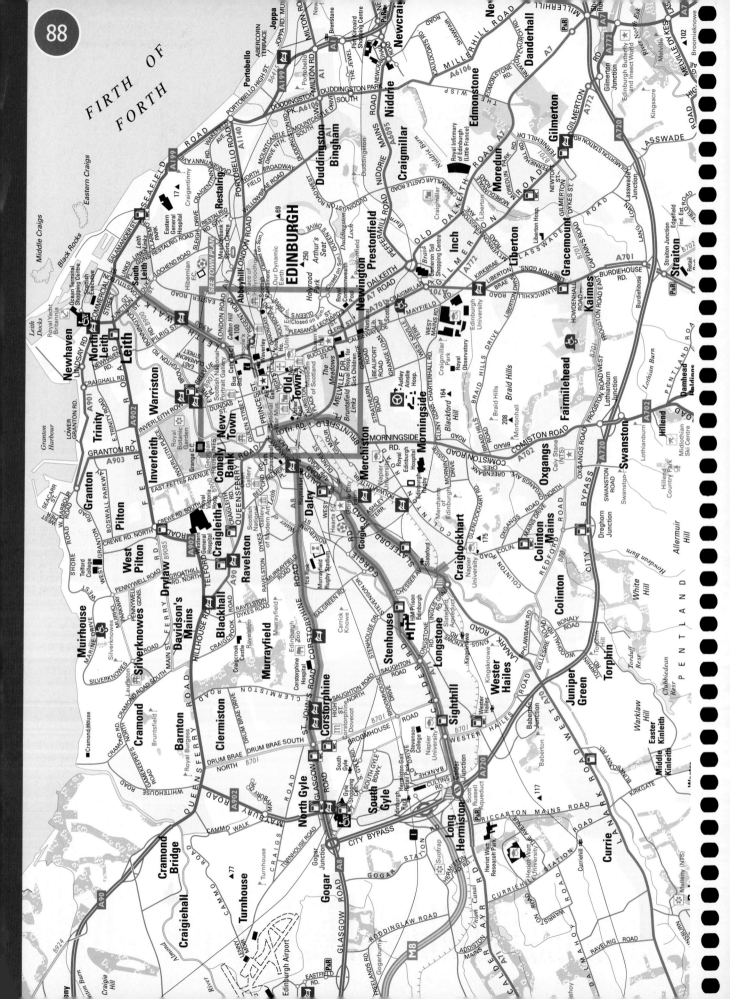

VISITOR INFORMATION

3 PRINCES STREET,
EDINBURGH,
EH2 2QP

☎ 0845 22 55 121

HOSPITAL

ROYAL INFIRMARY OF
EDINBURGH,
51 LITTLE FRANCE CRESCENT,
OLD DALKEITH ROAD,
EDINBURGH,
EH16 4SA

☎ 0131 536 1000

ADMINISTRATION

CITY OF EDINBURGH
COUNCIL,
CITY CHAMBERS,
HIGH STREET,
EDINBURGH, EH1 1YJ
www.edinburgh.gov.uk
☎ 0131 200 2323

INDEX TO STREET NAMES

Edinburgh *Edin.*
Population: 430,082.

Historic city and capital of Scotland, with the Old Town and New Town making a World Heritage Site, built on a range of rocky crags and extinct volcanoes, on S side of Firth of Forth, 41m/66km E of Glasgow. Administrative, financial and legal centre of Scotland. Medieval castle (Historic Scotland) on rocky eminence overlooks central area and was one of main seats of Royal court, while Arthur's Seat (largest of the volcanoes) guards eastern approaches. Three universities. Port at Leith, where Royal Yacht Britannia is now docked and open to public. Important industries include brewing, distilling, food and electronics. Palace of Holyroodhouse (Historic Scotland) is chief royal residence of Scotland. Old Town typified by Gladstone's Land (Historic Scotland), 17c six-storey tenement with arcaded front, outside stair and stepped gables. Numerous literary associations including Sir Arthur Conan Doyle who was born here. Many galleries and museums including National Gallery of Scotland. Annual arts festival attracts over a million visitors each year and is largest such event in the world.

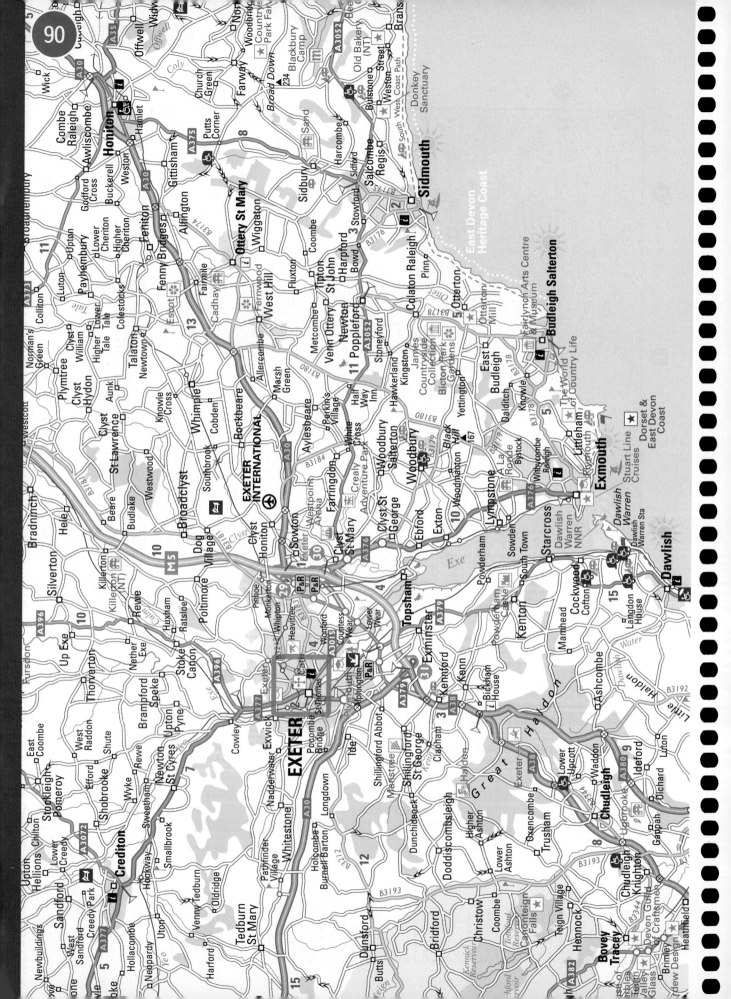

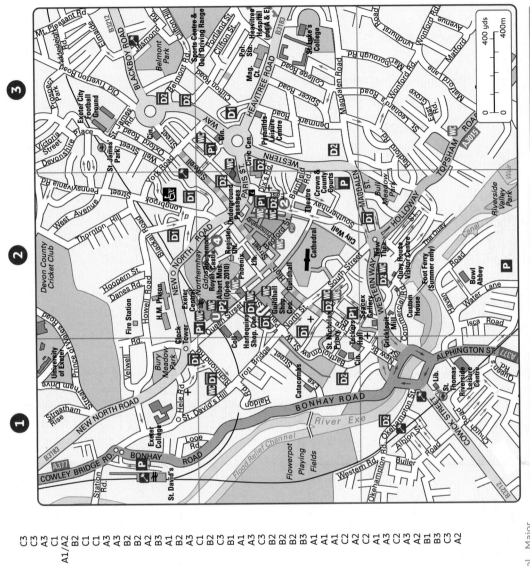

Exeter *Devon*
Population: 106,772.

City and county town on River Exe, 64m/103km SW of Bristol. Major administrative, business and financial centre on site of Roman town Isca Dumnoniorum. Cathedral is Decorated, with Norman towers and façade with hundreds of stone statues. 15c guildhall. Modern buildings in centre built after extensive damage from World War II. Beneath the city lie remains of medieval water-supply system built in 14c to supply fresh water to city centre. Royal Albert Memorial Museum and Art Gallery. Early 16c mansion of Bowhill (English Heritage), with preserved Great Hall, 2m/3km SW. University 1m/2km N of city centre. Airport 5m/8km E at Clyst Honiton.

VISITOR INFORMATION

DIX'S FIELD,
EXETER,
EX1 1GF

☎ 01392 265700

HOSPITAL

ROYAL DEVON & EXETER
HOSPITAL (WONFORD),
BARRACK ROAD,
EXETER,
EX2 5DW

☎ 01392 411611

ADMINISTRATION

EXETER CITY COUNCIL,
CIVIC CENTRE,
PARIS STREET,
EXETER,
EX1 1JN

www.exeter.gov.uk
☎ 01392 277888

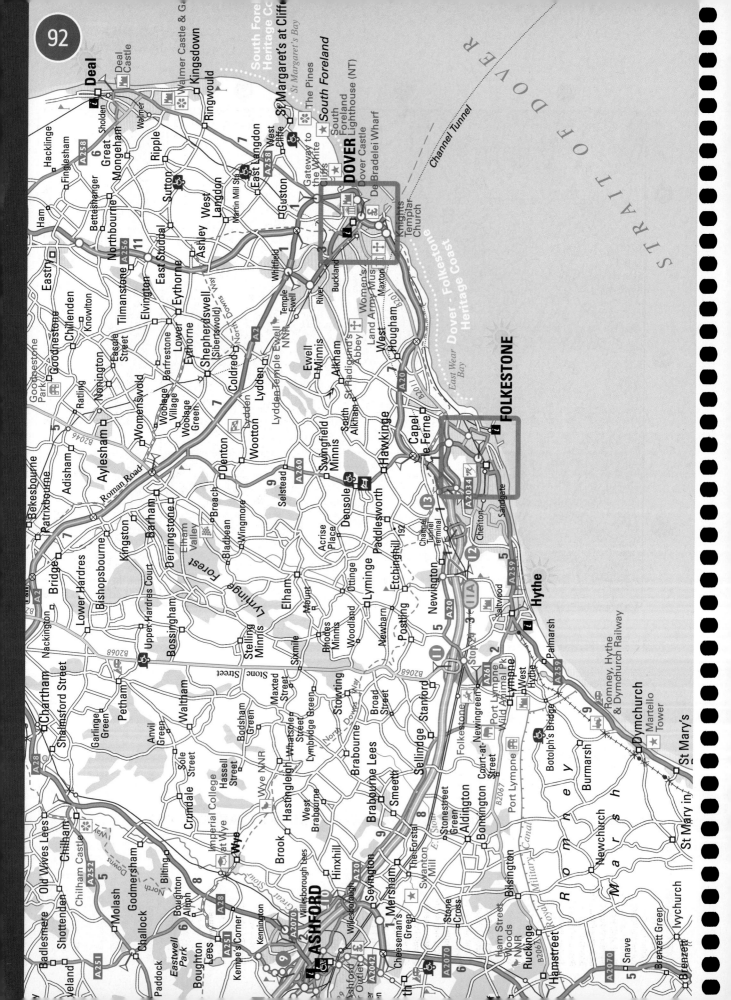

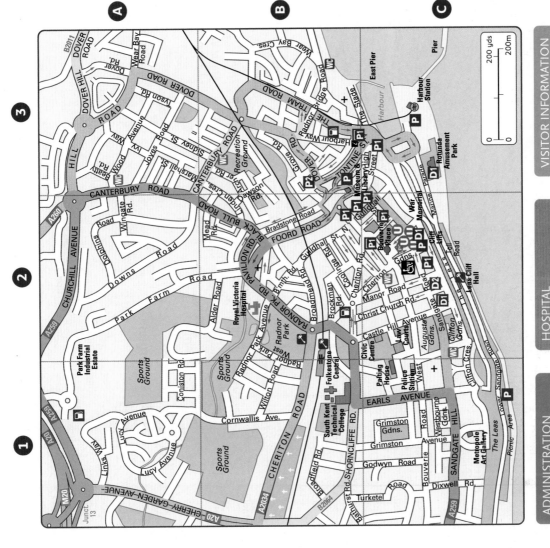

Folkestone *Kent*
Population: 45,273.

Town, Channel port and resort, 14m/22km E of Ashford. The Lear marine promenade accessed by Victorian cliff lift. Ornate Victorian hotels. Martello tower on East Cliff. Kent Battle of Britain Museum at Hawkinge airfield 3m/5km N. Channel Tunnel terminal on N side.

VISITOR INFORMATION

HARBOUR STREET,
FOLKESTONE,
CT20 1QN

☎ 01303 258594

HOSPITAL

WILLIAM HARVEY HOSPITAL,
KENNINGTON ROAD,
WILLESBOROUGH,
ASHFORD,
TN24 0LZ

☎ 01233 633331

ADMINISTRATION

SHEPWAY DISTRICT COUNCIL,
CIVIC CENTRE,
CASTLE HILL AVENUE,
FOLKESTONE,
CT20 2QY

www.shepway.gov.uk
☎ 01303 853000

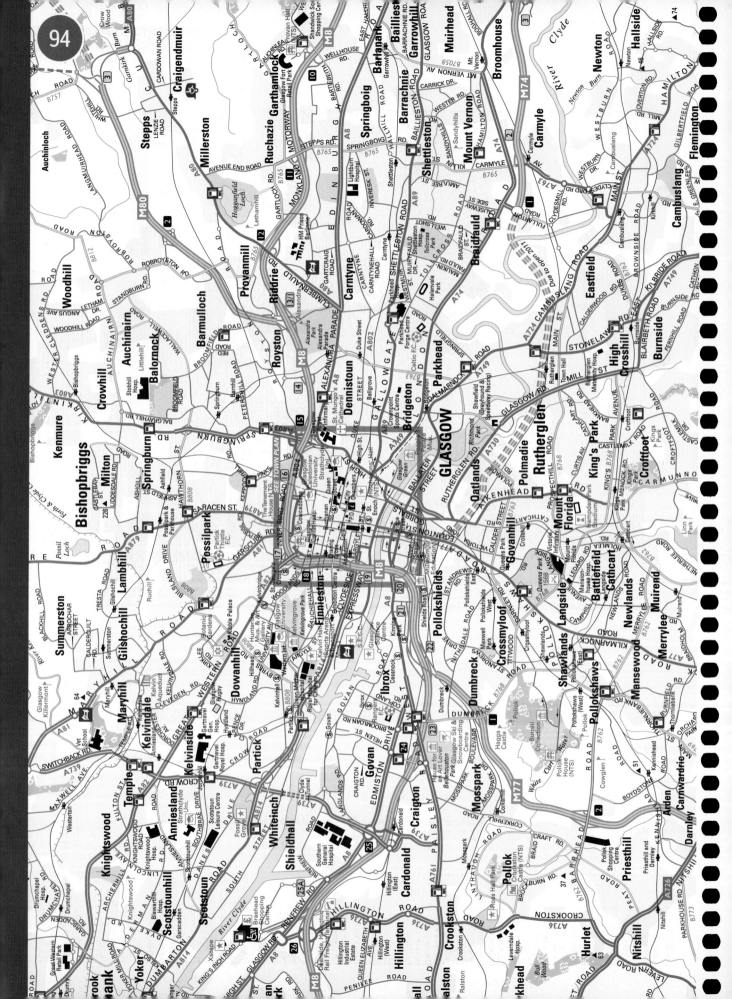

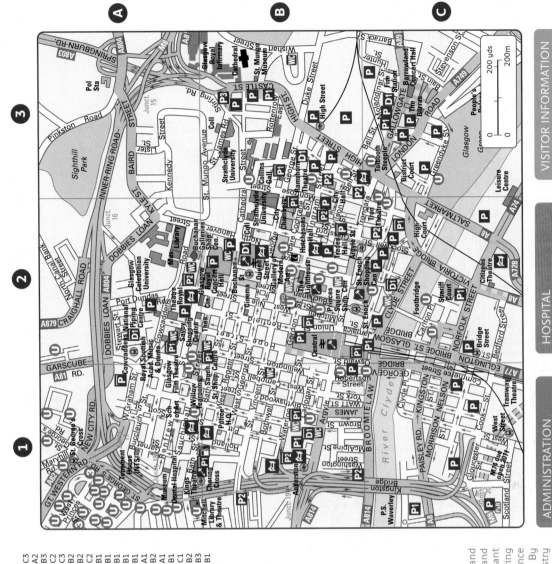

Glasgow *Glas.*
Population: 629,501.

Largest city in Scotland. Port and commercial, industrial, cultural and entertainment centre on River Clyde, 41m/66km W of Edinburgh and 346m/557km NW of London. Major industrial port and important trading point with America until War of Independence. During industrial revolution, nearby coal seams boosted Glasgow's importance and its population increased ten-fold between 1800 and 1900. By beginning of 20c shipbuilding dominated the city, although industry went into decline in 1930s. Glasgow is now seen to be a city of culture and progress. It has a strong performing arts tradition and many museums and galleries including Burrell Collection (set in Pollok Country Park). Cathedral is rare example of an almost complete 13c church. Early 19c Hutcheson's Hall (National Trust for Scotland) in Ingram Street is one of city's most elegant buildings; Tenement House (National Trust for Scotland) is late Victorian tenement flat retaining many original features. Three universities. Airport 7m/11km W.

VISITOR INFORMATION

11 GEORGE SQUARE,
GLASGOW,
G2 1DY

☎ 0141 204 4400

HOSPITAL

WESTERN INFIRMARY,
DUMBARTON ROAD,
GLASGOW,
G11 6NT

☎ 0141 211 2000

ADMINISTRATION

GLASGOW CITY COUNCIL,
CITY CHAMBERS,
GEORGE SQUARE,
GLASGOW,
G2 1DU

www.glasgow.gov.uk
☎ 0141 287 2000

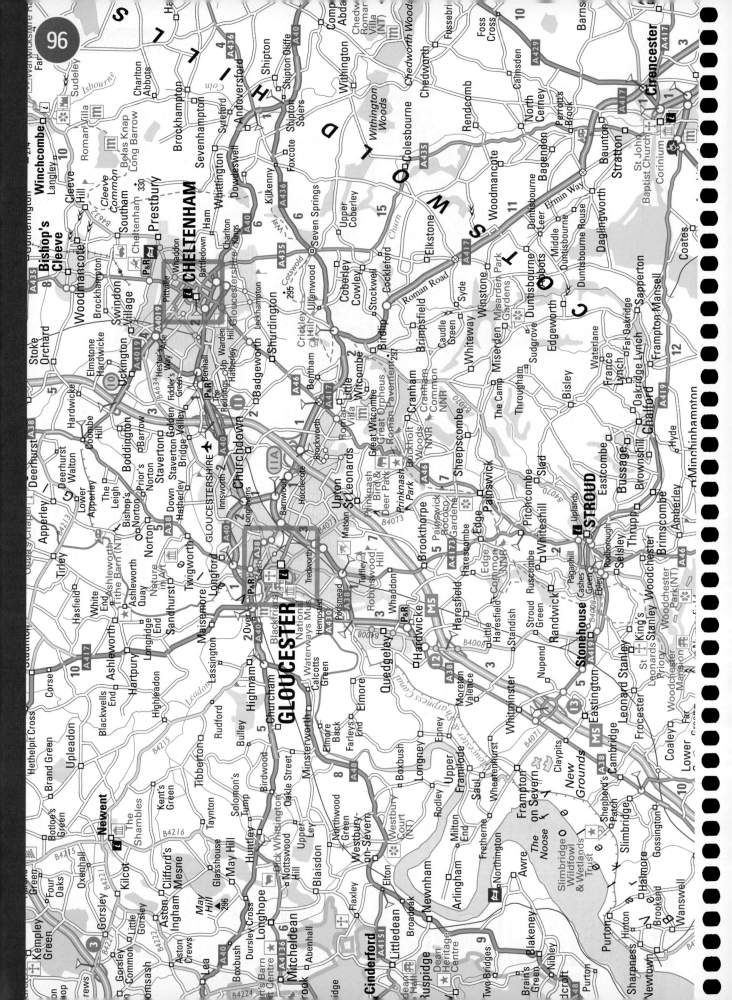

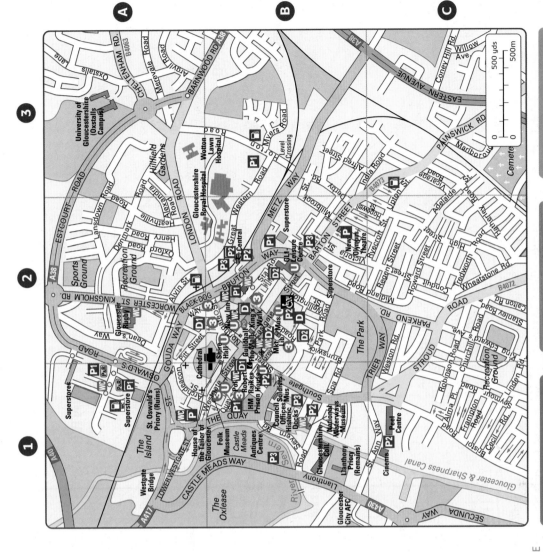

Gloucester *Glos.*
Population: 123,205.

City, on River Severn, on site of Roman town of Glevum, 32m/52km NE of Bristol. Norman era saw Gloucester grow in political importance, from here William the Conqueror ordered survey of his Kingdom which resulted in Domesday Book of 1086. City became a religious centre during middle ages. Cathedral built in mixture of Norman and Perpendicular styles, has cloisters and England's largest stained glass window, dating from 14c. Remains of 15c-16c Franciscan friary, Greyfriars, (English Heritage). Historic docks, now largely redeveloped, on Gloucester and Sharpness Canal. Three Choirs Festival held every third year. Airport at Staverton 4m/7km NE of city centre.

VISITOR INFORMATION

28 SOUTHGATE STREET,
GLOUCESTER,
GL1 2DP

☎ 01452 396672

HOSPITAL

GLOUCESTERSHIRE
ROYAL HOSPITAL,
GREAT WESTERN ROAD,
GLOUCESTER,
GL1 3NN

☎ 01452 528555

ADMINISTRATION

GLOUCESTER CITY COUNCIL,
COUNCIL OFFICES,
NORTH WAREHOUSE,
THE DOCKS,
GLOUCESTER, GL1 2EP
www.gloucester.gov.uk
☎ 01452 522232

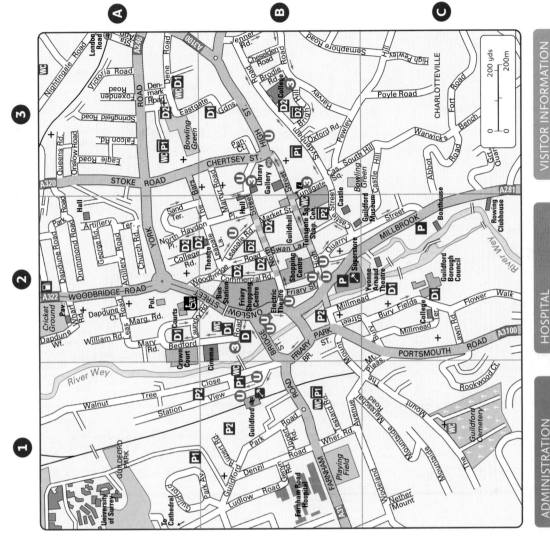

VISITOR INFORMATION

14 TUNSGATE,
GUILDFORD,
GU1 3QT

☎ 01483 444333

HOSPITAL

ROYAL SURREY COUNTY
HOSPITAL,
EGERTON ROAD,
GUILDFORD,
GU2 7XX

☎ 01483 571122

ADMINISTRATION

GUILDFORD BOROUGH
COUNCIL,
MILLMEAD HOUSE,
MILLMEAD,
GUILDFORD, GU2 4BB

www.guildford.gov.uk
☎ 01483 505050

INDEX TO STREET NAMES

Guildford *Surr.*
Population: 69,400.

County town and former weaving centre on River Wey, 27m/43km SW of London. High Street lined with Tudor buildings, the Guildhall the most impressive. Remains of Norman castle keep built c.1173, on an 11c motte, used as county gaol for 400 years. Cathedral consecrated in 1961 and built of red brick, the interior is designed in a modern gothic style. University of Surrey. Royal Grammar School noted for its chained library.

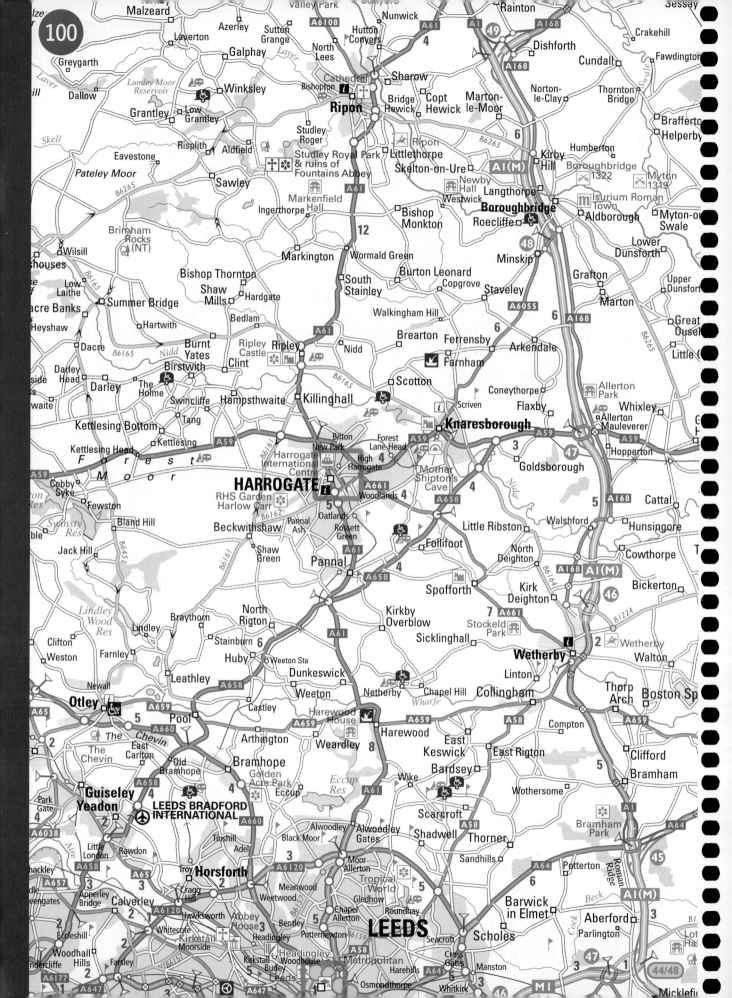

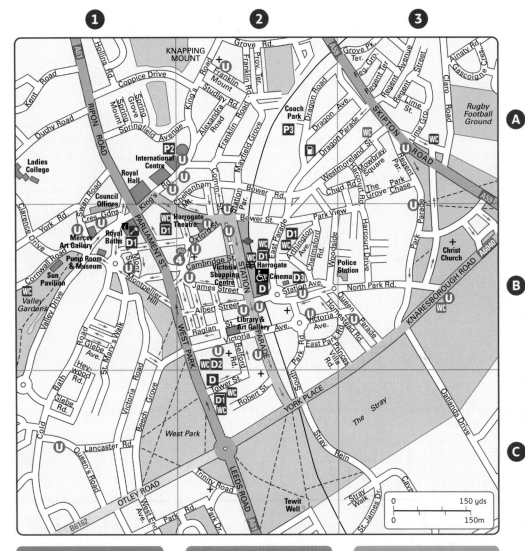

ADMINISTRATION

HARROGATE BOROUGH
COUNCIL,
COUNCIL OFFICES,
CRESCENT GARDENS,
HARROGATE, HG1 2SG

www.harrogate.gov.uk
☎ 01423 500600

HOSPITAL

HARROGATE DISTRICT
HOSPITAL,
LANCASTER PARK ROAD,
HARROGATE,
HG2 7SX

☎ 01423 885959

VISITOR INFORMATION

ROYAL BATHS,
CRESCENT ROAD,
HARROGATE,
HG1 2RR

☎ 0845 389 3223

Harrogate *N.Yorks.*
Population: 70,811.

Spa town and conference centre, 12m/21km N of
Leeds. Fashionable spa town of 19c with many
distinguished Victorian buildings, extensive gardens
and pleasant tree-lined streets. Royal Baths (1897)
open for Turkish baths and Health Spa. Royal Pump
Room (1842) now a museum. The Stray park and
gardens are S of town centre. The Valley Gardens to the
SW are the venue for band concerts and flower shows.
Harlow Carr Botanical Gardens and Museum of
Gardening 2m/3km SW. Mother Shipton's cave,
reputed home to the 16c prophetess, near
Knaresborough, 4m/6km NW.

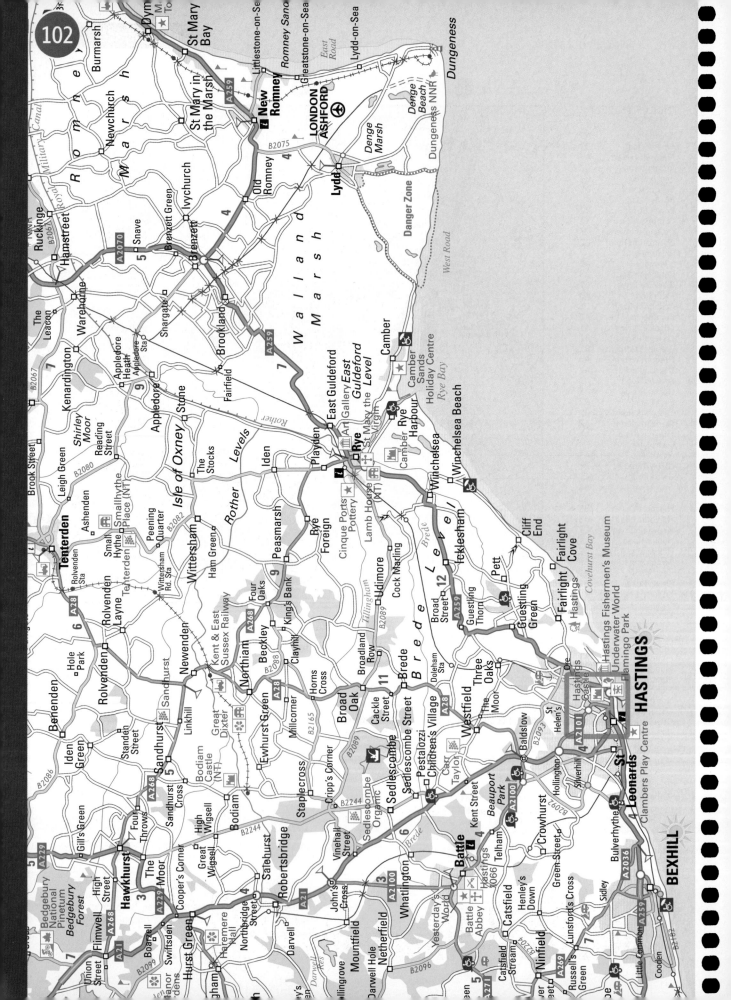

A B C

3 2 1

Frederick Road
OLD LONDON RD A259
Farley Bank
Chiltern Drive
Malvern Way
Ore
Bloomsgrove Rd
Fellows Rd.
Parker Road
Wood Road
Head's
Linley Drive
St. Helen's Down
Beaconsfield Road
St. Thomas's Rd
Elphinstone Road
Hughenden Rd.
Mount Rd
St. George's
Pleasant Rd
St. Mary's Terr.
St. Mary's Rd
Vicarage Road
Milward Road
Priory
QUEEN'S ROAD
Baldslow Road
A2101
Wood-brook Rd.
Downs Road
St. Helen's Park Rd
Laton Road
Fearon Rd.
St. Helen's Park Rd
Freshwater Ave.
St. Helen's Road
Hillside Road
Ashford Way
Ashford Road
Park Crescent
Park Way
Park View
ST. HELEN'S ROAD
A2101
Parkstone Rd.
Alexandra Park
Lower Park Road
Upper Park Road
Amherst Road
A21
BOHEMIA ROAD
Horntye Park Sports Complex
Fire Station
Police Station
Priory Avenue
Wykeham Rd
Linton Rd
Linton Gardens
Braybrooke Road
College
Hastings
University
Sports Centre
Museum & Art Gallery
Cambers
Play Cen.
Falaise Rd.
CAMBRIDGE RD.
Denmark Rd
WHITE ROCK
White Rock
White Rock Theatre
EVERSFIELD PLACE
Magdalen Road
Warrior Square
St. Margaret's Road
St. John's Road
Church Rd
De
Cram
A259
Pier
Harold Road
ASHBURNHAM ROAD
Priory Rd
Bembrook Road
St. George's Rd
Croft Rd
Collier Rd
Old Town Hall
Stables Theatre
Smugglers' Adventure in St Clements Caves
Hastings Castle (Ruins)
St. Clements Church
1066
Hastings Road Experience
PELHAM PL
St. Mary-in-the-Castle
East Hill
East Hill Lift
Flower Makers Museum
Fishermen's Museum
Shipwreck Heritage Centre
Underwater World
Harbour
West Hill
GEORGE ST
Marine Parade
High Street
THE BOURNE
George St
Wellington Rd
Cornwallis Terrace
Robertson Street
DENMARK PL
PELHAM RD.

500 yds
0
500m
0

Hastings *E.Suss.*
Population: 85,828.

Town, Cinque port and seaside resort 32m/52km E of Brighton. Remains of Norman castle built 1068-1080 on hill in town centre, houses the 1066 exhibition which relates the history of castle and Norman invasion. Battle of 1066 fought at Battle, 6m/9km NW. Former smugglers' caves have a display on smuggling, once a vital part of the town's economy.

VISITOR INFORMATION

QUEENS SQUARE,
PRIORY MEADOW,
HASTINGS,
TN34 1TL

☎ 0845 274 1001

HOSPITAL

CONQUEST HOSPITAL,
THE RIDGE,
ST. LEONARDS-ON-SEA,
TN37 7RD

☎ 01424 755255

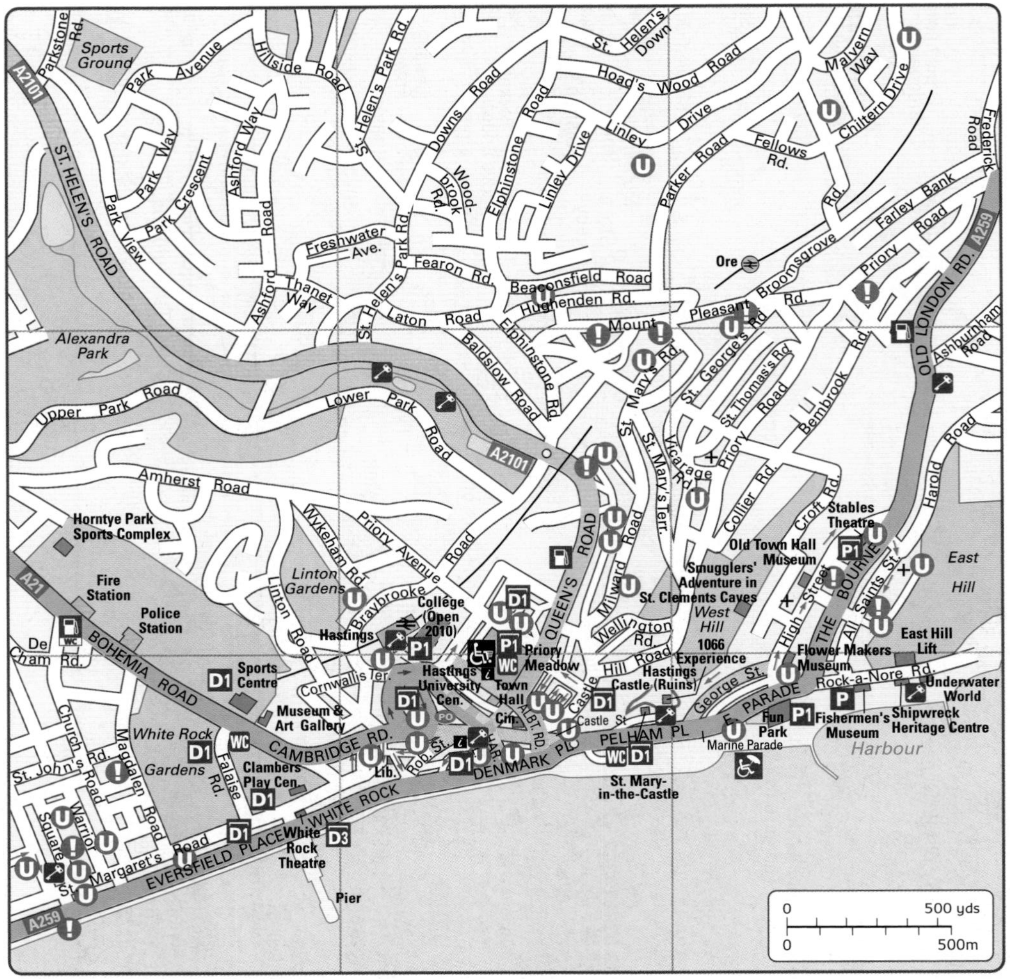

ADMINISTRATION

HASTINGS BOROUGH
COUNCIL,
TOWN HALL,
QUEENS ROAD,
HASTINGS, TN34 1QR

www.hastings.gov.uk
☎ 0845 274 1066

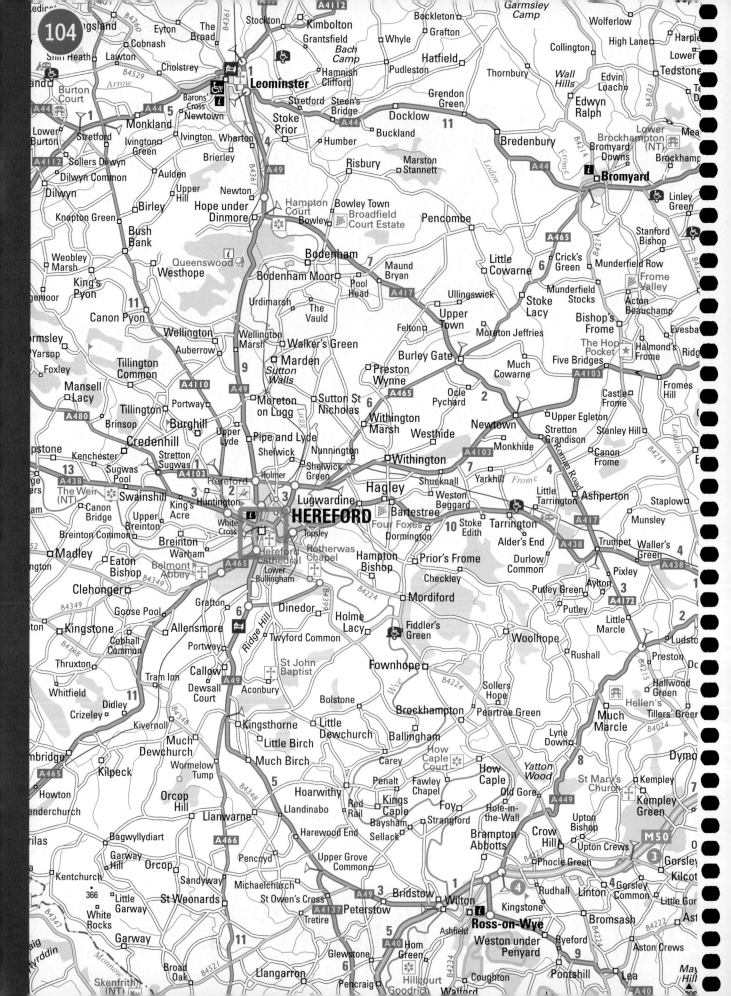

INDEX TO STREET NAMES

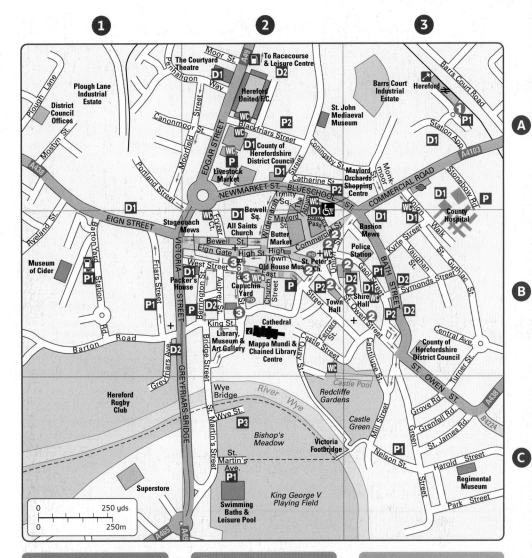

ADMINISTRATION

HEREFORDSHIRE COUNCIL,
BROCKINGTON,
35 HAFOD ROAD,
HEREFORD,
HR1 1SH

www.herefordshire.gov.uk
☎ 01432 260000

HOSPITAL

HEREFORD COUNTY
HOSPITAL,
UNION WALK,
HEREFORD,
HR1 2ER

☎ 01432 355444

VISITOR INFORMATION

1 KING STREET,
HEREFORD,
HR4 9BW

☎ 01432 268430

Hereford *Here.*
Population: 56,373.

City, county town and cathedral city on River Wye, 45m/72km SW of Birmingham. Many old buildings and museums, including Waterworks museum and City Museum and Art Gallery. 1621 Old House is a museum of local history. Medieval Wye Bridge. Cathedral includes richly ornamented Early English style Lady chapel. New building houses Chained Library of 1500 volumes and 1289 Mappa Mundi Map of the world. Three Choirs Festival every third year. Cider Museum and King Offa Distillery W of city centre depicts history of cider making.

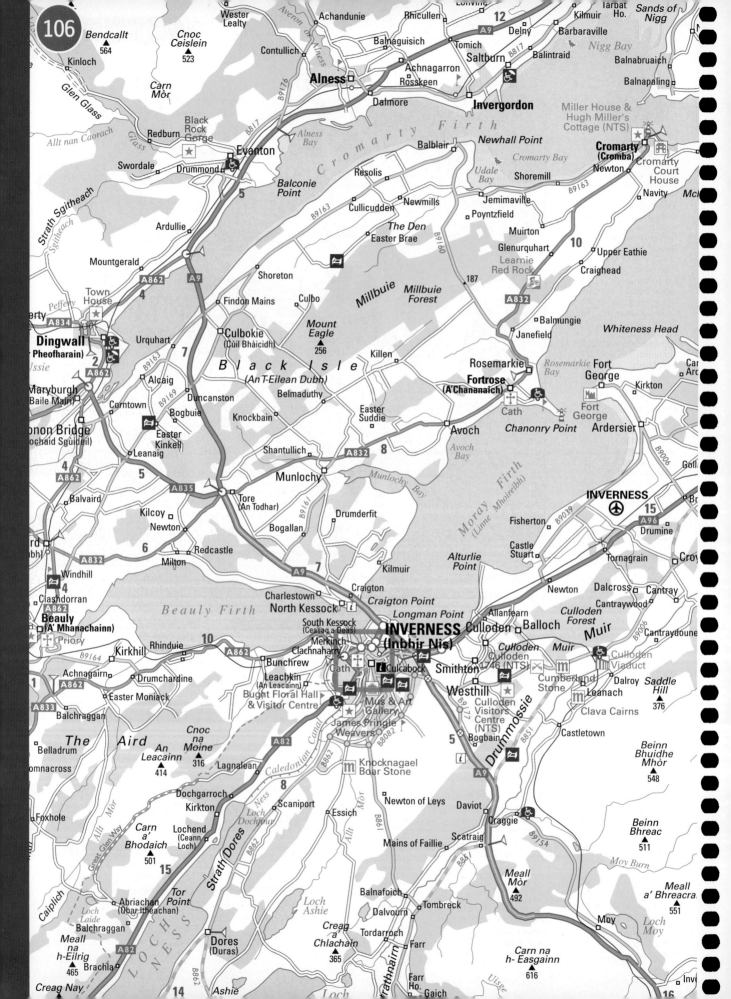

INDEX TO STREET NAMES

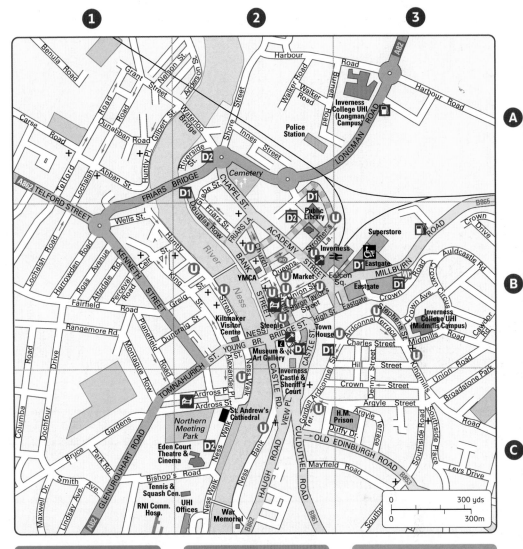

ADMINISTRATION

HIGHLAND COUNCIL,
COUNCIL OFFICES,
GLENURQUHART ROAD,
INVERNESS,
IV3 5NX

www.highland.gov.uk
☎ 01463 702000

HOSPITAL

RAIGMORE HOSPITAL,
OLD PERTH ROAD,
INVERNESS,
IV2 3UJ

☎ 01463 704000

VISITOR INFORMATION

CASTLE WYND,
INVERNESS,
IV2 3BJ

☎ 0845 22 55 121

Inverness *High.*
Population: 40,949.

City, at mouth of River Ness at entrance to Beauly Firth, 105m/169km NW of Aberdeen and 113m/181km NW of Edinburgh. Administrative, commercial and tourist centre. Caledonian Canal passes to W of city. Victorian castle in city centre used as law courts. Inverness Museum and Art Gallery depicts history of Highlands. Balnain House is a museum of Highland music and musical instruments. University of the Highlands and Islands. 1746 Culloden battle site 5m/8km E. Airport at locality of Dalcross, 7m/11km NE of city.

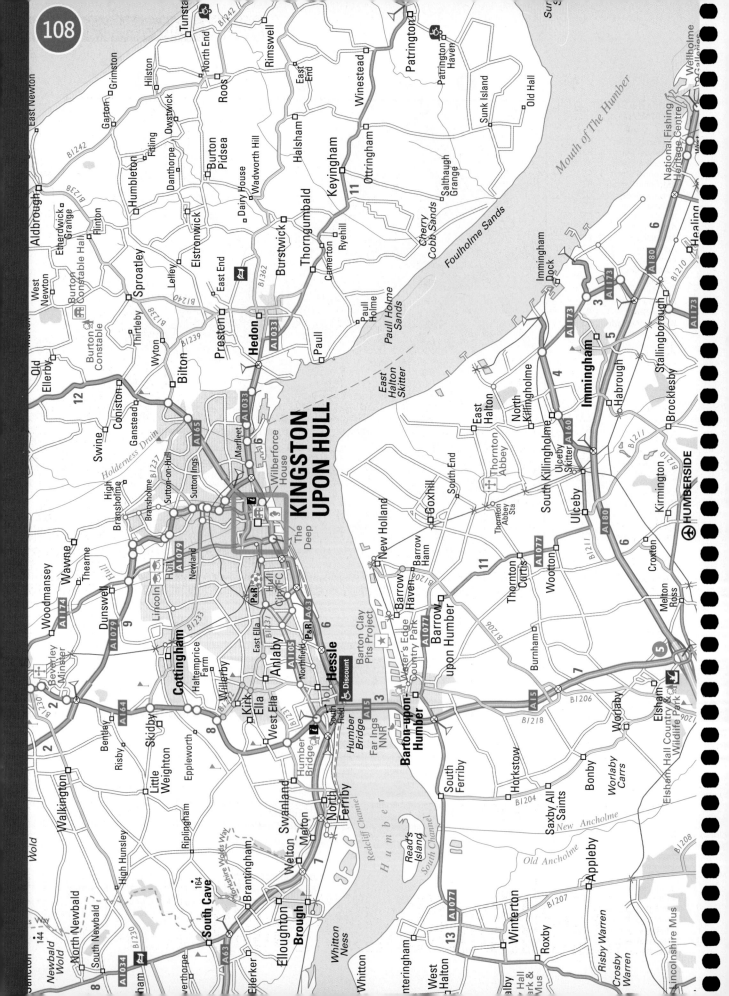

KINGSTON UPON HULL

HUMBERSIDE

Mouth of The Humber

Foulholme Sands

Immingham

Barton-upon-Humber

Hessle

Hedon

Cottingham

Brough

South Cave

Aldbrough

VISITOR INFORMATION

1 PARAGON STREET,
KINGSTON UPON HULL,
HU1 3NA

☎ 01482 223559

HOSPITAL

HULL ROYAL INFIRMARY,
ANLABY ROAD,
KINGSTON UPON HULL,
HU3 2JZ

☎ 01482 328541

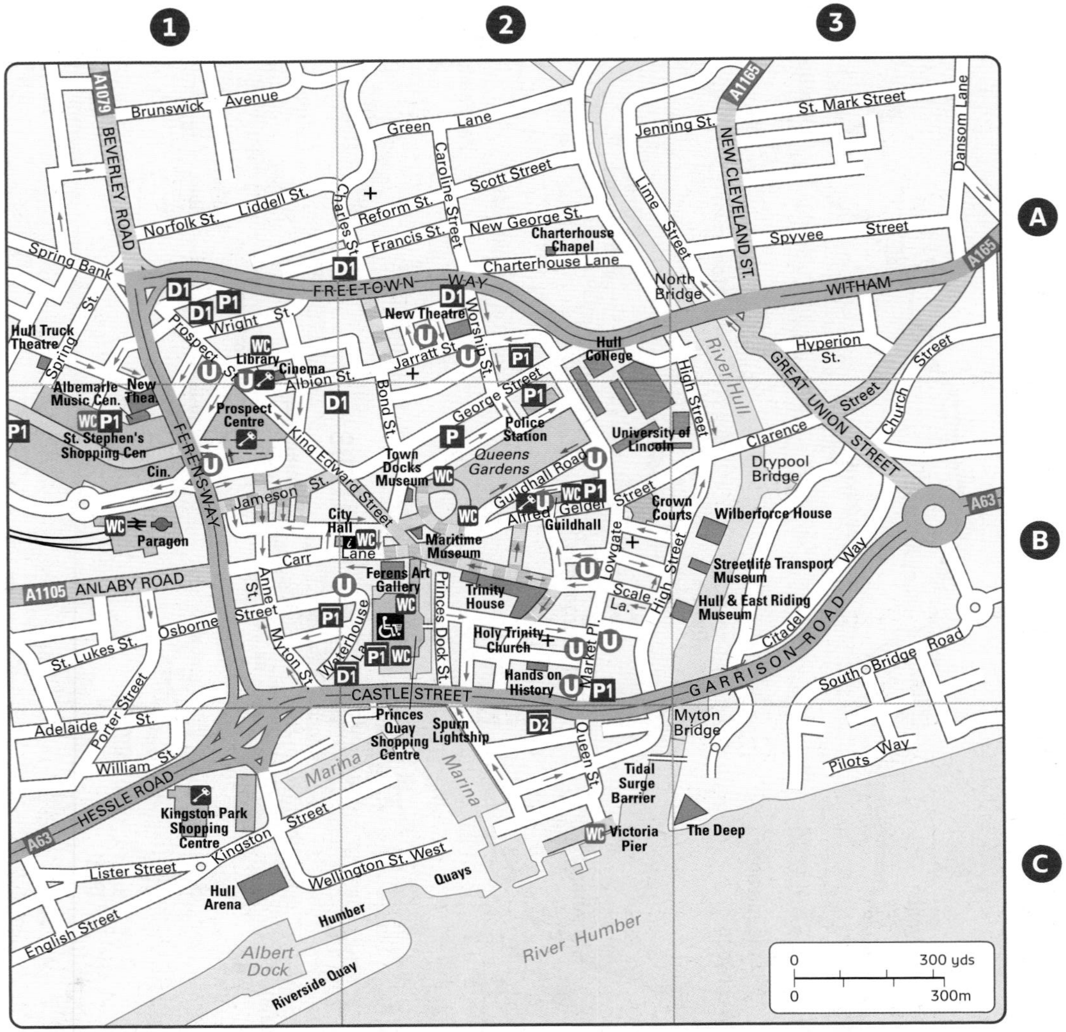

ADMINISTRATION

HULL CITY COUNCIL,
GUILDHALL,
ALFRED GELDER STREET,
KINGSTON UPON HULL,
HU1 2AA

www.hullcc.gov.uk
☎ 01482 300300

Kingston upon Hull (Commonly known as Hull.) *Hull*
Population: 301,416.

City, port at confluence of Rivers Humber and Hull, 50m/80km E of Leeds. City centre rebuilt after bombing in World War II. Formerly had a thriving fishing industry. Major industry nowadays is frozen food processing. Restored docks, cobble streeted Old Town and modern marina. Universities. Birthplace of William Wilberforce, slavery abolitionist, 1759. Wilberforce Museum covers history of slavery. Streetlife Transport Museum. Town Docks Museum explores city's maritime history. Famous for associations with poets Andrew Marvell, Stevie Smith and Philip Larkin.

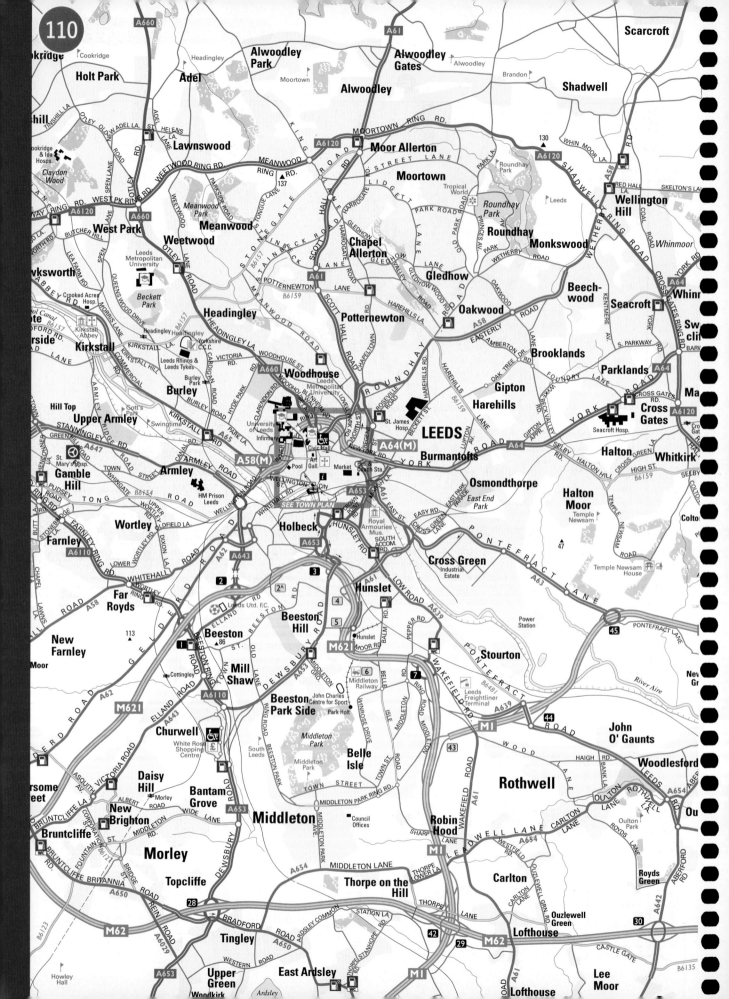

INDEX TO SELECTIVE STREET NAMES

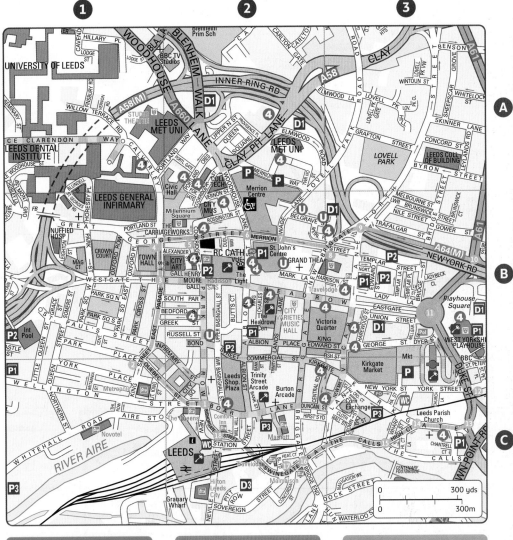

ADMINISTRATION

LEEDS CITY COUNCIL,
CIVIC HALL,
CALVERLEY STREET,
LEEDS,
LS1 1UR

www.leeds.gov.uk
☎ 0113 234 8080

HOSPITAL

LEEDS GENERAL INFIRMARY,
GREAT GEORGE STREET,
LEEDS,
LS1 3EX

☎ 0113 243 2799

VISITOR INFORMATION

THE ARCADE,
CITY STATION,
LEEDS,
LS1 1PL

☎ 0113 242 5242

Leeds *W.Yorks.*
Population: 443,247.

Commercial and industrial city on River Aire and on Leeds and Liverpool Canal, 36m/58km NE of Manchester and 170m/274km NW of London. Previously important for textile industry. Prospered during Victorian period, the architecture of a series of ornate arcades containing some magnificent clocks reflecting the affluence of this time. City Art Gallery has a fine collection of 20c British Art. Edwardian Kirkgate Market is the largest in north of England. Royal Armouries Museum houses arms and armour collection from the Tower of London. Universities. Leeds Bradford International Airport at Yeadon, 7m/11km NW.

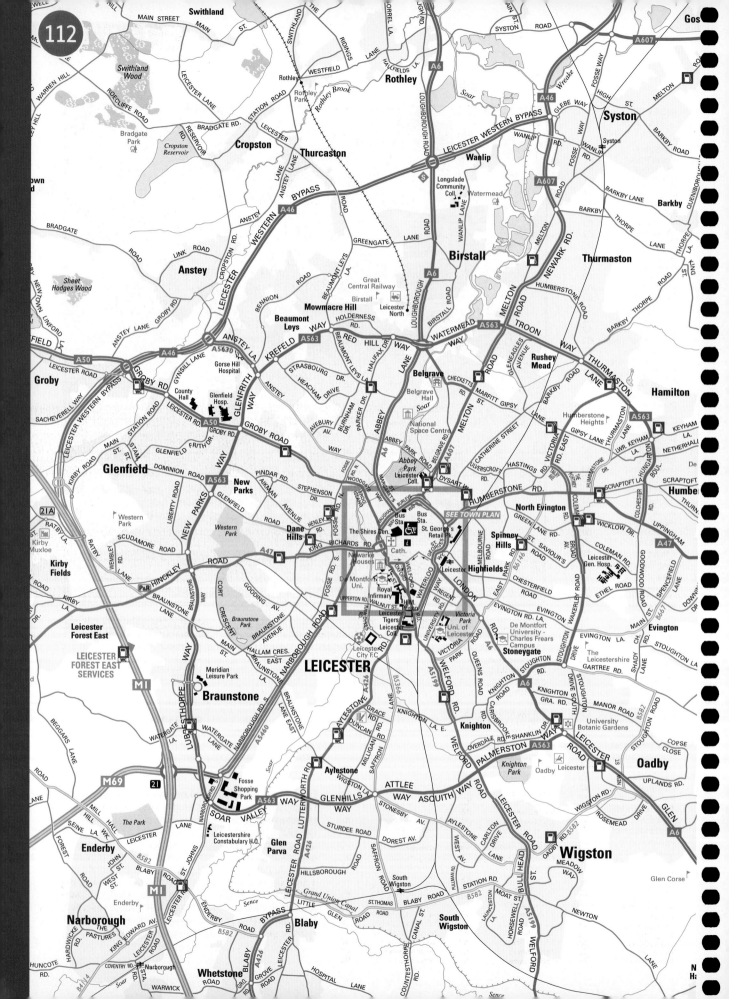

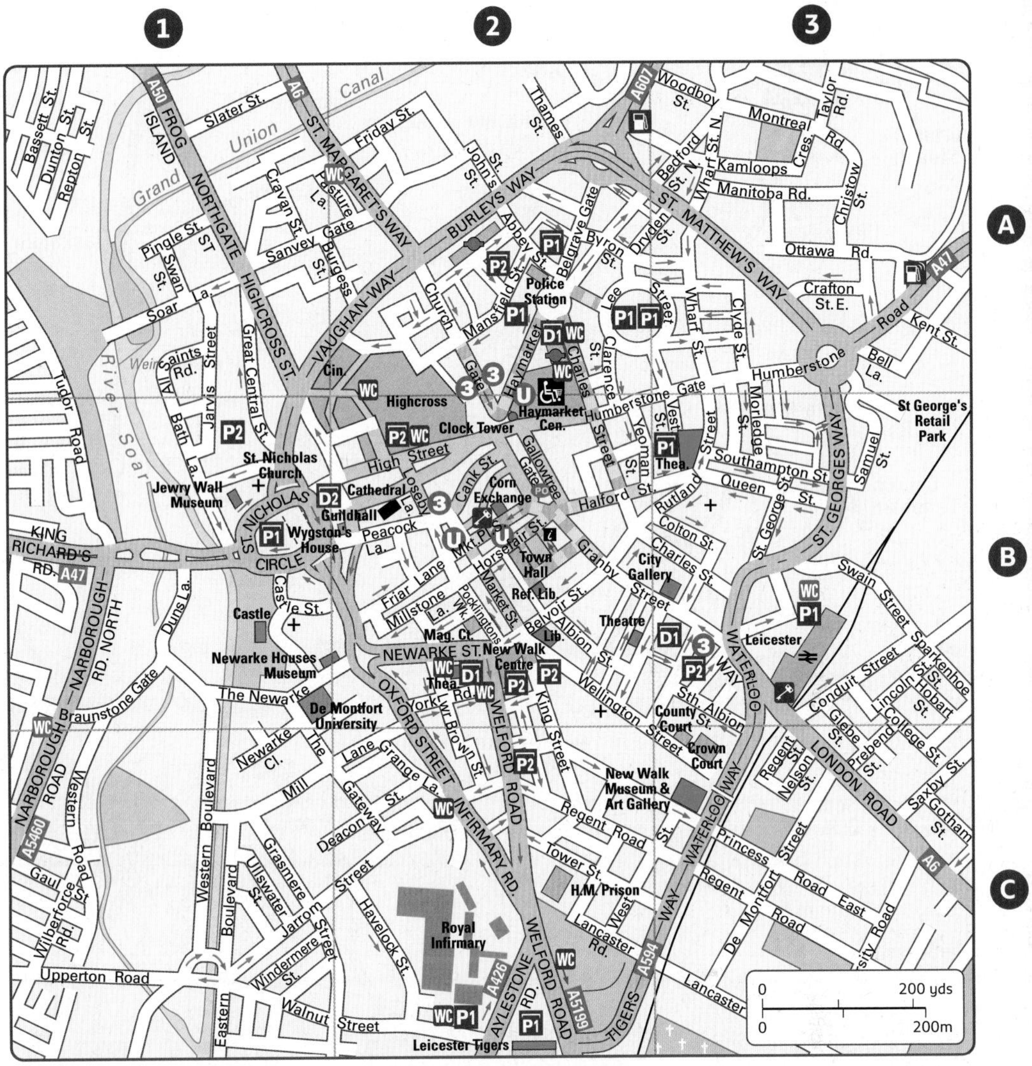

ADMINISTRATION

LEICESTER CITY COUNCIL,
COUNCIL OFFICES,
NEW WALK CENTRE,
WELFORD PLACE,
LEICESTER, LE1 6ZG

www.leicester.gov.uk
☎ 0116 252 7000

HOSPITAL

LEICESTER ROYAL INFIRMARY,
INFIRMARY SQUARE,
LEICESTER,
LE1 5WW

☎ 0116 254 1414

VISITOR INFORMATION

7-9 EVERY STREET,
TOWN HALL SQUARE,
LEICESTER,
LE1 6AG

☎ 0906 294 1113

Leicester *Leic.*
Population: 330,574.

City, county town and commercial and industrial centre on River Soar, on site of Roman town of Ratae Coritanorum, 89m/143km NW of London. Industries include hosiery and footwear, alongside more modern industries. Universities. Many historic remains including Jewry Wall (English Heritage), one of largest surviving sections of Roman wall in the country, Roman baths and a medieval guildhall. Saxon Church of St. Nicholas. 11c St. Martin's Cathedral. Victorian clock tower. Newarke Houses Museum explores the city's social history. Home to England's second biggest street festival after Notting Hill Carnival. Joseph Merrick, the 'Elephant Man' born and lived here.

INDEX TO STREET NAMES

Abbey Street	A2
Albion Street	B2
All Saints Road	B1
Aylestone Road	C2
Bassett Street	A1
Bath Lane	B1
Bedford Street North	A3
Belgrave Gate	A2
Bell Lane	A3
Belvoir Street	B2
Braunstone Gate	B1
Burgess Street	A2
Burleys Way	A2
Byron Street	A2
Cank Street	B2
Castle Street	B1
Charles Street	B3
Christow Street	A3
Church Gate	A2
Clarence Street	A2
Clyde Street	A3
College Street	B3
Colton Street	B3
Conduit Street	B3
Crafton Street East	A3
Cravan Street	A1
De Montfort Street	C3
Deacon Street	C2
Dryden Street	A2
Duns Lane	B1
Dunton Street	A1
Eastern Boulevard	C1
Friar Lane	B2
Friday Street	A2
Frog Island	A1
Gallowtree Gate	B2
Gaul Street	C1
Glebe Street	B3
Gotham Street	C3
Granby Street	B2
Grange Lane	C2
Grasmere Street	C1
Great Central Street	A1
Halford Street	B2
Havelock Street	C2
Haymarket	A2
High Street	B2
Highcross Street	A1
Hobart Street	B3
Horsfair Street	B2
Humberstone Gate	B2
Humberstone Road	A3
Infirmary Road	C2
Jarrom Street	C1
Jarvis Street	B1
Kamloops Crescent	A3
Kent Street	A3
King Richard's Road	B1
King Street	B2
Lancaster Road	C2
Lee Street	A2
Lincoln Street	B3
London Road	C3
Loseby Lane	B2
Lower Brown Street	B2
Manitoba Road	A3
Mansfield Street	A2
Market Place South	B2
Market Street	B2
Mill Lane	C1
Millstone Lane	B2
Montreal Road	A3
Morledge Street	B3
Narborough Road	C1
Narborough Road North	B1
Nelson Street	C3
Newarke Close	C1
Newarke Street	B2
Northgate Street	A1
Ottawa Road	A3
Oxford Street	B2
Pasture Lane	A1
Peacock Lane	B2
Pocklingtons Walk	B2
Prebend Street	C3
Princess Road East	C3
Pringle Street	A1
Queen Street	B3
Regent Road	C2
Regent Street	C3
Repton Street	A1
Rutland Street	B3
Samuel Street	B3
Sanvey Gare	A1
Saxby Street	C3
Slater Street	A1
Soar Lane	A1
South Albion Street	B3
Southampton Street	B3
Sparkenhoe Street	B3
St. George Street	B3
St. George's Way	B3
St. John's Street	A2
St. Margaret's Way	A1
St. Matthew's Way	A3
St. Nicholas Circle	B1
Swain Street	B3
Swan Street	A1
Taylor Road	A3
Thames Street	A2
The Gateway	C1
The Newarke	B1
Tigers Way	C2
Tower Street	C2
Tudor Road	A1
Ullswater Street	C1
University Road	C3
Upperton Road	C1
Vaughan Way	A1
Vestry Street	B3
Walnut Street	C1
Waterloo Way	C3
Welford Road	B2
Wellington Street	B2
West Street	C2
Western Boulevard	C1
Western Road	C1
Wharf Street	A3
Wharf Street North	A3
Wilberforce Road	C1
Windermere Street	C1
Woodboy Street	A3
Yeoman Street	B2
York Road	B2

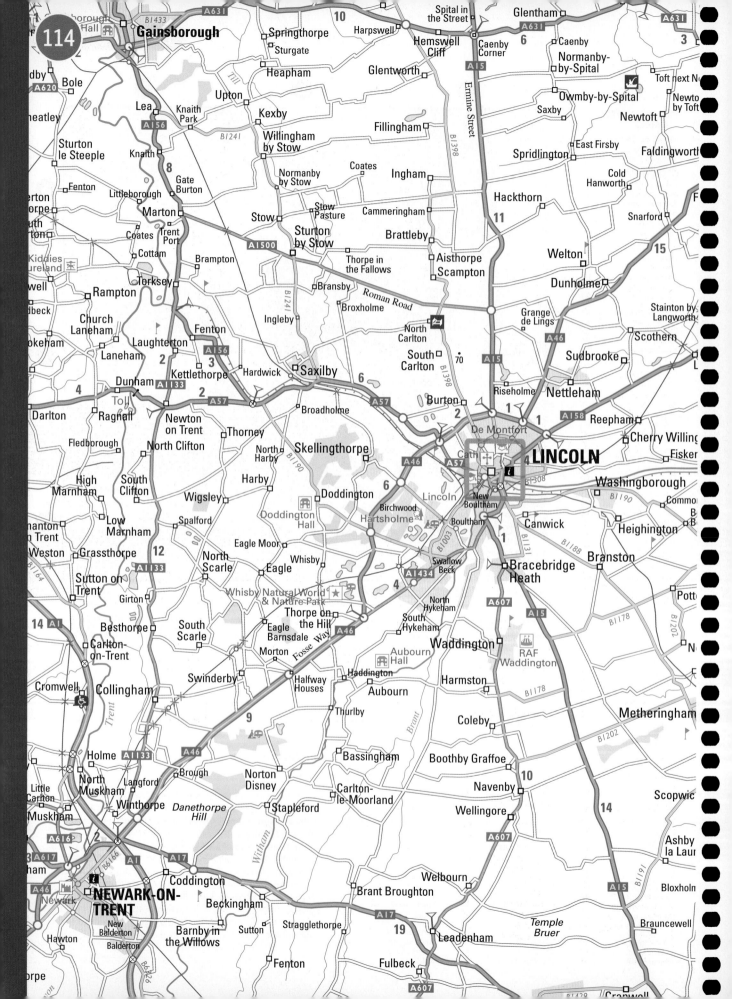

INDEX TO STREET NAMES

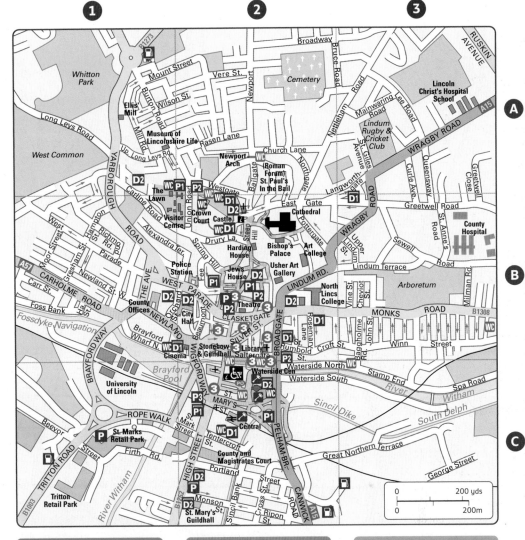

ADMINISTRATION

CITY OF LINCOLN COUNCIL,
CITY HALL,
BEAUMONT FEE,
LINCOLN,
LN1 1DD

www.lincoln.gov.uk
☎ 01522 881188

HOSPITAL

LINCOLN COUNTY HOSPITAL,
GREETWELL ROAD,
LINCOLN,
LN2 5QY

☎ 01522 512512

VISITOR INFORMATION

9 CASTLE HILL,
LINCOLN,
LN1 3AA

☎ 01522 873213

Lincoln *Lincs.*
Population: 85,963.

County town and cathedral city on River Witham, on site of Roman town of Lindum, 120m/193km N of London. City grew as a result of strategic importance in the wool trade. Many ancient monuments and archaeological features. Castle built by William I. 13c cathedral, is the third largest in Britain with its three towers on hilltop dominating the skyline. Carvings in the Angel Choir include the stone figure of the Lincoln Imp which is the city's emblem. Lincoln Bishop's Old Palace (English Heritage) is medieval building on S side of cathedral. 12c Jew's House. Museum of Lincolnshire Life. Universities.

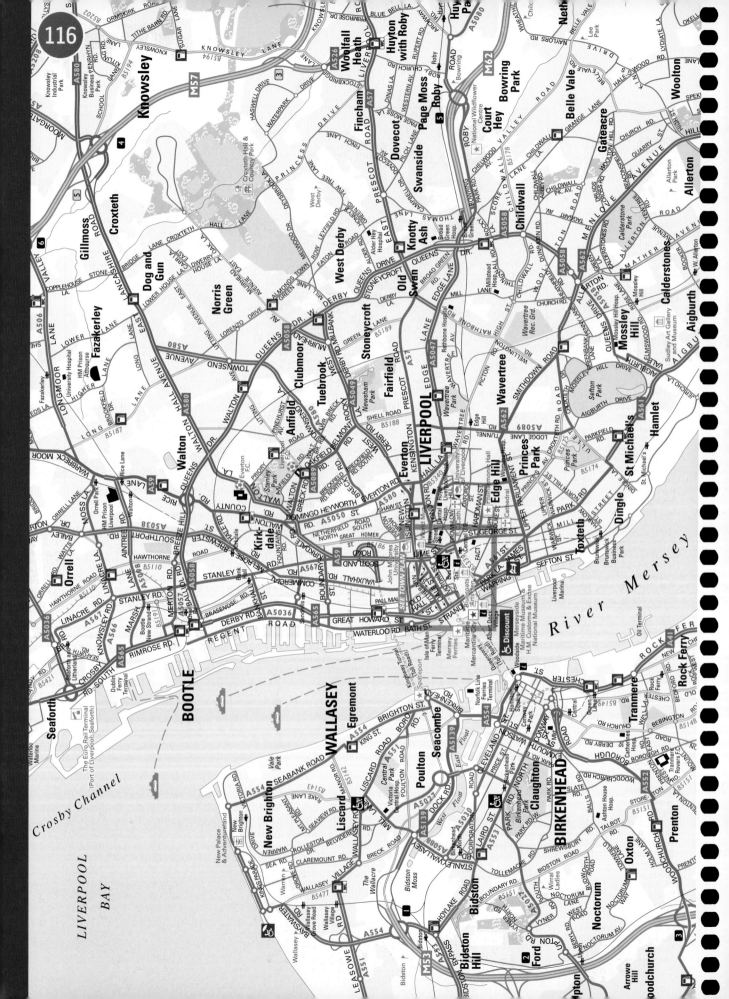

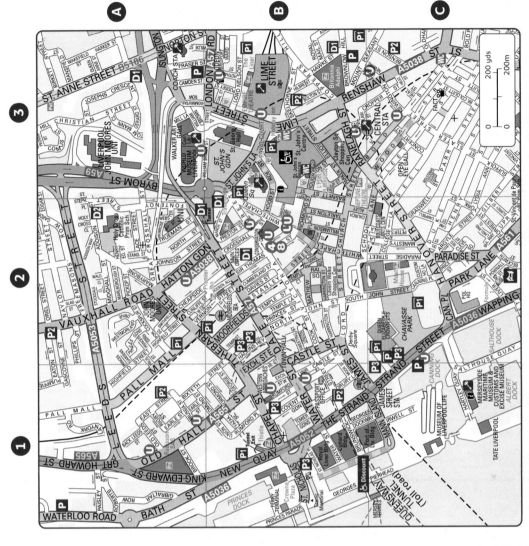

VISITOR INFORMATION

THE 08 PLACE,
WHITECHAPEL,
LIVERPOOL,
L1 6DZ

☎ 0151 233 2008

HOSPITAL

UNIVERSITY HOSPITAL OF
AINTREE,
LONGMOOR LANE,
LIVERPOOL,
L9 7AL

☎ 0151 525 5980

ADMINISTRATION

LIVERPOOL CITY COUNCIL,
MUNICIPAL BUILDINGS,
DALE STREET,
LIVERPOOL,
L69 2DH
www.liverpool.gov.uk
☎ 0151 233 3000

INDEX TO SELECTIVE STREET NAMES

Liverpool *Mersey.*
Population: 469,017.

Major port and industrial city, now a World Heritage Site, on River Mersey estuary, 178m/286km NW of London. Originally a fishing village it experienced rapid expansion during early 18c due to transatlantic trade in sugar, spice and tobacco and was involved in slave trade. Docks declined during 20c, now Albert Dock is home to shops, museums and Tate Liverpool. In 19c a multicultural city developed as Liverpool docks were point of departure for Europeans emigrating to America and Australia. Also became home to refugees from Irish potato famine of 1845. Present day Liverpool is home to variety of industries and many museums and art galleries. Also home of the Beatles, who performed at Liverpool's Cavern Club. Universities. Modern Anglican and Roman Catholic cathedrals. On Pier Head the famous Royal Liver Building is situated, topped by Liver Birds. Railway tunnel and two road tunnels under River Mersey to Wirral peninsula.

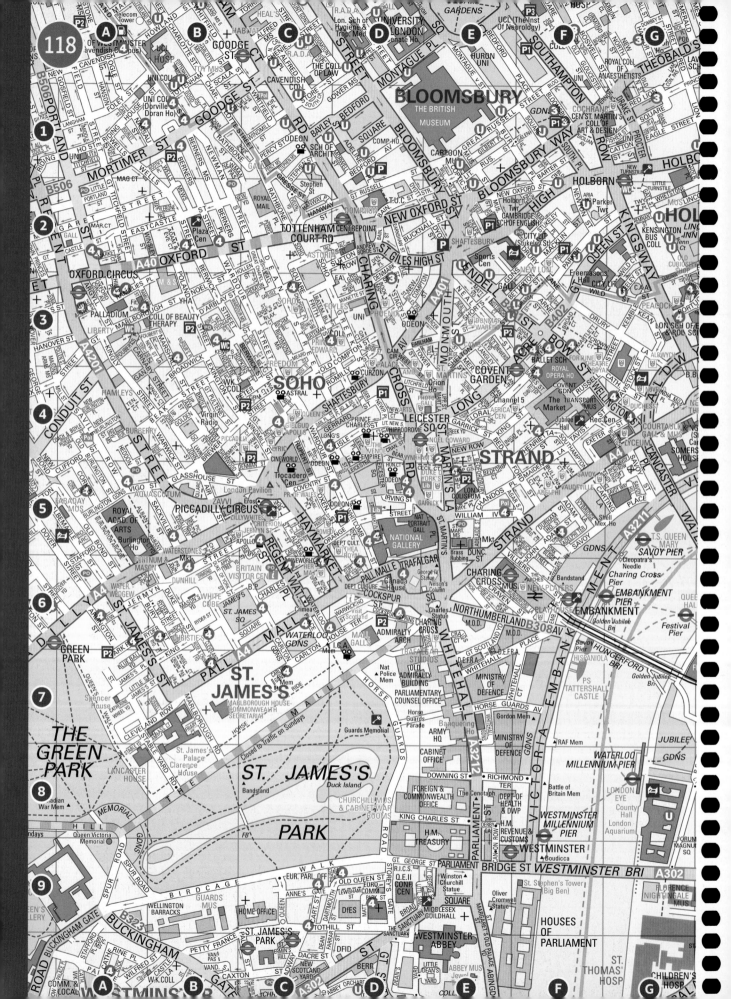

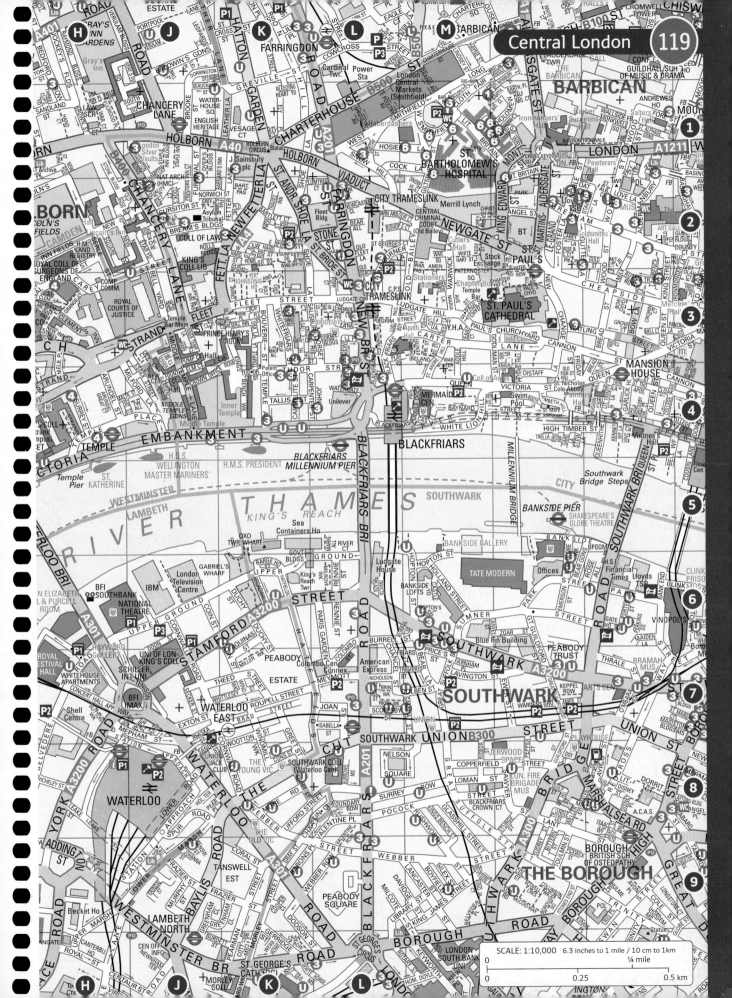

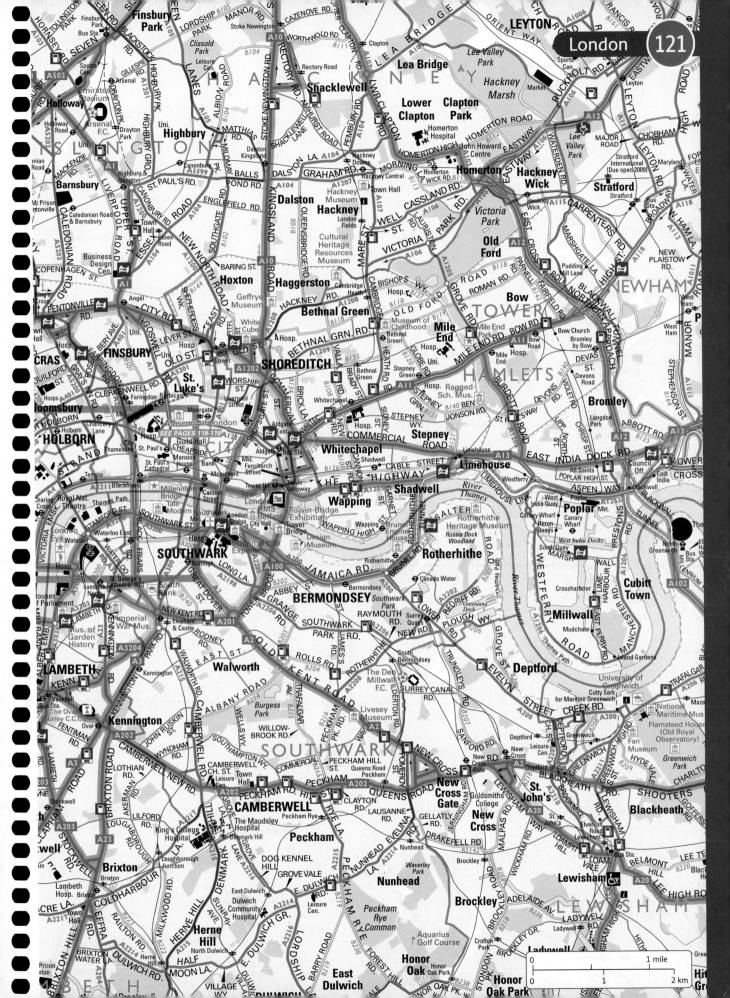

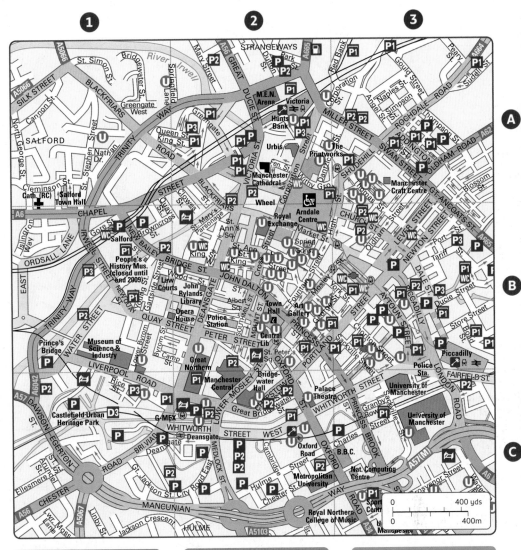

ADMINISTRATION

MANCHESTER CITY COUNCIL,
TOWN HALL,
ALBERT SQUARE,
MANCHESTER,
M60 2LA

www.manchester.gov.uk

☎ 0161 234 5000

HOSPITAL

MANCHESTER ROYAL
INFIRMARY,
OXFORD ROAD,
MANCHESTER,
M13 9WL

☎ 0161 276 1234

VISITOR INFORMATION

TOWN HALL EXTENSION,
LLOYD STREET,
MANCHESTER,
M60 2LA

☎ 0871 222 8223

Manchester *Gt.Man.*
Population: 394,269.

City, important industrial, business, cultural and commercial centre and port, 164m/264km NW of London. Access for ships by River Mersey and Manchester Ship Canal, opened in 1894. 15c cathedral, formerly parish church, has widest nave in England. Experienced rapid growth during industrial revolution. In 1750, Manchester was essentially still a village. During Victorian era, city was global cotton milling capital. Present day city is home to wide range of industries and is unofficial capital of nation's 'youth culture'. Major shopping centres include Arndale and Trafford Centres. Universities. International airport 9m/14km S of city centre.

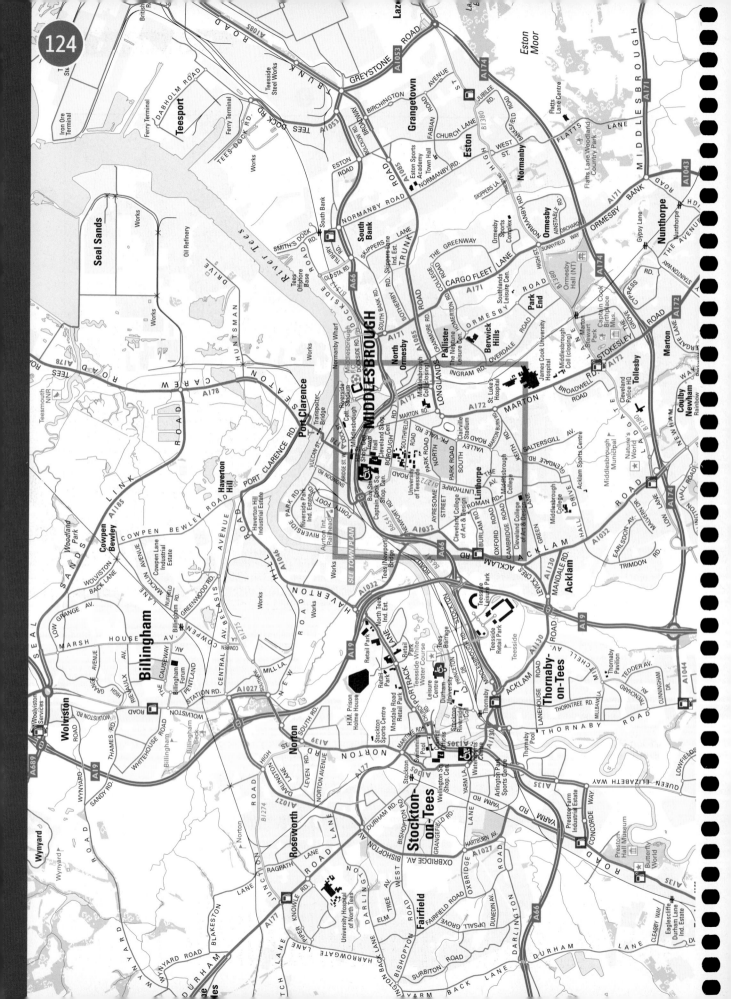

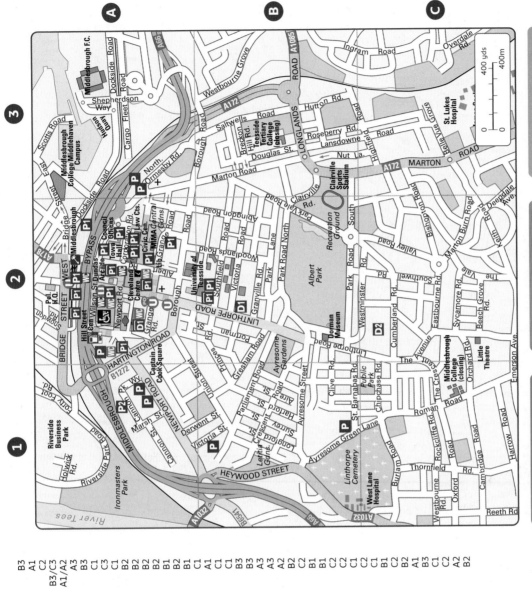

Middlesbrough *Middbro*.
Population: 142,691.

Town, port, with extensive dock area, on S bank of River Tees, forming part of Teesside urban complex. A former iron and steel town, its chief industries now involve oil and petrochemicals. Unusual 1911 transporter bridge over River Tees. University of Teesside. Captian Cook Birthplace Museum in Stewart Park at Marton.

VISITOR INFORMATION

TOWN HALL,
ALBERT ROAD,
MIDDLESBROUGH,
TS1 2QQ

☎ 01642 729700

HOSPITAL

UNIVERSITY HOSPITAL OF
NORTH TEES,
HARDWICK ROAD,
STOCKTON-ON-TEES,
TS19 8PE

☎ 0844 8118222

ADMINISTRATION

MIDDLESBROUGH COUNCIL,
PO BOX 99A,
TOWN HALL,
RUSSELL STREET,
MIDDLESBROUGH, TS1 2QQ
www.middlesbrough.gov.uk
☎ 01642 245432

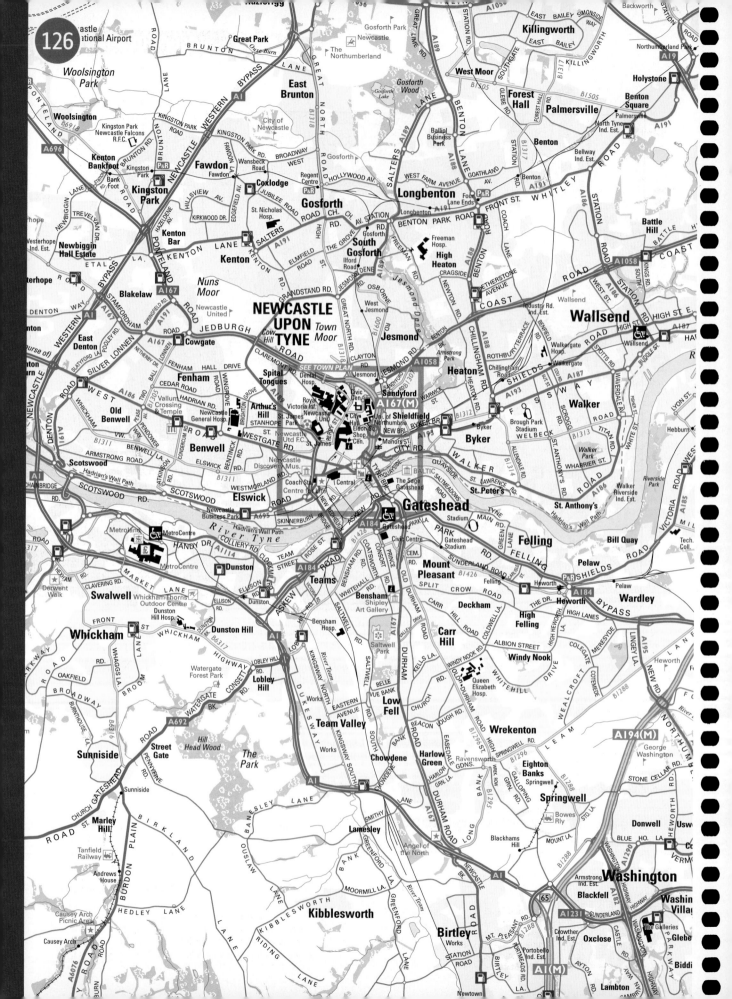

INDEX TO STREET NAMES

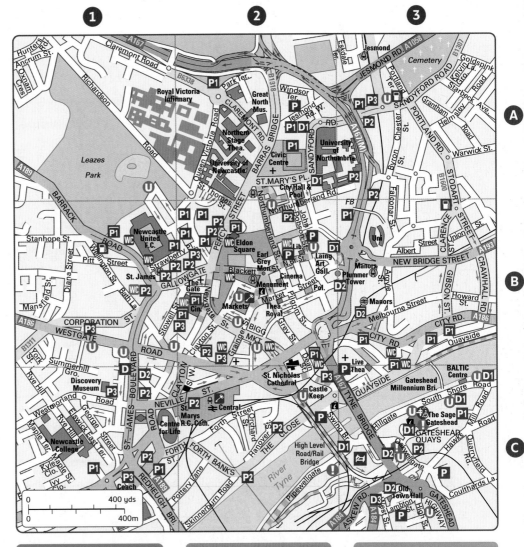

ADMINISTRATION

NEWCASTLE CITY COUNCIL,
CIVIC CENTRE,
BARRAS BRIDGE,
NEWCASTLE UPON TYNE,
NE99 1RD

www.newcastle.gov.uk
☎ 0191 232 8520

HOSPITAL

NEWCASTLE GENERAL
 HOSPITAL,
WESTGATE ROAD,
NEWCASTLE UPON TYNE,
NE4 6BE

☎ 0191 233 6161

VISITOR INFORMATION

8-9 CENTRAL ARCADE,
NEWCASTLE UPON TYNE,
NE1 5BQ

☎ 0191 277 8000

Newcastle upon Tyne *T. & W.*
Population: 189,863.

City, on northern bank of River Tyne about 11m/17km upstream from river mouth and 80m/129km N of Leeds. The 'new castle' of city's name started in 1080 by Robert Curthose, eldest son of William the Conqueror. 13c castle gatehouse known as 'Black Gate'. Commercial and industrial centre, previously dependent upon coalmining and shipbuilding. In its heyday, 25 percent of world's shipping built here. Cathedral dates from 14 to 15c. Bessie Surtees House (English Heritage) comprises 16c and 17c merchants' houses. Tyne Bridge, opened in 1928 and longest of its type at the time. Venerable Bede (AD 672-735) and Catherine Cookson (1906-1998) were born to the east in Jarrow. Universities. Newcastle International Airport 7m/11km.

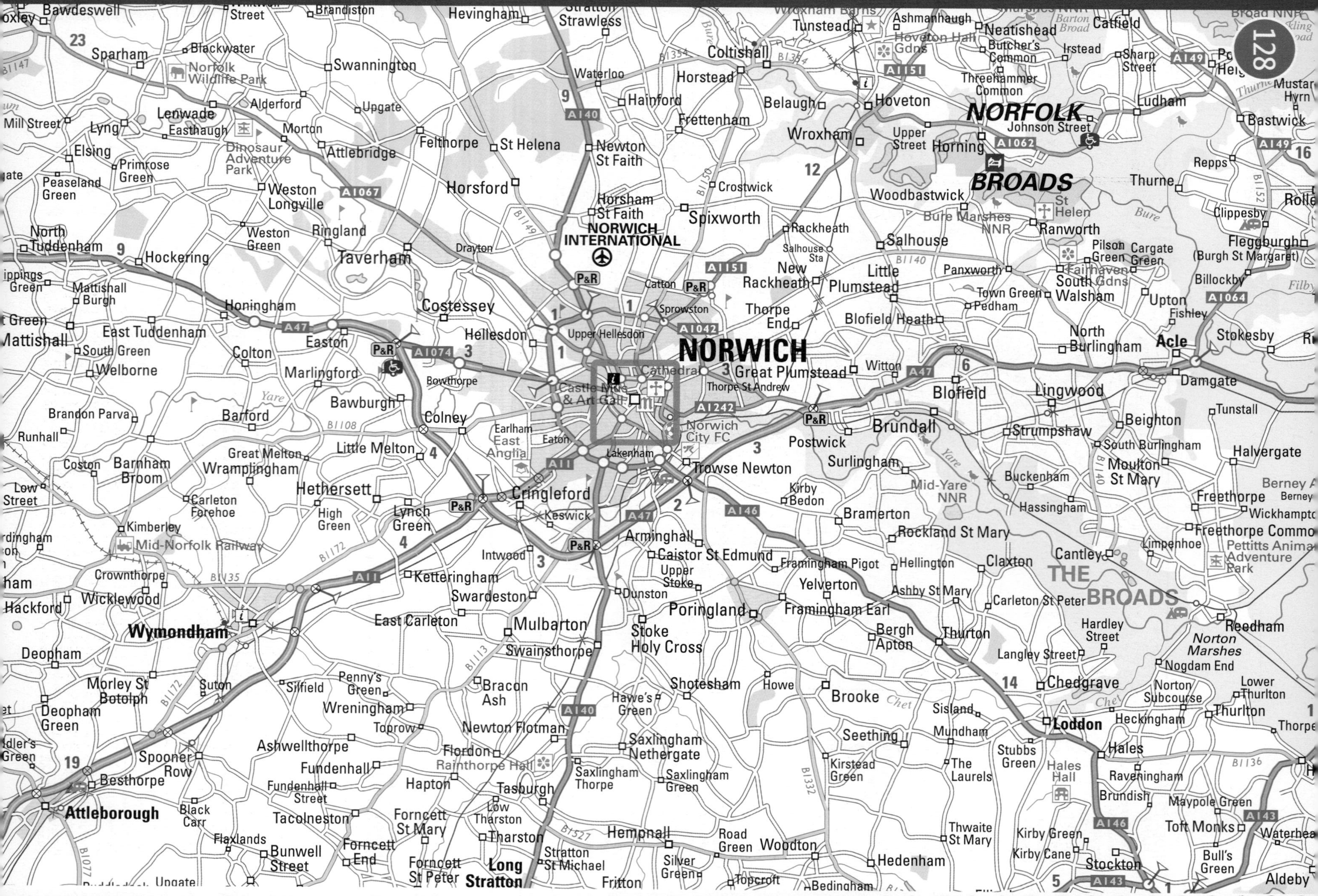
NORWICH
NORWICH INTERNATIONAL
NORFOLK
BROADS
THE BROADS
Wymondham
Attleborough
Long Stratton
Acle
Loddon
Bawdeswell
Sparham
Swannington
Hevingham
Strawless
Coltishall
Tunstead
Ashmanhaugh
Neatishead
Catfield
Ludham
Horning
Hoveton
Wroxham
Horstead
Hainford
Frettenham
Belaugh
Horsford
St Helena
Felthorpe
Newton St Faith
Horsham St Faith
Spixworth
Crostwick
Rackheath
Salhouse
Woodbastwick
Ranworth
South Walsham
Upton
Stokesby
Blofield
Lingwood
Brundall
Strumpshaw
Beighton
Halvergate
Freethorpe
Reedham
Cantley
Claxton
Chedgrave
Thurlton
Hales
Brooke
Poringland
Framingham Earl
Yelverton
Rockland St Mary
Bramerton
Surlingham
Postwick
Trowse Newton
Arminghall
Caistor St Edmund
Stoke Holy Cross
Shotesham
Mulbarton
Swardeston
Ketteringham
Hethersett
Cringleford
Colney
Costessey
Hellesdon
Taverham
Drayton
Ringland
Weston Longville
Attlebridge
Lenwade
Lyng
Elsing
Honingham
Easton
Marlingford
Bawburgh
Colton
Barford
East Tuddenham
Mattishall
Welborne
Barnham Broom
Wramplingham
Little Melton
East Carleton
Swainsthorpe
Newton Flotman
Tasburgh
Flordon
Hapton
Fundenhall
Ashwellthorpe
Wreningham
Tacolneston
Bunwell Street
Spooner Row
Besthorpe
Deopham
Morley St Botolph
Wicklewood
Crownthorpe
Kimberley
Hempnall
Woodton
Hedenham
Seething
Thwaite St Mary
Stockton
Aldeby
Norwich City FC
East Anglia
Mid-Norfolk Railway
Norfolk Wildlife Park
Dinosaur Adventure Park
A47
A11
A140
A146
A1074
A1067
A1042
A1242
A1151
A1062
A149
A1064
A143

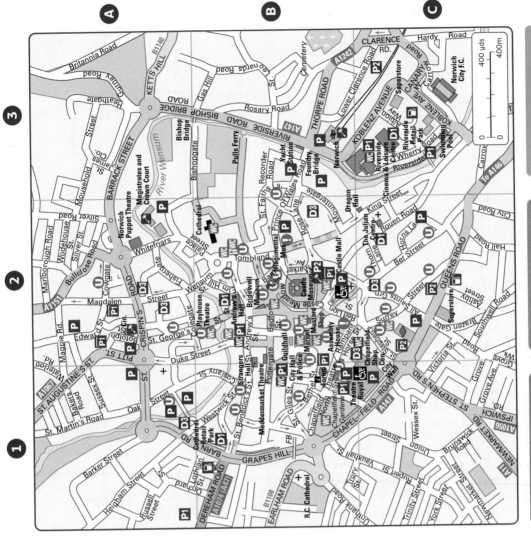

Norwich *Norf.*
Population: 174,047.

County town and cathedral city at confluence of River Wensum and River Yare, 98m/158km NE of London. Middle ages saw Norwich become second richest city in country through exporting textiles. Medieval streets and buildings are well preserved. Sections of 14c flint city wall defences still exist, including Cow Tower (English Heritage). Current chief industries are high technology and computer based. Notable buildings include partly Norman cathedral with second highest spire in Britain, Norman castle with keep (now museum and art gallery). 15c guildhall, modern city hall, numerous medieval churches. University of East Anglia 2m/4km W of city centre. Airport 3m/5km N.

VISITOR INFORMATION

THE FORUM,
MILLENNIUM PLAIN,
NORWICH,
NR2 1TF

☎ 01603 727927

HOSPITAL

NORFOLK & NORWICH
UNIVERSITY HOSPITAL,
COLNEY LANE,
NORWICH,
NR4 7UY

☎ 01603 286286

ADMINISTRATION

NORWICH CITY COUNCIL,
CITY HALL,
ST. PETER'S STREET,
NORWICH,
NR2 1NH

www.norwich.gov.uk
☎ 01603 212212

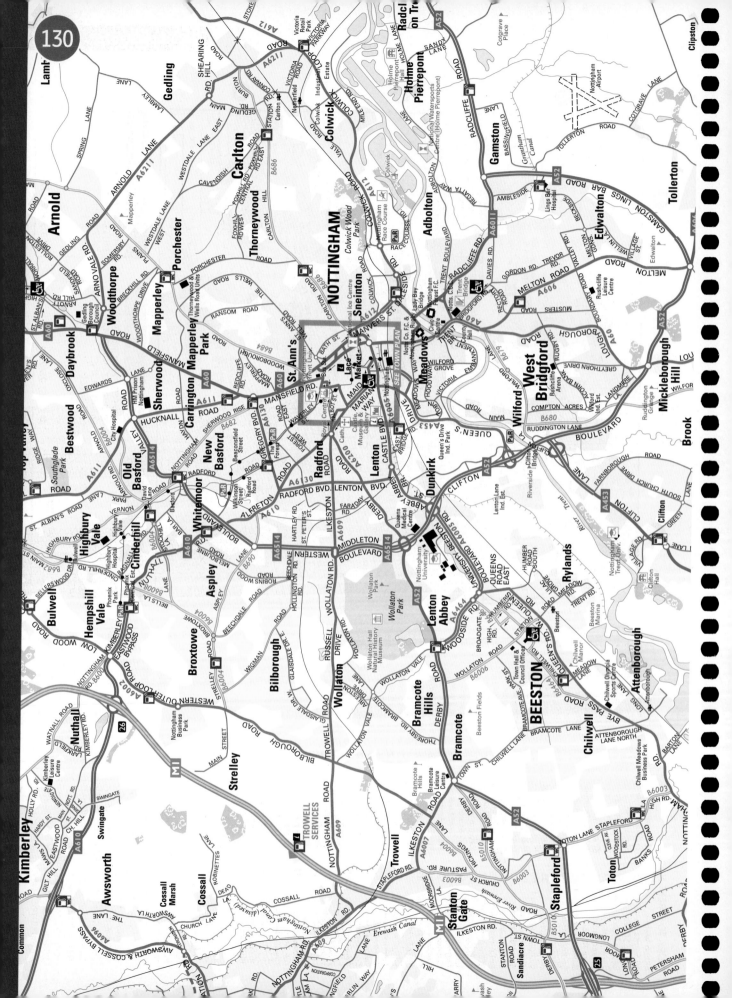

INDEX TO STREET NAMES

Street	Grid
Abbotsford Drive	A2
Albert Street	B2
Angel Row	B1
Barker Gate	B3
Bath Street	A3
Beacon Hill Rise	A3
Bellar Gate	B3
Belward Street	B3
Bridlesmith Gate	B2
Broad Street	B2
Brook Street	A3
Burton Street	A1
Canal Street	C2
Carlton Street	B2
Carrington Street	C2
Castle Boulevard	C1
Castle Gate	B2
Castle Meadow Road	C1
Castle Road	C1
Chapel Bar	B1
Chaucer Street	A1
Cheapside	B2
City Link	C3
Clarendon Street	A1
Cliff Road	C2
Clumber Street	B2
College Street	B1
Collin Street	C2
Cranbrook Street	B3
Cromwell Street	A1
Curzon Street	A2
Derby Road	B1
Dryden Street	A1
Fisher Gate	B3
Fishpond Drive	C1
Fletcher Gate	B2
Forman Street	B2
Friar Lane	B1
Gedling Street	B3
George Street	B2
Gill Street	A1
Glasshouse Street	A2
Goldsmith Street	A1
Goose Gate	B3
Hamilton Drive	C1
Hampden Street	A1
Handel Street	B3
Heathcote Street	B2
High Pavement	B2
Hockley	B3
Hollowstone	B3
Hope Drive	C1
Huntingdon Drive	B1
Huntingdon Street	A2
Instow Rise	A3
Kent Street	A2
King Edward Street	B2
King Street	B2
Lamartine Street	A3
Lenton Road	C1
Lincoln Street	B2
Lister Gate	C2
London Road	C3
Low Pavement	B2
Lower Parliament Street	B2
Maid Marian Way	B1
Mansfield Road	A2
Manvers Street	B3
Market Street	B2
Middle Pavement	B2
Milton Street	A2
Mount Street	B1
North Church Street	A2
North Sherwood Street	A2
Park Row	B1
Park Terrace	B1
Park Valley	B1
Peel Street	A1
Pelham Street	B2
Pennyfoot Street	B3
Peveril Drive	C1
Pilcher Gate	B2
Plantagenet Street	A3
Popham Street	C2
Poplar Street	B3
Queens Road	C2
Queen Street	B2
Regent Street	B1
Robin Hood Street	A3
Roden Street	A3
St. Ann's Well Road	A3
St. James Street	B1
St. Mary's Gate	B2
St. Peter's Gate	B2
Shakespeare Street	A1
Shelton Street	A2
Smithy Row	B2
Sneinton Road	B3
South Parade	B2
South Sherwood Street	A2
Southwell Road	B3
Station Street	C2
Stoney Street	B3
Talbot Street	A1
The Great Northern Close	C3
The Rope Walk	B1
Union Road	A2
Upper Parliament Street	B1
Victoria Street	B2
Warser Gate	B2
Waverley Street	A1
Wheeler Gate	B2
Wilford Street	C1
Wollaton Street	B1
Woolpack Lane	B3

Nottingham *Nott.*
Population: 249,584.

City, on River Trent, 45m/72km NE of Birmingham. Originally Saxon town built on one of a pair of hills. In 1068, Normans built castle on other hill and both communities traded in valley between. Legendary home to the world's best-loved outlaw, Robin Hood. Historically important as lace making centre. Important commercial, industrial, entertainment and sports centre. Key industries now include manufacture of clothing and textiles, pharmaceuticals, food, drink, tobacco and engineering. Designated a Science City in recognition of past scientific achievements and growing success as centre of scientific research. Nottingham Castle is a restored 17c mansion on site of original Norman castle, housing museum and art gallery. Two universities. Repertory theatre. Racecourse 2m/3km E of city centre.

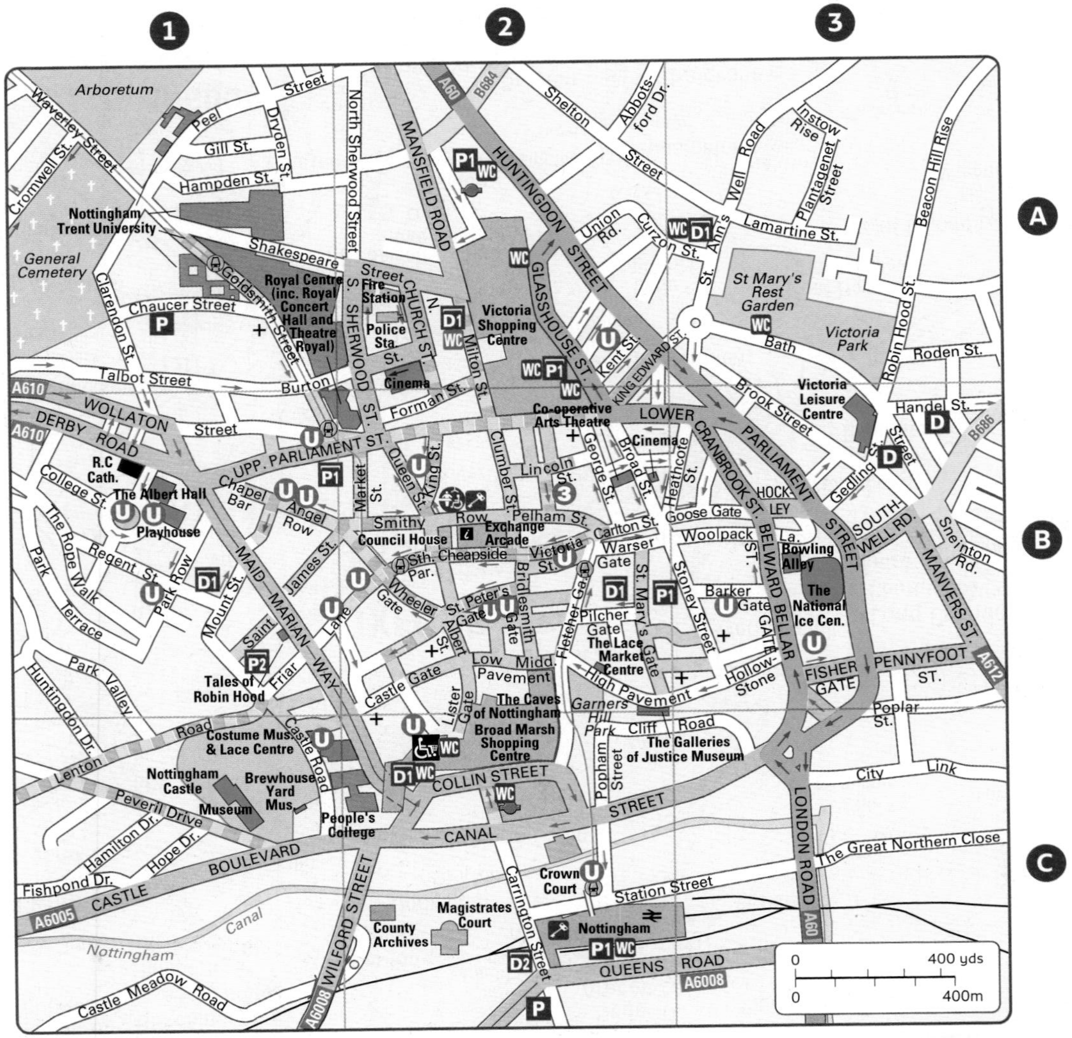
1
2
3
A
B
C
Arboretum
General Cemetery
Nottingham Trent University
Royal Centre (inc. Royal Concert Hall and Theatre Royal)
Fire Station
Police Sta.
Victoria Shopping Centre
Victoria Leisure Centre
St Mary's Rest Garden
Victoria Park
Co-operative Arts Theatre
Cinema
Council House
Exchange Arcade
R.C Cath.
The Albert Hall
Playhouse
Tales of Robin Hood
Costume Mus. & Lace Centre
Nottingham Castle
Museum
Brewhouse Yard Mus.
People's College
The Caves of Nottingham
Broad Marsh Shopping Centre
The Lace Market Centre
The Galleries of Justice Museum
Bowling Alley
The National Ice Cen.
Crown Court
Magistrates Court
County Archives
Nottingham
HUNTINGDON STREET
MANSFIELD ROAD
GLASSHOUSE ST.
LOWER PARLIAMENT STREET
UPP. PARLIAMENT ST.
MAID MARIAN WAY
DERBY ROAD
WOLLATON STREET
CASTLE BOULEVARD
CANAL STREET
COLLIN STREET
LONDON ROAD
QUEENS ROAD
WILFORD STREET
CRANBROOK ST.
BELWARD ST.
SOUTHWELL RD.
MANVERS ST.
PENNYFOOT ST.
FISHER GATE
A60
A610
A6005
A6008
A612
B684
B686
0
400 yds
400m

ADMINISTRATION

NOTTINGHAM CITY COUNCIL,
THE GUILDHALL,
SOUTH SHERWOOD STREET,
NOTTINGHAM, NG1 4BT

www.nottinghamcity.gov.uk
☎ 0115 915 5555

HOSPITAL

QUEENS MEDICAL CENTRE,
UNIVERSITY HOSPITAL,
DERBY ROAD,
NOTTINGHAM,
NG7 2UH

☎ 0115 924 9924

VISITOR INFORMATION

1-4 SMITHY ROW,
NOTTINGHAM,
NG1 2BY

☎ 0115 915 5330

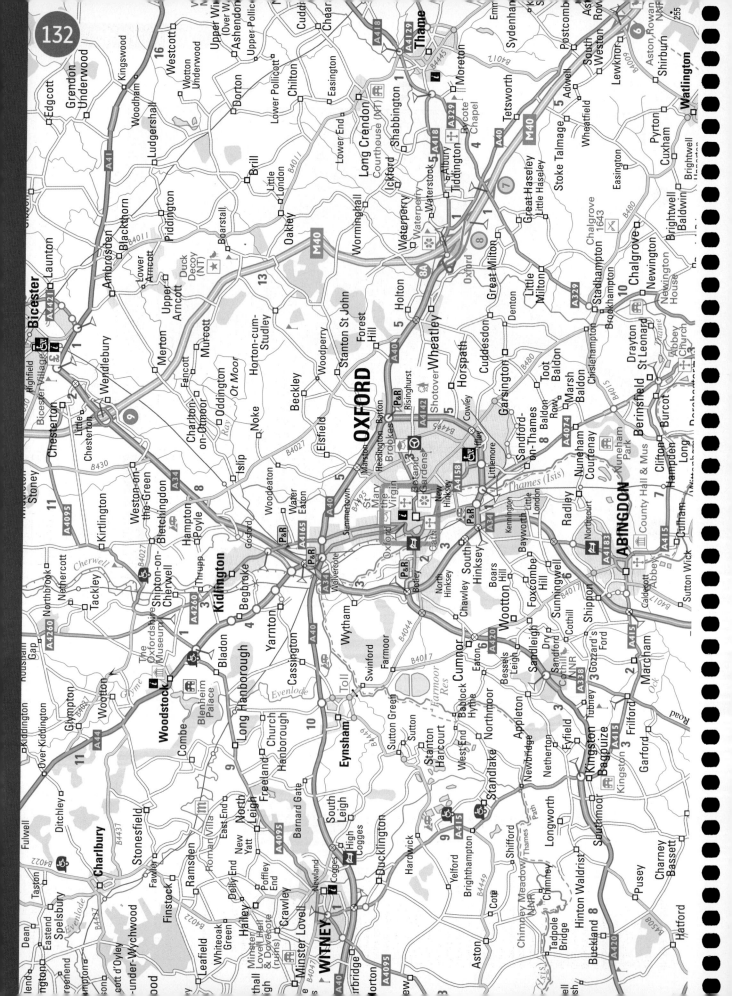

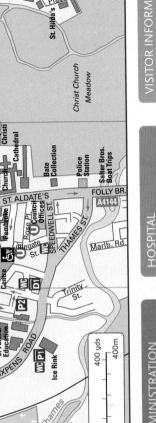

Oxford *Oxon.*
Population: 143,016.

City, at confluence of Rivers Thames and Cherwell, 52m/84km NW of London. Began as Saxon settlement, flourished under Normans when it was chosen as royal residence. University dating from 13c, recognised as being among best in the world. Many notable buildings create spectacular skyline. Cathedral. Bodleian Library, second largest in UK. Ashmolean museum, oldest public museum in country. Tourist and commercial centre. Ancient St. Giles Fair held every September. Oxford Brookes University at Headington, 2m/4km E of city centre. Airport at Kidlington.

VISITOR INFORMATION

15-16 BROAD STREET,
OXFORD,
OX1 3AS

☎ 01865 726871

HOSPITAL

JOHN RADCLIFFE HOSPITAL,
HEADLEY WAY,
HEADINGTON,
OXFORD,
OX3 9DU

☎ 01865 741166

ADMINISTRATION

OXFORD CITY COUNCIL,
PO BOX 10,
OXFORD,
OX1 1EN

www.oxford.gov.uk
☎ 01865 249811

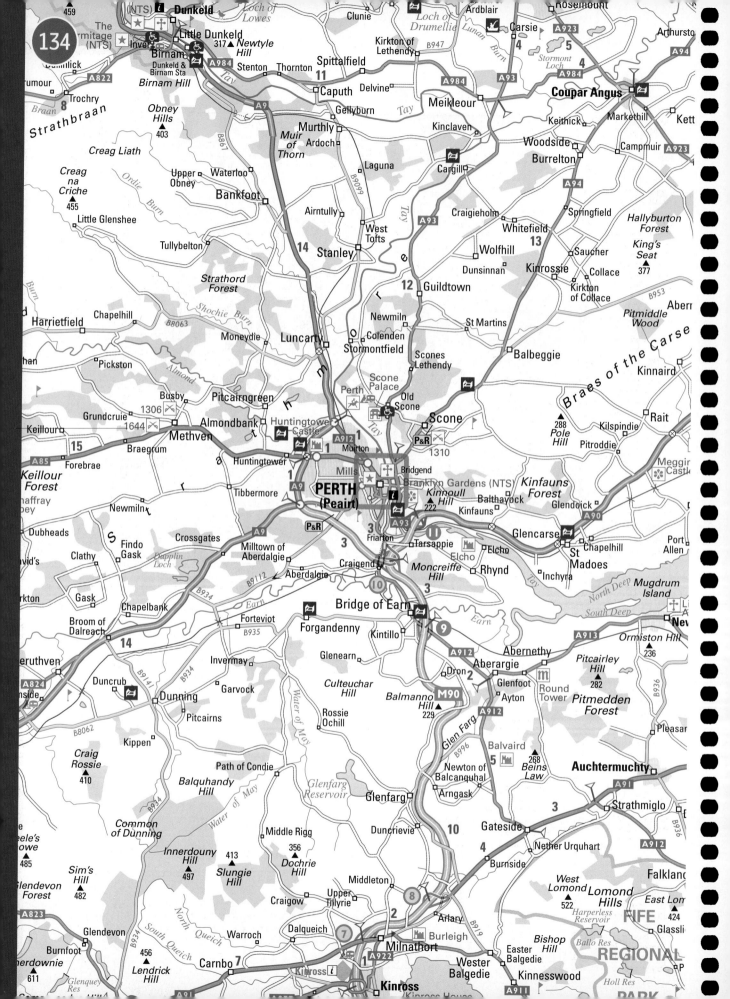

INDEX TO STREET NAMES

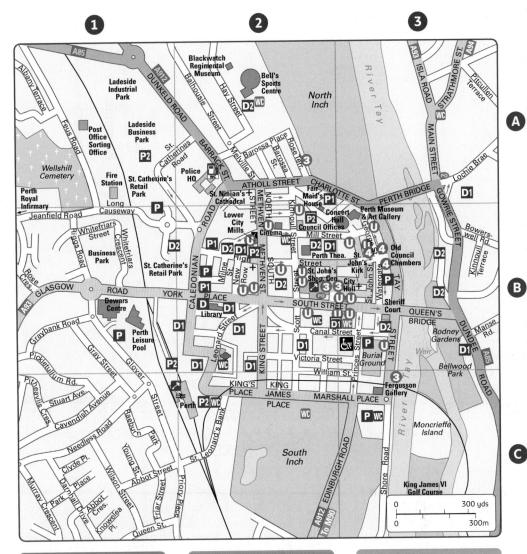

ADMINISTRATION

PERTH & KINROSS COUNCIL,
2 HIGH STREET,
PERTH,
PH1 5PH

www.pkc.gov.uk
☎ 01738 475000

HOSPITAL

PERTH ROYAL INFIRMARY,
TAYMOUNT TERRACE,
PERTH,
PH1 1NX

☎ 01738 623311

VISITOR INFORMATION

LOWER CITY MILLS,
WEST MILL STREET,
PERTH,
PH1 5QP

☎ 01738 450600

Perth P. & K.
Population: 43,450.

Ancient cathedral city (Royal Charter granted 1210) on River Tay, 31m/50km N of Edinburgh. Once capital of Medieval Scotland. Centre of livestock trade. Previously cotton manufacturing centre; now important industries include whisky distilling. St. John's Kirk founded 1126. 15c Balhousie Castle houses regimental headquarters and Museum of the Black Watch. Art Gallery and Museum. 16c Fair Maid's House. Gothic mansion Scone Palace 2m/3km N contains collections of furniture, needlework and porcelain with site of Coronation Stone of Destiny in its grounds. Airfield (Scone) to NE.

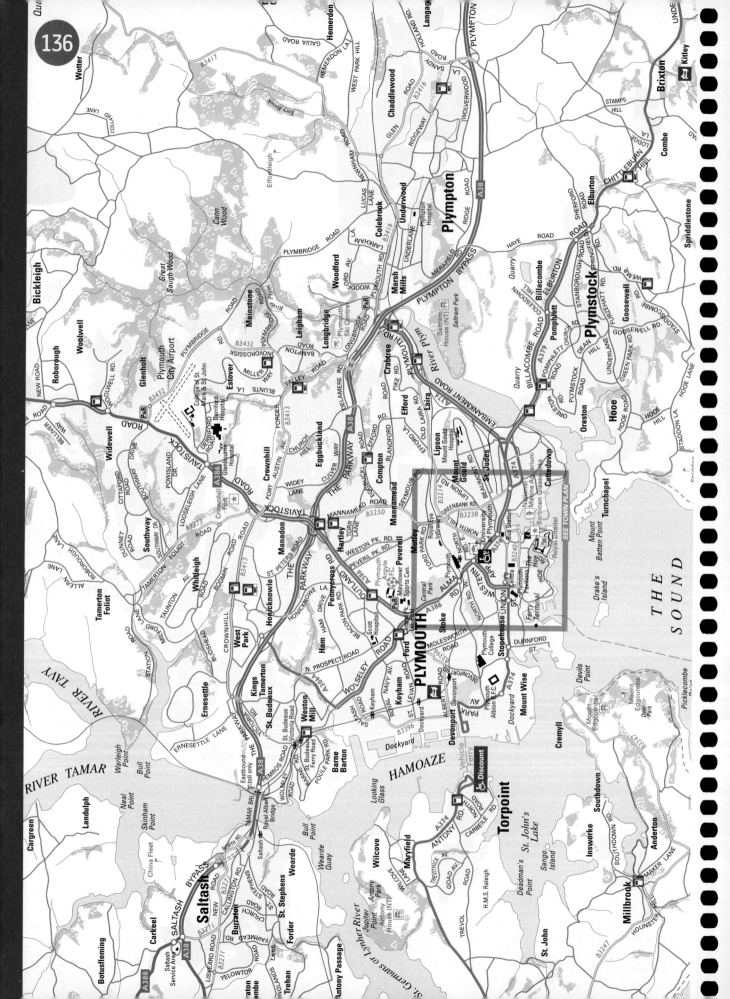

A B C

3

2

1

Central Park

Cemetery

ALMA ROAD

A386

Ponsonby Road

MUTLEY PLAIN

GREENBANK ROAD

Freedom Fields Park

Beaumont Park

B3214
B3250
B3238

ALEXANDRA ROAD

TOTHILL AVE.

TOTHILL RD.

GDYNIA WAY

EMBANKMENT ROAD

A374

Sutton Road

Sutton Harbour

Fish Quay

National Marine Aquarium

Mayflower Memorial

Barbican Theatre

Royal Citadel

Plymouth Hoe

The Hoe

Smeaton's Tower

Plymouth Dome (closed)

Tinside Lido

West Hoe Road

Recreation Ground

Great Western Docks

Inner Basin

Outer Basin

Car Ferry Terminal

Victoria Park

R.C. Cathedral

University of Plymouth

Royal Eye Infirmary

DRAKE CIRCUS

Museum & Art Gallery Library

Police HQ

Charles Church (Ruin)

St Andrews Church

Theatre Royal

Guildhall

Civic Centre

Law Courts

Pavilions

Athenaeum Thea.

Elizabeth House

Mayflower Visitor Centre

Chapters

Cin. Bowling Abbey

WESTERN APPROACH

0 400 yds
0 400m

Plymouth *Plym.*
Population: 243,795.

Largest city in SW England, 100m/160km SW of Bristol. Port and naval base. Regional shopping centre. City centre rebuilt after bombing in World War II. Has strong commercial and naval tradition. In 1588 Sir Francis Drake sailed from Plymouth to defeat Spanish Armada. Captain Cook's voyages to Australia, South Seas and Antarctica all departed from here. University. Plymouth City Airport to N of city.

VISITOR INFORMATION

PLYMOUTH MAYFLOWER CENTRE,
3-5 THE BARBICAN,
PLYMOUTH,
PL1 2LR
☎ 01752 306330

HOSPITAL

DERRIFORD HOSPITAL,
DERRIFORD ROAD,
CROWNHILL,
PLYMOUTH,
PL6 8DH
☎ 0845 155 8155

ADMINISTRATION

PLYMOUTH CITY COUNCIL,
CIVIC CENTRE,
ARMADA WAY,
PLYMOUTH,
PL1 2AA
www.plymouth.gov.uk
☎ 01752 668000

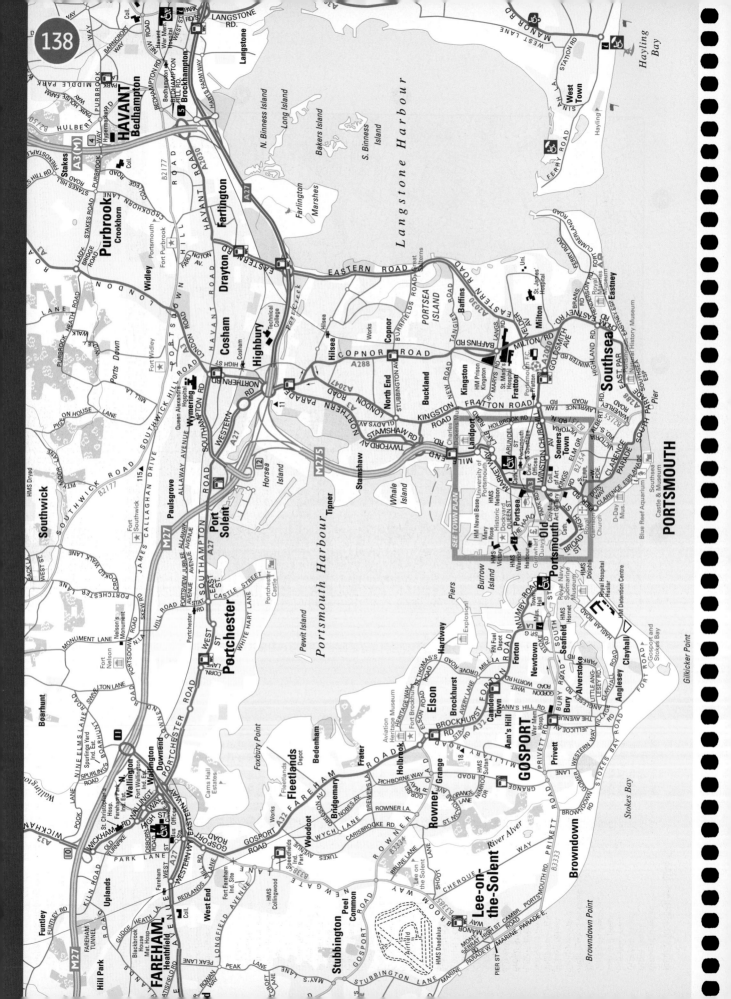

VISITOR INFORMATION

THE HARD,
PORTSMOUTH,
PO1 3QJ

☎ 023 9282 6722

HOSPITAL

QUEEN ALEXANDRA
HOSPITAL,
SOUTHWICK HILL ROAD,
COSHAM,
PORTSMOUTH,
PO6 3LY

☎ 023 9228 6000

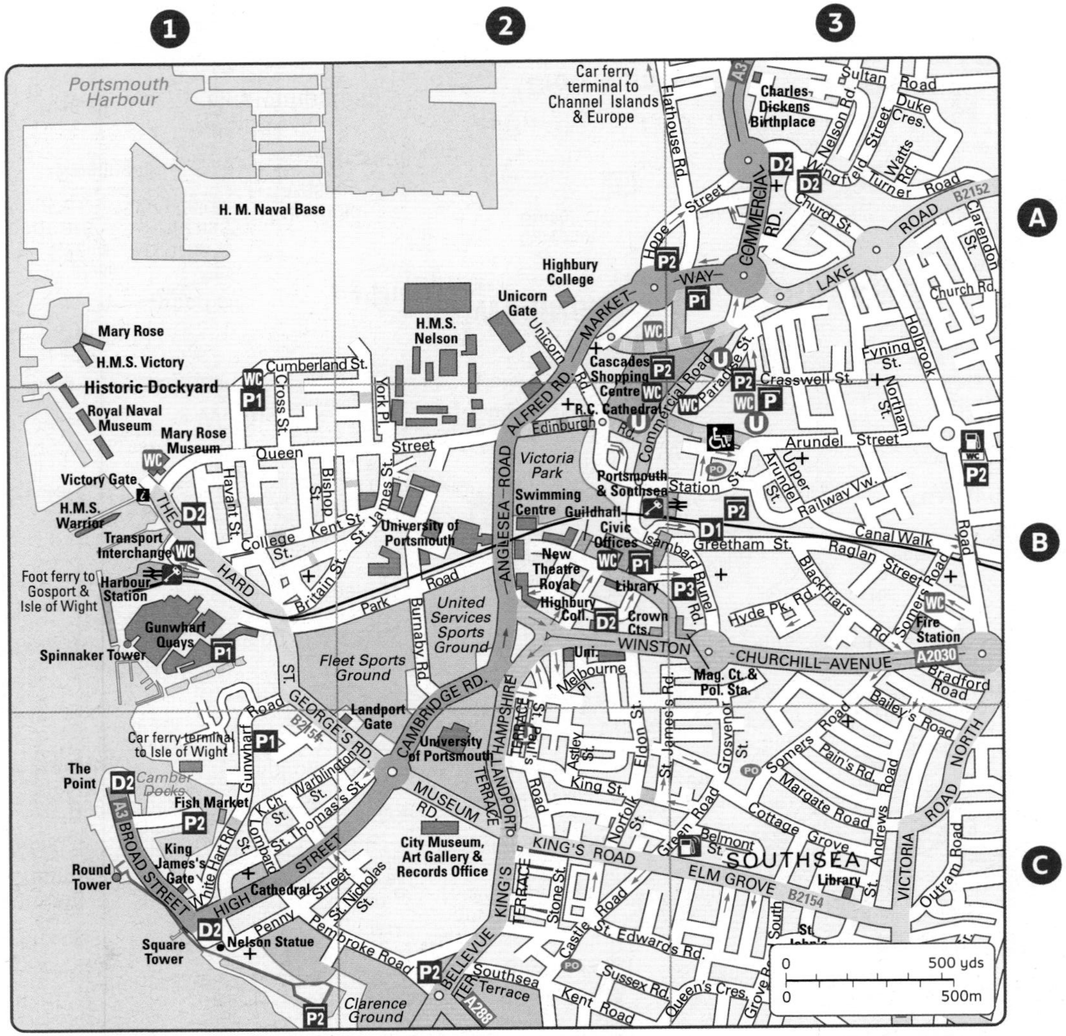

ADMINISTRATION

PORTSMOUTH CITY
COUNCIL,
CIVIC OFFICES,
GUILDHALL SQUARE,
PORTSMOUTH, PO1 2BG
www.portsmouth.gov.uk
☎ 023 9282 2251

INDEX TO STREET NAMES

Portsmouth *Ports.*
Population: 187,056.

City, port and naval base (Portsmouth Harbour, on W side of city) 65m/105km SW of London, extending from S end of Portsea Island to S slopes of Ports Down. Various industries, including tourism, financial services and manufacturing. Partly bombed in World War II and now rebuilt; however, some 18c buildings remain. Boat and hovercraft ferries to Isle of Wight. University. Two cathedrals. Nelson's ship, HMS Victory, in harbour, alongside which are remains of Henry VIII's flagship, Mary Rose, which sank in 1545. King James's Gate and Landport Gate were part of 17c defences, and Fort Cumberland is 18c coastal defence at Eastney (all English Heritage). Royal Garrison Church (English Heritage) was 16c chapel prior to Dissolution. Museums, many with nautical theme.

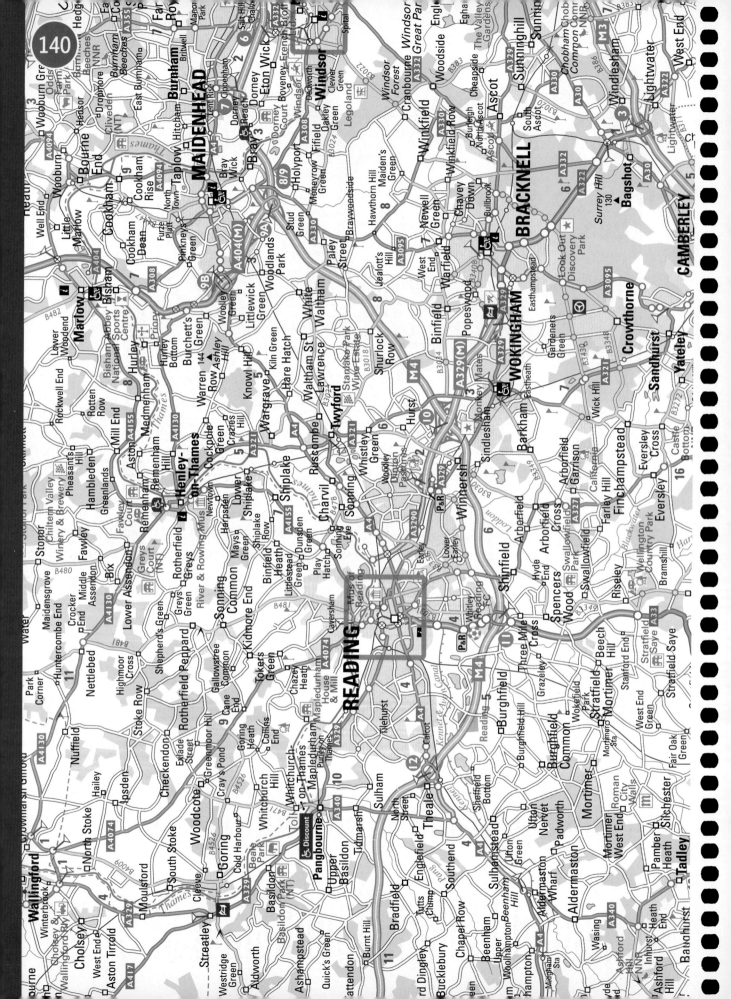

INDEX TO STREET NAMES

Addington Road	C3	Fobney Street	B2	St. Anne's Road	A2
Addison Road	A1	Forbury Road	B2	St. John's Road	A3
Alexandra Road	B3	Friar Street	B2	St. Mary's Butts	B2
Allcroft Road	C3	Gas Work Road	B3	St. Peters Avenue	A1
Alpine Street	C2	George Street		St. Saviours Road	C1
Amersham Road	A3	*Caversham*	A2	Silver Street	C2
Amity Road	B1	George Street		South Street	B2
Ardler Road	A2	*Reading*	B1	Southampton	
Ashley Road	C1	Gosbrook Road	A2	Street	C2
Audley Street	B1	Gower Street	B1	South View Road	A2
Baker Street	B1	Great Knollys		Star Road	A3
Basingstoke Road	C2	Street	B1	Station Hill	B2
Bath Road	C1	Greyfriars Road	B2	Station Road	B2
Bedford Road	B1	Hemdean Road	A2	Swansea Road	A2
Berkeley Avenue	C1	Hill Street	C2	Tessa Road	A1
Blagrave Street	B2	Holybrook Road	C1	The Warren	A1
Blenheim Road	B3	Kenavon Drive	B3	Tilehurst Road	B1
Briant's Avenue	A3	Kendrick Road	C2	Upper Redlands	
Bridge Street	B2	King's Road		Road	C3
Broad Street	B2	*Caversham*	A2	Vastern Road	A2
Cardiff Road	A1	King's Road		Waldelk Street	C2
Castle Hill	B1	*Reading*	B2	Waterloo Road	C2
Castle Street	B2	Lesford Road	C1	Wensley Road	C1
Catherine Street	B1	London Road	B3	Western Elms	
Caversham Road	B2	London Street	B2	Avenue	B1
Chatham Street	B1	Lower Henley		Westfield Road	A2
Cheapside	B2	Road	A3	West Street	B2
Cholmeley Road	B3	Mill Road	A3	Whitley Street	C2
Christchurch Road	C2	Milford Road	A1	Wolsey Road	A2
Church Road	A1	Milman Road	C2	York Road	A2
Church Street	A2	Minster Street	B2		
Coley Avenue	C1	Morgan Road	C3		
Coley Place	B2	Napier Road	B2		
Cow Lane	B1	Orts Road	B3		
Craven Road	B3	Oxford Road	B1		
Crown Place	B3	Pell Street	C2		
Crown Street	C2	Portman Road	A1		
Cumberland Road	B3	Priest Hill	A2		
Curzon Street	B1	Prospect Street			
De Beauvoir Road	B3	*Caversham*	A2		
Donnington Road	B3	Prospect Street			
Duke Street	B2	*Reading*	B1		
East Street	B2	Queen's Road			
Eldon Road	B3	*Caversham*	A2		
Eldon Terrace	B3	Queen's Road			
Elgar Road	C2	*Reading*	B2		
Elgar Road South	C2	Richfield Avenue	A1		
Elmhurst Road	C3	Rose Kiln Lane	C2		
Erleigh Road	B3	Russell Street	B1		

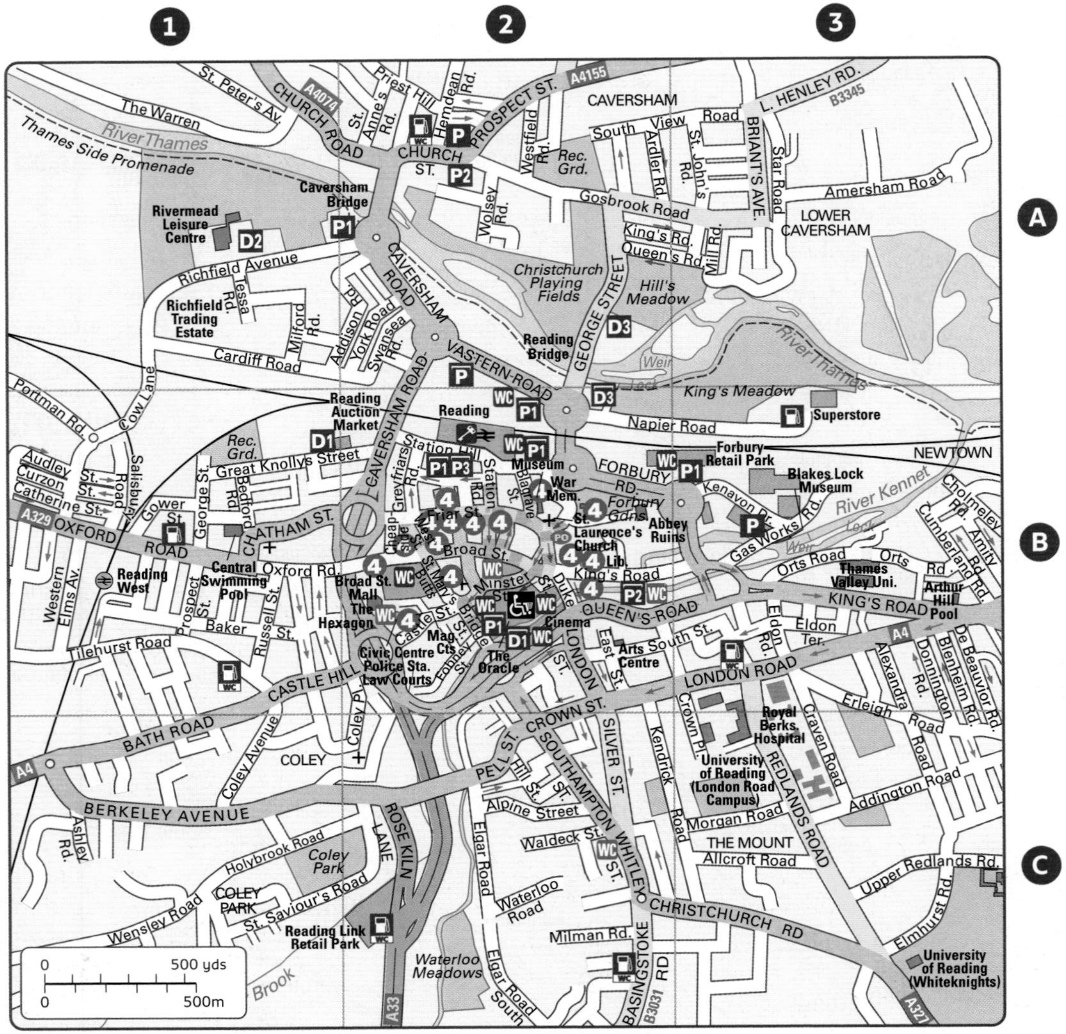

ADMINISTRATION

READING BOROUGH COUNCIL,
CIVIC CENTRE, CIVIC OFFICES (OFF CASTLE STREET),
READING, RG1 7AE

www.reading.gov.uk
☎ 0118 939 0900

HOSPITAL

ROYAL BERKSHIRE HOSPITAL,
LONDON ROAD,
READING,
RG1 5AN

☎ 0118 322 5111

Reading *Read.*
Population: 232,662.

County town and railway centre on River Thames, 36m/58km W of London. During Victorian times Reading was an important manufacturing town, particularly for biscuit-making and brewing. University. Remains of Norman abbey, founded by Henry I who lies buried there.

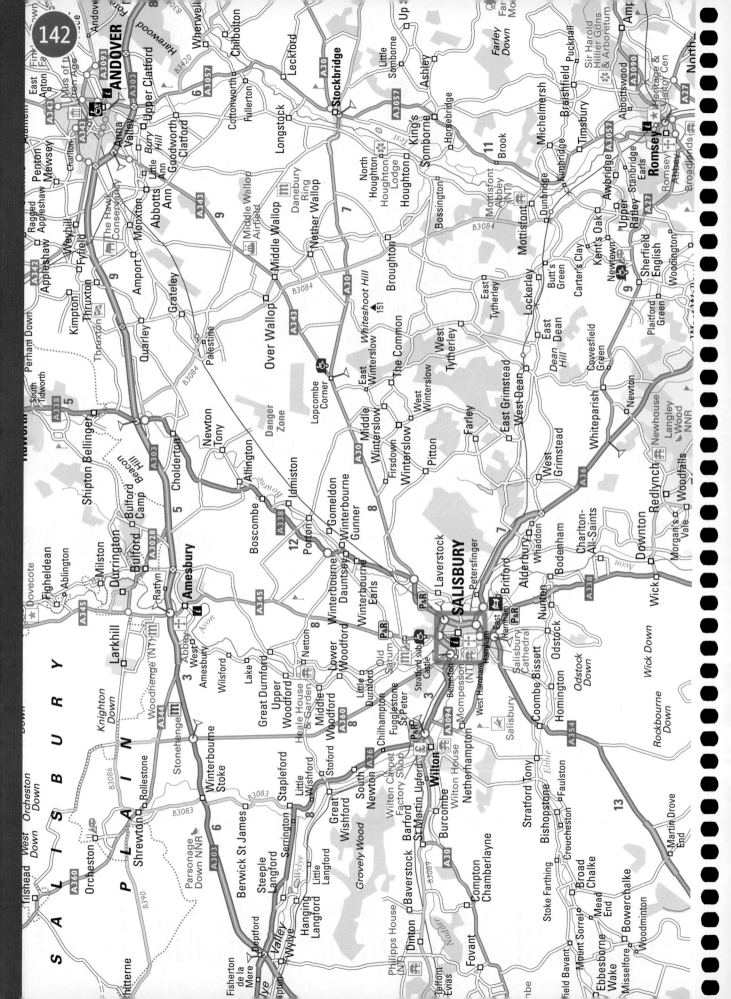

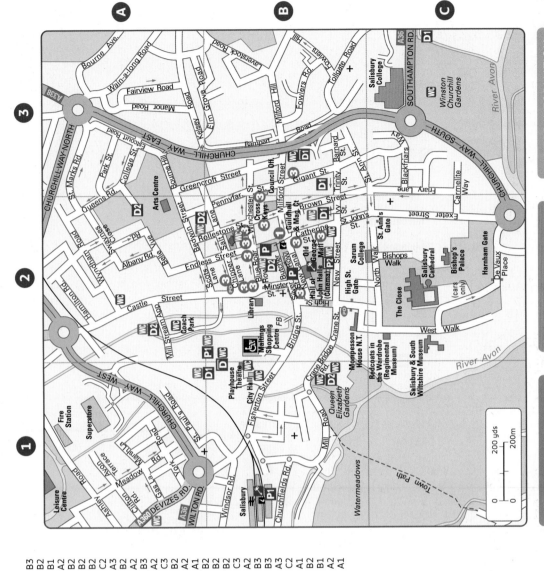

VISITOR INFORMATION

FISH ROW,
SALISBURY,
SP1 1EJ

☎ 01722 334956

HOSPITAL

SALISBURY DISTRICT
HOSPITAL,
ODSTOCK ROAD,
SALISBURY,
SP2 8BJ

☎ 01722 336262

ADMINISTRATION

SALISBURY DISTRICT
COUNCIL,
PENNYFARTHING HOUSE,
18 PENNYFARTHING STREET,
SALISBURY, SP1 1HJ
www.salisbury.gov.uk
☎ 01722 336272

INDEX TO STREET NAMES

Salisbury (Former and official name New Sarum) Wilts.
Population: 43,355.

Cathedral city at confluence of Rivers Avon and Nadder, 21m/34km
NW of Southampton. Shopping centre and market town, with buildings
ranging from medieval to Victorian; several medieval churches.
Cathedral, in Early English style, built between 1220 and 1260, has the
tallest spire in England at 123m/404ft.

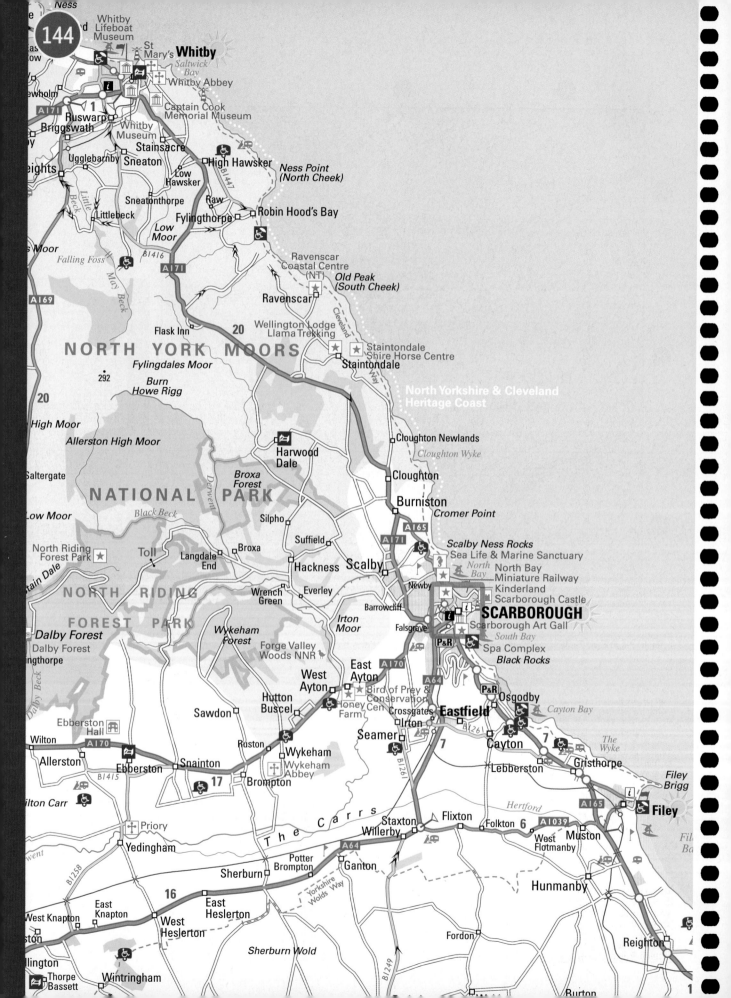

INDEX TO STREET NAMES

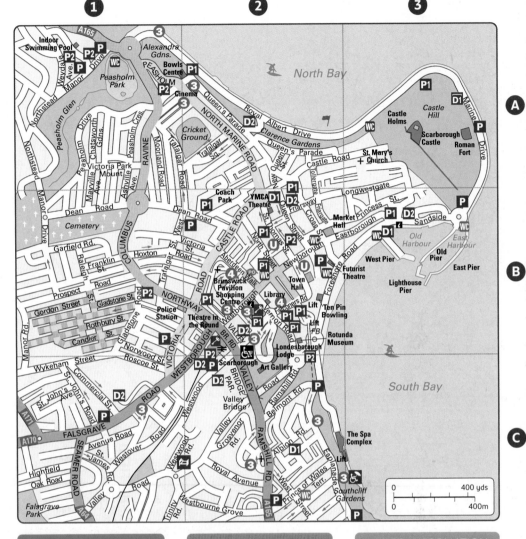

ADMINISTRATION

SCARBOROUGH BOROUGH
  COUNCIL,
TOWN HALL,
ST NICHOLAS STREET,
SCARBOROUGH, YO11 2HG

www.scarborough.gov.uk
☎ 01723 232323

HOSPITAL

SCARBOROUGH GENERAL
  HOSPITAL,
WOODLANDS DRIVE,
SCARBOROUGH,
YO12 6QL

☎ 01723 368111

VISITOR INFORMATION

BRUNSWICK SHOPPING
  CENTRE,
UNIT 15A,
WESTBOROUGH,
SCARBOROUGH,
YO11 1UE

☎ 01723 383636

Scarborough *N. Yorks.*
Population: 38,364.

Old North sea fishing port and spa town built on steep cliff side, now large resort and conference town, 35m/57km NE of York. Remains of 12c castle (English Heritage) and of Roman signal station on Castle Cliff, between North Bay and South Bay. Piers, harbour and Victorian esplanade. Restored Spa Complex is a venue for conferences, exhibitions and entertainment.

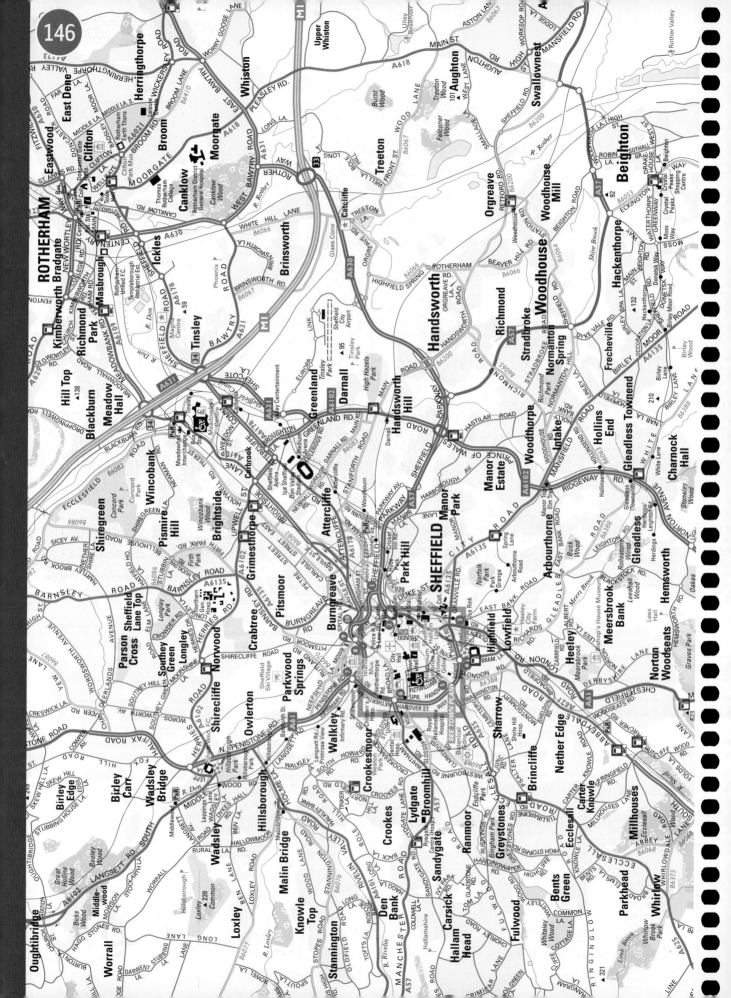

VISITOR INFORMATION
14 NORFOLK ROW,
SHEFFIELD,
S1 2PA
☎ 0114 221 1900

HOSPITAL
NORTHERN GENERAL
HOSPITAL,
HERRIES ROAD,
SHEFFIELD,
S5 7AU
☎ 0114 243 4343

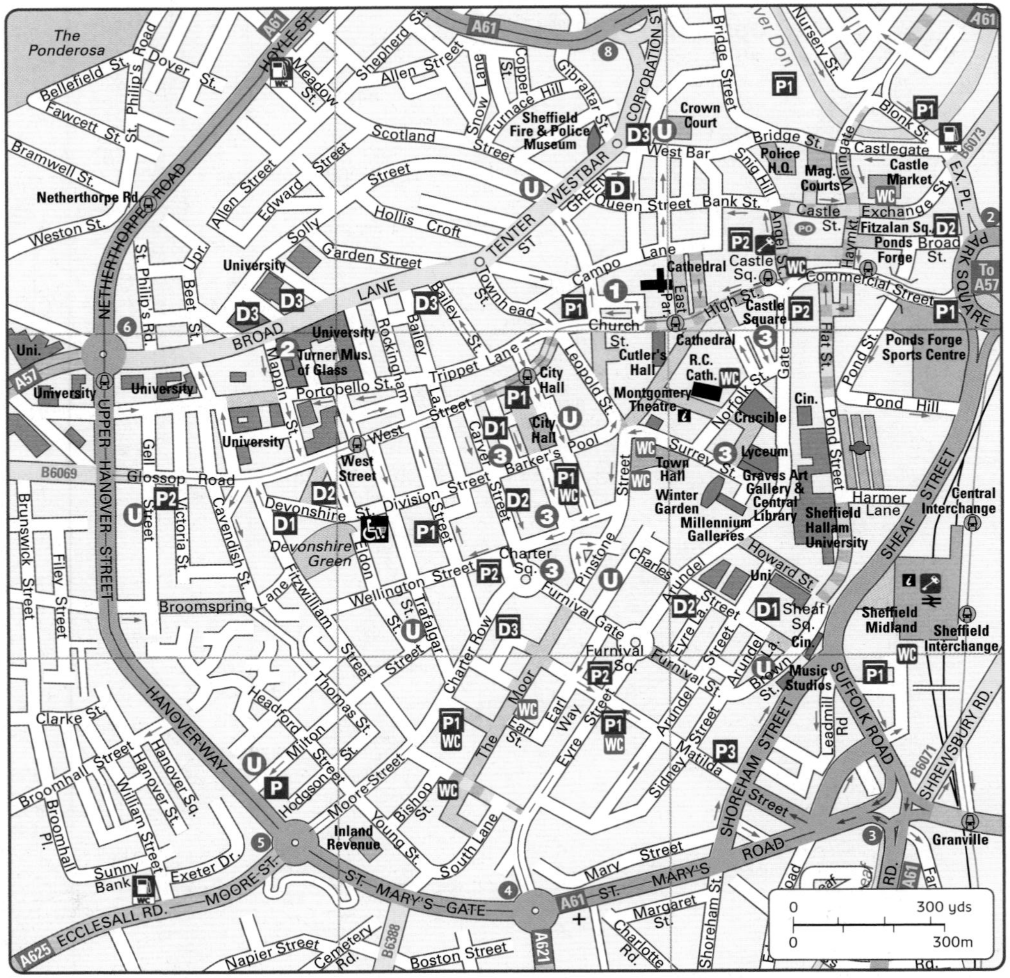

ADMINISTRATION
SHEFFIELD CITY COUNCIL,
TOWN HALL,
PINSTONE STREET,
SHEFFIELD,
S1 2HH
www.sheffield.gov.uk
☎ 0114 272 6444

INDEX TO STREET NAMES

Allen Street	A2	Fawcett Street	A2	Snow Lane	A2
Angel Street	A3	Filey Street	B1	Solly Street	A1
Arundel Gate	B2	Fitzwilliam Street	B1	South Lane	C2
Arundel Lane	C3	Flat Street	A3	Spring Street	A2
Arundel Street	C2	Furnace Hill	C2	Suffolk Road	C3
Bailey Lane	A2	Furnival Gate	B2	Sunny Bank	C1
Bailey Street	B2	Furnival Square	B2	Surrey Street	B2
Bank Street	A3	Furnival Street	B2	Tenter Street	A2
Barker's Pool	B2	Garden Street	A1	The Moor	C2
Beet Street	A1	Gell Street	B1	Thomas Street	C1
Bellefield Street	A1	Gibraltar Street	A2	Townhead Street	A2
Bishop Street	C2	Glossop Road	B1	Trafalgar Street	B1
Blonk Street	A3	Hanover Square	C1	Trippet Lane	B2
Boston Street	C2	Hanover Street	C1	Upper Allen Street	A1
Bower Street	A2	Hanover Way	C1	Upper Hanover Street	B1
Bramwell Street	A1	Harmer Lane	B3	Victoria Street	B1
Bridge Street	A3	Haymarket	A3	Waingate	A3
Broad Lane	B1	Headford Street	C1	Wellington Street	B2
Broad Street	A3	High Street	A3	West Bar	A2
Broomhall Street	C1	Hodgson Street	C1	West Street	B2
Broomhall Place	C1	Hollis Croft	A2	Westbar Green	A2
Broomspring Lane	B1	Howard Street	B2	Weston Street	A1
Brown Street	C3	Hoyle Street	A1	William Street	C1
Brunswick Street	B1	Leadmill Road	B3	Young Street	C2
Campo Lane	A2	Leopold Street	B2		
Carver Street	B2	Mappin Street	B1		
Castle Square	A3	Margaret Street	C2		
Castle Street	A3	Mary Street	C2		
Castlegate	A3	Matilda Street	C2		
Cavendish Street	B1	Meadow Street	A1		
Cemetery Road	C1	Milton Street	C1		
Charles Street	B2/B3	Moore Street	C1		
Charlotte Road	C2	Napier Street	C1		
Charter Row	C2	Netherthorpe Road	A1		
Charter Square	B2	Norfolk Street	B3		
Church Street	A2	Nursery Street	A3		
Clarke Street	B1	Pinstone Street	B2		
Commercial Street	A3	Pond Hill	B3		
Copper Street	A2	Pond Hill	B3		
Corporation Street	A2	Portobello Street	B1		
Devonshire Street	B1	Queen Street	A2		
Division Street	B2	Queens Road	C3		
Dover Street	A1	Rockingham Street	B2		
Duchess Road	C3	St. Mary's Gate	C2		
Earl Street	C2	St. Mary's Road	C2		
Earl Way	A3	St. Philip's Road	A1		
East Parade	A3	Scotland Street	A2		
Ecclesall Road	C1	Sheaf Gardens	C3		
Edmund Road	C3	Sheaf Square	B3		
Edward Street	A1	Sheaf Street	B3		
Eldon Street	B2	Shepherd Street	A2		
Exchange Street	A3	Shoreham Street	C3		
Exeter Drive	C1	Shrewsbury Road	C3		
Eyre Lane	B3	Sidney Street	C2		
Eyre Street	C2	Snig Hill	A3		
Farm Road	C3				

Sheffield S.Yorks.
Population: 439,866.

City, on River Don, 144m/232km NW of London. Former centre of heavy steel industry, now largely precision steel and cutlery industries. University of Sheffield and Sheffield Hallam University. Various museums dedicated to Sheffield's industrial past. Meadowhall shopping centre and Sheffield City Airport, 3m/5km NE of city centre.

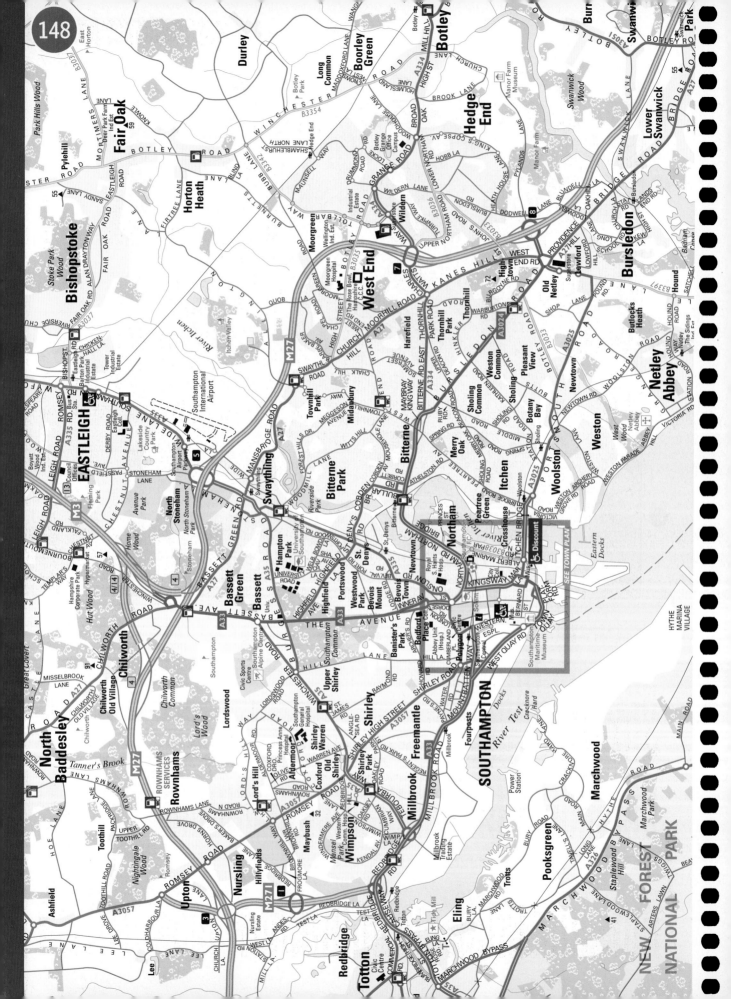

A · B · C
1 · 2 · 3

VISITOR INFORMATION

9 CIVIC CENTRE ROAD,
SOUTHAMPTON,
SO14 7FJ

☎ 023 8083 3333

HOSPITAL

SOUTHAMPTON GENERAL
HOSPITAL,
TREMONA ROAD,
SHIRLEY,
SOUTHAMPTON,
SO16 6YD

☎ 023 8077 7222

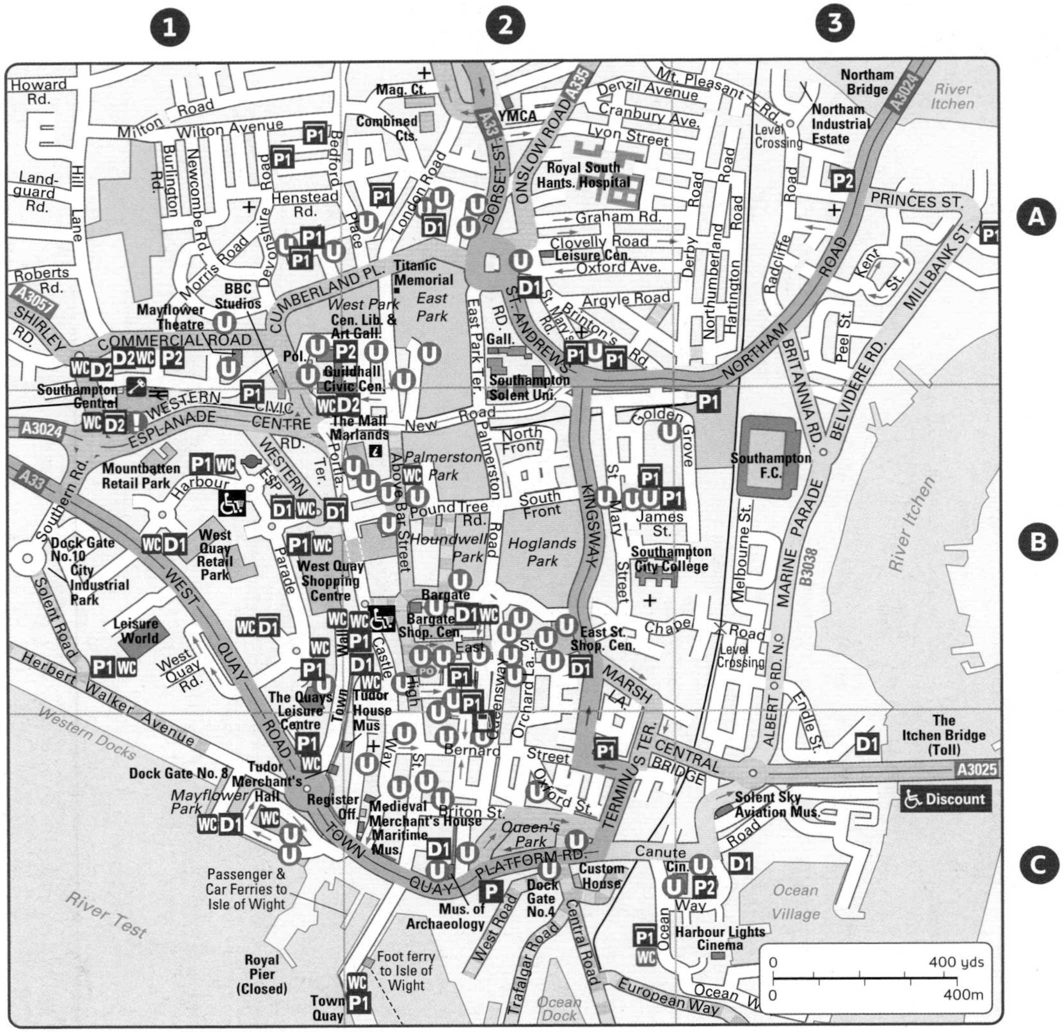

ADMINISTRATION

SOUTHAMPTON CITY
COUNCIL,
CIVIC CENTRE,
CIVIC CENTRE ROAD,
SOUTHAMPTON, SO14 7LY

www.southampton.gov.uk
☎ 023 8022 3855

INDEX TO STREET NAMES

Southampton *Soton City*
Population: 234,224.

City, at confluence of Rivers Itchen and Test at head of Southampton Water, 70m/113km SW of London. Southern centre for business, culture and recreation. Container and transatlantic passenger port, dealing with 7 percent of UK's seaborne trade. Site of many famous departures: Henry V's army bound for Agincourt; the Pilgrim Fathers sailed to America on the Mayflower in 1620; maiden voyage of Queen Mary and the fateful voyage of Titanic. Jane Austen lived here 1806-1809. Remains of medieval town walls. Medieval Merchant's House (English Heritage) has authentically recreated furnishings. Car and foot (Hi Speed) ferries to Isle of Wight. Host to many international boating events including The Southampton Boat Show. Universities. Southampton International Airport 1m/2km S of Eastleigh.

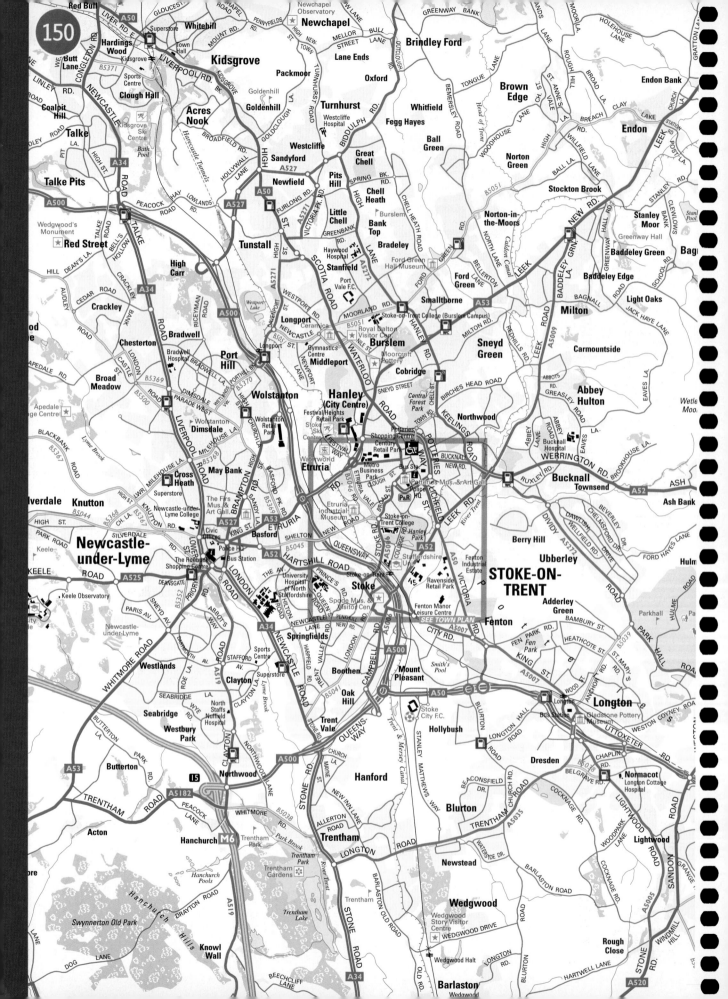

INDEX TO STREET NAMES

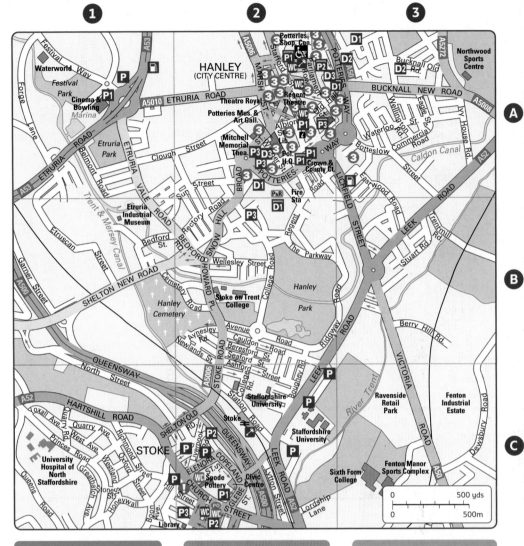

ADMINISTRATION

STOKE-ON-TRENT
 CITY COUNCIL,
TOWN HALL,
CIVIC CENTRE, GLEBE STREET,
STOKE-ON-TRENT, ST4 1RN

www.stoke.gov.uk
☎ 01782 234567

HOSPITAL

UNIVERSITY HOSPITAL OF
 NORTH STAFFORDSHIRE,
PRINCE'S ROAD,
STOKE-ON-TRENT,
ST4 7LN

☎ 01782 715444

VISITOR INFORMATION

VICTORIA HALL,
BAGNALL STREET,
HANLEY,
STOKE-ON-TRENT,
ST1 3AD

☎ 01782 236000

Stoke-on-Trent *Stoke*
Population: 259,252.

City, on River Trent, 135m/217km NW of London. Centre for employment, shopping and leisure. Created by an amalgamation of six towns in 1910: former Stoke-upon-Trent (now Stoke), Burslem, Fenton, Hanley (the city centre), Longton and Tunstall. They are collectively known as 'The Potteries' and were once the largest claywear producer in the world. Wedgwood and Spode offer pottery factory tours. Potteries Museum in Hanley charts history of the potteries. Gladstone Pottery Museum in Longton is centred around large bottle-kiln and demonstrates traditional skills of pottery production. Staffordshire University.

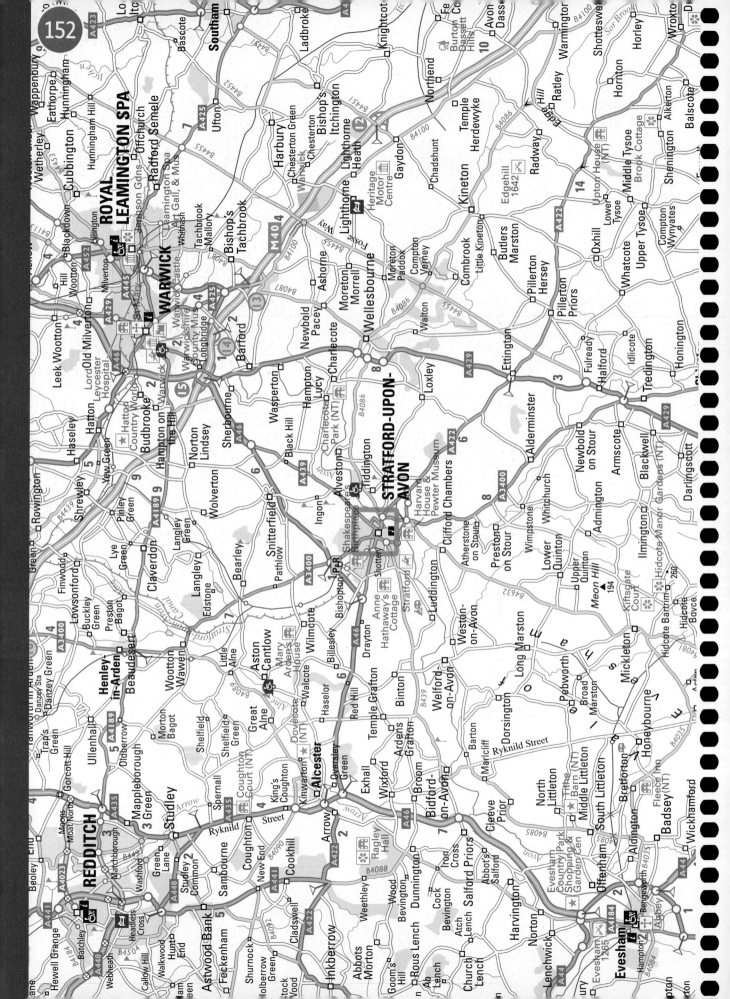

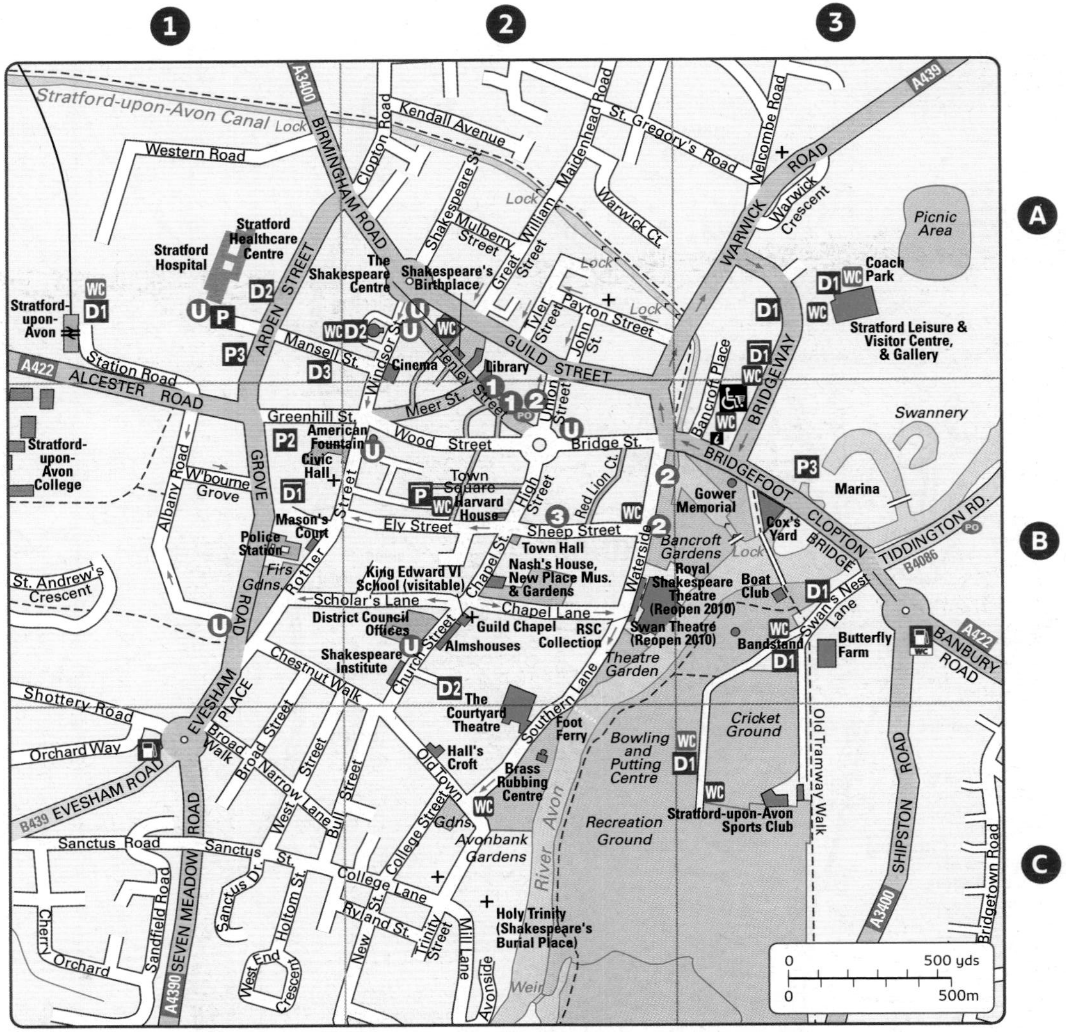

Stratford-upon-Avon (Also called Stratford-on-Avon.) *Works.*
Population: 22,187.

Town, on River Avon, 8m/13km SW of Warwick. Tourist centre. Many attractive 16c buildings. Reconstructed Shakespeare's Birthplace. Elizabethan garden at New Place. Hall's Croft Elizabethan town house and doctor's dispensary. Royal Shakespeare Theatre. Shakespeare's grave at Holy Trinity Church. Anne Hathaway's Cottage to W, at Shottery.

VISITOR INFORMATION

BRIDGEFOOT,
STRATFORD-UPON-AVON,
CV37 6GW

☎ 0870 160 7930

HOSPITAL

WARWICK HOSPITAL,
LAKIN ROAD,
WARWICK,
CV34 5BW

☎ 01926 495321

ADMINISTRATION

STRATFORD-ON-AVON
DISTRICT COUNCIL,
ELIZABETH HOUSE,
CHURCH STREET,
STRATFORD-UPON-AVON,
CV37 6HX
☎ 01789 267575
www.stratford.gov.uk

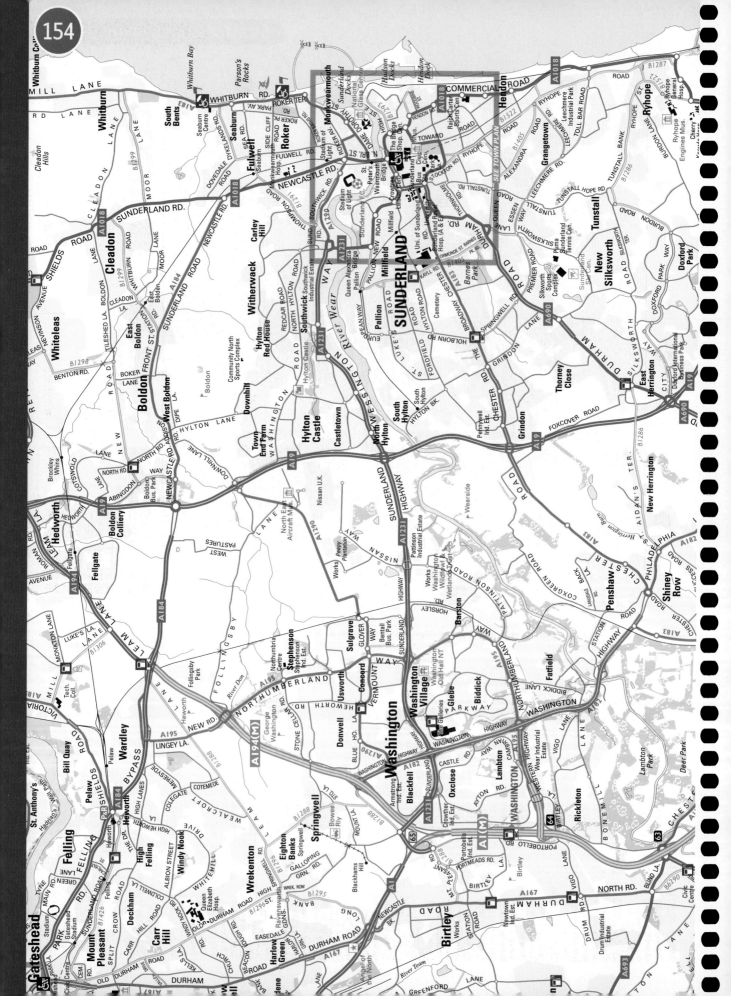

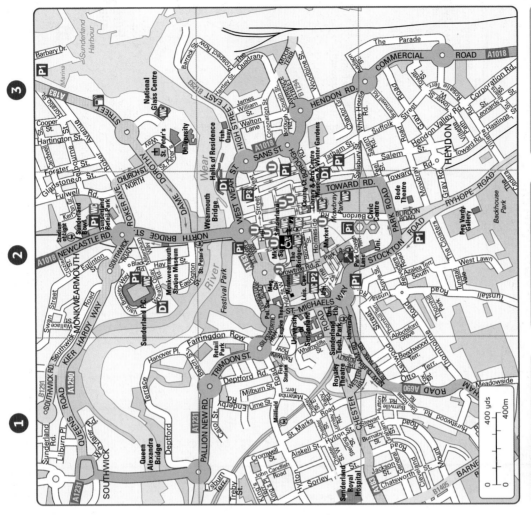

Sunderland *T. & W.*
Population 177,739.

Industrial city and seaport at mouth of River Wear, 11m/17km SE of Newcastle upon Tyne. Previously largest ship-building town in the world; coal mining was also important. Several museums celebrate city's industrial past. Service sector and manufacturing account for largest contribution to local economy. National Glass Centre commemorates importance of stained glass to area. University. Airport 4m/6km W.

VISITOR INFORMATION
50 FAWCETT STREET,
SUNDERLAND,
SR1 1RF
☎ 0191 553 2000

HOSPITAL
SUNDERLAND ROYAL
HOSPITAL,
KAYLL ROAD,
SUNDERLAND,
SR4 7TP
☎ 0191 565 6256

ADMINISTRATION
SUNDERLAND CITY COUNCIL,
CIVIC CENTRE,
BURDON ROAD,
SUNDERLAND,
SR2 7DN
www.sunderland.gov.uk
☎ 0191 520 5555

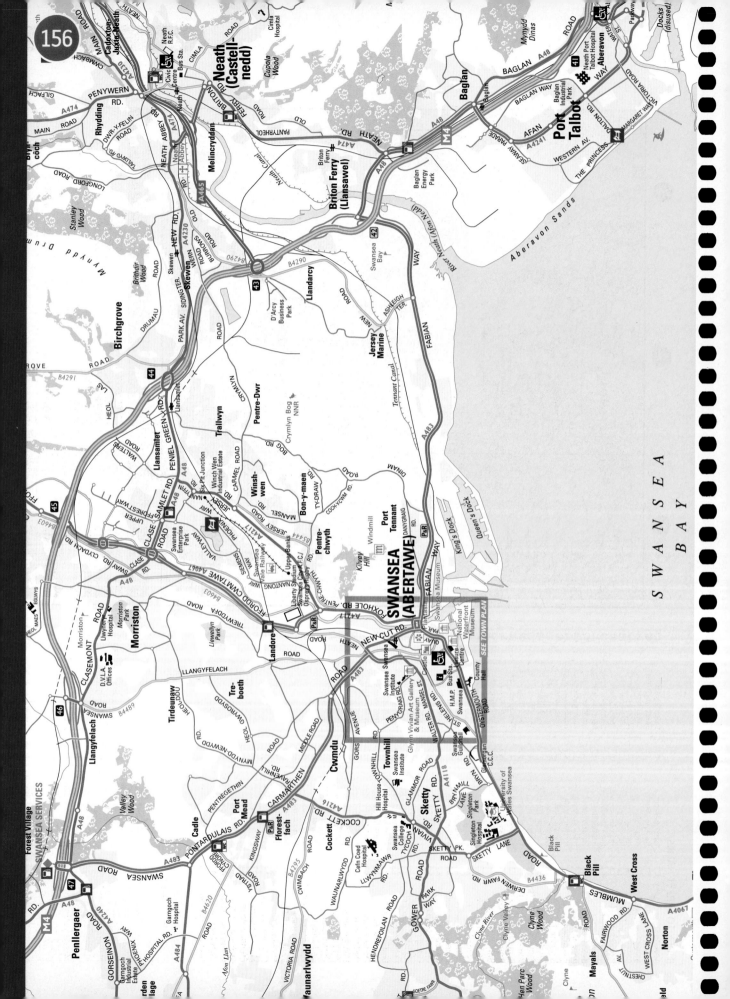

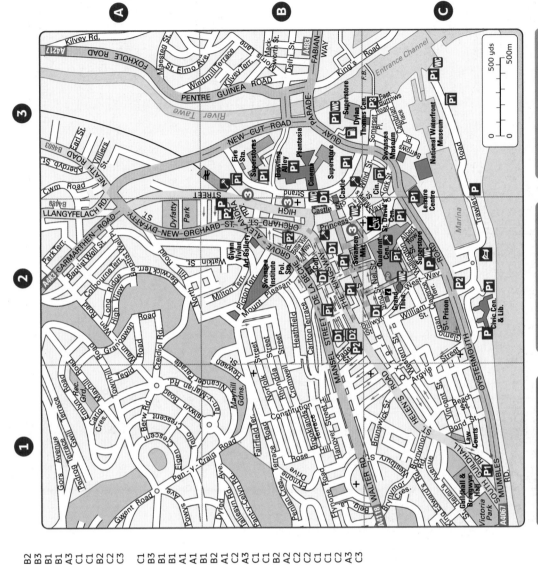

Swansea (Abertawe).
Population: 169,880.

City, port on Swansea Bay at mouth of River Tawe, and Wales' second city, 35m/57km W of Cardiff. Settlement developed next to Norman castle built in 1099, but claims made that a Viking settlement existed before this date. Previously a port for local metal smelting industries. Bombed in World War II, and city centre rebuilt. Birthplace of Dylan Thomas, who described it as 'an ugly, lovely town'. Remains of 14c castle (Cadw) or fortified manor house. University of Wales. Tropical plant and wildlife leisure centre, Plantasia. Airport 5m/9km W at Fairwood Common.

VISITOR INFORMATION

PLYMOUTH STREET,
SWANSEA,
SA1 3QG

☎ 01792 468321

HOSPITAL

MORRISTON HOSPITAL,
HEOL MAES EGLWYS,
MORRISTON,
SWANSEA,
SA6 6NL

☎ 01792 702222

ADMINISTRATION

CITY & COUNTY OF
SWANSEA,
COUNTY HALL,
OYSTERMOUTH ROAD,
SWANSEA, SA1 3SN

www.swansea.gov.uk
☎ 01792 636000

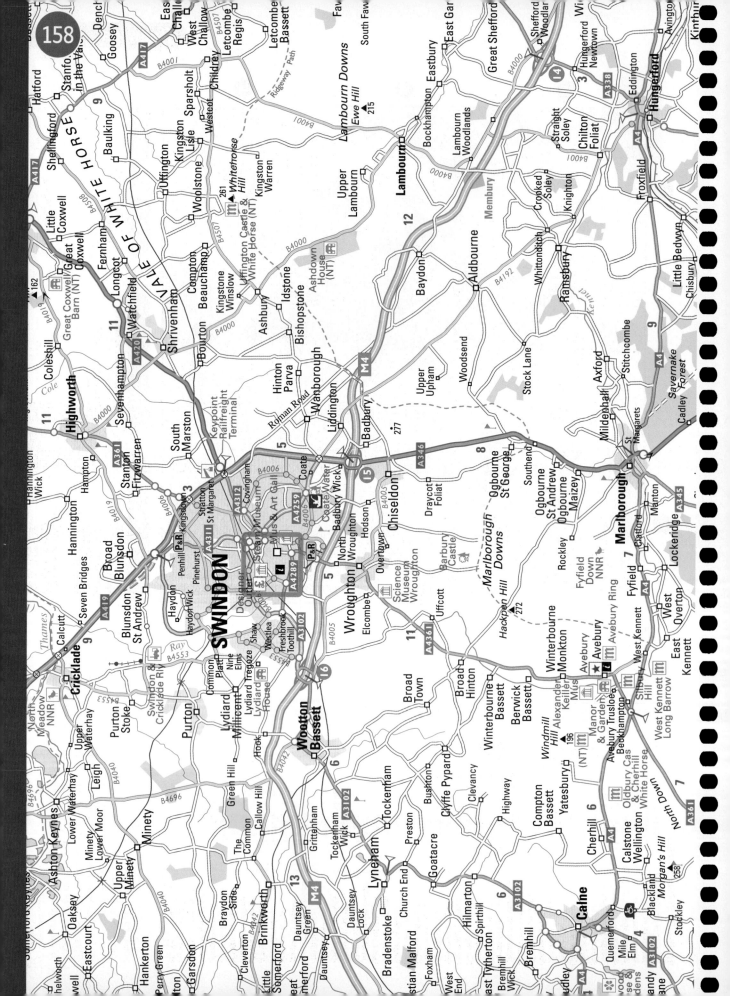

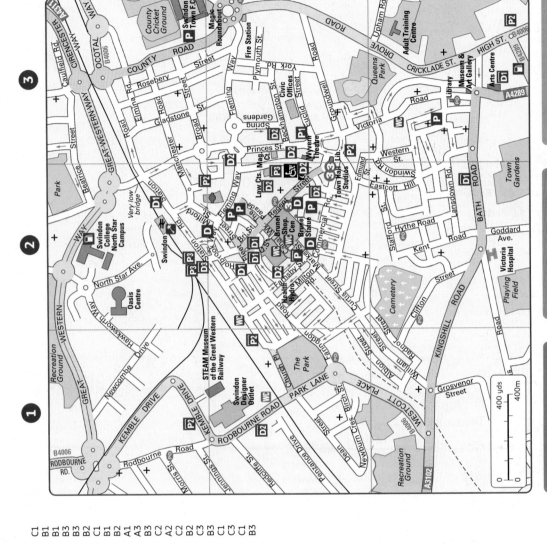

Swindon *Swin.*
Population: 155,432.

Town, industrial and commercial centre, 70m/113km W of London. Large, modern shopping centre. Town expanded considerably in 19c with arrival of the railway. The Steam Museum of the Great Western Railway exhibits Swindon built locomotives and documents the history of the railway works.

VISITOR INFORMATION

37 REGENT STREET, SWINDON, SN1 1JL

☎ 01793 530328

HOSPITAL

THE GREAT WESTERN HOSPITAL, MARLBOROUGH ROAD, SWINDON, SN3 6BB

☎ 01793 604020

ADMINISTRATION

SWINDON BOROUGH COUNCIL, CIVIC OFFICES, EUCLID STREET, SWINDON, SN1 2JH
www.swindon.gov.uk
☎ 01793 463000

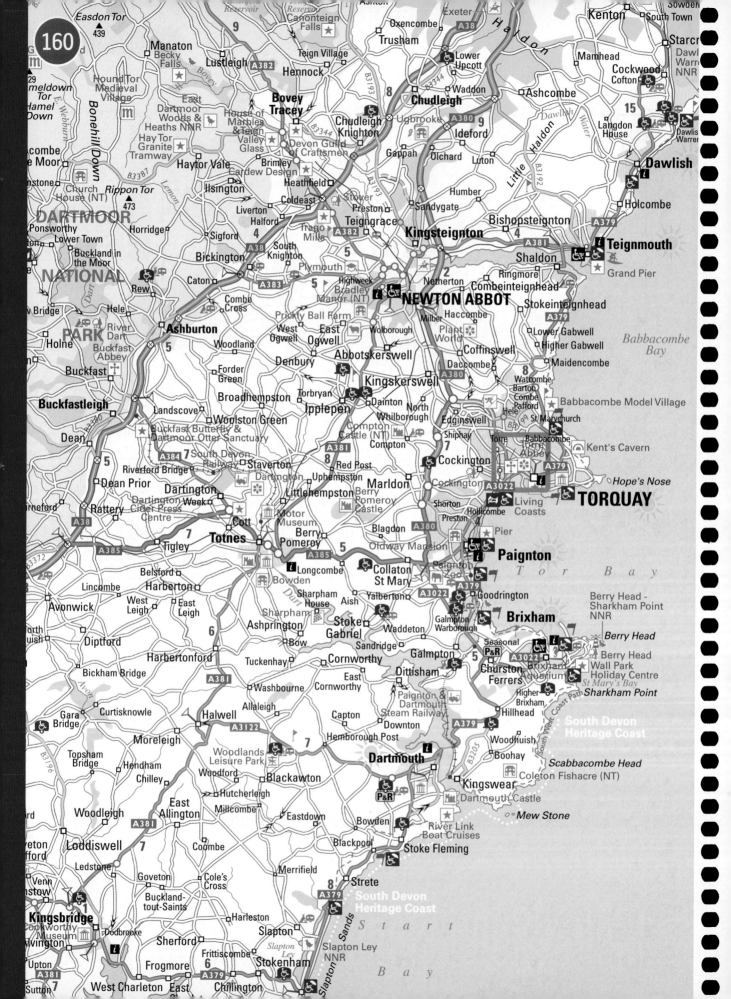

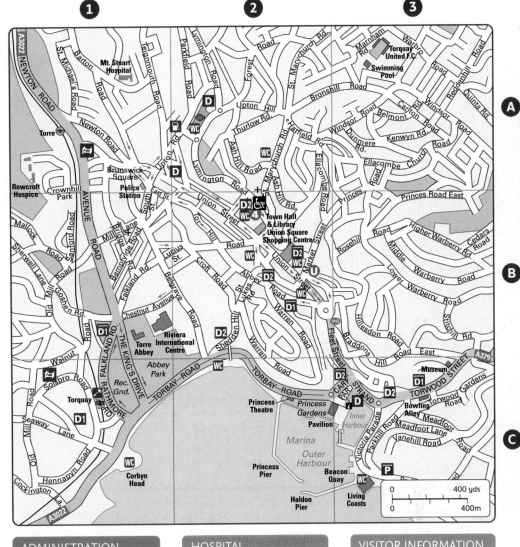

ADMINISTRATION

TORBAY COUNCIL,
TOWN HALL,
CASTLE CIRCUS,
TORQUAY,
TQ1 3DS

www.torbay.gov.uk
☎ 01803 201201

HOSPITAL

TORBAY DISTRICT GENERAL
 HOSPITAL,
NEWTON ROAD,
TORQUAY,
TQ2 7AA

☎ 01803 614567

VISITOR INFORMATION

VAUGHAN PARADE,
TORQUAY,
TQ2 5JG

☎ 0870 70 70 010

Torquay *Torbay*
Population: 62,968.

Town, 18m/30km S of Exeter. Chief town and resort of Torbay English Riviera district, with harbour and several beaches. Noted for mild climate. Torre Abbey with 15c gatehouse, is a converted monastery housing a collecion of furniture and glassware. Torquay Museum has display on crimewriter Agatha Christie who was born in Torquay. Kent's Cavern showcaves are an important prehistoric site. Babbacombe Model village 2m/3km N.

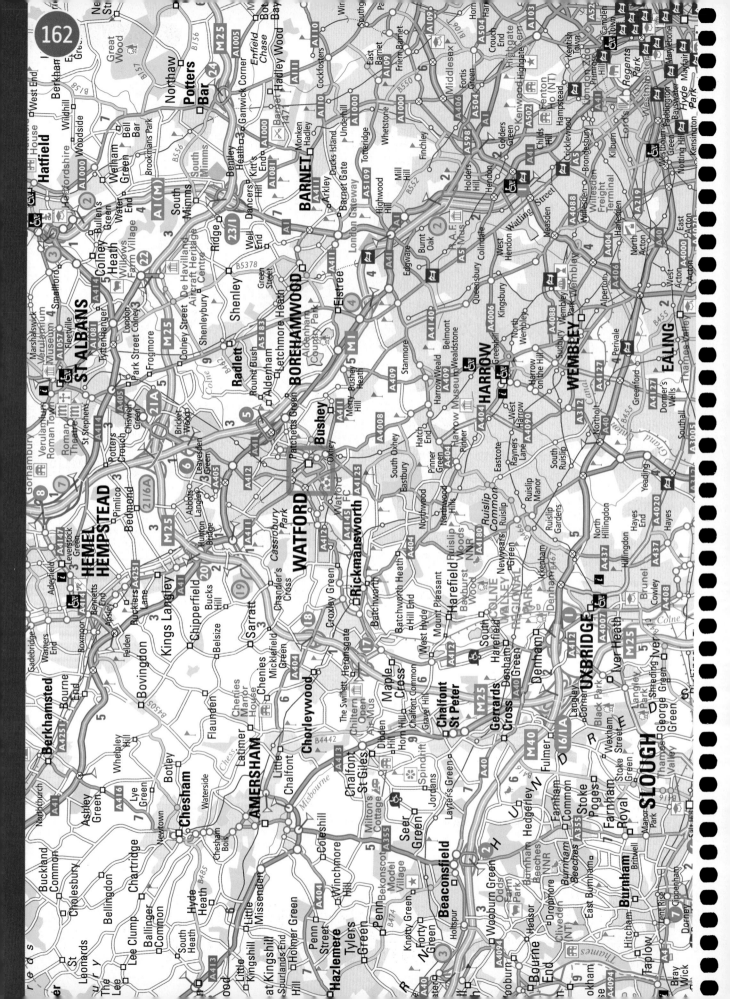

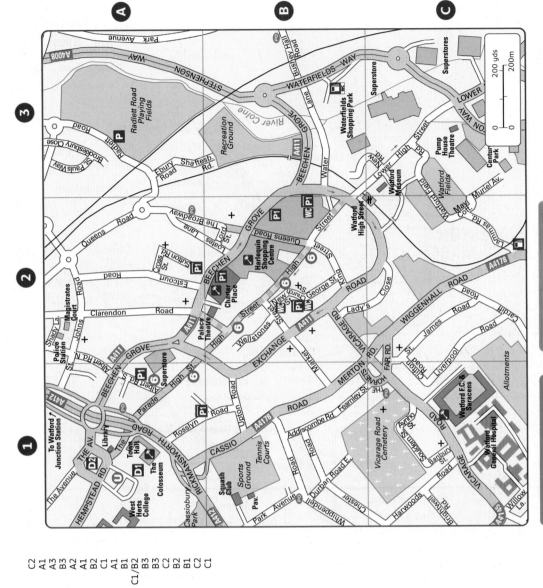

Watford *Herts.*
Population: 120,960.

Old market town on River Colne, 16m/26km NW of London. Printing and brewing developed as the main industries; now the industrial base is more diverse. Shopping and leisure centre with modern sculptures in redeveloped central area. Parish church of Saint Mary's has 16c chapel. Local history museum housed in Georgian house. Edwardian Palace Theatre originally opened as a music hall in 1908.

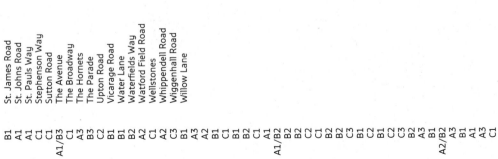

ADMINISTRATION

WATFORD BOROUGH
COUNCIL,
TOWN HALL,
WATFORD,
WD17 3EX

www.watford.gov.uk
☎ 01923 226400

HOSPITAL

WATFORD GENERAL
HOSPITAL,
VICARAGE ROAD,
WATFORD,
WD18 0HB

☎ 01923 244366

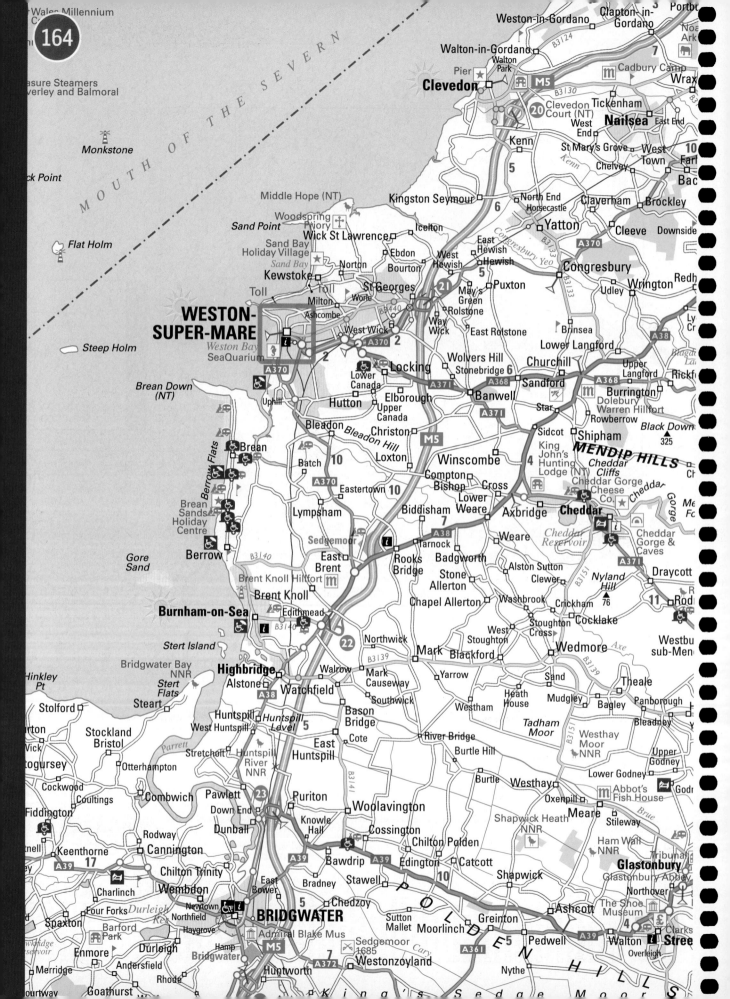

INDEX TO STREET NAMES

ADMINISTRATION

NORTH SOMERSET COUNCIL,
TOWN HALL,
WALLISCOTE GROVE ROAD,
WESTON-SUPER-MARE,
BS23 1UJ

www.n-somerset.gov.uk
☎ 01934 888888

HOSPITAL

WESTON GENERAL HOSPITAL,
GRANGE ROAD,
UPHILL,
WESTON-SUPER-MARE,
BS23 4TQ

☎ 01934 636363

VISITOR INFORMATION

BEACH LAWNS,
WESTON-SUPER-MARE,
BS23 1AT

☎ 01934 888800

Weston-super-Mare *N.Som.*
Population: 78,044.

Town and popular resort on the Bristol Channel, 18m/28km SW of Bristol, situated on Weston Bay and first developed in the 19c. Over 1m/2km of sands with traditional beach donkeys; promenade, marine lake, miniature steam railway and Winter Gardens. Amusement park located on the central Grand Pier, built in 1904. The Aquarium houses ocean and coastal waters display tanks. Local history and heritage museums give an insight into the town as a Victorian seaside resort. Annual motorbike beach race, Enduro, is held in October. International Helicopter Museum at Locking 2m/3km E.

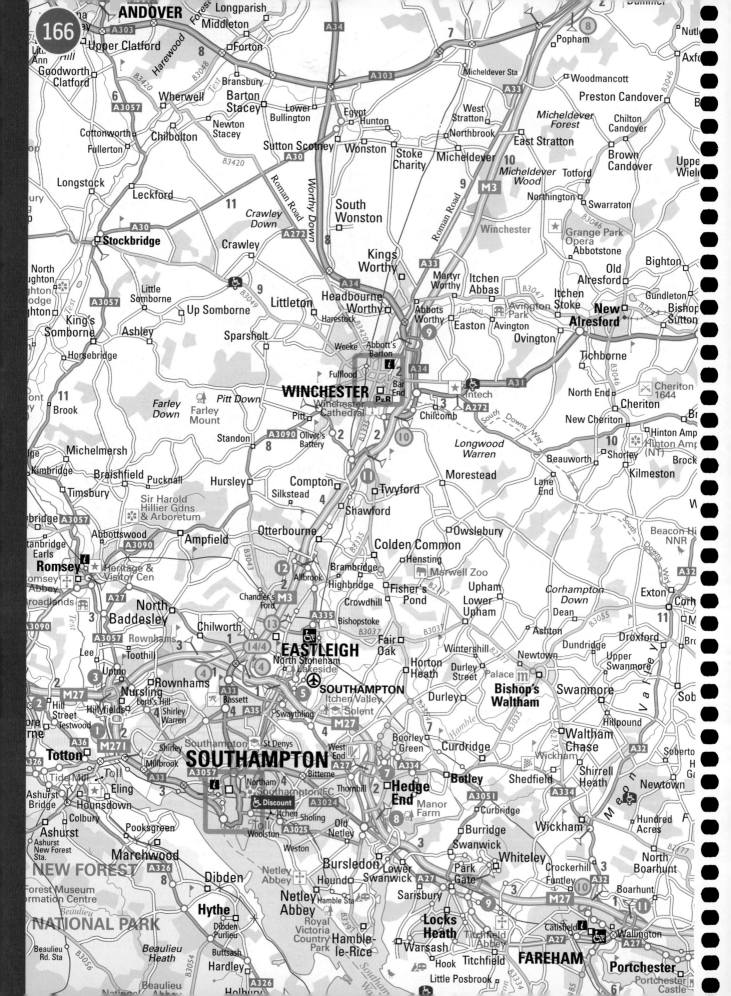

INDEX TO STREET NAMES

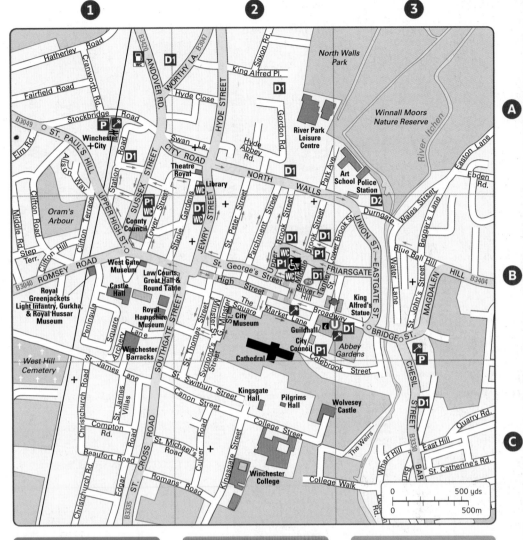

ADMINISTRATION

WINCHESTER CITY COUNCIL,
CITY OFFICES,
COLEBROOK STREET,
WINCHESTER,
SO23 9LJ

www.winchester.gov.uk
☎ 01962 840222

HOSPITAL

ROYAL HAMPSHIRE COUNTY
 HOSPITAL,
ROMSEY ROAD,
WINCHESTER,
SO22 5DG

☎ 01962 863535

VISITOR INFORMATION

GUILDHALL,
HIGH STREET,
WINCHESTER,
HAMPSHIRE,
SO23 9GH

☎ 01962 840500

Winchester *Hants.*
Population: 41,420.

Cathedral city and county town on River Itchen on site of Roman town of Venta Belgarum, 12m/19km N of Southampton. Ancient capital of Wessex and of Anglo-Saxon England. 11c cathedral, longest in Europe with carved Norman font and England's oldest complete choir-stalls. Winchester College, boys' public school founded 1382. 13c Great Hall is only remaining part of Winchester Castle. Westgate Museum is in 12c gatehouse in medieval city wall, once a debtors' prison. 12c hospital of St. Cross. City Mill (National Trust), built over river in 18c. To S across river, St. Catherine's Hill, Iron Age fort. Extensive ruins of medieval Wolvesey Castle, also known as Old Bishop's Palace (English Heritage).

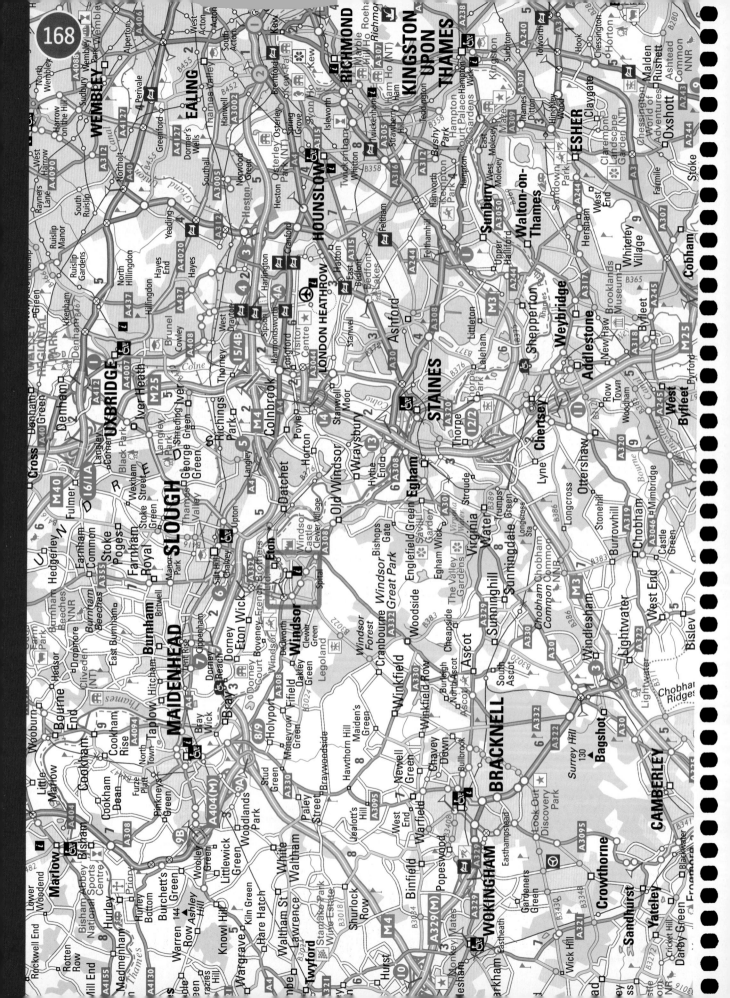

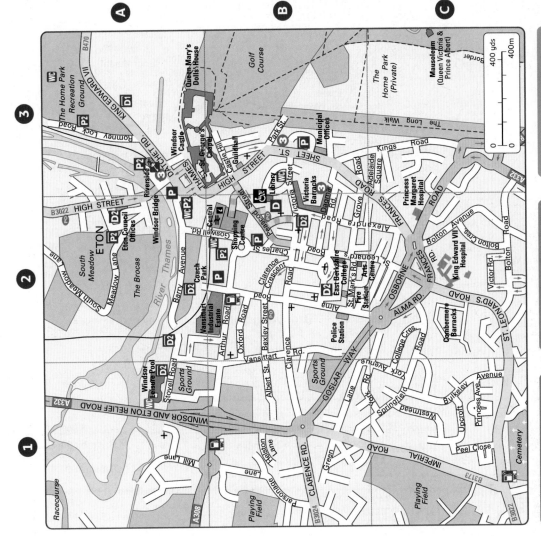

Windsor W. & M.
Population: 26,747.

Attractive market town on S bank of River Thames, 2m/3km S of Slough and 21m/34km W of London. Castle is royal residence. Great Park to S of town is open to public; Home Park bordering river is private. St. George's Chapel is impressive. Many Georgian houses, and guildhall designed by Sir Christopher Wren.

VISITOR INFORMATION
OLD BOOKING HALL, CENTRAL STATION, WINDSOR, SL4 1PJ
☎ 01753 743900

HOSPITAL
WEXHAM PARK HOSPITAL, WEXHAM STREET, SLOUGH, SL2 4HL
☎ 01753 633000

ADMINISTRATION
ROYAL BOROUGH OF WINDSOR & MAIDENHEAD, COUNCIL OFFICES, YORK HOUSE, SHEET STREET, WINDSOR, SL4 1DD
www.rbwm.gov.uk
☎ 01753 810525

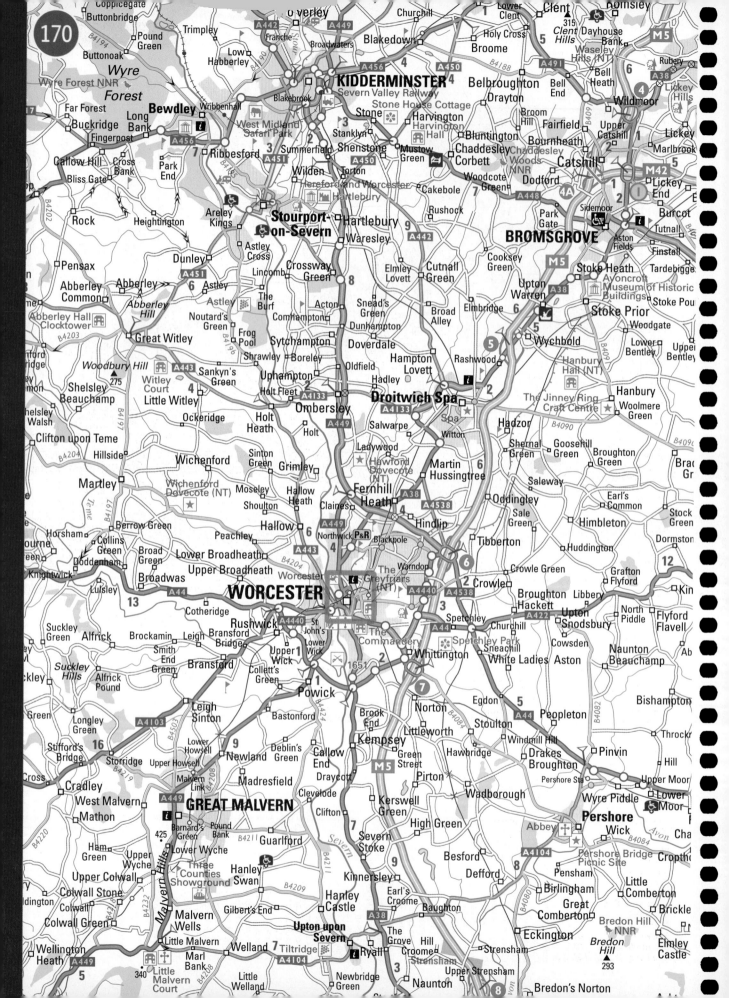

INDEX TO STREET NAMES

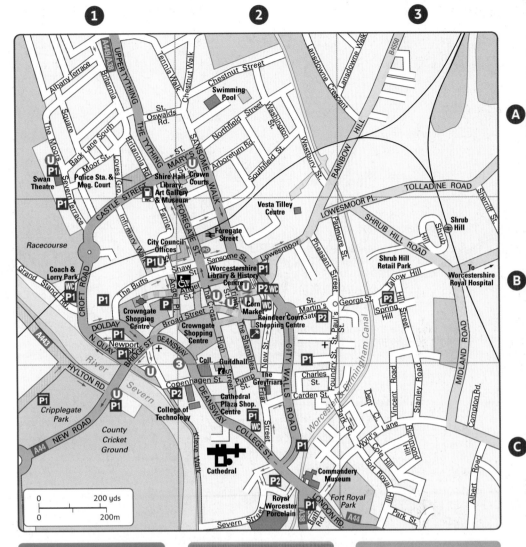

ADMINISTRATION

WORCESTER CITY COUNCIL,
ORCHARD HOUSE,
FARRIER STREET,
WORCESTER,
WR1 3BB

www.cityofworcester.gov.uk
☎ 01905 722233

HOSPITAL

WORCESTERSHIRE ROYAL
 HOSPITAL,
CHARLES HASTINGS WAY,
NEWTOWN ROAD,
WR5 1DD

☎ 01905 763333

VISITOR INFORMATION

THE GUILDHALL,
HIGH STREET,
WORCESTER,
WR1 2EY

☎ 01905 726311

Worcester *Worcs.*
Population: 94,029.

Cathedral city and county town on River Severn, 24m/38km SW of Birmingham. Shopping, cultural, sports and industrial centre; industries include porcelain and sauces and condiments. 18c Guildhall. Cathedral mainly Early English includes England's largest Norman crypt, 13c choir and Lady Chapel and tomb of King John. Three Choirs Festival held here every third year. Civil War Centre at the Commandery, headquarters for Charles II during Battle of Worcester. Factory tours and museum at Royal Worcester Porcelain. Elgar's Birthplace, home of composer Sir Edward Elgar, in Broadheath, 3m/5km W.

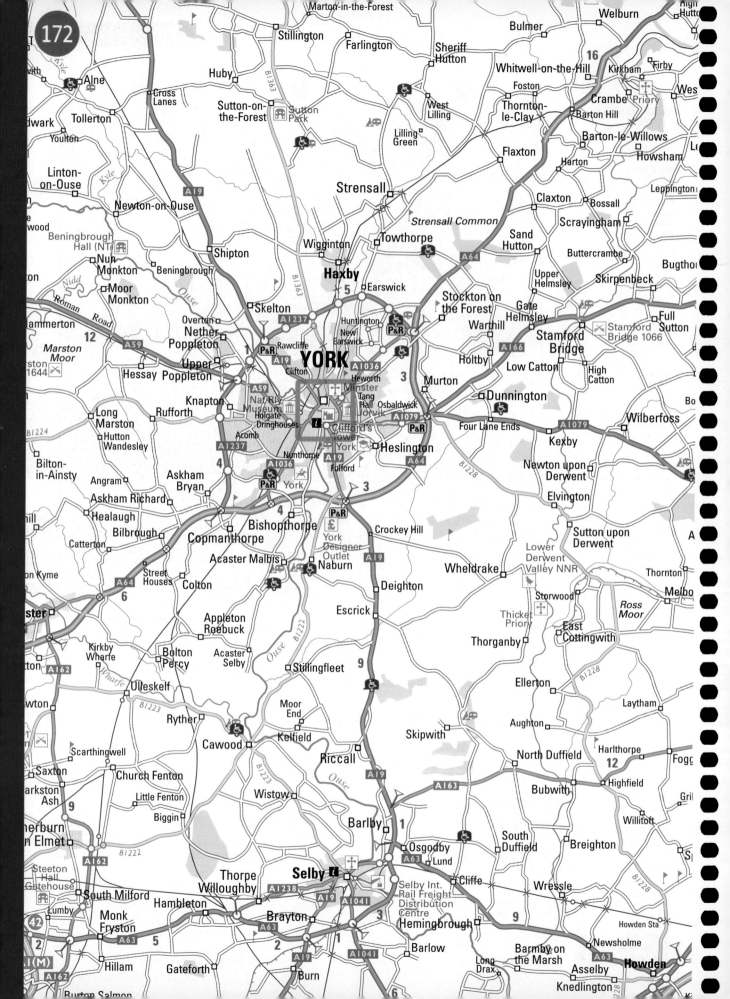

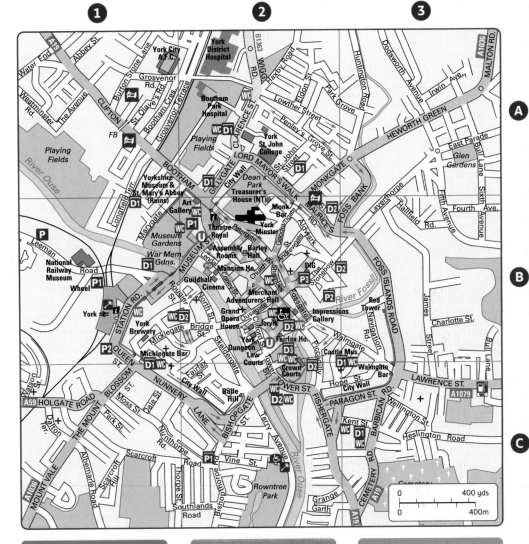

ADMINISTRATION

CITY OF YORK COUNCIL,
THE GUILDHALL,
YORK,
YO1 9QN

www.york.gov.uk
☎ 01904 551550

HOSPITAL

YORK HOSPITAL,
WIGGINTON ROAD,
YORK,
YO31 8HE

☎ 01904 631313

VISITOR INFORMATION

DE GREY ROOMS,
EXHIBITION SQUARE,
YORK,
YO1 2HB

☎ 01904 550099

York

Population: 137,505.

Ancient city and archiepiscopal see on River Ouse, 22m/36km NE of Leeds. On site of Roman Eboracum. Constantine the Great proclaimed Roman Emperor in York in AD 306; only emperor to be enthroned in Britain. City fell to Danes in AD 867 and became known as Jorvik. Medieval wall largely intact, other fortifications including Clifford's Tower (English Heritage). York Minster's medieval stained glass window was damaged by fire in 1984 and took four years to repair. Previously a wool trading, craft and railway centre. Home to National Railway Museum. Jorvik Viking Centre in Coppergate. Merchant Adventurers' Hall in Fossgate is finest remaining guildhall in Europe. University of York at Heslington. Racecourse at Knavesmire.

Abbreviations

All	Alley	Co	County	Exhib	Exhibition	Int	International	Pl	Place	TA	Territorial Army
Allot	Allotments	Coll	College	FB	Footbridge	Junct	Junction	Pol	Police	TH	Town Hall
Amb	Ambulance	Comm	Community	FC	Football Club	La	Lane	Prec	Precinct	Tenn	Tennis
App	Approach	Conv	Convent	Fld	Field	Las	Lanes	Prim	Primary	Ter	Terrace
Apts	Apartments	Cor	Corner	Flds	Fields	Lib	Library	Prom	Promenade	Thea	Theatre
Arc	Arcade	Coron	Coroners	Fm	Farm	Lo	Lodge	Pt	Point	Trd	Trading
Av	Avenue	Cors	Corners	Gall	Gallery	Lwr	Lower	Quad	Quadrant	Twr	Tower
Bdy	Broadway	Cotts	Cottages	Gar	Garage	Mag	Magistrates	RC	Roman Catholic	Twrs	Towers
Bk	Bank	Cov	Covered	Gdn	Garden	Mans	Mansions	Rd	Road	Uni	University
Bldgs	Buildings	Crem	Crematorium	Gdns	Gardens	Mem	Memorial	Rds	Roads	Vil	Villas
Boul	Boulevard	Cres	Crescent	Govt	Government	Mkt	Market	Rec	Recreation	Vil	Villa
Bowl	Bowling	Ct	Court	Gra	Grange	Mkts	Markets	Res	Reservoir	Vw	View
Br	Bridge	Cts	Courts	Grd	Ground	Ms	Mews	Ri	Rise	W	West
C of E	Church of England	Ctyd	Courtyard	Grds	Grounds	Mt	Mount	S	South	Wd	Wood
Cath	Cathedral	Dep	Depot	Grn	Green	Mus	Museum	Sch	School	Wds	Woods
Cem	Cemetery	Dev	Development	Grns	Greens	N	North	Sec	Secondary	Wf	Wharf
Cen	Central, Centre	Dr	Drive	Gro	Grove	NT	National Trust	Shop	Shopping	Wk	Walk
Cft	Croft	Dws	Dwellings	Gros	Groves	Nat	National	Sq	Square	Wks	Works
Cfts	Crofts	E	East	Gt	Great	PH	Public House	St.	Saint	Yd	Yard
Ch	Church	Ed	Education	Ho	House	PO	Post Office	St	Street		
Chyd	Churchyard	Elec	Electricity	Hos	Houses	Par	Parade	Sta	Station		
Cin	Cinema	Embk	Embankment	Hosp	Hospital	Pas	Passage	Sts	Streets		
Circ	Circus	Est	Estate	Hts	Heights	Pav	Pavilion	Sub	Subway		
Cl	Close	Ex	Exchange	Ind	Industrial	Pk	Park	Swim	Swimming		

Administrative area abbreviations

Aber.	Aberdeenshire	*Flints.*	Flintshire	*N.Yorks.*	North Yorkshire	*Som.*	Somerset
Arg. & B.	Argyll & Bute	*Glos.*	Gloucestershire	*Norf.*	Norfolk	*Staffs.*	Staffordshire
B'burn.	Blackburn with Darwen	*Gt.Lon.*	Greater London	*Northants.*	Northamptonshire	*Stir.*	Stirling
Beds.	Bedfordshire	*Gt.Man.*	Greater Manchester	*Northumb.*	Northumberland	*Suff.*	Suffolk
Bucks.	Buckinghamshire	*Hants.*	Hampshire	*Notts.*	Nottinghamshire	*Surr.*	Surrey
Cambs.	Cambridgeshire	*Here.*	Herefordshire	*Ork.*	Orkney	*T. & W.*	Tyne & Wear
C. & W.Ches.	Chester & West Cheshire	*Herts.*	Hertfordshire	*Oxon.*	Oxfordshire	*Tel. & W.*	Telford & Wrekin
		High.	Highland	*P. & K.*	Perth & Kinross	*V. of Glam.*	Vale of Glamorgan
Ches.E.	Cheshire East	*I.o.M.*	Isle of Man	*Pembs.*	Pembrokeshire	*W'ham*	Wokingham
Cornw.	Cornwall	*I.o.W.*	Isle of Wight	*Peter.*	Peterborough	*W.Isles*	Western Isles
Cumb.	Cumbria	*Lancs.*	Lancashire	*R.C.T.*	Rhondda Cynon Taff		(Na h-Eileanan an Iar)
D. & G.	Dumfries & Galloway	*Leics.*	Leicestershire	*S.Ayr.*	South Ayrshire	*W.Loth.*	West Lothian
Derbys.	Derbyshire	*Lincs.*	Lincolnshire	*S.Glos.*	South Gloucestershire	*W.Suss.*	West Sussex
Dur.	Durham	*Med.*	Medway	*S.Lan.*	South Lanarkshire	*W.Yorks.*	West Yorkshire
E.Ayr.	East Ayrshire	*Mersey.*	Merseyside	*S.Yorks.*	South Yorkshire	*Wilts.*	Wiltshire
E.Loth.	East Lothian	*Mon.*	Monmouthshire	*Sc.Bord.*	Scottish Borders	*Worcs.*	Worcestershire
E.Riding	East Riding of Yorkshire	*N.Lan.*	North Lanarkshire	*Shet.*	Shetland	*Wrex.*	Wrexham
Edin.	Edinburgh	*N.Lincs.*	North Lincolnshire	*Shrop.*	Shropshire		

A

Abbeytown **27** G3
Abbots Bromley **18** C3
Abbotsbury **6** B5
Aberaeron **10** D1
Aberaman **11** G4
Aberavon **11** F5
Abercanaid **11** G4
Aberchirder **41** E3
Abercynon **11** G5
Aberdare **11** G4
Aberdaron **16** A4
Aberdeen **41** G5
Aberdeen Airport **41** F5
Aberdour **32** C1
Aberdyfi **16** C6
Aberfeldy **36** B2
Aberffraw **16** B2
Aberfoyle **31** H1
Abergavenny
 (Y Fenni) **12** A4
Abergele **22** A6
Abergynolwyn **16** C5
Aberkenfig **11** F5
Aberlady **32** D1
Aberlemno **37** F2
Aberlour **40** C3
Abernethy **36** D4
Aberporth **10** C2
Abersoch **16** B4
Abersychan **11** H4
Abertillery **11** H4
Aberuthven **36** C4
Aberystwyth **16** C6
Abhainnsuidhe **44** C4
Abingdon **13** F5
Abington **32** B4
Aboyne **41** E6
Abram **22** D4
Accrington **23** E3
Achadh Mòr **44** E3
Achahoish **30** D3
Acharacle **34** D1
Achavanich **43** G3
Achfary **42** B3
Achiltibuie **42** A5
Achintee **39** E3
Achnacroish **35** E2
Achnasheen **39** F3
Achosnich **34** C1
Achriesgill **42** B3
Ackworth Moor Top **24** B4
Acle **21** G4
Acomb **28** C2
Adderbury **13** F3
Addingham **23** F2
Addlestone **14** A6

Adlington **22** D4
Adwick le Street **24** C4
Ainsdale **22** C4
Aintree **22** C5
Aird Asaig **44** D4
Aird of Sleat **38** C5
Airdrie **32** A2
Airidh a'Bhruaich **44** D4
Airth **32** A1
Airton **23** E2
Aith *Ork.* **45** D2
Aith *Shet.* **45** H4
Akeld **33** G4
Albrighton **18** B4
Alcester **12** D2
Aldbourne **13** E6
Aldbrough **25** F3
Aldeburgh **15** H2
Aldenham **14** B5
Alderbury **7** E3
Alderholt **7** E4
Alderley Edge **23** E6
Alderney Airport **5** H5
Aldershot **7** H2
Aldingham **22** B1
Aldington **9** F4
Aldridge **18** C4
Alexandria **31** G3
Alford *Aber.* **41** E5
Alford *Lincs.* **25** G6
Alfreton **19** E2
Allanton **32** A3
Allendale Town **28** B3
Allenheads **28** B3
Allhallows **15** E6
Allnabad **42** C3
Alloa **32** A1
Allonby **27** F3
Alloway **31** G6
Almondsbury **12** B5
Alness **39** H2
Alnmouth **33** H5
Alnwick **33** H5
Alresford **15** F3
Alrewas **18** D4
Alsager **18** B2
Alston **28** B3
Altnafeadh **35** G2
Altnaharra **42** D4
Alton *Hants.* **7** H3
Alton *Staffs.* **18** C2
Altrincham **23** E5
Alva **32** A1
Alvechurch **12** D1
Alveley **18** B5
Alves **40** C2
Alveston **12** B5

Alvie **40** A5
Alyth **36** D2
Ambergate **19** E2
Amble **33** H5
Amblecote **18** B5
Ambleside **27** H5
Ambrosden **13** G4
Amersham **14** A5
Amesbury **7** E2
Amlwch **16** B1
Ammanford **11** E4
Ampthill **14** A3
Amulree **36** B3
Ancaster **19** H2
Ancroft **33** G3
Ancrum **33** E4
Andover **7** F2
Andreas **26** C5
Angle **10** A4
Angmering **8** A5
Anlaby **25** E3
Annan **27** G2
Annbank **31** G5
Annfield Plain **28** D3
Anstey **19** F4
Anstruther **37** F4
Aoradh **30** A3
Appleby Magna **19** E4
Appleby-in-Westmorland
 28 A4
Applecross **38** D3
Appledore *Devon* **4** C2
Appledore *Kent* **9** F4
Appleton Thorn **22** D5
Appley Bridge **22** D4
Arbirlot **37** F2
Arbroath **37** F2
Ardchiavaig **30** B1
Arden **31** G2
Ardentinny **31** F2
Ardeonaig **36** A3
Ardersier **40** A3
Ardfern **30** D1
Ardgay **39** H1
Ardleigh **15** F3
Ardlui **31** G1
Ardlussa **30** C2
Ardmair **39** F1
Ardminish **30** C4
Ardmolich **35** E1
Ardrishaig **30** D2
Ardrossan **31** F4
Ardtalnaig **36** A3
Ardtoe **34** D1
Ardvasar **38** C5
Arinagour **34** B2
Arisaig **38** C6

Alvie **40** A5
Armadale **32** B2
Armitage **18** C4
Armthorpe **24** C4
Arncliffe **23** F1
Arnisdale **38** D5
Arnol **44** E2
Arnold **19** F2
Arnprior **31** H2
Arrochar **31** G1
Arundel **8** A5
Ascot **14** A6
Asfordby **19** G4
Ash *Kent* **9** G3
Ash *Surr.* **7** H2
Ashbourne **18** D2
Ashburton **5** E5
Ashbury **13** E5
Ashby de la Zouch **19** E4
Ashchurch **12** D3
Ashcott **6** A3
Ashford *Kent* **9** F3
Ashford *Surr.* **14** A6
Ashington **28** D1
Ashkirk **32** D4
Ashley **14** D1
Ashton **22** D6
Ashton-in-Makerfield
 22 D5
Ashton-under-Lyne **23** F5
Ashurst *Hants.* **7** F4
Ashurst *Kent* **8** D4
Ashwick **6** B2
Askern **24** C4
Aspatria **27** G3
Aston Clinton **13** H4
Aston on Trent **19** E3
Astwood Bank **12** D1
Atherington **4** D2
Atherstone **19** E5
Atherton **22** D4
Attadale **39** E4
Attleborough **21** E5
Attlebridge **21** F4
Auchallater **40** C6
Auchenblae **37** G1
Auchenbreck **31** E2
Auchencairn **27** E3
Auchencrow **33** F2
Auchindrain **31** E1
Auchinleck **31** H5
Auchmull **37** F1
Auchnagatt **41** G3
Aucholzie **40** D6
Auchterarder **36** C4
Auchtermuchty **36** D4
Auchtertool **32** C1
Audlem **18** A2

Audley **18** B2
Aughton *Lancs.* **22** C4
Aughton *S.Yorks.* **24** B5
Auldearn **40** B3
Aultbea **38** D1
Aultguish Inn **39** G2
Aveley **14** D5
Aviemore **40** A5
Avoch **39** H3
Avonbridge **32** B2
Avonmouth **12** B6
Awre **12** C4
Awsworth **19** E2
Axminster **5** G4
Aycliffe **28** D4
Aylesbury **13** H4
Aylesford **9** E3
Aylesham **9** G3
Aylsham **21** F3
Ayr **31** G5
Aysgarth **28** C6
Aywick **45** J2

B

Babworth **24** C5
Backaland **45** D2
Backwell **12** A6
Bacup **23** E3
Badcaul **39** E1
Badenscoth **41** E4
Badintagairt **42** C5
Badlipster **43** G3
Badsey **12** D2
Bagillt **22** B6
Baglan **11** F5
Bagshot **14** A6
Baildon **24** A3
Baile Mhartainn **44** B6
Baile Mòr **34** B3
Bainbridge **28** C6
Bainton **25** E2
Bakewell **24** A6
Bala (Y Bala) **17** E4
Balallan **44** D3
Balbeggie **36** D3
Balblair **40** A2
Balcombe **8** C4
Balderton **19** G2
Baldock **14** B3
Baldslow **9** E5
Balemartine **34** A2
Balephuil **34** A2
Balfour **45** C3
Balfron **31** H2
Balgown **38** B2
Balintore **40** A2
Balivanich **44** B7

Administrative area abbreviations

Banbr. Banbridge

enjoyEngland.com™

National Accessible Scheme

Operators of accommodation taking part in the National Accessible Scheme (NAS) have gone out of their way to ensure a comfortable stay for guests with hearing, visual or mobility needs.

NAS means:
- Accommodation is independently assessed by trained assessors against demanding criteria.
- Facilities such as handrails, ramps, level-access showers and colour contrast.
- Members of staff will have completed disability training and will know what assistance you may need.

Look out for the National Accessible Scheme symbols which are included throughout the accommodation directory. Using the NAS could help make the difference between a good holiday and a perfect one!

Search for NAS accredited accommodation at **www.enjoyengland.com**.

For tips and advice on holiday travel in Britain, go to **www.visitbritain.com/access**

How to use this directory

To assist the user to find locations within a small area we have referenced the entries by the map page number and grid reference. To locate an entry, determine the area you wish to visit and note the map page number and grid reference. Using this information the user can search the directory by the page and grid square to locate a list of locations appearing within the designated grid square.

Please note that in a few cases where there is a large overlap between map pages a location is only referenced to one page. Therefore if you cannot see an entry for a particular grid square that contains a symbol please check the overlapping map page grid reference.

Example White Hart Inn, Redditch appears on pages 12 D1 and 18 C6 and is only referenced to page 12 D1.

🛏 Accessible Accommodation-England

We recommend when booking any accommodation you check that your specific requirements can be met prior to confirming your booking. The symbols shown will enable people with disabilities to make an informed choice.

ACCESSIBILITY CATEGORIES

The National Accessible Scheme is a comprehensive quality assurance scheme for those with mobility, hearing and visual impairments. Under the scheme, properties are carefully assessed by advisors using strict criteria and awarded one or more of the following gradings outlined below. Where an establishment has a rating at least one bedroom in the hotel, B&B or hostel is accessible to the level given.

Relatively few properties in London have applied for the NAS scheme, however the London Development Agency have undertaken an in depth survey of access etc. These hotels are not assessed under the NAS scheme but all have a high level of access.

Typically suitable for a person with sufficient mobility to climb a flight of steps but who would benefit from fixtures and fittings to aid balance.

Typically suitable for a person with restricted walking ability and for those who may need to use a wheelchair some of the time and can negotiate a maximum of three steps.

Typically suitable for a person who depends on the use of a wheelchair and requires assistance from a carer, and maybe a hoist, when transferring to and from the wheelchair in a seated position.

Typically suitable for a person who depends on the use of a wheelchair and transfers unaided to and from the wheelchair in a seated position. This person may be an independent traveller.

Access Exceptional is awarded to establishments that meet the requirements of independent wheelchair users or assisted wheelchair users and also fulfil more demanding requirements with reference to the British Standard BS 8300:2001.

Category 1: Wheelchair access without assistance

* Self catering accommodation

Pg	Ref	Town name	Accommodation name	Type	Telephone No.
3	E5	Penzance	Penzance Youth Hostel		01736 362666
3	E5	Penzance	Hotel Penzance		01736 363117
3	E5	St Just	Swallows End*		01736 787011
3	F3	St Marys	Isles of Scilly Country Guest House		01720 422440
3	F4	Redruth	Trengove Farm Cottages*		01209 843008
3	F4	Redruth	Higher Laity Farm*		01209 842317
3	F5	Helston	Tregoose Farmhouse*		01209 714314
3	F5	Marazion	Ocean Studios*		01736 711040
3	G4	Truro	Tregoninny Farm		01872 520529
3	H2	Boscastle	The Old Coach House		01840 250398
3	H2	Boscastle	Reddivallen Farm		01840 250854
3	H3	Bodmin	Lanhydrock Hotel and Golf Club		01208 262570
3	H3	Padstow	Woodlands Country House		01841 532426
3	H3	Port Isaac	Tolraggott Farm Cottages*		01208 880927
3	H3	Roche	Owls Reach*		01208 831597
3	H3	Wadebridge	The Olde House*		01208 813219
3	H4	Ruan High Lanes	Trelagossick Farm - Barnowl Cottage*		01872 501338
4	B3	Bude	Forda Lodges & Cottages*		01288 321413
4	B6	Fowey	Penquite Farm Holidays*		01726 833319

Pg	Ref	Town name	Accommodation name	Type	Telephone No.
4	C3	Bideford	West Hele*		01237 451044
4	C4	Beaworthy	Blagdon Farm Country Holidays*		01409 211509
4	C5	Callington	Berrio Mill*		01579 363252
4	C6	Plymouth	Haddington House Apartments*		07966 256984
4	D2	Umberleigh	Country Ways*		01769 560503
4	D4	Okehampton	Beer Farm*		01837 840265
4	D5	Yelverton	Overcombe House		01822 853501
4	D6	Plymouth	Kitley House Hotel and Restaurant		01752 881555
5	E2	Exford	Westermill Farm*		01643 831238
5	E2	South Molton	Stable Cottage*		01598 740130
5	E3	Crediton	Ashridge Farm		01363 774292
5	E3	Crediton	Creedy Manor*		01363 772684
5	E4	Moretonhampstead	Budleigh Farm*		01647 440835
5	E5	Ashburton	Wren & Robin Cottages*		01364 631421
5	E6	Kingsbridge	Beeson Farm Holiday Cottages*		01548 581270
5	F1	Minehead	Woodcombe Lodges*		01643 702789
5	F3	Wellington	Old Lime Kiln Cottages*		01823 672339
5	F4	Exeter	Hues Piece*		01392 466720
5	F5	Torquay	Crown Lodge		01803 298772

* Self catering accommodation

Accessible Accommodation-England

Pg	Ref	Town name	Accommodation name	Telephone No.
5	F5	Torquay	South Sands Apartments*	01803 293521
5	F5	Torquay	Atlantis Holiday Apartments*	01803 607929
5	G1	Williton	Stilegate Bed and Breakfast	01984 639119
5	G2	Bridgwater	Blackmore Farm	01278 653442
5	G4	Colyton	Smallcombe Farm	01404 831310
5	G4	Colyton	Smallcombe Farm*	01404 831310
6	A2	Cheddar	Cheddar YHA	01934 742494
6	A2	Godney	Double-Gate Farm	01458 832217
6	A3	Bridgwater	Walkers Farm Cottages*	01823 698229
6	A3	Stoke St Gregory	Holly Farm Cottages*	01823 490828
6	A4	Beaminster	Lewesdon Farm Holidays*	01308 868270
6	A4	Beaminster	Stable Cottage*	01308 862305
6	A5	Charmouth	The Poplars*	01297 560697
6	B2	Bristol	Greyfield Farm Cottages*	01761 471132
6	B2	Wells	St Marys Lodge*	01749 342157
6	B3	Clanville	Clanville Manor Tallet and Lone Oak Cottage*	01963 350124
6	B5	Dorchester	Whatcombe Stables*	01305 789000
6	B5	Abbotsbury	Tamarisk Farm Cottages*	01308 897784
6	B5	Weymouth	Character Farm Cottages*	01305 871347
6	C3	Gillingham	Top Stall*	01258 820022
6	C3	Templecombe	Half Moon Inn	01963 370140
6	C4	Blandford Forum	Ellwood Cottages*	01258 818196
6	C4	Blandford Forum	Houghton Lodge*	01258 882170
6	C4	Dorchester	Bookham Court*	01300 345511
6	C4	Shaftesbury	Hartgrove Farm*	01747 811830
6	C5	Dorchester	Tincleton Lodge and Clyffe Dairy Cottage*	01305 848391
6	D5	Corfe Castle	Mortons House Hotel	01929 480988
6	D6	Swanage	9 Quayside Court*	01454 311178
7	E3	Salisbury	The Old Stables*	01722 349002
7	E5	Lymington	The Nurses Cottage	01590 683402
7	F5	Norton	The Savoy*	01983 760355
7	F6	Chale	Atherfield Green Farm Holiday Cottages*	01983 867613
7	G5	Sandown	Borthwood Cottages*	01983 403967
7	G5	Shanklin	Sunny Bay Apartments*	01983 866379
7	G5	Shanklin	Laramie*	01983 862905
7	H2	Farnham	High Wray*	01252 715589
7	H3	Liss	The Jolly Drover	01730 893137
7	H4	Chichester	Chichester Park Hotel	01243 786351
8	A5	Arundel	YHA Arundel	01903 882204
8	A5	Pulborough	The Labouring Man	01798 872215
8	B3	Dorking	Bulmer Farm*	01306 731871
8	D3	Edenbridge	Hay Barn & Straw Barn*	07770 762076
8	D3	Golden Green	Goldhill Mill Cottages*	01732 851626
8	D4	Royal Tunbridge Wells	The Brew House Hotel	01892 520587
8	D6	Eastbourne	Hydro Hotel	01323 720643
9	E4	Ashford	Heron Cottage	01580 291358
9	E4	Tenterden	Little Silver Country Hotel	01233 850321
9	F4	Ashford	The Granary*	01233 850871
9	G3	Folkestone	Garden Lodge	01303 893147
12	A1	Stokesay	Upper Onibury Cottages*	01584 856206
12	A1	Ludlow	Mocktree Barns Holiday Cottages*	01547 540441
12	A2	Leominster	YHA Leominster	01568 620517
12	A3	Hereford	Grafton Villa Farm Cottages*	01432 268689
12	A6	Weston-super-Mare	Beverley Guest House	01934 622956
12	A6	Weston-super-Mare	Milton Lodge Guest House	01934 623161
12	A6	Weston-super-Mare	Spreyton Guest House	01934 416887
12	A6	Weston-super-Mare	Royal Hotel	01934 423100
12	B4	Lydney	The Fountain Inn	01594 562189
12	B4	Lydney	2 Danby Cottages*	0117 942 2301
12	B4	Newnham	The Priory Cottages*	07919 407128
12	B4	Ross-on-Wye	Portland House	01600 890757
12	C1	Kidderminster	Brockencote Hall	01562 777876
12	C3	Tewkesbury	Deerhurst Cottages*	01684 275845
12	C6	Bath	The Carfax	01225 462089
12	C6	Bradford-on-Avon	Church Farm Country Cottages*	01225 722246
12	D1	Redditch	White Hart Inn	01527 545442
12	D3	Cheltenham	The Prestbury House	01242 529533
13	E3	Stow-on-the-Wold	YHA Stow-on-the-Wold*	01451 830497
13	F2	Warwick	Church Hill Farm B & B	01926 651251
13	F4	Witney	Springhill Farm Bed & Breakfast	01993 704919
13	F4	Witney	Swallows Nest*	01993 704919
13	G4	Oxford	YHA Oxford	01865 727275
13	G5	Abingdon	Abbey Guest House	01235 537020
13	G5	Reading	Streatley On Thames YHA*	01491 872278
13	H3	Buckingham	Weatherhead Farm	01280 860502
13	H6	Bracknell	Coppid Beech Hotel	01344 303333
14	A6	Hayes	Premier Travel Inn - Heathrow (M4)	0870 990 6612
14	A6	London, West Drayton	Crowne Plaza London Heathrow	0870 400 9140
14	A6	London, Heathrow	Hilton London Heathrow Airport	020 8759 7755
14	A6	London, West Drayton	Holiday Inn London Heathrow	020 899 00000
14	A6	London, Hayes	Holiday Inn London Heathrow Ariel	0870 400 9040
14	A6	London, West Drayton	Holiday Inn London Heathrow M4 (Jct 4)	0870 400 8595
14	A6	London, Hayes	Ibis London Heathrow Airport	020 8759 4888
14	A6	London, West Drayton	Novotel London Heathrow	01895 431431
14	A6	London, Hayes	Radisson Edwardian Heathrow Hotel	0800 37 44 11
14	B2	Sandy	Acorn Cottage*	01767 682332
14	B5	London, Mayfair	Browns Hotel	020 7493 6020
14	B5	London, Cricklewood	Crown Moran Hotel	020 8452 4175
14	B5	London, Wembley	Days Hotel London North	020 8906 7000
14	B5	London, Church Street	Hilton London Metropole	020 7402 4141
14	B5	London, Brent Cross	Holiday Inn	0870 400 9112

Pg Ref	Town name	Accommodation name	Type	Telephone No.
14 B5	London, Camden Town	Holiday Inn Camden Lock	♿	020 7485 4343
14 B5	London, Regent's Park	Holiday Inn	♿	0870 400 9111
14 B5	London, Euston	Novotel London St Pancras	♿	020 7666 9000
14 B5	London, Hayes	Premier Travel Inn - Hayes Heathrow	♿	0870 1977132
14 B5	London, Euston	Premier Travel Inn	♿	0870 238 3301
14 B5	London, Greenford	Premier Travel Inn	♿	020 8998 8820
14 B5	London, Hampstead	Premier Travel Inn	♿	0870 850 6328
14 B5	London, Wembley	Premier Travel Inn	♿	0870 990 6484
14 B5	London, Bayswater	Ramada Hyde Park	♿	020 7229 1212
14 B5	London, Marble Arch	Thistle Marble Arch	♿	0871 376 9027
14 B5	London, West End	YHA London Central*	♿	01629 592633
14 B5	London	Premier Travel Inn - Edgware	♿	0870 990 6522
14 B6	London, Kensington	Copthorne Tara Hotel	♿	020 7937 7211
14 B6	London, St James	Crowne Plaza	♿	020 7834 6655
14 B6	London, West Kensington	Express by Holiday Inn Earls Court	♿	020 7384 5151
14 B6	London, Hammersmith	Express by Holiday Inn	♿	020 8746 5100
14 B6	London, Victoria	Express by Holiday Inn	♿	020 7630 8888
14 B6	London, Battersea	Express by Holiday Inn Wandsworth	♿	870 720 1298
14 B6	London, South Wimbledon	Express by Holiday Inn Wimbledon South	♿	020 8545 7300
14 B6	London, Kensington	Holiday Inn Kensington	♿	020 7373 2222
14 B6	London, Chessington	Holiday Inn	♿	0870 890 0567
14 B6	London, Sutton	Holiday Inn London Sutton	♿	0870 400 9113
14 B6	London, West Brompton	Ibis London Earls Court	♿	020 7610 0880
14 B6	London, South Kensington	Meininger City Hostel & Hotel London*	♿	020 3051 8173
14 B6	London, Fulham Road	Millennium & Copthorne Hotels at Chelsea Football Club	♿	0870 300 1212
14 B6	London, Hammersmith	Novotel London West	♿	020 8741 1555
14 B6	London, Victoria	Park Plaza Victoria	♿	020 7769 9999
14 B6	London, Chessington	Premier Travel Inn - Chessington	♿	0870 197 7057
14 B6	London, Hammersmith	Premier Travel Inn	♿	0870 850 6310
14 B6	London, Brentford	Premier Travel Inn - London Kew	♿	0870 990 6304
14 B6	London, London	Premier Travel Inn - London Putney Bridge	♿	0870 238 3302
14 B6	London, Wimbledon	Premier Travel Inn - London Wimbledon South	♿	0870 990 6342
14 B6	London, Whitton	Premier Travel Inn - Twickenham	♿	0870 990 6416
14 B6	London, Park Lane	The InterContinental Hotel	♿	020 7409 3131
14 B6	London, Feltham	Travelodge Feltham	♿	0870 191 1819
14 B6	London, Battersea	Travelodge	♿	0870 191 1688
14 B6	London, Morden	Travelodge London Wimbledon (Morden)	♿	0870 1911695
14 B6	London	Travelodge Chessington Tolworth	♿	0870 085 0950
14 C5	London, Pentonville	Crowne Plaza City	♿	0870 400 9190
14 C5	London, Royal Victoria Dock	Crowne Plaza London Docklands	♿	0870 990 9692
14 C5	London, Barking	Etap East Barking	♿	020 8507 8500
14 C5	London, Silvertown	Etap Hotel London City Airport	♿	020 7474 9106
14 C5	London, Chingford	Express by Holiday Inn	♿	0870 444 2789
14 C5	London, Limehouse	Express by Holiday Inn	♿	020 77913850
14 C5	London, City	Express by Holiday Inn	♿	020 7300 4300
14 C5	London, Silvertown	Express by Holiday Inn London Royal Docks	♿	020 7540 4040
14 C5	London, Stratford	Express By Holiday Inn	♿	0870 240 5708
14 C5	London, Southwark	Express by Holiday Inn	♿	020 7401 2525
14 C5	London, Barking	Formule 1 East Barking	♿	020 8507 0789
14 C5	London, Islington	Hilton London Islington	♿	020 7354 7700
14 C5	London, Bloomsbury	Holiday Inn	♿	0870 400 9222
14 C5	London, King's Cross	Holiday Inn	♿	020 7833 3900
14 C5	London, Whitechapel	Ibis London City	♿	020 7422 8400
14 C5	London, Royal Victoria Dock	Ibis London ExCel	♿	020 7055 2300
14 C5	London, Stratford	Ibis	♿	020 8535 3700
14 C5	London, Islington	Jurys Inn	♿	020 7282 5500
14 C5	London, London Bridge	London Bridge Hotel	♿	020 7855 2200
14 C5	London, Southwark	Mercure London City Bankside Hotel	♿	020 7902 0800
14 C5	London, Southwark	Novotel London City South	♿	020 7089 0400
14 C5	London, Barking	Premier Travel Inn	♿	0870 990 6318
14 C5	London, Enfield	Premier Travel Inn	♿	0870 238 3306
14 C5	London, Docklands	Premier Travel Inn	♿	0870 238 3322
14 C5	London, Southwark	Premier Travel Inn	♿	0870 990 6402
14 C5	London, Kings Cross	St Pancras YHA*	♿	020 7388 9998
14 C5	London, Aldwych	The Waldorf Hilton	♿	0870 400 8484
14 C5	London, Silvertown	Travelodge London City Airport	♿	0870 085 0950
14 C5	London, Finsbury	Travelodge London City Road	♿	0871 984 6333
14 C5	London, Covent Garden	Travelodge	♿	020 7208 9988
14 C5	London, Docklands	Travelodge	♿	0870 191 1691
14 C5	London, Ilford	Travelodge	♿	0870 1911693
14 C5	London, Kings Cross	Travelodge	♿	0870 1911757
14 C5	London, City	Travelodge London Liverpool Street	♿	0870 191 1689
14 C5	London, Rotherhithe	YHA London Thameside*	♿	0870 770 6010
14 C5	Romford	Premier Travel Inn - Romford West	♿	0870 990 6450
14 C6	Bromley	Best Western Bromley Court Hotel	♿	020 8461 8600
14 C6	London, Belgravia	City Inn Westminster	♿	020 7630 1000
14 C6	London, Blackheath	Clarendon Hotel	♿	020 8318 4321
14 C6	London, Vauxhall	Comfort Inn	♿	020 7735 9494
14 C6	London, Waterloo	Days Hotel	♿	020 7922 1331
14 C6	London, Marsh Wall	Hilton London Canary Wharf	♿	020 3002 2300
14 C6	London, Bexley	Holiday Inn	♿	0870 400 9006
14 C6	London, Croydon	Jurys Inn	♿	020 8448 6000
14 C6	London, Waterloo	Novotel London	♿	020 7793 1010
14 C6	London, Croydon	Premier Travel Inn - Croydon South	♿	0870 197 7069
14 C6	London, Croydon	Premier Travel Inn - Croydon West	♿	020 8633 9300
14 C6	London, London	Premier Travel Inn - London County Hall	♿	0870 238 3300
14 D2	Saffron Walden	Hill Farm Holiday Cottages*	♿	01799 584881

* Self catering accommodation

Pg Ref	Town name	Accommodation name	Telephone No.
14 D5	London, Rainham	Premier Travel Inn	0870 197 7217
14 D5	London, Romford	Premier Travel Inn - Romford Central	0870 197 7220
14 D5	London, Romford	Travelodge Romford Central Hotel	0870 191 1756
15 E3	Halstead	The White Hart	01787 475657
15 E4	Chelmsford	Boswell House Hotel	01245 287587
15 F1	Diss	Jayes Holiday Cottages*	01359 251255
15 F1	Eye	Netus Barn*	01449 766275
15 F1	Stowmarket	Coda Cottages*	01449 780076
15 F1	Stowmarket	Leys Farmhouse Annexe*	01449 711750
15 F1	Stowmarket	Red House Farm Cottages*	01449 673323
15 F2	Sudbury	Sherbourne Farm Lodge Cottages*	01787 210885
15 F2	Wattisham	Wattisham Hall Holiday Cottages*	01449 740240
15 F3	Colchester	Gladwins Farm*	01206 262261
15 G2	Ipswich	Damerons Farm Holidays*	01473 832454
15 G2	Woodbridge	Grove House Bed & Breakfast	01394 382202
15 G3	Frinton-on-Sea	Bufo Villae Guest House	01255 672644
15 G3	Manningtree	Curlews	01255 870890
15 G4	Clacton-on-Sea	The Cartlodge at Lee Wick Farm*	01255 823031
15 H1	Beccles	The Plough Inn	01353 698000
15 H1	Halesworth	Wissett Lodge*	01986 873173
15 H1	Hatfield	School Farm Cottages*	01986 798844
15 H1	Hatfield	Holly Tree Farm Barns*	01986 798062
15 H1	Saxmundham	Bluebell Bonny Buttercup & Bertie*	01728 668324
15 H1	Southwold	Newlands Country House	01502 722164
15 H2	Aldeburgh	Brudenell Hotel	01728 452071
15 H2	Woodbridge	Blaxhall YHA	0870 770 5702
17 G3	Chester	Grosvenor Pulford Hotel & Karma Spa	01244 570560
17 G5	Shrewsbury	Lyth Hill House	01743 874660
17 G6	Church Stretton	Botvyle Farm Holiday Cottages*	01694 722869
17 G6	Craven Arms	Strefford Hall Self Catering - Robins & Swallows Nest*	01588 672383
17 G6	Craven Arms	Goosefoot Barn Cottages*	01584 861326
18 A5	Craven Arms	Tugford Farm B&B	01584 841259
18 A5	Ludlow	Sutton Court Farm Cottages*	01584 861305
18 C2	Stoke-on-Trent	Dimmingsdale YHA	0870 770 5794
18 D2	Ashbourne	Ilam Hall YHA	0870 770 5879
19 F4	Loughborough	imago at Burleigh Court	01509 211515
19 H3	Grantham	Farrier Cottage*	01476 861057
19 H5	Peterborough	Oundle Cottage Breaks*	01832 273531
20 A2	Boston	Elms Farm Cottages*	01205 290840
20 A2	Martin, Nr. Metheringham	The Manor House Stables*	01526 378717
20 A3	Donington	Browntoft House	01775 822091
20 B2	Boston	Crewyard Cottages*	01205 871389
20 B4	Wisbech	Common Right Barns*	01945 410424
20 C2	Hunstanton	Caley Hall Hotel	01485 533486
20 C2	Hunstanton	Foxgloves Cottage*	01485 532460
20 C3	Sandringham	Park House Hotel	01485 543000
20 C5	Ely	Casa Nostra Guesthouse	01353 862495
20 D2	Brancaster	Titchwell Manor Hotel	01485 210221
20 D3	Nr. Fakenham	Oyster House	01485 528327
21 E2	Kelling	The Pheasant Hotel	01263 588382
21 E3	Fakenham	Jex Farm Barns*	01328 878257
21 E3	Bawdeswell	Moor Farm Stable Cottages*	01362 688523
21 E4	Dereham	Greenbanks Country Hotel (A47)	01362 687747
21 E4	Kings Lynn	Holmdene Farm*	01328 701284
21 E5	East Harling	Berwick Cottage*	01787 372343
21 F2	Cromer	Incleborough House Luxury Bed and Breakfast	01263 515939
21 F2	Sheringham	Sheringham YHA	0870 770 6024
21 F2	Sheringham	Roman Camp Inn	01263 838291
21 F3	Holt	Wood Farm Cottages*	01263 587347
21 F5	Diss	Malthouse Farm Cottages*	01379 658021
21 G3	Happisburgh	Boundary Stables*	01692 650171
21 G3	Mundesley	Overcliff Lodge	01263 720016
21 G3	Nr. Happisburgh	Primrose Cottage*	01692 650667
21 G3	Stalham	The Piggeries*	01480 890216
21 G4	Bradwell	Fritton Lake Country World*	01493 488208
21 G4	Horning	King Line Cottages*	01692 630297
21 H5	Lowestoft	Hotel Victoria	01502 574433
21 H6	Southwold	Hightide*	01502 724033
22 C1	Grange-over-Sands	Netherwood Hotel	01539 532552
22 C1	Morecambe	Eden Vale Luxury Holiday Flats*	07739 008301
22 C2	Blackpool	Norbreck Castle Hotel	01253 352341
22 C3	Blackpool	The Lawton	01253 753471
22 C3	Blackpool	Holmsdale	01253 621008
22 C3	Blackpool	Big Blue Hotel	0845 367 3333
22 C3	Blackpool	Burbage Holiday Lodge*	01253 356657
22 C3	Blackpool	The Beach House*	01253 826555
22 C3	Blackpool	The Berkeley*	01253 623218
22 C3	Lytham St Annes	The Chadwick Hotel	01253 720061
22 C3	Poulton-le-fylde	Hardhorn Breaks*	01253 890422
22 C4	Scarisbrick	Sandy Brook Farm	01704 880337
22 C4	Scarisbrick	Sandy Brook Farm*	01704 880337
22 C5	Liverpool	YHA Liverpool International	0870 770 5924
22 C5	Liverpool	Ibis Hotel	0151 706 9800
22 C6	Ellesmere Port	Holiday Inn Ellesmere Port/ Cheshire Oaks	0151 356 8111
22 D1	Caton	Croft (The) - Ground Floor Apartment*	01524 770725
22 D1	Ingleton	Riverside Lodge	01524 241359
22 D2	Nr. Longridge	The Gibbon Bridge Hotel	01995 61456
22 D2	Nr. Garstang	Barnacre Cottages*	01995 600918
22 D2	Nr. Garstang	Bleasdale Cottages*	01995 61343
22 D3	Preston	Proven House*	01772 782653
22 D3	Ribchester	Riverside Barn*	01254 878095
22 D3	Ribchester	Pinfold Farm*	01254 820740

Pg	Ref	Town name	Accommodation name	Type	Telephone No.
22	D6	Warrington	Tall Trees Lodge		01928 790824
23	E1	Clapham	New Inn Hotel		01524 251203
23	E2	Newton Great Harwood	Stonefold Holiday Cottage*		07966 582834
23	E3	Nr. Blackburn	Mytton Fold Hotel		01254 240662
23	E3	Nr. Haslingden	Clough Head Farm - Self Catering*		01254 704758
23	E5	Manchester	Luther King House		0161 224 6404
23	E5	Manchester	Manchester YHA		0870 770 5950
23	E5	Manchester, Manchester Airport	Bewleys Hotel		0161 498 1390
23	E5	Manchester	Midland Hotel		0161 236 3333
23	E5	Manchester	Macdonald Manchester Hotel		0870 194 2137
23	E5	Manchester, Deansgate	Hilton		0161 870 1600
23	E5	Salford	Lowry Hotel		0161 827 4000
23	E6	Congleton	Sandhole Farm		01260 224419
23	F6	Macclesfield	Strawberry Duck Cottage*		01260 223591
23	F6	Macclesfield	The Old Byre*		01260 223293
23	F4	Saddleworth	Cherry Clough Farm House Accommodation		01457 874369
24	A3	Shaw	The Lodge at Birkby Hall		01484 400321
24	A6	Buxton	Ash Tree Cottage*		01298 84247
24	A6	Buxton	Wheeldon Trees Farm*		01298 83219
24	B6	Chesterfield	Abbeydale Hotel		01246 277849
24	C2	York	The Groves		01904 559777
24	C2	York	Best Western Monkbar Hotel		01904 638086
24	C2	York	The Grange Hotel		01904 644744
24	D1	Malton	The Old Post Office*		01944 758047
24	D5	Gainsborough	Blyton (Sunnyside) Ponds		01427 628240
25	E3	Nr. South Cave	Rudstone Walk Country B&B		01430 422230
25	E6	North Carlton	Cliff Farm Cottage*		01522 730475
25	F1	Bridlington	Providence Place		01262 603840
25	F1	Bridlington	The Bay View Hotel		01262 674225
25	F3	Hedon	Little Weghill Farm		01482 897650
25	F6	Belchford	Poachers Hideaway*		01507 533555
25	F6	Horncastle	Best Western Admiral Rodney Hotel		01507 523131
25	F6	Louth	Bay Tree Cottage*		01507 343230
25	F6	Woodhall Spa	Mill Lane Holiday Cottage*		01526 353101
25	F6	Woodhall Spa	Wayside Cottage*		01526 353101
25	G4	Cleethorpes	Tudor Terrace Guest House		01472 600800
25	G5	Covenham St Bartholomew	Westfield Mews & Lodges*		01507 363217
25	G5	Louth	Copthorne Lodge*		01507 313540
25	G6	Alford	Half Moon Hotel		01507 463477
25	G6	Hagworthingham, Nr. Horncastle	Kingfisher Lodge*		01205 870210
25	H6	Ingoldmells	Ingoldale Park*		01754 872335
25	H6	Skegness	Chatsworth		01754 764177
27	G2	Bowness-on-Solway	The Old Chapel		01697 351126
27	G5	Borrowdale	Borrowdale YHA		0870 770 5706
27	H4	Threlkeld	Scales Farm Country Guest House		01768 779660
27	H5	Ambleside	Rothay Manor		01539 433605

Pg	Ref	Town name	Accommodation name	Type	Telephone No.
27	H5	Ambleside	Crop Howe*		01539 433251
27	H6	Windermere	Linthwaite House Hotel		01539 488600
28	B1	Falstone	Falstone Barns*		01434 240251
28	B2	Haydon Bridge	Grindon Cartshed (B6318)		01434 684273
28	B2	Haydon Bridge	Shaftoes		01434 684664
28	B2	Newbrough	Carr Edge Farm		01434 674788
28	B3	Allendale Town	Station House Flat*		01434 683362
28	C2	Hexham	The Hytte*		01434 672321
28	C3	Hexham	Old Byre*		01434 673259
28	C5	Nr. Bowes	Mellwaters Barn*		01833 628181
28	D1	Longhorsley	Macdonald Linden Hall Hotel		0870 194 2123
28	D1	Longhorsley	Beacon Hill*		01670 780900
28	D1	Pegswood	Longhirst Hall		01670 791348
28	D2	Gateshead	Hilton Newcastle Gateshead		01914 909700
28	D4	Cockfield	Stonecroft and Swallows Nest*		01388 718251
28	D4	Ingleton	Mill Granary Cottages*		01325 730339
28	D5	Gainford	East Greystone Farm Cottages*		01325 730236
28	D5	Winston	Alwent Mill Cottage*		01325 730479
29	E4	High Hesleden	The Ship Inn		01429 836453
29	E6	Northallerton	Lovesome Hill Farm		01609 772311
29	F6	Helmsley	Helmsley YHA		01439 770433
29	F6	Kirkbymoorside	Low Hagg Holidays*		01751 430500
29	G5	Hinderwell	Ellerby		01947 840342
29	G6	Kirkbymoorside	The Cornmill		01751 432000
29	G6	Lockton	YHA Lockton		01751 460376
29	G6	Wrelton	Beech Farm Cottages*		01751 476612
29	G6	Pickering	Keld Head Farm Cottages*		01751 473974
29	G6	Pickering	North Yorkshire Cottages*		01751 476653
29	G6	Nr. Lockton	Mel House Cottages*		01751 475396
29	G6	Nr. Lockton	Sunset Cottage*		01751 472172
29	G6	Nr. Snainton	Cow Pasture & Swallow-Tail Cottages*		01723 859285
29	G6	Thornton-le-Dale	Easthill Farm House and Gardens*		01751 474561
29	H5	Whitby	Whitby YHA		01947 602878
29	H6	Nr. Staintondale	The Grainary		01723 870026
29	H6	Scarborough	The Scarborough Travel and Holiday Lodge		01723 363537
33	G3	Berwick-upon-Tweed	Meadow Hill Guest House		(01289) 306325
33	G3	Berwick-upon-Tweed	West Ord Holiday Cottages* (A698)		01289 386631
33	G4	Kirknewton	Crookhouse*		01668 216113
33	G4	Doddington	Fenton Hill Farm Cottages*		01668 216228
33	G5	Nr. Netherton	The Byre Vegetarian B&B		01669 650476
33	H4	Belford	Elwick Farm Cottages*		01668 213242
33	H4	Belford	Lucker Hall Steading* (B1341)		01668 219941
33	H5	Stillbottle	Village Farm*		01665 575591
33	H5	Alnwick	Bog Mill Farm Holiday Cottages*		01665 604529
33	H5	Craster	Craster Pine Lodges*		01665 576286

We recommend when booking any accommodation you check that your specific requirements can be met prior to confirming your booking. The symbols shown will enable people with disabilities to make an informed choice.

ACCESSIBILITY CATEGORIES

A comprehensive quality assurance scheme for those with mobility impairment has been in place in Scotland for the past two decades. Under the scheme, properties are carefully assessed by VisitScotland Quality Advisors using strict criteria and awarded one or more of the following gradings outlined below. Where an establishment holds an award, at least one bedroom in a hotel or guest, B&B or hostel is accessible to the level given.

 Category 1: Wheelchair access without assistance

 Category 2: Wheelchair access with assistance

 Category 3: Limited mobility

Pg	Ref	Town name Accommodation name	Type	Telephone No.
26	A1	Ballentrae Glenapp Castle		01465 831212
26	A1	Girvan Downanhill Cottage		01465 831368
26	A3	Portpatrick Braefield Guest House		01776 810255
26	A3	Portpatrick Portpatrick Hotel		01776 810333
26	A3	Portpatrick The Fernhill Hotel		01776 810220
26	B1	Girvan Garryloop		01465 871393
26	B3	Stranraer Culmore Bridge		01776 830539
26	B4	Drummore Harbour Row		01776 840631
26	B4	Drummore Old Diary Cottage		01776 840242
26	C3	Newton Stewart East Culkae Farm House		01988 850214
26	D3	Gatehouse of Fleet Garden Cottage		01557 814215
26	D3	Gatehouse of Fleet Rusko Holidays		01557 814215
27	E2	Nr. Castle Douglas Craigadam Lodge		01556 650233
27	E2	Castle Douglas Chapelerne Farmhouse		01556 650270
27	E2	Castle Douglas Redcastle House		01556 660475
27	E3	Auchencairn, Nr. Castle Douglas Balcary Bay Hotel		01556 640217
27	E3	Castle Douglas Barncrosh Farm		01556 680216
27	E3	Castle Douglas Rose Cottage		01556 502 513
27	E3	Colvend Dalbeattie Clonyard House Hotel		01556 630372
27	E3	Dalbeattie Kippford Holiday Park		01556 620636
27	F1	Nr. Parkgate Gubhill Farm		01387 860648
27	F1	Dumfries Wallamhill House		01387 248249
27	F1	Lochmaben The Crown Hotel		01387 811750
27	F2	Carrutherstown Hetland Hall Hotel (A75)		01387 840201
27	F2	Clarencefield Alder and Acorn (B724)		01387 870608
27	F2	Dumfries Cairnyard Holiday Lodges		01387 730218
27	F2	Glencaple Conheath Gatelodge		01387 770205
27	F2	Dumfries Glenlossie Guest House (A711)		01387 254305
27	F2	Lockfoot Nunland Country Holidays		01387 730214
27	F3	Southwick Clifton Farm		01387 780206
27	G1	Lockerbie Dryfesdale Country House Hotel		01576 202427
27	G2	Eastriggs The Graham Arms Guest House		01461 40031
27	H1	Newburgh Mosspaul		01450 850245
27	H2	Gretna Hunters Lodge Hotel		01461 338214
27	H2	Gretna The Garden House Hotel		01461 337621
27	H2	Gretna Green Days Inn		01461 337566
27	H2	Gretna Green Smiths at Gretna Green		0845 367 6768
30	A3	Kilchoman Bruichladdich Coull Farm Holiday Cottage & Flat		01496 850317
30	B3	Ballygrant Craigard Holiday Accommodation		01496 810728

Pg	Ref	Town name Accommodation name	Type	Telephone No.
30	B3	Bridgend 2 Mulindry Cottages		01496 810397
30	B3	Islay The Meadows		01496 810567
30	B3	Isle of Islay Glen-na-airidh & Blackpark Croft		01496 810376
30	B4	Bowmore, Isle of Islay The Old Stables Flats		01496 810414
30	B4	Glenegedale Laggan View		01764 663316
30	C5	Campbeltown The Dairy Rhoin Farm		01586 820220
30	C5	Kilkenzie Dalnaspidal Guest House		01586 820466
30	D1	Ardmaddy Ardmaddy Castle Holiday Cottages		01852 300353
30	D1	Isle of Seil Oban Oban Seil Croft Cottages		01852 300457
30	D2	Ardrishaig Brenfield Shores		01546 603284
30	D2	Lochgilphead Empire Travel Lodge		01546 602381
30	D3	Lochgilphead Barnlongart House & Ormsary Lodges		01880 770222
30	D5	Carradale Dunvalanree		01583 431226
31	E1	Inveraray Loch Fyne Hotel		01499 302148
31	E2	Minard Minard Castle		01546 886272
31	E5	Brodick Auchrannie Country House Hotel		01770 302234
31	E5	Brodick Auchrannie Spa Resort		01770 302234
31	E5	Brodick Belvedere		01770 302397
31	E5	Brodick Belvedere Guest House		01770 302397
31	E5	Brodick Strathwhillan House		01770 302331
31	E5	Glen Cloy Brodick Bluebird Peacock & Finch Cottage		01770 302219
31	E5	Glenashdale Strathconon		01586 830323
31	E5	Kildonan, Nr. Lagg Grianan House and Grianan Cottage		01770 820236
31	E5	Kildonan Kildonan Hotel		01770 820207
31	E5	Kildonan Kildonan School & Schoolhouse		01436 820956
31	E5	Kildonan The Beach House		01770 820392
31	E5	Lamlash Clauchlands View Holiday Cottage		01770 600317
31	E5	Lamlash Lilybank		01770 600230
31	E5	Lamlash Oakbank Farm		01770 600404
31	E5	Lamlash, Isle of Arran Ghillies and Drovers		01770 600291
31	E5	Whiting Bay Sandbraes Lodge		01770 700235
31	F1	Arrochar Village Inn		01301 702279
31	F2	Nr. Dunoon Stronchullin Holiday Cottages		01369 810246
31	F2	Rhu Rosslea Hall Hotel		01436 439955
31	F3	Gourock Spinnaker Hotel		01475 633107
31	F3	Greenock Express by Holiday Inn		01475 786666
31	F3	Greenock James Watt College		01475 731360
31	F3	Greenock Tontine Hotel		01475 723316

Pg	Ref	Town name	Accommodation name	Type	Telephone No.
31	F3	Largs	Seger Property Mgnt		01475 686 369
31	F3	Toward, Nr. Dunoon	Egmont		0141 639 3129
31	F4	Kilwinning	Ailsa Craig View		01294 552361
31	F4	Millport	The Cathedral of the Isles		01475 530353
31	F6	Maybole	Royal Artillery Cottage		0131 243 9331
31	F6	Turnberry	The Westin Turnberry Resort		01655 331000
31	G1	Kinlochard	Lochside Cottages		01360 449060
31	G1	Tarbet	Stewart House		01301 702230
31	G2	Alexandria	De Vere Cameron House		01389 755565
31	G2	Drymen	Winnock Hotel		01360 660245
31	G2	Drymen Loch Lommond Glasgow	Foxglove Cottages		01360 661128
31	G2	Gartocharn	Greystonelea Lodge		01389 830419
31	G2	Helensburgh	RSR Braeholm		01436 671880
31	G2	Loch Lomond	Culag Lochside Guest House		01436 860248
31	G3	Abbotsinch Paisley	Ramada Glasgow Airport		0141 840 2200
31	G3	Clydebank	The Beardmore Hotel & Conference Centre		0141 951 6000
31	G3	Duntocher	West Park Hotel		01389 872333
31	G3	Erskine	Erskine Bridge Hotel		0141 812 0123
31	G3	Milton, Nr. Dumbarton	Milton Inn		01389 761401
31	G3	Paisley	Ardgowan Town House Hotel		0141 889 4763
31	G3	Paisley	Express by Holiday Inn Glasgow Airport		0141 842 1100
31	G4	Fenwick	Fenwick Hotel		01560 600478
31	G4	Irvine	Donegal Self Catering		01294 211676
31	G4	Lochwinnoch	East Lochhead Cottages		01505 842610
31	G5	Ayr	Fairfield House Hotel		01292 267461
31	G5	Ayr	Horizon Hotel		01292 264384
31	G5	Ayr	Ramada Jarvis		01292 269331
31	G5	Gailes, Nr. Irvine	The Gailes Lodge		01294 204040
31	G5	Irvine	Thistle Irvine		01294 274272
31	G5	Prestwick	Parkstone Hotel		01292 477286
31	G5	Troon	Barcelo Troon Marine Hotel		01292 314444
31	G5	Troon	Piersland House Hotel		01292 314747
31	G5	Troon	South Beach Hotel		01292 312033
31	G6	Alloway	South Lodge		01292 441313
31	G6	Nr. Ayr	Alt-Na-Craig		01292 560555
31	G6	Dalrymple	Springwater Chalets Ltd		01292 560343
31	G6	Straiton, Nr. Crosshill	Balbeg House		01655 770665
31	H1	Aberfoyle	Crannaig House		01877 382276
31	H1	Aberfoyle	Rob Roy Hotel		01877 382245
31	H1	Callander	Roman Camp Hotel		01877 330003
31	H1	Callander	The Crags Hotel		01877 330257
31	H1	Callander	The Old Rectory Guest House		01877 339215
31	H3	Glasgow	Carlton George Hotel		0141 353 6373
31	H3	Glasgow, Finnieston	Crowne Plaza Hotel		0870 443 4691
31	H3	Glasgow	Fraser Suites Glasgow		0141 553 4288
31	H3	Glasgow	Glasgow Hilton		0141 204 5555
31	H3	Glasgow, Finnieston	Glasgow Marriott		0141 226 5577
31	H3	Glasgow	Holiday Inn		0141 352 8300
31	H3	Glasgow	Ibis Hotel Glasgow		0141 225 6000
31	H3	Glasgow	Novotel Glasgow Centre		0141 222 2775
31	H3	Glasgow, Oatlands	Premier Inn Glasgow City Centre South		0870 423 6452
31	H3	Glasgow, Riddrie	The Knowes		0141 770 5213
31	H3	Glasgow	The Ramada Glasgow City		0141 248 4401
31	H3	Maryhill Road	Wolfson Hall		0141 3303773
31	H5	Drumclog	Drumboy Lodge		01357 440544
31	H6	Glen Afton, Nr. Craigdarroch	Ashmark Farm Cottage		01290 338830
31	H6	New Cumnock	Lochside House Hotel		01290 333000
32	A1	Alloa	Orchard Lodge		01259 226400
32	A1	Alva	Boll Holiday Cottages		01259 769638
32	A1	Bridge of Allan	Lynedoch		01786 832178
32	A1	Bridge of Allan	The Queens Hotel		01786 833268
32	A1	Stirling	Express by Holiday Inn		01786 449922
32	A1	Stirling	Hawthorn Cottage		01786 472523
32	A1	Stirling	Stirling Management Centre		01786 451666
32	A2	Bellshill	Hilton Strathclyde		01698 395500
32	A2	Bonnybridge	Antonine Wall Cottages		01324 811875
32	A3	Canderside Toll, Nr. Larkhall	Shawlands Hotel		01698 791111
32	A3	Motherwell	Express By Holiday Inn		01698 852375
32	A3	Motherwell	Moorings Hotel		01698 258131
32	A3	Motherwell	Motherwell College Stewart Hall		01698 261890
32	A3	Motherwell	The Alona Hotel		0870 112 3888
32	A3	New Lanark	New Lanark Mill Hotel		01555 667200
32	A3	Strathaven	Rissons at Springvale		01357 521131
32	A5	Sanquhar	Newark		01659 50263
32	A5	Sanquhar	Nith Riverside Lodges		01659 50270
32	B1	Dollar	Arndean Cottages		01259 743525
32	B1	Dunfermline	Best Western Keavil House Hotel		01383 736258
32	B1	Grangemouth	Leapark Hotel		01324 486733
32	B2	Livingston	Ramada Livingston		01506 431222
32	B2	Polmont	Inchyra Grange Hotel		01324 711911
32	B2	Whitburn	Best Western Hilcroft Hotel		01501 740818
32	B3	Nr. West Calder	Crosswoodhill Farm		01501 785205
32	B4	Biggar	Crossridge Country Cottages		01555 880589
32	B5	Moffat	Limetree House		01683 220001
32	B5	Moffat	Lochhouse Farm Retreat Centre		01683 300451
32	B5	Moffat	Lochhouse Farm Retreat Centre		01683 300451
32	C1	Aberdour	Aberdour Hotel		01383 860325
32	C1	Burntisland	Kingswood Hotel		01592 872329
32	C1	Dunfermline	Garvock House Hotel		01383 621067
32	C1	Dunfermline	Pitbauchlie House Hotel		01383 722282
32	C2	Corstorphine	Featherhall Garden Court		0845 430 1430
32	C2	Edinburgh, Gilmerton	Abbey Lodge Hotel		0131 6649548

Pg	Ref	Town name	Accommodation name	Type	Telephone No.
32	C2	Edinburgh, Leith Walk	Atholl Brae	♿	07732 730177
32	C2	Edinburgh, Liberton	Brae Lodge Guest House	🚶	0131 6722876
32	C2	Edinburgh	Caledonian Hilton Hotel	♿	0131 222 8888
32	C2	Edinburgh	Canon Court	🚶	0131 474 7000
32	C2	Edinburgh	Edinburgh Apartments City Central	🚶	07950 018865
32	C2	Edinburgh	Edinburgh City Centre (Morrison St) Premier Inn	♿	0870 238 3319
32	C2	Edinburgh, Corstorphine	Edinburgh Marriott	♿	0870 400 7293
32	C2	Edinburgh, Leith	Express By Holiday Inn	♿	0131 555 4422
32	C2	Edinburgh	Express By Holiday Inn	♿	0131 5582300
32	C2	Edinburgh, Edinburgh Airport	Hilton	♿	0131 519 4400
32	C2	Edinburgh	Hilton Edinburgh Grosvenor	♿	0131 226 6001
32	C2	Edinburgh, Corstorphine	Holiday Inn	♿	0870 400 9026
32	C2	Edinburgh, Blackhall	Holiday Inn Edinburgh-North		0870 400 9025
32	C2	Edinburgh, Holyrood Park	Holland House	🚶	0131 651 2007
32	C2	Edinburgh, Holyrood Park	Holyrood Aparthotel	🚶	0131 524 3200
32	C2	Edinburgh	Jurys Inn	♿	0131 200 3300
32	C2	Edinburgh, Blackhall	Kellys Guest House	🚶	0131 3323894
32	C2	Edinburgh, Murrayfield	Lindsay Guest House	🚶	0131 337 1580
32	C2	Edinburgh, Holyrood Park	Masson House	🚶	0131 651 2007
32	C2	Edinburgh, Murrayfield	Napier University	♿	0131 455 3738
32	C2	Edinburgh	Novotel Edinburgh Centre	♿	0131 656 3500
32	C2	Edinburgh, St. James	Ramada Mount Royal Hotel	♿	0131 225 7161
32	C2	Edinburgh, St. James	Royal Garden Apartments	🚶	0131 625 2345
32	C2	Edinburgh	Thistle Edinburgh	♿	0131 556 0111
32	C2	Edinburgh, Corstorphine	Toby Carvery & Innkeepers Lodge	♿	0870 243 0500
32	C2	Loanhead	Aaron Glen Guest House	🚶	0131 440 1293
32	C2	Rosewell	Park Neuk	🚶	0131 440 2411
32	C2	South Queensferry	Priory Lodge	🚶	0131 331 4345
32	C3	Peebles	Courtyard Cottages	🚶	01721 721264
32	C3	Romannobridge, West Linton	Mill Cottage	🚶	01968 660887
32	C3	West Linton	Drochil Castle Farm	♿	01721 752249
32	C4	Broughton, Nr. Biggar	The Glenholm Centre	♿	01899 830408
32	C5	Selkirk	Crook Cottage and Elspinhope	♿	01750 62259
32	D2	Edinburgh, Portobello	Ardgarth Guest House	♿	0131 669 3021
32	D2	Eskbank, Nr. Dalkeith	Glenarch House	🚶	0131 6631478
32	D2	Gorebridge	Ivory House	♿	01875 820755
32	D2	Macmerry	Adniston Manor	🚶	01875 611190
32	D2	Musselburgh	Carberry Tower	🚶	0131 665 3135
32	D4	Ashkirk	Synton Mains Farm	♿	01750 32388
32	D4	Galashiels	Ettrickvale	🚶	01896 755224
32	D5	Hawick	Mansfield Mills	🚶	01450 374435
32	D5	Hawick	Whitchester Guest House	♿	01450 377477
33	E1	Dirleton	Denis Duncan House	♿	01787 372343
33	E2	Haddington	Maitlandfield House Hotel	♿	01620 826513
33	E4	Jedburgh	Allerton House	🚶	01835 869633
33	E4	Newton St Boswells	Roxburgh Newtown Farm	🚶	01573 450250
33	E4	Melrose	Dimpleknowe Mill & Cottage	♿	01835 870333
33	E4	Melrose	Easter Cottage	🚶	01835 870281
33	E4	Melrose	Eildon Holiday Cottages	♿	01896 823258
33	E4	Nenthorn, Nr. Kelso	Burnbrae Holidays	🚶	01573 225570
33	E5	Hawick	Elm House Hotel	♿	01450 372866
33	E5	Hawick	Jos Cottage	🚶	01450 860656
33	F2	Duns	Greenhope Cottage	♿	01361 890242
33	F3	Coldstream	Little Swinton Cottages Cotoneaster & Honeysuckle	♿	01890 882173
33	F3	Swinton	The Wheatsheaf at Swinton	♿	01890 860257
33	F4	Ednam	Plumbraes Barn	🚶	01573 225028
33	F4	Kelso	Cross Keys Hotel	🚶	01573 223303
33	F4	Kelso	Edenmouth Farm	🚶	01890 830391
33	F4	Nr Kelso	Edenmouth Farm Holiday Cottages	🚶	01890 830391
33	G2	Coldingham	Dunlaverock	🚶	01890 771450
33	G3	West Fishwick	Bunnahabhain Strathisla and Tomatin	♿	01289 386279
34	C3	Bunessan	Salachran	🚶	01786 472900
34	C3	Fionnphort	Taigh Foise	🚶	01681 700509
34	D2	Salen	Ard Mhor House	♿	01680 300255
34	D2	Tobermory	Highland Cottage	🚶	01688 302030
34	D2	Tobermory	Tobermory Hotel	🚶	01688 302091
35	E1	Strontian	Bluebell Croft	♿	01967 402226
35	E2	Benderloch	Isle of Eriska Hotel	♿	01631 720371
35	E3	Benderloch, Oban	Tunnag Cottage	🚶	01631 720700
35	E3	Nr. Oban	Cologin Country Chalets	♿	01631 564501
35	E3	Connel, Nr. Oban	Wide Mouthed Frog	♿	01631 567005
35	E3	Oban	The Caledonian Hotel	🚶	01631 563133
35	F1	Nr. Clovullin	The Inn at Ardgour	🚶	01855 841225
35	F1	Fort William	Clan MacDuff Hotel	♿	01397 702341
35	F2	Ballachulish	Isles of Glencoe Hotel & Leisure Centre	♿	01855 811602
35	F2	Ballachulish	The Ballachulish Hotel	♿	01855 811606
35	F3	Connel	Tigh Grianach	🚶	01631 710288
35	F3	Kilchrenan	Roineabhal Country House	♿	01866 833207
35	F3	Taynuilt	Sithean	♿	01866 822110
35	F3	Taynuilt	Tigh an Daraich	♿	01866 822693
35	G1	Fort William	Craig Nevis West	🚶	01397 702023
35	G1	Fort William	Lochan Cottage Guest House	🚶	01397 702695
35	G1	Kinlochleven	Tigh-Na-Cheo	♿	01855 831434
35	G2	Glencoe	Glencoe Cottages	🚶	01855 811207
35	G3	Dalmally	Glenorchy Lodge Hotel	🚶	01838 200312
36	A2	Kinloch Rannoch	Dunalastair Hotel	♿	01882 632323
36	A3	Balquhidder	Lochside Cottages	♿	01877 384219
36	A3	St Fillans	Achray House Hotel	🚶	01764 685231
36	A3	Killin, Nr. Morenish	Killin Highland Lodges	🚶	01567 820334
36	A3	Killin, Nr. Strathyre	Tigh an Eilean and Wee Dalerb	🚶	01567 820961
36	A3	Lochearnhead	Earnknowe	🚶	01567 830238

Pg	Ref	Town name	Accommodation name	Type	Telephone No.
36	B2	Aberfeldy	Drumcroy Lodges	♿	01887 820978
36	B2	Aberfeldy, Nr. Kenmore	Loch Tay Lodges	♿	01887 830209
36	B2	Aberfeldy	Tomvale	♿	01887 820171
36	B2	Nr. Aberfeldy	The Ghillies Cottage	♿	01887 829553
36	B2	Tummel Bridge	Kynachan Loch Tummel Hotel	♿	01796 484848
36	B3	Comrie	Highland Heather Lodges	♿	01764 670440
36	B3	Crieff	Comely Bank Guest House	♿	01764 653409
36	B3	Crieff	Crieff Hydro Hotel	♿	01764 655555
36	B3	Crieff	Crieff Hydro Hotel Chalets	♿	01764 655555
36	B3	Crieff	Murraypark Hotel	♿	01764 658000
36	B4	Blackford	Blackford Hotel	♿	01764 682497
36	C2	Nr. Pitlochry	East Haugh House Country Hotel & Res	♿	01796 473121
36	C2	Dunkeld	Erigmore Estate Leisure Park	♿	01350 727236
36	C2	Kirkmichael	Rocksite	♿	01250 881298
36	C2	Pitlochry	Craigatin House & Courtyard	♿	01796 472478
36	C2	Pitlochry	Craigvrack Hotel	♿	01796 472399
36	C2	Bailinluig	Cuil -an- Daraich Guest House	♿	01796 482750
36	C2	Pitlochry	Dalshian Chalets	♿	01796 473080
36	C2	Pitlochry	Green Park Hotel	♿	01796 473248
36	C2	Pitlochry	The Poplars	♿	01796 472911
36	C2	Pitlochry	The Well House	♿	01796 472239
36	C3	Crieff	Fendoch Guest House	♿	01764 655619
36	C3	Perth	Huntingtower Hotel	♿	01738 583771
36	C3	Perth	Orchard Cottage	♿	01738 620783
36	C4	Auchterarder	Duchally Country Estate	♿	01764 663071
36	C4	Auchterarder	The Gleneagles Hotel	♿	01764 662231
36	C4	Dunning	Duncrub Holidays Ltd	♿	01764 684368
36	C4	Forgandenny	Battledown Bed & Breakfast	♿	01738 812471
36	D1	Blairgowrie	Glenbeag Mountain Lodges	♿	01250 885204
36	D2	Alyth	The Reed & The Toftin	♿	01828 632547
36	D2	Blairgowrie	Holmrigg	♿	01250 884309
36	D2	Coupar Angus	Red House Hotel	♿	01828 628500
36	D2	Cragisla	Lochside Lodge & Roundhouse Restaurant	♿	01575 560340
36	D3	Glencarse	Glencarse Hotel	♿	01738 860206
36	D3	Cargill	Ballathie House Hotel	♿	01250 883268
36	D3	Perth	Sunbank House	♿	01738 624882
36	D3	Scone	Perth Airport Skylodge	♿	01738 555700
36	D4	Bridge of Earn	River Edge Lodges	♿	01738 812370
36	D4	Markinch, Nr. Glenrothes	Balbirnie House Hotel	♿	01592 610066
37	E1	Kirriemuir	Glenprosen Cottages	♿	01575 540302
37	E2	Glenisla, Nr. Kirriemuir	Tipperwhig & Brankam	♿	01575 560213
37	E2	Kirriemuir	Pearsie Lodge	♿	01575 540234
37	E2	Westmuir	Westmuir Holiday	♿	01828 632568
37	E3	Broughty Ferry	Forbes of Kingennie	♿	01382 350777
37	E3	Rathillet	St Andrews Country Cottages	♿	01382 330318
37	E3	Dundee	Hilton Dundee	♿	01382 229271
37	E3	Dundee	Seabraes Self Catering Flats	♿	01382 573111
37	E3	Dundee	West Park Centre	♿	01382 647177
37	E3	Kellas	Main Wing	♿	01382 350 239
37	E4	St Andrews	Rufflets Country House Hotel	♿	01334 472594
37	E4	Elie	Elie Letting	♿	01333 330219
37	E4	Leven	Bayview	♿	01333 360454
37	F1	Brechin	Northern Hotel	♿	01356 625400
37	F3	Carnoustie	Carnoustie Coach House B&B	♿	01241 857319
37	F4	Anstruther	Lobster Pot Cottage	♿	01333 340640
37	F4	Nr. St Andrews	Balmashie Holiday Cottages (A917)	♿	01334 880666
37	F4	St Andrews	Pitmilly West Lodge	♿	01334 880581
37	F4	St Andrews	The Old Station Country Guest House	♿	01334 880505
37	G1	Montrose	Brawliemuir Farm	♿	01561 362453
37	G2	Montrose	Best Western Links Hotel	♿	01674 671000
38	A3	Waternish	Auld Orwell Cottage	♿	01470 592363
38	A3	Waternish	La Bergerie	♿	01470 592282
38	B3	Nr. Bernisdale	Auchendinny	♿	01470 532470
38	B3	Portree	Cuillin Hills Hotel	♿	01478 612003
38	B3	Portree	Viewfield House Hotel	♿	01478 612217
38	B3	Carbost	Taigh Na H-Aibhne	♿	01313 32 6622
38	C4	Broadford	Corriegorm Beag	♿	01471 822515
38	C4	Kyle of Lochalsh	Borodale House	♿	01478 660222
38	D1	Aultbea, Nr. Achnasheen	31 Mellon Charles	♿	01445 731382
38	D2	Gairloch	Willow Croft	♿	01445 712448
38	D3	Achnasheen	The Torridon	♿	01445 791242
38	D4	Nr. Achmore	Soluis Mu Thuath	♿	01599 577219
39	E1	Laide	Rocklea Little Gruinard	♿	01314 416053
39	F1	Lochbroom	Taigh a Braoin	♿	01560 484003
39	F1	Ullapool	Dromnan Guest House	♿	01854 612333
39	F6	Nr. Spean Bridge	Dreamweavers	♿	01397 712548
39	F6	Roy Bridge	The Stronlossit Inn	♿	01397 712253
39	F6	Spean Bridge	Old Pines Hotel and Restaurant	♿	01397 712324
39	F6	Spean Bridge	The Heathers	♿	01397 712077
39	G4	Glenurquhart	Old Stables	♿	01456 476367
39	G5	Whitebridge	Kinbrylie	♿	01456 486658
39	H2	Culbokie, Nr. Dingwall	Wester Brae Highland Lodges and Chalets	♿	01349 877609
39	H3	Nr. Beauly	Dunsmore Lodges	♿	01463 782424
39	H3	Nr. Conon Bridge	Kinkell Country House	♿	01349 861270
39	H3	Inverness	Avalon Guest House	♿	01463 239075
39	H3	Inverness	Express by Holiday Inn	♿	01463 732700
39	H3	Inverness	Glencairn and Ardross House	♿	01463 232965
39	H3	Inverness	Kingsmills Hotel Inverness Ltd	♿	01463 237166
39	H3	Inverness	Ramada Jarvis Inverness	♿	01463 235181
39	H3	Inverness	Rookery Nook	♿	01463 237085
39	H3	Muir-of-Ord	Hillview Park	♿	01463 870787
39	H4	Drumnadrochit	Woodlands	♿	01456 450356

200

Accessible Accommodation-Scotland

Pg Ref	Town name	Accommodation name	Type	Telephone No.
39 H6	Falls of Truim	Crubenbeg House	♿	01540 673300
40 A3	Daviot	The Lodge at Daviot Mains	♿	01463 772215
40 A3	Nairn	Windsor Hotel	♿	01667 453108
40 A3	Westhill	Firthview House Links View & The Gatehouse	♿	01463 790620
40 A5	Aviemore	Avielochan Farm Holiday Cottages	🚶	01479 810846
40 A5	Aviemore	High Range Self Catering Chalets	♿	01479 810636
40 A5	Aviemore	Macdonald Academy	♿	01479 810781
40 A5	Aviemore	Pine Bank Chalets	🚶	01479 810000
40 A5	Aviemore	Silverglades Holiday Homes	♿	01479 810165
40 A5	Aviemore	Waverley	🚶	01479 811226
40 A5	Kincraig	Loch Insh Chalets	♿	01540 651272
40 A5	Kingussie	The Hermitage Guest House	🚶	01540 662137
40 B3	Auldearn	Covenanters Inn	♿	01667 452456
40 B3	Littlemill	Hidden Glen Holidays	♿	01667 454630
40 B4	Grantown-On-Spey	Muckrach Lodge Hotel	♿	01479 851257
40 B4	Nethybridge	Fhuarain Forest Cottages	♿	01479 821642
40 B4	Nethybridge	Nethybridge Hotel	♿	01479 821203
40 B4	Nethybridge	Osprey House & Red Kite House	🚶	01330 844344
40 B5	Aviemore	Aviemore Holiday Homes	🚶	01479 810499
40 B5	Nethybridge	Dell of Abernethy Cottages	🚶	01479 821643
40 C2	Nr. Elgin	Carden Self-Catering	♿	01343 850222
40 C2	Lossiemouth	Ceilidh B&B	♿	01343 815848
40 C2	Lossiemouth	Links Lodge	🚶	01343 813815
40 C4	Ballindalloch	Easter Corrie	🚶	01807 590241
40 C6	Braemar	Braemar Lodge Hotel	🚶	01339 741627
40 C6	Crathie	Crathie Opportunity Holidays	♿	01339 742100
40 D2	Buckie	10 Great Eastern Road	🚶	01542 831277
40 D3	Dufftown Keith	Parkmore Farm Holiday Cottages	♿	01340 820072
40 D3	Huntly	Drumdelgie house	♿	01466 760346
40 D4	Dufftown	Braehead Villa	🚶	01340 820461
40 D6	Ballater	Darroch Learg Hotel	🚶	01339 755443
40 D6	Ballater	Glenernan	♿	01339 753111
40 D6	Glen Tanar Aboyne	Glen Tanar Estate	♿	01339 886451
41 E5	Alford	Craich Cottage	🚶	01975 562584
41 E5	Kemnay	Grant Arms Hotel	♿	01467 651226
41 E6	Aboyne	Chesterton House	🚶	01339 886740
41 E6	Banchory	Birch & Willow Lodges	🚶	01330 822622
41 E6	Nr. Banchory	Woodend Chalet Holidays	♿	01339 882562
41 F3	Turriff	Delgatie Castle	♿	01888 563479
41 F3	Turriff	Deveron Lodge B&B Guesthouse	♿	01888 563613
41 F3	New Blyth	Garden Cottage	♿	01888 544230
41 F3	Fyvie	Stonefolds Farm Cottage	🚶	01651 891267
41 F4	Inverurie	Strathburn Hotel	🚶	01467 624422
41 F5	Aberdeen, Airport	Britannia Hotel	🚶	01224 409988
41 F5	Aberdeen, Airport	Thistle Aberdeen Airport Hotel	♿	01224 725252
41 F5	Blairs Aberdeen	Ardoe House Hotel	♿	01224 860600
41 F5	Dyce Aberdeen	Speedbird Inn	♿	01224 772883
41 F5	Kintore	The Greenknowe	🚶	01467 632366
41 F5	Westhill Aberdeen	Holiday Inn Aberdeen West	♿	01224 270300
41 F6	Banchory	Bridge of Bennie Cottage	🚶	01330 824288
41 G3	Nr. Peterhead	Greenbrae Farmhouse	🚶	01779 821051
41 G5	Aberdeen, Old Aberdeen	Aberdeen Patio Hotel	♿	01224 633339
41 G5	Aberdeen, Ruthrieston	Copthorne Hotel	♿	01224 630404
41 G5	Aberdeen, Old Aberdeen	Crombie House	♿	01224 273444
41 G5	Aberdeen, Ruthrieston	Express by Holiday Inn	♿	01224 623500
41 G5	Aberdeen, Old Aberdeen	Hillhead Halls	♿	01224 274000
41 G5	Aberdeen, Old Aberdeen	Kings Hall	♿	01224 273444
41 G5	Aberdeen, Old Aberdeen	Northern Hotel	🚶	01224 483342
41 G5	Aberdeen	Woolmanhill Flats	♿	01224 262134
41 G5	Altens Aberdeen	Thistle Aberdeen Altens	♿	01224 877000
41 G5	Pitfodels Aberdeen	The Marcliffe Hotel and Spa	♿	01224 861000
41 G5	Bamedie	The Byre	♿	01358 742673
41 H3	Peterhead	Invernettie Guest House	♿	01779 473530
42 A4	Nr. Lochinver	Glendarroch House	🚶	01431 821207
42 A4	Lochinver	Cathair Dhubh Estate	🚶	01571 855277
42 B4	Nr. Lairg	Ruddyglow Park Country House	🚶	01571 822216
42 D2	Talmine	Cloisters	♿	01847 601286
42 D2	Talmine	Post Office Flat	🚶	01847 601250
42 D4	Altnaharra	Invermudale Annexe	🚶	01549 411250
43 F2	Nr. Thurso	Forss House Hotel	🚶	01847 861201
43 F5	Brora	Tigh Fada Apartment & The Eyrie	🚶	01408 621332
43 G2	Thurso	Park Hotel	♿	01847 893251
43 G2	Thurso	Pentland Lodge House	♿	01847 895103
43 G2	Thurso	Weigh Inn Hotel	♿	01847 893722
43 G2	Weydale, Nr. Thurso	Curlew Cottage	🚶	01847 895638
44 B7	Lochcarnan	Orasay Inn	♿	01870 610298
44 B8	Isle of South Uist	Caloraidh	🚶	01878 710365
44 B8	South Uist, Nr. Stilligarry	Crossroads	♿	01870 620321
44 B9	Northbay	Airds Guest House	🚶	01871 890720
44 C5	Isle of Harris	Carminish House	🚶	01859 520400
44 C6	Isle of North Uist	Redburn House	🚶	01876 500301
44 C6	Isle of North Uist	Tigh Dearg Hotel	♿	01876 500700
44 D3	Uig	Riof Ocean Cottage	♿	01851 672732
44 D4	Isle of Harris	Ardhasaig House	🚶	01859 502500
44 D5	Isle of Harris	Croft Cottage	♿	01859 502338
44 E2	Back	Broad Bay House	♿	01851 820990
44 E3	Stornoway	Herbridean Self Catering	♿	01851 700190
44 E3	Uig	Valtos Cottage	🚶	01851 703957
44 F1	Isle of Lewis	The Cross Inn	♿	01851 810152
45 B2	Dounby	Lochland Chalets	🚶	01856 771340
45 C1	Westray	The Kilnmans Cottage	🚶	01857 677482
45 C3	Kirkwall	Lav rockha Guest House	♿	01856 876103

Pg	Ref	Town name	Accommodation name	Type	Telephone No.
45	C3	Orkney	14 Buttquoy Park		01856 872454
45	C3	Orphir	Cullya-Quoy		01856 811244
45	C3	Orphir Scapa Flow	Houton Bay Lodge		01856 811320
45	C3	Rendall, Nr. Tingwall	Widefirth Cottages		01856 761891
45	C4	Hoy	Stromabank		01856 701494
45	D3	Tankerness	Sebay Mill Holiday Apartments		01856 872281
45	E1	North Ronaldsay	Observatory Guest House		01857 633200

Pg	Ref	Town name	Accommodation name	Type	Telephone No.
45	G4	Walls	Burrastow House		01595 809307
45	H4	Lerwick	63 Burgh Road & Decca		01595 696651
45	H4	Lerwick	Glen Orchy Guest House		01595 692031
45	H4	Lerwick	Shetland Hotel		01595 695515
45	H4	Aith	Langbiggin		01595 810361
45	H5	Gulberwick	Virdafjell		01595 694336

✈ Accessible Accommodation-Wales

We recommend when booking any accommodation you check that your specific requirements can be met prior to confirming your booking. The symbols shown will enable people with disabilities to make an informed choice.

ACCESSIBILITY CATEGORIES

Visit Wales do not offer a disability assessment for accommodation types in Wales. The current policy is to encourage each property to have an Accessibility Statement. Using alternative sources we have included details of properties and their self assessment of disabled facilities.

 Category 1: Wheelchair access without assistance

 Category 2: Wheelchair access with assistance

 Category 3: Limited mobility

Pg	Ref	Town name	Accommodation name	Type	Telephone No.
10	A3	St Davids	Hendre Eynon Park		01437 720474
10	A3	St Davids	Ocean Haze Hotel		01437 720826
10	A3	St Davids	Tretio Park		01437 781359
10	A4	Haverfordwest	Rosemoor Cottage (A327)		01437 781326
10	A4	Nr. Camrose	Keeston Hill Cottage		01437 710440
10	B3	Nr. Newport	Gellifawr		01239 820343
10	B3	Clarbeston Road	Ivy Court Cottage		01437 532473
10	B3	Nr. Greenway	Salutation Inn		01239 820564
10	B4	Tenby	Greenhills Country Hotel		01834 871291
10	B4	Pembroke Dock	Cleddau Bridge Hotel		01646 685961
10	B4	Haverfordwest	Dreenhill Farm		01437 764494
10	B4	Tenby	Milton Manor Hotel (A477)		01646 651398
10	B4	Narberth	Highl d Grange Farm Guest House		01834 860952
10	B5	Pembroke	Rosedene Guest House (A4139)		01646 672586
10	B5	Pembroke	Stackpole Trust (B4319)		01646 661425
10	B5	Manorbier	YHA Manorbier		01834 871803
10	C2	Aberporth	Ffynon Wen Gst House		01239 810312
10	C2	Aberporth	Gorslwyd Farm		01239 810593
10	C2	Cardigan	Canllefaes Ganol Cottage		01239 613712
10	C2	St Dogmaels	Trenewydd Farm Cottage		01239 612370
10	C2	Nr. Cardigan	The Gwbert Hotel		01239 612638
10	C2	Newcastle Emlyn	Cenarth Falls		01239 710345
10	C3	Boncath	Clynfyw Country Centre (A478)		01239 841236
10	C3	Newport	Llwyngwair Manor Park		01446 774845
10	C4	Red Roses	Homeleigh Country Cottage		01834 831765
10	C4	Saundersfoot	Saundersfoot Bay		01834 812284
10	C4	Nr. Clunderwen	Latchygors Cottage		01994 240460
10	C4	Tenby	Heywood Ldge Hotel		01834 842684

Pg	Ref	Town name	Accommodation name	Type	Telephone No.
10	C4	Tenby	Clarence House Hotel		01834 844371
10	C4	Tenby	Atlantic Hotel		01834 842881
10	C4	Saundersfoot	Merlewood Hotel		01834 812421
10	C4	Saundersfoot	Smugglers Cottage		01348 837742
10	C4	Whitland	Pantglas Farm Park		01834 831618
10	D2	Cardigan	Penbontbren Farm Hotel		01239 810248
10	D2	Nr. Plwmp	Quay West Resort		01545 560477
11	E2	Lampeter	Bryn Castell		01570 422447
11	E3	LLanarthney	Hamdden Llety Mieri		01558 823059
11	E3	Llandeilo	Plough Inn		01558 823431
11	E3	Nr. Llandeilo	Maerdy Cottages (B4302)		01550 777448
11	E5	Swansea	Swansea Marriot Hotel		01792 642020
11	E5	LLansamlet	Hilton National		01792 310330
11	F2	Llandovery	Rhandirmwyn Camping		01550 760257
11	F4	Ystradgynlais	Maes y Gwernen Hotel		01639 730218
11	F5	Port Talbot	Aberavon Beach Hotel		01639 884949
11	F5	Neath	Cwmbach Cottages		01639 639825
11	F5	Nr. Port Talbot	Ty n Y Caeau House		01639 883897
11	F6	Porthcawl	Glamorgan Holiday Hotel		01656 785375
11	F6	Porthcawl	Rest Convalescent Home		01656 772066
11	G1	Llandrindod Wells	Hotel Metropole		01597 823700
11	G1	Cross Gates	Guidfa House		01597 851241
11	G1	Llandrindod Wells	Bell Inn		01597 823959
11	G2	Builth Wells	Pencerrig Gardens		01982 553226
11	G2	Garth	Lake Country House		01591 620202
11	G3	Brecon	Castle of Brecon Hotel		01874 624611
11	G3	Brecon	Plough & Harrow Inn		01874 622709
11	G4	Nr. Merthyr Tydfil	Nant Ddu Lodge Hotel (A470)		01685 379111

Pg Ref	Town name	Accommodation name	Type	Telephone No.
11 G4	Merthyr Tydfil	Tregenna Hotel		01685 723627
11 G5	Bridgend	Welcome Break Sarn Park		01656 659218
11 G5	Coychurch	Coed y Mwstwr Hotel		01656 860621
11 G6	Llantwit Major	Acorn Caravan Park		01446 794024
11 G6	Cardiff	Parc Coed Machen Ctry Cottaget		01446 760684
11 H2	Kington	Offas Dyke Lodge		01544 370341
11 H4	Nantyglo	Lamb House		01495 290179
11 H5	Cwmbran	Parkway Hotel		01633 871199
11 H6	Cardiff	Novotel Cardiff		02920 475 000
11 H6	Caerau	Copthorne Cardiff		02920 599100
12 A4	Skenfirth	Lower Green Farm		01873 821219
12 A5	Nr. Usk	Cwrt-Y-Gaer		01291 650700
12 A5	Newport	Hilton Newport		01633 413737
16 A4	Abersoch	Rhydolion		01758 712342
16 B1	Amlwch	Beudygwyn Farm Holidays		01407 711433
16 B1	Benllech	Treysgawen Hall		01248 750750
16 B3	Llanllyfni	Hen Ysgol		01286 660701
16 B3	Pwllheli	Rhosydd		01758 612956
16 B4	Nr. Pwllheli	Y Beudy & Ysgubor		01766 810259
16 B4	Nr. Pwllheli	Afonwen Cottages		01766 810939
16 B4	Pwllheli	Gwynfryn Farm		01758 612536
16 C1	Benllech	Bryn Meirion Lodge		01248 853118
16 C2	Llanddeiniolen	Ty n Rhos Country House		01248 670489
16 C2	Llanfairfechan	Aber Falls Hotel		01248 680579
16 C2	Bangor	British Hotel		01248 364911
16 C2	Llanberis	Royal Victoria Hotel		01286 870253
16 C2	Beaumaris	The Bulkeley Hotel		01248 810415
16 C3	Llanberis	Pen y Pass YHA		01286 870428
16 C3	Caernarfon	The Stables Hotel		01286 830711
16 C4	Nr. Llanbedr	Ystumgwern Farm		01341 247249
16 C4	Nr. Llanbedr	Byrdir		01341 247200
16 C4	Porthmadog	Greenacres Park		01766 512781
16 C4	Harlech	The Estuary Motel		01766 771155
16 C4	Harlech	Hotel Maes Y Neuadd		01766 780200
16 C5	Llwyngwril	Pentre Bach Cottage		01341 250294
16 C5	Tywyn	Corbett Arms Hotel		01654 710264
16 C5	Tywyn	Pant y Neuadd		01654 711393
16 C5	Barmouth	The Sandpiper		01341 280318
16 C5	Opposite Barmouth	Graig Wen		01341 250482
16 C5	Nr. Abergynolwyn	Eisteddfa		01654 782385
16 C5	Nr. Dolgellau	George III Hotel		01341 422525
16 C6	Nr. Machynlleth	Penmaendyfi House		01654 791616
16 C6	Aberystwyth	Marine Hotel		01970 612444
16 C6	Aberystwyth	Glan Y Mor Park		01970 828900
16 C6	Borth	Cambrain Coast		01970 871233
16 C6	Aberdyfi	Hillside Village		01654 767522
16 C6	Aberystwyth	Ocean View Park		01970 623361
16 D1	Llandudno	Marlborough Hotel		01492 875846
16 D1	Llandudno	RBS Belmont Hotel		01492 877770
16 D1	Llandudno	West Shore Hotel		01492 876833
16 D1	Llandudno	Dunoon Hotel		01492 860787
16 D1	Llandudno	Four Oaks Hotel		01492 876506
16 D1	Colwyn Bay	Beachmount		01492 549314
16 D1	Llandudno	Epperstone Hotel		01492 878746
16 D1	Llandudno	Royal Hotel		01492 876476
16 D1	Llandudno	Bay Court Hotel		01492 877356
16 D1	Llandudno	Esplanade Hotel		01492 860300
16 D1	Llandudno	Ambassador Hotel		01492 876886
16 D1	Llandudno	Evans Hotel		01492 860784
16 D1	Llandudno	Grafton Hotel		01492 876814
16 D1	Colwyn Bay	Ashmount Hotel		01492 544582
16 D1	Colwyn Bay	Northwood Hotel		01492 549931
16 D2	Llanrwst	Glan Y Borth Holidays		01492 641543
16 D2	Colwyn Bay	Hwylfa Ddafydd Farm		01492 516965
16 D2	Nr. Caerhun	The Lodge Hotel		01492 660766
16 D2	Colwyn Bay	Holcombe Hotel		01492 530423
16 D2	Colwyn Bay	Edelweiss Hotel		01492 532314
16 D3	Nr. Betws Y Coed	Plas Hall Manor Hotel		01690 750206
16 D4	Trawsfynydd	Old Mill Farm House		01766 540397
16 D5	Machynlleth	Warren Parc		01654 702054
17 E4	Llandderfel	Bryncelyn Holiday Park		01678 530212
17 E5	Llangadfan	Brynllys		01938 820347
17 F3	Llangollen	Bryn Howel Hotel		01978 860331
17 F3	Cefn-mawr	Eirianfa Park		01978 860919
17 F5	Llanfair Caereinion	Madogs Wells Farm		01938 810446
17 G3	Gresford	Forte Travelodge		01978 365705
17 G3	Rossett	Corner House Farm		01829 270452
22 A5	Rhyl	Sandy Shores Guest House		01745 351989
22 A6	Abergele	Dolhyfryd Lodge Hotel		01745 826505
22 A6	Abergele	Ty Mawr Holiday Park		01745 832079
22 A6	Bodelwyddan	Bodelwyddan Castle Hotel		01745 585088
22 B5	Prestatyn	Presthaven Sands		01745 856471
22 B6	Mold	Forte Travelodge		01244 816473
22 B6	Ewloe	St Davids Park Hotel		01244 520800
22 B6	Halkyn	Forte Travelodge		01352 780952
22 B6	Mold	Beaufort Park Hotel		01352 758646
22 B6	Mold	Holiday Inn Garden Court		01244 550011

How to use this directory

To assist the user to find locations within a small area we have referenced the entries by the map page number and grid reference. To locate an entry, determine the area you wish to visit and note the map page number and grid reference. Using this information the user can search the directory by the page and grid square to locate a list of locations appearing within the designated grid square.

Please note that in a few cases where there is a large overlap between map pages a location is only referenced to one page. Therefore if you cannot see an entry for a particular grid square that contains a symbol please check the overlapping map page grid reference.

Example Tower Esplanade Beach, Skegness appears on pages 20 C1and 25 H6 and is only referenced to page 25 H6.

Pg	Ref	Beach name	Town name	Parking
3	E5	Sennen Cove	Sennen Cove	P
3	E5	Porthcurno	St Buryan	
3	F4	Gwithian/Godrevy	Gwithian	
3	F4	Porthtowan	Porthtowan	
3	F4	Portreath	Portreath	P
3	F4	Porthmeor	St Ives	
3	F4	Porthminster	St Ives	P
3	F5	Praa Sands	Breage	
3	F5	Towans Beach	Hayle	
3	G3	Fistral	Newquay	
3	G3	Great Western	Newquay	
3	G3	Porth	Newquay	
3	G3	Towan Beach	Newquay	P
3	G3	Porthcothan	Porthcothan	P
3	G3	Constantine Bay	St Merryn	P
3	G3	Harlyn Bay	St Merryn	
3	G3	Treyarnon Bay	St Merryn	P
3	G3	Mawgan Porth	Trenance	P
3	G3	Trevone Bay	Trevone	P
3	G5	Gyllyngvase	Falmouth	P
3	G6	Kennack Sands (west)	Lizard	
3	H2	Trebarwith Strand	Tintagel	P
3	H3	Polzeath	Polzeath	P
3	H4	Par Sands	Par	
3	H4	Porthpean	St Austell	
4	B3	Crooklets	Bude	P
4	B3	Sandymouth	Bude	P
4	B3	Summerleaze	Bude	P
4	B3	Widemouth Sands	Bude	P
4	B4	Crackington Haven	Bude	P
4	B6	Readymoney	Fowey	
4	C1	Putsborough Sands	Putsborough	
4	C1	Woolacombe Sands	Woolacombe	P
4	C2	Westward Ho	Bideford	P
4	C2	Croyde Bay	Croyde	
4	C6	Seaton	Seaton	P
4	D1	Tunnels Beaches	Ilfracombe	
4	D6	Bantham	Bigbury-on-Sea	
4	D6	Bigbury-on-Sea	Bigbury-on-Sea	
4	D6	Challaborough	Bigbury-on-Sea	
4	D6	Mouthwell Sands	Galmpton	
4	D6	Thurlestone South Milton	Galmpton	
4	D7	Hope Cove	Galmpton	
5	E5	Paignton Sands	Paignton	
5	E5	Preston	Paignton	
5	E6	Blackpool Sands	Blackpool	P
5	E6	Broadsands	Brixham	
5	E6	Goodrington South Sands	Paignton	
5	E6	Beesands	Stokenham	
5	E6	Slapton Sands, Torcross	Stokenham	
5	E6	Strete Gate	Strete	
5	E7	North Sands	Salcombe	
5	E7	South Sands	Salcombe	
5	F5	Coryton Cove	Dawlish	P
5	F5	Dawlish Warren	Dawlish	P
5	F5	Ness Cove Shaldon	Teignmouth	P
5	F5	Teignmouth Town	Teignmouth	P
5	F5	Babbacombe	Torquay	
5	F5	Corbyn Head (Torre Abbey)	Torquay	
5	F5	Maidencombe	Torquay	
5	F5	Meadfoot Beach	Torquay	
5	F5	Oddicombe Beach	Torquay	

Pg	Ref	Beach name	Town name	Parking
5	F5	Watcombe	Torquay	
5	F6	Breakwater Beach	Brixham	
5	F6	St Marys Bay	Brixham	
5	G1	Brean	Berrow	
5	G1	Brean Cove	Berrow	
5	G1	Berrow	Burnham on Sea	P
5	G5	Cobo Bay	Castel	
5	G5	L'Eree	Castel	
5	G5	Port Soif Bay	Castel	
5	G5	Vazon	Castel	
5	G6	Petit Bot Bay	St Martin	
5	G6	Portelet Bay	St Martin	
5	H5	Pembroke/L'Ancresse	Vale	
5	H6	Fermain	St Martin	
6	A2	Burnham on Sea	Burnham on Sea	P
6	A2	Weston-super-Mare	Weston-super-Mare	P
6	A5	Charmouth West	Lyme Regis	P
6	B6	Central	Weymouth	
6	D5	Alum Chine	Bournemouth	
6	D5	Bournemouth Pier	Bournemouth	P
6	D5	Durley Chine	Bournemouth	
6	D5	Branksome Chine	Canford Cliffs	P
6	D5	Canford Cliffs Chine	Canford Cliffs	
6	D5	Shore Road	Canford Cliffs	P
6	D5	Rockley Sands	Poole	P
7	E5	Fisherman's Walk	Boscombe	
7	E5	Durley Chine	Bournemouth	
7	E5	Southbourne Beach	Southbourne	P
7	F5	Colwell Bay	Freshwater	
7	F5	Gurnard	Northwood	
7	F5	Totland Bay	Totland	
7	G5	St Helens Duver	Bembridge	P
7	G5	Cowes East	East Cowes	
7	G5	West Beachlands West	Hayling Island	P
7	G5	Ryde East	Ryde	P
7	G5	Seagrove Bay	Ryde	
7	G5	Springvale	Ryde	
7	G5	Sandown	Sandown	P
7	G5	Yaverland	Sandown	P
7	G6	Ventnor	Ventnor	P
7	H5	West Wittering Beach	East Wittering	P
7	H5	Eastoke	Hayling Island	P
7	H5	West Beachlands Central	Hayling Island	P
8	A5	Littlehampton Coastguards	Littlehampton	
8	A6	East of Pier	Bognor Regis	P
8	B5	Town Beach	Worthing	
8	C6	Seaford Bay	Seaford	P
8	D5	Normans Bay Beach	Bexhill on Sea	
8	D5	Pevensey Bay	Pevensey	P
8	D6	Pier to Wish Tower	Eastbourne	P
8	D6	Tower to Holywell	Eastbourne	P
8	D6	Birling Gap	Seaford	
9	E5	Bexhill on Sea	Bexhill on Sea	
9	E5	Cooden Beach	Bexhill on Sea	
9	E5	Pelham Beach	Hastings	
9	F5	Camber Sands	Rye	P
9	F5	Winchelsea	Winchelsea	P
10	A3	Abereiddy	Berea	

Pg	Ref	Beach name	Town name	Parking
10	A3	Newgale	Newgale	P
10	A3	Caerfai	St Davids	
10	A3	White Sands	St Davids	P
10	A4	West Angle Bay	Angle	
10	A4	Broadhaven	Broad Haven	P
10	A4	Little Haven	Broad Haven	
10	A4	St Brides Haven	Broad Haven	
10	A4	Dale	Dale	
10	A4	Marloes	Dale	
10	A4	Martins Haven	Dale	
10	A4	Gelliswick	Milford Haven	
10	A4	Sandy Haven	Milford Haven	
10	A4	Nolton Haven	Nolton Haven	P
10	B2	Dinas Cross Cwm-yr-Eglwys	Dinas	
10	B3	Pwll - Gwaelod	Dinas	
10	B3	Goodwick Sands	Fishguard	P
10	B3	Newport Sands	Newport	
10	B5	Barafundle Bay	Freshwater East	
10	B5	Freshwater East	Freshwater East	
10	B5	Manorbier	Manorbier	
10	B5	Lydstep	Penally	P
10	C2	Aberporth	Aberporth	
10	C2	Mwnt	Ferwig	
10	C2	Poppit Sands	St Dogmaels	P
10	C2	Penbryn	Tresaith	
10	C2	Tresaith	Tresaith	P
10	C4	Amroth	Saundersfoot	P
10	C4	Coppet Hall	Saundersfoot	
10	C4	Saundersfoot	Saundersfoot	P
10	C4	Wisemans Bridge	Saundersfoot	
10	C4	Tenby Castle	Tenby	P
10	C5	Penally	Penally	
10	C5	Tenby South	Tenby	P
10	D1	Traeth y Harbwr	New Quay	
10	D2	Aberaeron South	Llangrannog	
10	D2	Llangrannog	Llangrannog	
10	D2	Llangrannog Cilborth	Llangrannog	
10	D2	Cwmtydu	Nanternis	
10	D2	New Quay Traeth y Dolau	New Quay	
10	D4	Pembrey Country Park Cefn Sidan	Pembrey	
10	D5	Port Eynon	Port Eynon	P
11	E1	Aberystwyth South	Aberystwyth	P
11	E1	Llanrhystud	Llanrhystud	
11	E5	Bracelet Bay	Mumbles	P
11	E5	Caswell Bay	Mumbles	P
11	E5	Langland Bay	Mumbles	P
11	E5	Limeslade	Mumbles	
11	F6	Trecco Bay	Portcawl	
11	F6	Rest Bay	Portcawl	P
11	F6	Southerndown	St Brides Major	P
11	H6	Whitmore Bay, Barry Island	Barry	P
15	E5	Bell Wharf, Leigh on Sea	Southend-on-Sea	
15	E5	Three Shells	Southend-on-Sea	
15	F4	Brightlingsea Beach	St Osyth	P
15	F5	Shoeburyness East	Shoeburyness	
15	F5	Shoebury Common	Shoeburyness	
15	F6	Leysdown Beach	Leysdown-on-Sea	P
15	F6	Beach Street	Sheerness	P
15	F6	Minster Leas	Sheerness	
15	G3	Felixstowe South	Felixstowe	P

Accessible beaches

Pg	Ref	Beach name	Town name	Parking
15	G3	Dovercourt	Harwich	P
15	G3	Albion Beach	Walton on the Naze	P
15	G4	Clacton West Beach	Clacton-on-Sea	P
15	G4	Frinton on Sea	Frinton-on-Sea	
15	G6	Minnis Bay	Birchington	P
15	G6	Herne Bay	Herne Bay	
15	G6	Reculver	Herne Bay	P
15	G6	Tankerton	Whitstable	
15	H1	Sizewell Beach	Leiston	P
15	H2	Aldeburgh	Aldeburgh	P
15	H2	Thorpeness Beach	Thorpeness	P
15	H3	The Dip	Felixstowe	
15	H6	West Bay, Westgate	Birchington	
15	H6	Botany Bay	Broadstairs	P
15	H6	Joss Bay	Broadstairs	P
15	H6	Main Sands	Margate	P
15	H6	St Mildred's Bay, Westgate	Margate	P
15	H6	Walpole Bay	Margate	P
15	H6	Westbrook Bay	Margate	P
15	H6	Main Sands	Ramsgate	P
16	A1	Porth Trwyn	Llanfaethlu	
16	A1	Llanfwrog Sandy Beach	Llanfwrog	
16	A2	Treaddur Bay	Holyhead	P
16	A2	Trearddur Bay, Porth Dafarch	Holyhead	P
16	A2	Borth Wen	Rhoscolyn	
16	A2	Silver Bay	Rhoscolyn	
16	A4	Aberdaron	Aberdaron	
16	B1	Llaneilian Porth Eilian	Amlwch	
16	B1	Cemlyn	Cemlyn	
16	B1	Cemaes Traeth Mawr	Llanbadrig	P
16	B1	Dulas Traeth Lligwy	Moelfre	
16	B1	Church Bay	Rhydwyn	
16	B2	Traeth Mawr	Aberffraw	
16	B2	Cable Bay	Llanfaelog	
16	B2	Porth Nobla	Llanfaelog	
16	B2	Porth Tyn Tywn	Llanfaelog	
16	B2	Rhosneigr Broad Beach	Llanfaelog	
16	B2	Newborough	Newborough	P
16	B2	Traith Crigyll	Rhosneigr	
16	B3	Dinas Dinlle (Morfa Dinlle) Liandwrog		P
16	B4	Abersoch	Abersoch	
16	B4	Machroes	Abersoch	
16	B4	Llanbedrog	Llanbedrog	
16	B4	Pwllheli Marian y De	Pwllheli	P
16	C1	Benllech	Benllech	
16	C1	Red Wharf Bay St David's	Benllech	
16	C1	Red Wharf Bay Traeth Coch	Benllech	
16	C1	Llanddona	Llanddona	P
16	C1	Moelfre	Moelfre	
16	C2	Beaumaris	Beaumaris	
16	C2	Llanfairfechan	Llanfairfechan	P
16	C2	Penmon	Penmon	
16	C4	Criccieth	Criccieth	P
16	C4	Criccieth West	Criccieth	
16	C4	Harlech	Harlech	P
16	C4	Traeth Bennar Morfa Dyffryn Llanbedr		P
16	C4	Llandanwg	Llandanwg	P
16	C5	Abermaw	Barmouth	P
16	C5	Fairbourne Ffriog	Fairbourne	P
16	C6	Aberdyfi	Aberdyfi	P
16	C6	Aberystwyth North	Aberystwyth	P
16	C6	Borth	Aberystwyth	P
16	C6	Clarach	Aberystwyth	
16	D1	Colwyn Bay Rhos on Sea Colwyn Bay		P
16	D1	Northshore	Llandudno	P
16	D1	Westshore	Llandudno	P
16	D2	Tywyn	Conwy	P

Pg	Ref	Beach name	Town name	Parking
16	D2	Old Colwyn	Old Colwyn	P
16	D2	Penmaenmawr	Penmaenmawr	P
20	C2	Hunstanton	Hunstanton	P
20	C3	Heacham Beach	Heacham	
21	F2	Cromer	Cromer	P
21	F2	Sheringham	Sheringham	P
21	G3	Mundesley	Mundesley	P
21	G3	Sea Palling	Stalham	P
21	H4	Central	Great Yarmouth	P
21	H4	Gorleston on Sea	Hopton	P
21	H5	Kessingland	Kessingland	
21	H5	North of Claremont Pier	Lowestoft	P
21	H5	South of Claremont Pier	Lowestoft	P
21	H6	Denes	Southwold	
21	H6	Pier Beach	Southwold	P
22	A5	Kinmel Bay	Kinmel Bay	P
22	A5	Central	Prestatyn	
22	A5	Rhyl	Rhyl	P
22	A6	Pensarn/Abergele	Abergele	
22	B4	Lifeboat Road	Formby	P
22	B5	Talacre/ Gronant	Prestatyn	P
22	B5	Wallasey Beach	Wallasey	
22	B5	West Kirby	West Kirby	P
22	C1	Morecambe South	Morecambe	P
22	C3	Central Pier to Tower	Blackpool	
22	C3	St Chads Road to South Pier Blackpool		
22	C3	Lytham St Annes	Lytham St Annes	P
22	C4	Ainsdale Beach	Southport	
22	C4	Southport	Southport	
25	F1	North Beach	Bridlington	P
25	F1	South Beach	Bridlington	P
25	F1	Danes Dyke Beach	Flamborough	
25	F1	South Landing	Flamborough	
25	F2	Barmston	Barmston	
25	F2	Hornsea	Hornsea	P
25	G3	Withernsea	Withernsea	P
25	G4	Central	Cleethorpes	P
25	H5	Central	Mablethorpe	
25	H5	Central	Sutton on Sea	P
25	H6	Tower Esplanade	Skegness	P
26	D3	Marina	Kirkcudbright	
27	F3	South Saltpans	Allonby	
27	F3	West Winds	Allonby	
27	F5	Seascale	Seascale	P
27	F5	St Bees	St Bees	P
27	G3	West Beach	Silloth	
27	G6	Silecroft	Millom	P
29	E2	Sandhaven	South Shields	P
29	E2	Whitburn North - Seaburn Sunderland		P
29	E2	Cullercoats	Tynemouth	
29	E2	King Edwards Bay	Tynemouth	
29	E2	Longsands South	Tynemouth	P
29	E2	Whitley Bay	Whitley Bay	P
29	E3	Whitburn South - Roker	Sunderland	P
29	F4	Seaton Carew Foreshore	Hartlepool	
29	F4	Redcar Lifeboat Station	Redcar	P
29	G5	Runswick Bay	Runswick	
29	G5	Sandsend	Sandsend	
29	G5	West Cliff	Whitby	
29	H5	Robin Hood's Bay	Robin Hoods Bay	
29	H6	Cayton Bay	Cayton	
29	H6	North Bay	Cayton	P
29	H6	Filey Town	Filey	P
29	H6	South Bay	Scarborough	P
31	F4	Saltcoats South Beach	Ardrossan	
31	F4	Newton Beach, Millport	Millport	
31	G5	South Ayr Beach	Ayr	
31	G5	Irvine	Irvine	
32	C1	Black Sands	Aberdour	P

Pg	Ref	Beach name	Town name	Parking
32	C1	Silver Sands	Aberdour	
32	C1	Burntisland Beach	Burntisland	
32	C1	Kinghorn & Pettycur Bay	Kinghorn	P
32	D1	Elie Harbour	Elie	
32	D1	Gullane Bents	Gullane	
32	D2	Gosford	Longniddry	
32	D2	Longniddry	Longniddry	
33	E1	Yellowcraig	Dirleton	
33	E1	Elie Ruby Bay	Elie	P
33	E1	Milsey Bay (East - Milsey Bay)	North Berwick	
33	E1	West Beach	North Berwick (West)	
33	E2	Belhaven Bay	Dunbar	
33	G2	Coldingham sands	Eyemouth	
33	H4	Bamburgh	Bamburgh	
33	H4	Beadnell Bay	Beadnell	
33	H4	Low Newton	Embleton	P
33	H4	St Aidens	Seahouses	
33	H5	Amble Links	Amble	
35	E3	Ganavan Sands	Near Oban	
37	F3	Carnoustie	Carnoustie	P
37	F4	Billowness	Anstruther	P
37	F4	Roome Bay	Crail	
37	F4	Kingsbarns Beach	Kingsbarns	P
37	F4	East Sands	St Andrews (East)	
37	F4	West Sands	St Andrews (West)	
37	G2	Seafront	Montrose	
38	D1	Firemore Beach	Poolewe	
38	D2	Big Sand	Gairloch	P
38	D2	Gairloch Beach	Gairloch	
39	E1	Gruinard Bay	Laide	P
39	H3	Redpoint North	Redpoint	P
40	A1	Dornoch Beach	Dornoch	
40	A1	Embo	Dornoch	
40	A1	Sango Sands	Durness	
40	A1	North Beach	Golspie	P
40	A1	South Beach	Golspie	
40	A2	Shandwick Bay	Balintore	
40	A2	Saltburn	Saltburn	P
40	A3	Central Beach	Nairn	
40	B1	Portmahomack	Portmahomack	P
41	E2	Inverboyndie Beach	Whitehills	
41	F6	Stonehaven Beach	Stonehaven	
41	G4	Cruden Bay	Cruden Bay	P
41	G5	Aberdeen Ballroom	Aberdeen	
41	G5	Balmedie Beach	Balmedie	
42	A4	Achmelvich Bay	Achmelvich	P
43	E2	Strathy Bay	Near Melvich	P
43	F5	Brora Beach	Brora	
43	H3	Broadhaven South	Wick	P
45	H5	St Ninian's Isle	Bigton	
46	D1	Benone Strand Magilligan Castlerock		P
47	E1	East Strand	Portrush	
47	E1	Strand	Portstewart	P
47	F1	Ballycastle	Ballycastle	
47	F5	Cranfield West	Kilkeel	P
47	G3	Lagoon	Millisle	
47	G4	Tyrella Beach	Ballykinler	P
48	E1	White Rocks	Portrush	
49	E1	West Strand	Portrush	

How to use this directory

To assist the user to find locations within a small area we have referenced the entries by the map page number and grid reference. To locate an entry, determine the area you wish to visit and note the map page number and grid reference. Using this information the user can search the directory by the page and grid square to locate a list of locations appearing within the designated grid square.

Please note that in a few cases where there is a large overlap between map pages a location is only referenced to one page. Therefore if you cannot see a entry for a particular grid square that contains a symbol please check the overlapping map page grid reference.

Example Darwin Forest Country Park, Matlock appears on pages 18 D1 and 24 A6 and is only referenced to 24 A6.

Pg	Ref	Caravan site name Town name	Telephone No.
3	E5	**Kelynack Caravan & Camping Park** Penzance	01736 787633
3	E5	**Kenegie Manor Holiday Park** Penzance	01271 866766
3	E5	**Tower Park Caravans & Camping Site** Penzance	01736 810286
3	F4	**Porthtowan Tourist Park** Truro	01209 890256
3	F4	**Tehidy Holiday Park** Portreath	01209 216489
3	F5	**Godrevy Park** Hayle	01736 753100
3	F5	**Little Trevarrack Holiday Park** St. Ives	01736 797580
3	F5	**Parbola Holiday Park** Hayle	01209 831503
3	F5	**St. Ives Holiday Village** St. Ives	01271 866766
3	G3	**Mother Iveys Bay Caravan Park** Nr. Padstow	01841 520990
3	G3	**Point Curlew Holiday Estate** Padstow	01841 520855
3	G3	**Tregurrian Camping & Caravanning Club Site** Nr. Newquay	01637 860448
3	G3	**Treloy Touring Park** Newquay	01637 872063
3	G3	**Watergate Bay Touring Park** Newquay	01637 860387
3	G4	**Carnon Downs Caravan Park** Truro	01872 862283
3	G4	**Chiverton Park** Truro	01872 560667
3	G4	**Liskey Holiday Park** Truro	01872 560274
3	G4	**Monkey Tree Holiday Park** Newquay	01872 572032
3	G4	**Newperran Holiday Park** Newquay	01872 572407
3	G4	**Penrose Farm Touring Park** Perranporth	01872 573185
3	G4	**Perran Sands Holiday Park** Perranporth	01872 573551
3	G4	**Perran View Holiday Park** St. Agnes	01271 866766
3	G4	**Riverside Holiday Park** Newquay	01637 873617
3	G4	**Summer Lodge Holiday Park** Newquay	01726 860415
3	G4	**Treamble Valley** Truro	01872 573675
3	G4	**Trevornick Holiday Park** Nr. Newquay	01637 830531
3	G4	**Valley View Touring Park** Nr. Truro	07974 737665
3	G4	**White Acres Holiday Park** Newquay	08716 412045
3	G5	**Merrose Farm** Truro	01872 580380
3	G5	**Retanna Holiday Park** Falmouth	01326 340643
3	H2	**Trewethett Farm Caravan Club Site** Tintagel	01840 770222
3	H2	**Valley Truckle** Camelford	01840 212206
3	H3	**Hengar Manor Country Park** Bodmin	01208 850382
3	H3	**Little Bodieve** Wadebridge	01208 812323
3	H3	**Mena Farm Caravan & Camping Site** Bodmin	01208 831845
3	H3	**Michaelstow Manor Holiday Park** St Tudy	01208 850244
3	H3	**Padstow Holiday Park** Padstow	01841 532289
3	H3	**St. Minver Holiday Park** Nr. Rock	08716 412045
3	H3	**Trewan Hall Camping & Caravanning Club Site** St Columb	01637 880261
3	H4	**Penhaven Touring Park** Mevagissey	01726 843687
3	H4	**Powderham Castle Tourist Park** Lostwithiel	01208 872277
3	H4	**Seaview International Holiday Park** St. Austell	01726 843425
3	H4	**Tregarton Park** St. Austell	01726 843666
3	H4	**Trencreek Farm Country Holiday Park** St Austell	01726 882540
3	H4	**Veryan Camping & Caravanning Club Site** Truro	01872 501658
4	B3	**Budemeadows Touring Park** Bude	01288 361646
4	B3	**Hedlywood Caravan & Camping Park** Holsworthy	01288 381404
4	B3	**Upper Lynstone Camping & Caravan Park** Bude	01288 352017
4	B3	**Widemouth Bay Caravan Park (John Fowler Holiday Park)** Bude	01288 361741
4	B3	**Wooda Farm Park** Bude	01288 352069
4	B6	**Looe** Looe	01503 264006
4	B6	**Looe Bay Holiday Park** Looe	08716 412045
4	B6	**Penmarlam Caravan & Camping Park** Fowey	01726 870088
4	B6	**Polborder House Caravan & Camping Park** Looe	01503 240265
4	B6	**Trelawne Manor Holiday Park** Looe	01503 272213
4	B6	**Trelay Farm Park** Looe	01503 220900
4	C1	**North Morte Farm C & C P** Woolacombe	01271 870381
4	C1	**Warcombe Farm Camping Park** Mortehoe	01271 870690
4	C1	**Willingcott** Woolacombe	01271 870554
4	C2	**Bideford** Near Bideford	01237 431271
4	C2	**Lobb Field** Park Braunton	01271 812090
4	C2	**Surf Bay Holiday Park** Westward Ho!	01237 471833
4	C2	**Westward Ho! Beach Holiday Park** Westward Ho!	01271 866766
4	C5	**Notter Mill Country Park** Saltash	01752 843694
4	C5	**Woodovis Park** Tavistock	01822 832968
4	D1	**Brook Lea** West Down	01271 862848
4	D1	**Combe Martin Beach Holiday Park** Combe Martin	01271 882563
4	D1	**Devon Coast Holiday Park** Ilfracombe	01271 866766
4	D1	**Golden Coast Holiday Park** Ilfracombe	01271 866766
4	D1	**Hele Valley Holiday Park** Ilfracombe	01271 862460
4	D1	**Hidden Valley Park** Nr. Ilfracombe	01271 813837
4	D1	**Ilfracombe Holiday Park** Ilfracombe	01271 866766
4	D1	**Mill Park and Lake** Ilfracombe	01271 882647
4	D1	**Sandaway Beach Holiday Park** Ilfracombe	01271 866766
4	D1	**Stowford Farm Meadows** Combe Martin	01271 882476
4	D2	**Ruda Holiday Park** Braunton	08716 412045
4	D2	**Umberleigh Camping and Caravanning Club Site** Umberleigh	01769 560009
4	D5	**Harford Bridge Holiday Park** Tavistock	01822 810349
4	D5	**Higher Longford Caravan and Camping Park** Tavistock	01822 613360
4	D6	**Broad Park Caravan Club Site** Ivybridge	01548 830714
4	D6	**Challaborough Bay Holiday Park** Bigbury on Sea	08716 412045
4	D6	**Plymouth Sound** Plymouth	01752 862325
5	E1	**Channel View Caravan & Camping Park** Lynton	01598 753349
5	E2	**Halse Farm Caravan And Tent Park** Exmoor	01643 851259
5	E4	**Barley Meadow Caravan and Camping Park** Crockernwell	01647 281629
5	E4	**Holmans Wood Caravan Park** Chudleigh	01626 853785
5	E5	**Ashburton Caravan Park** Ashburton	01364 652552
5	E5	**Bona Vista Holiday Park** Paignton	01803 551971
5	E5	**Byslades International Touring Park** Paignton	01803 555072
5	E5	**Dornafield** Newton Abbot	01803 812732
5	E5	**Finlake Holiday Park** Chudleigh	01626 855242
5	E5	**Ross Park** Newton Abbot	01803 812983
5	E5	**Widdicombe Farm Touring Park** Paignton	01803 558325
5	E5	**Woodville Caravan Park** Newton Abbott	01803 812240
5	E6	**Beverley Park** Paignton	01803 661939
5	E6	**California Cross Camping & Caravanning Club Site** Ivybridge	01548 821297
5	E6	**Deer Park Caravan & Camping** Dartmouth	01803 770253
5	E6	**Galmpton Touring Park** Brixham	01803 842066
5	E6	**Little Cotton Caravan Park** Dartmouth	01803 832558
5	E6	**Marine Park Holiday Centre** Paignton	01803 843887
5	E6	**Meadowside Luxury Lodges** Paignton	01803 843887
5	E6	**Parkland Caravan & Camping Site** Kingsbridge	01548 852723
5	E6	**Ramslade** Totnes	01803 782575
5	E6	**Start Bay** Kingsbridge	01548 580430
5	E6	**Woodlands Leisure & Caravan Park** Dartmouth	01803 712598
5	F1	**Beeches Holiday Park** Minehead	01984 640391
5	F1	**Doniford Bay Holiday Park** Watchet	01984 632423
5	F1	**Minehead** Minehead	01643 704345
5	F2	**Exmoor House Caravan Club Site** Dulverton	01398 323268
5	F2	**Lakeside** Dulverton	01398 324068
5	F4	**Cofton Country Holidays** Dawlish	08000 858649
5	F4	**Webbers Caravan Park** Exeter	01395 232276
5	F5	**Hazelwood Park** Dawlish Warren	08453 080800
5	F5	**Ladys Mile Holiday Park** Dawlish	01626 863411
5	F5	**Peppermint Park** Dawlish Warren	01626 863436
5	F5	**Welcome Family Holiday Park** Dawlish	01626 862070
5	F6	**Hillhead Holiday Park Caravan Club Site** Brixham	01803 853204
5	F6	**South Bay Holiday Park** Brixham	01803 853004
5	G1	**Beachside Holiday Park** Brean	01278 751346
5	G1	**Brightholme Holiday Park** Burnham On Sea	01278 751347
5	G1	**Holiday Resort Unity** Burnham-on-Sea	01278 751235
5	G1	**Hurn Lane** Burnham-on-Sea	01278 751412

Caravan sites

Pg	Ref	Caravan site name	Town name	Telephone No.
5	G1	Mill Farm Caravan and Camping Park	Bridgwater	01278 732286
5	G1	Northam Farm Caravan & Touring Park	Brean	01278 751244
5	G1	Sandyglade Holiday Park	Burnham-on-Sea	01278 751271
5	G1	St. Audries Bay Holiday Club	Minehead	01984 632515
5	G1	Warren Farm Holiday Centre	Burnham-on-Sea	01278 751227
5	G2	Cadeside Caravan Club Site	Nynehead	01823 663103
5	G2	Cornish Farm Touring Park	Taunton	01823 327746
5	G2	Quantock Orchard Caravan Park	Taunton	01984 618618
5	G2	Somerset View Caravan Park	Bridgwater	01278 661294
5	G3	Five Acres Caravan Club Site	Chard	01460 234519
5	G3	Forest Glade Holiday Park	Cullompton	01404 841381
5	G4	Andrewshayes Caravan Park	Axminster	01404 831225
5	G4	Kings Down Tail C & C P	Sidmouth	01297 680313
5	G4	Leacroft Touring Park	Colyton	01297 552823
5	G4	Putts Corner Caravan Club Site	Sidmouth	01404 428750
6	A2	Broadway House Holiday Cvn & Cmpg Park Cheddar		01934 742610
6	A2	Bucklegrove Caravan & Camping Park	Cheddar	01749 870261
6	A2	Cheddar	Cheddar	01934 740207
6	A2	Cheddar Bridge Touring Park	Cheddar	01934 743048
6	A2	Fairways International Park	Bridgwater	01278 685569
6	A2	Home Farm Holiday Park & Country Club Burnham On Sea		01278 788888
6	A2	Southfield Farm Caravan Park	Burnham On Sea	01278 751233
6	A2	Weston-super-Mare Camping and Caravanning Club Site Weston-super-Mare		01934 822548
6	A3	Bowdens Crest Limited	Langport	01458 250553
6	A5	Binghams Farm Caravan Park	Bridport	01308 488234
6	A5	Freshwater Beach Holiday Park	Bridport	01308 897317
6	A5	Highlands End Holiday Park	Bridport	01308 422139
6	A5	Monkton Wyld Farm	Charmouth	01297 631131
6	A5	West Bay Holiday Park	Bridport	08716 412045
6	A5	Wood Farm Caravan Park	Charmouth	01297 560697
6	B2	Bath Chew Valley Caravan Park	Bath	01275 332127
6	B3	Long Hazel Park	Yeovil	01963 440002
6	B3	The Old Oaks Touring Park	Glastonbury	01458 831437
6	B5	Bagwell Farm Touring Park	Weymouth	01305 782575
6	B5	Morn Gate Caravan Park	Dorchester	01305 889284
6	B6	Chesil Beach Holiday Park	Weymouth	01305 773233
6	B6	Cove Park	Portland	01305 821286
6	B6	East Fleet Farm Touring Park	Weymouth	01305 785768
6	C2	Brokerswood Country Park	Westbury	01373 822238
6	C2	Longleat Caravan Club Site	Warminster	01342 327490
6	C3	Wincanton Racecourse Caravan Club Site Wincanton		01963 342760
6	C4	The Inside Park	Blandford	01258 453719
6	C5	Crossways Caravan Club Site	Dorchester	01305 852032
6	C5	Hunters Moon	Wareham	01929 556605
6	C5	Manor Farm Caravan Park	Wareham	01929 462870
6	C5	Moreton Camping and Caravanning Club Site Dorchester		01305 853801
6	C5	Sandyholme Holiday Park	Dorchester	01305 852677
6	C5	Wareham Forest Tourist Park	Wareham	01929 551393
6	C5	Waterside Holiday Park & Spa	Weymouth	01305 833103
6	D4	St Leonards Farm Caravan & Camping Park Ferndown		01202 872637
6	D5	Beacon Hill Touring Park	Poole	01202 631631
6	D5	Haycraft Caravan Club Site	Swanage	01929 480572
6	D5	Merley Court Touring Park	Poole	01590 648331
6	D5	Sandford Holiday Park	Poole	08716 412045
6	D5	South Lytchett Manor Caravan & Camping Park Poole		01202 622577
7	E3	Hill Farm Caravan Park	Romsey	01794 340402
7	E3	Hillside	Salisbury	01980 862527
7	E3	Salisbury Camping and Caravanning Club Site Salisbury		01722 320713
7	E4	Black Knowl	Brockenhurst	01590 623600
7	E4	Hollands Wood Caravan & Camp Site Brockenhurst		01313 146505
7	E4	Oakdene Forest Park	Ringwood	01590 648331
7	E4	Red Shoot Camping Park	Ringwood	01425 473789
7	E4	Sandy Balls Holiday Centre	Fordingbridge	01425 653042
7	E4	Shamba Holidays	St. Leonards	01202 873302
7	E5	Carrington Park	Lymington	01590 642654
7	E5	Hoburne Naish	New Milton	01425 273586
7	E5	Holmsley Caravan & Camping Site	Christchurch	01313 146505
7	E5	Lytton Lawn Touring Park	Milford-on-Sea	01590 648331
7	E5	Meadowbank Holidays	Christchurch	01202 483597
7	E5	Mount Pleasant Touring Park	Christchurch	01202 475474
7	E5	New Forest	Christchurch	01425 673638
7	E5	Sandhills Holiday Park	Christchurch	08458 159710
7	F3	Morn Hill Caravan Club Site	Winchester	01962 869877
7	F4	Green Pastures Caravan Park	Romsey	02380 814444
7	F5	Orchards Holiday Park	Yarmouth	01983 531331
7	F5	Thorness Bay Holiday Park	Near Cowes	08716 649779
7	G3	Morn Hill	Winchester	01962 869877
7	G4	Rookesbury Park	Fareham	01329 834085
7	G4	Solent Breezes Holiday Park	Nr. Southampton	01489 559739
7	G5	Adgestone Camping and Caravanning Club Site Adgestone		01983 403432
7	G5	Beaper Farm Caravan & Camping Site	Ryde	01983 615210
7	G5	Hillgrove Park	Ryde	01983 721606
7	G5	Landguard Camping	Shanklin	08716 649806
7	G5	Landguard Holidays	Shanklin	01983 863100
7	G5	Lower Hyde Holiday Park	Shanklin	08716 649751
7	G5	Old Barn Touring Park	Sandown	01983 866414
7	G5	Old Mill Caravan Park	Ryde	01983 872507
7	G5	Southland Camping Park	Newchurch	01983 865385
7	G5	Whitecliff Bay Holiday Park	Bembridge	01983 872671
7	H4	Hayling Island Holiday Park	Hayling Island	08716 412045
7	H5	Fishery Creek Caravan & Camping Park Hayling Island		02392 462164
7	H5	Red House Farm Camping Site	Chichester	01243 512959
7	H5	Warner Farm Touring Park (Bunn Leisure Holidays) Selsey		01243 604499
8	A5	Rowan Park Caravan Club Site	Bognor Regis	01243 828515
8	A5	The Lillies Caravan Park	Bognor Regis	01243 552081
8	A5	White Rose Touring Park	Littlehampton	01903 716176
8	B3	Alderstead Heath Caravan Club Site	Redhill	01737 644629
8	B4	Amberley Fields	Crawley	01293 524834
8	B4	Sumners Ponds Campsite & Fishery	Horsham	01403 732539
8	B5	Honeybridge Park	Nr. Horsham	01403 710923
8	B5	Northbrook Farm Caravan Club Site	Worthing	01903 502962
8	C4	Stairs Farm	Hartfield	01892 654884
8	C5	Sheepcote Valley	Brighton	01273 626546
8	C5	Sheepcote Valley Caravan Club Site	Brighton	01273 626546
8	D3	Gate House Wood Touring Park	Wrotham Heath	01732 843062
8	D3	Little Venice Country Park and Marina	Maidstone	01622 814158
8	D4	Crowborough Camping & Caravanning Club Site Crowborough		01892 664827
8	D5	Bay View Park	Eastbourne	01323 768688
8	D5	Martello Beach Park	Pevensey Bay	01323 761424
8	D5	Normans Bay Camping and Caravanning Club Site Pevensey		01323 761190
9	E3	Bearsted	Maidstone	01622 730018
9	E3	Tanner Farm Touring Caravan & Camping Park Marden		01622 832399
9	E5	Beauport Holiday Park	St. Leonards-on-Sea	08458 159777
9	E5	Combe Haven Holiday Park	Hastings	01424 426771
9	E5	Crazy Lane Tourist Park	Battle	01424 870147
9	E5	Crowhurst Park	Battle	01424 773344
9	E5	Fairlight Wood	Hastings	01424 812333
9	E5	Kloofs Caravan Park	Bexhill-on-Sea	01424 842839
9	E5	Normanhurst Court Caravan Club Site	Battle	01424 773808
9	F4	Broadhembury Caravan and Camping Park Ashford		01233 620859
9	F5	Frenchmans Beach Holiday Park	Rye	08458 159730
9	G3	Black Horse Farm Caravan Club Site	Folkestone	01303 892665
9	G3	Canterbury Camping & Caravanning Club Site Canterbury		01227 463216
9	G3	Yew Tree Park	Canterbury	01227 700306
9	G4	Daleacres	Hythe	01303 267679
9	H3	Hawthorn Farm	Dover	01304 852658
9	H3	Sandwich Leisure Park	Sandwich	01304 612681
9	H3	St Margarets Bay (Formerly St Margarets)	Dover	08716 649774
9	H3	Sutton Vale Caravan Park	Sutton By Dover	01304 374155
10	A3	Caerfai Bay Caravan & Tent Park	St Davids	01437 720274
10	A3	Lleithyr Meadow	St Davids	01437 720401
10	A4	Creampots Touring Caravan & Camping Park Haverfordwest		01437 781776
10	B4	Freshwater East Caravan Club Site Westhill Lamphey Pembroke		01646 672341

Pg Ref	Caravan site name	Town name	Telephone No.
10 B4	Masterland Farm Touring Caravan Park	Kilgetty	01834 813298
10 B5	Freshwater East	Pembroke	01646 672341
10 B5	Manorbier Country Park	Tenby	01834 871952
10 C2	Brongwyn Caravan and Camping Park	Cardigan	01239 613644
10 C2	Cenarth Falls Holiday Park	Newcastle Emlyn	01239 710345
10 C4	Gower Villa Caravan Park	Clynderwen	01437 562059
10 C4	Moreton Farm Leisure Park	Saundersfoot	01834 812016
10 C4	Pantglas Farm Caravan Park	Amroth	01834 831618
10 C4	Pendeilo Leisure Park	Narbeth	01834 831259
10 C4	Pendine Sands Holiday Park	Carmarthen	08716 410246
10 C4	Saltern Caravan Park	Tenby	01834 842157
10 C4	Scar Farm Holiday Home Park	Saundersfoot	01834 810181
10 C5	Crackwell Holiday Park	Tenby	01834 842688
10 D2	Bardsey View Holiday Park	Nr. Newquay	01545 560749
10 D2	Brownhill Caravan Park	Llandysul	01545 560288
10 D2	Brynawelon Touring & Camping Park	Llandysul	01239 654584
10 D2	Cardigan Bay Camping and Caravanning Club Site Llandysul		01545 560029
10 D2	Cwmsaeson Caravan Park	Aberaeron	01545 581067
10 D2	Shawsmead	Llanarth	01545 580423
10 D4	Carmarthen Bay Holiday Park	Kidwelly	08716 649722
10 D4	Pembrey Country Park	Llanelli	01554 834369
10 D4	Sunrise Bay Holiday Park	Llansteffan	01267 241394
10 D5	Bank Farm Leisure Park	Gower	01792 390452
10 D5	Gower Holiday Village	Gower	01792 390431
10 D5	New Park Holiday Park	Gower	01792 390292
10 D5	Pitton Cross Caravan & Camping Park	Rhossili	01792 390593
11 E2	Springwater Lakes	Llanwrda	01558 650788
11 E4	Black Lion Caravan & Camping Park	Llanelli	01269 845365
11 E4	River View Touring Park	Pontarddulais	01269 844876
11 E5	Gowerton	Swansea	01792 873050
11 F3	Erwlon Caravan & Camping	Llandovery	01550 721021
11 F6	Trecco Bay Holiday Park	Porthcawl	08716 412045
11 G1	Pines Caravan Park	Llandrindod Wells	01597 810068
11 G1	Wyeside Caravan & Camping Park	Rhayader	01597 810183
11 G3	Bishops Meadow Caravan Park	Brecon	01874 610000
11 G3	Brynich	Brecon	01874 623325
11 G3	Pencelli Castle Caravan & Camp Park	Brecon	01874 665451
11 G6	Acorn Caravan & Camping Park	Llantwit Major	01446 794024
11 G6	Fontygary Parks Ltd	Barry	01446 710386
11 G6	Llandow Touring Caravan Park	Cowbridge	01446 794527
11 H1	Rockbridge Park	Presteigne	01547 560300
11 H2	Penlan Caravan Park	Nr. Hay on Wye	01497 831485
11 H3	Anchorage Caravan Park	Brecon	01874 711246
11 H3	Riverside International Caravan & Camping Park Brecon		01874 711320
11 H5	Tredegar House Country Park	Newport	01633 815600
12 A1	Ashlea Pools Country Park	Craven Arms	01547 530430
12 A1	Pearl Lake Leisure Park	Leominster	01568 708326
12 A2	Arrow Bank HolidayPark	Leominster	01544 388312
12 A2	Moorhampton	Hereford	01544 318594
12 A2	Townsend Touring Park	Leominster	01544 388527
12 A3	Pandy	Abergavenny	01873 890370
12 A3	Poston Mill Park	Peterchurch	01981 550225
12 A4	Glen Trothy Caravan Park	Monmouth	01600 712295
12 B1	Blakehouse Farm Caravan Park	Tenbury Wells	01584 881313
12 B2	Boyce Caravan Park	Bromyard	01886 884248
12 B2	Bromyard Downs Caravan Club Site	Bromyard	01885 482607
12 B2	Hereford Camping & Caravanning Club Site Hereford		01432 890243
12 B2	Rowley Farm	Leominster	01568 616123
12 B2	The Millpond	Herefordshire	01432 890243
12 B3	Lucksall Caravan & Camping Park	Hereford	01432 870213
12 B3	Symonds Yat Caravan Park	Nr. Ross on Wye	01600 890883
12 B4	Braceland Camping And Caravan Park	Coleford	01594 833376
12 B6	Baltic Wharf Caravan Club Site	Bristol	01179 268030
12 C1	Lickhill Manor Caravan Park	Stourport On Severn	01299 871041
12 C1	Redstone Caravan Park	Stourport On Severn	01299 871711
12 C2	Blackmore	Worcester	01684 310505
12 C3	Kingsgreen Caravan Park	Malvern	01531 650272
12 C3	Tewkesbury Abbey Caravan Club Site	Tewkesbury	01684 294035
12 C6	Newton Mill Caravan & Camping Park	Bath	01225 333909
12 D1	Chapel Lane Caravan Park	Birmingham	01564 826483
12 D1	Clent Hills Caravanning Club Site Halesowen		01562 710015

Pg Ref	Caravan site name	Town name	Telephone No.
12 D2	The Springs Lakeside Holiday Home Park Pershore		01386 861851
12 D3	Broadway	Broadway	01386 858786
12 D3	Leedons Park Broadway	Broadway	01386 852423
12 D4	Cirencester Park	Cirencester	01285 651546
12 D5	Burton Hill Caravan & Camping Park	Malmesbury	01666 826880
12 D6	Blackland Lakes Holiday & Leisure Centre	Calne	01249 813672
12 D6	Devizes Camping & Caravanning Club Site Melksham		01380 828839
12 D6	Plough Lane Caravan Park (Adults Only) Chippenham		01249 750146
13 E1	Warwick Racecourse	Warwick	01926 495448
13 E2	Island Meadow Caravan Park	Aston Cantlow	01789 488273
13 E2	Riverside Caravan Park	Stratford Upon Avon	01789 292312
13 E3	Moreton-in-Marsh Caravan Club Site Moreton-in-Marsh		01608 650519
13 E4	Burford Caravan Club Site	Burford	01993 823080
13 F1	Lairhillock Park	Marton	01926 632119
13 F3	Chipping Norton Camping and Caravanning Club Site Chipping Norton		01608 641993
13 F3	Cotswold View Caravan & Camping Park Charlbury		01608 810314
13 F4	Bladon Chains	Woodstock	01993 812390
13 F4	Greenhill Farm Caravan & Camping Leisure Park Bletchingdon		01869 351600
13 F4	Hardwick Park Ltd	Witney	01865 300501
13 F4	Lincoln Farm Park Oxfordshire	Standlake	01865 300239
13 G1	Bush Hill Park	Flecknoe	01788 891808
13 H5	Four Oaks	Henley-on-Thames	01491 572312
14 A5	Highclere Farm Country Touring Park Beaconsfield		01494 874505
14 A5	Wyatts Covert	Uxbridge	01895 832729
14 A6	Amerden Caravan & Camping Park	Maidenhead	01628 627461
14 A6	Chertsey Camping & Caravanning Club Site Chertsey		01932 562405
14 B1	Grafham Water	Huntingdon	01480 810264
14 B1	Houghton Mill Caravan Club Site	Huntingdon	01342 336732
14 B1	Houghton Mill Caravan Site	Huntingdon	01480 466716
14 B1	Quiet Waters Caravan Park	Huntingdon	01480 463405
14 B2	St Neots Camping & Caravanning Club Site St Neots		01480 474404
14 B3	Ashridge Farm	Baldock	01462 742527
14 B4	Commons Wood	Welwyn Garden City	01707 260786
14 C1	Stroud Hill Park	Pidley	01487 741333
14 C2	Cherry Hinton Caravan Club Site	Cherry Hinton	01342 336732
14 C5	Lee Valley Campsite	Chingford	020 8529 5689
14 C5	Lee Valley Campsite	Leyton	020 8536 0959
14 C6	Abbey Wood Caravan Club Site	London	020 8311 7708
14 C6	Crystal Palace Caravan Club Site	London	020 8778 7155
14 D6	Thriftwood Caravan & Camping Park Stansted Sevenoaks		01732 822261
15 E1	Round Plantation Caravan Club Site	Mildenhall	01342 336732
15 E3	The Bell Inn Panfield	Braintree	01376 324641
15 E6	Allhallows Place House Touring Park	Rochester	01634 270106
15 F1	Dell Caravan & Camping Park	Bury St. Edmunds	01359 270121
15 F3	Colchester Holiday Park	Colchester	01206 545551
15 F4	Coopers Beach Holiday Park	Mersea Island	01206 383236
15 F4	Seaview Holiday Park	West Mersea	01206 382534
15 F4	St. Lawrence Caravans Ltd	St. Lawrence Bay	01621 779434
15 F4	Waldegraves Holiday Park	Colchester	01206 382898
15 F4	Waterside at St Lawrence Bay	Southminster	08716 649794
15 F6	Ashcroft Coast Holiday Park	Sheerness	08716 649700
15 F6	Elmhurst Caravan Park	Isle Of Sheppey	01795 880250
15 F6	Golden Leas Holiday Park & Hollybush Farm Sheerness		01795 874874
15 F6	Homing Park	Whitstable	01227 771777
15 F6	Oasis Park	Sheerness	01795 510094
15 F6	Seacliff Holiday Park	Minster on sea	01795 877299
15 F6	Warden Springs Holiday Park	Isle of Sheppey	01795 880888
15 G2	Orwell Meadows Leisure Park	Ipswich	01473 726666
15 G2	Stonham Barns Caravan & Camping Park Stowmarket		01449 711901
15 G2	Westwood Caravan Park	Nr. Ipswich	01473 659637
15 G3	Naze Marine Holiday Park	Walton-on-the-Naze	08716 649756
15 G3	Peewit Caravan Park	Felixstowe	01394 284511
15 G3	Suffolk Sands Holiday Park	Felixstowe	01394 284777

Pg Ref	Caravan site name Town name	Telephone No.
15 G4	Hutleys Caravan Parks Clacton On Sea	01255 820712
15 G4	Martello Beach Holiday Park Clacton on Sea	01255 820372
15 G4	Oaklands Holiday Park Clacton On Sea	08458 159785
15 G4	Valley Farm Holiday Park Clacton On Sea	08716 649788
15 G6	Seaview Holiday Park Swalecliffe	08458 159756
15 H2	Run Cottage Touring Park Woodbridge	01394 411309
15 H6	Quex Caravan Park Margate	01843 841273
15 H6	Two Chimneys Caravan Park Birchington	01843 843157
16 B1	Minffordd Caravan Park Dulas	01248 410678
16 B1	Penrhos Benllech	01248 852617
16 B1	Tyddyn Isaf Camping & Caravan Park Dulas	01248 410203
16 B2	Cwm Cadnant Valley Caravan & Camping Park Caernarfon	01286 673196
16 B2	Glan Gwna Country Holiday Park Caernarfon	01286 671740
16 B3	Dinlle Caravan Park Caernarfon	01286 830324
16 B4	Abererch Sands Holiday Centre Pwllheli	01758 612327
16 C1	Home Farm Caravan Park Marianglas	01248 410614
16 C1	St. Davids Park Pentraeth	01248 852341
16 C1	Ty Newydd Leisure Park Benllech	01248 450677
16 C2	Kingsbridge Caravan Park Beaumaris	01248 490636
16 C3	Beddgelert Forest Holidays Caravan & Camping Site Beddgelert	01313 146505
16 C3	Bryn Gloch Caravan Park Caernarfon	01286 650216
16 C4	Barmouth Bay Holiday Village Talybont	01341 247350
16 C4	Coed-y-llwyn Blaenau Ffestiniog	01766 590254
16 C4	Garreg Goch Caravan Park Porthmadog	01766 512210
16 C4	Islawrffordd Caravan Park Barmouth	01341 247269
16 C4	Murmur Yr Afon Touring Caravan & Camping Site Dyffryn Ardudwy	01341 247353
16 C4	Sarnfaen Holiday Park Barmouth	01341 247241
16 C4	Sunnysands Caravan Park Barmouth	01341 247301
16 C5	Hendre Mynach Touring Caravan & Camping Park Barmouth	01341 280262
16 C5	Sunbeach Holiday Estate Llwyngwril	01341 250263
16 C5	Trawsdir Touring Caravan & Camping Park Barmouth	01341 280999
16 C6	Glan-Y-Mor Leisure Park Aberystwyth	01970 828900
16 D1	Penrhyn Hall Farm Caravan Park Llandudno	01492 549207
16 D2	Berthlwyd Hall Holiday Park Conwy	01492 592270
16 D2	Bron Derw Touring Caravan Site Llanrwst	01492 640494
16 D2	Bryn Gynog Park Conwy	01492 650302
16 D2	Conwy Touring Park Conwy	01492 592856
16 D2	Tyddyn Du Touring Park Penmaenmawr	01492 622300
16 D4	Dolhendre Caravan Park Bala	01678 540629
16 D4	Glanllyn Lakeside Caravan & Camping Park Bala	01678 540227
16 D5	Garth Holiday Park Machynlleth	01654 702194
17 E3	Woodlands Hall Caravan Park Ruthin	01824 702066
17 E4	Bala Camping and Caravanning Club Site Bala	01678 530324
17 E4	Pale Wood Holiday Park Bala	01678 530212
17 E4	Penybont Touring & Camping Park Bala	01678 520549
17 F3	Eryrys Park Mold	01824 780866
17 F3	Station Camp Site Corwen	01490 430347
17 F4	Lady Margarets Park Wrexham	01691 777200
17 F5	Bank Farm Caravans Welshpool	01938 570526
17 F5	Fir View & Tan Y Fridd Caravan Park Welshpool	01938 810575
17 F5	Henllan Caravan Park Welshpool	01938 810554
17 F5	Hidden Valley Caravan Park Welshpool	01938 850300
17 G3	Plassey Leisure Park Wrexham	01978 780277
17 G6	Daisy Bank Touring Park Bishops Castle	01588 620471
18 A4	Beaconsfield Farm (Adults Only) Shrewsbury	01939 210030
18 A4	Church Farm Telford	01952 770381
18 A4	Severn Gorge Park Telford	01952 684789
18 A5	Presthope Caravan Club Site Much Wenlock	01746 785234
18 C2	Blackshaw Moor Caravan Club Site Leek	01538 300203
18 C2	Glencote Caravan Park Leek	01538 360745
18 C2	Leek Camping and Caravanning Club Site Leek	01538 300285
18 C2	Rudyard Vale Caravan Park Leek	01538 306178
18 C2	The Star Caravan & Camping Park Alton	01538 702219
18 C3	Uttoxeter Racecourse Uttoxeter	01889 564172
18 D2	Blackwall Plantation Caravan Club Site Ashbourne	01335 370903
18 D2	Callow Top Holiday Park Ashbourne	01335 344020
18 D2	Rivendale Ashbourne	01335 310311
18 D5	Kingsbury Water Park Camping & Caravanning Club Site Sutton Coldfield	01827 874101

Pg Ref	Caravan site name Town name	Telephone No.
19 E2	Golden Valley Camping & Caravan Park Golden Valley, Ripley	01773 513881
19 E2	Lickpenny Matlock	01629 583040
19 E2	The Firs Belper	01773 852913
19 E3	Elvaston Castle Caravan Club Site Derby	01332 571342
19 F2	New Hall Farm Edingley	01623 883041
19 F2	Robin Hood View Caravan Park Newark	07882 397217
19 G4	Ranksborough Hall Caravan Park Rutland	01572 722984
19 H4	Tallington Lakes Tallington	01778 347000
19 H5	Top Lodge Caravan Club Site Corby	01780 444617
19 H5	Yarwell Mill Caravan Park Peterborough	01780 782344
20 A2	Tattershall Lakes Country Park Tattershall	01526 348800
20 A2	Willow Holt Ltd Caravan & Camping Park Lincoln	01526 343111
20 A3	Walnut Lake and lodges Boston /Spalding	01205 460482
20 A5	Ferry Meadows Peterborough	01733 233526
20 B2	Pilgrims Way Camping Boston	01205 366646
20 B2	The White Cat Caravan & Camping Park Boston	01205 870121
20 B3	Silverhill Caravan and Holiday Park Spalding	01406 365673
20 B4	Foremans Bridge Caravan Park Long Sutton Spalding	01945 440346
20 C3	Heacham Beach Holiday Park Nr. Kings Lynn	08716 649742
20 C3	Sandringham Camping & Caravanning Club Site Sandringham	01485 542555
20 C3	Searles Leisure Resort Hunstanton	01485 534211
20 C3	The Sandringham Estate Sandringham	01553 631614
20 C3	The Sandringham Estate Caravan Club Site Sandringham	01342 336732
20 C4	Pentney Lakes Caravan & Leisure Park Kings Lynn	01760 338668
20 C4	Virginia Lake & Caravan Park Wisbech	01945 430167
20 C5	Lode Hall Caravan Park Wisbech	01354 638476
20 D3	Manor Park Touring Caravans Kings Lynn	01485 528808
20 D4	Breckland Meadows Touring Park Swaffham	01760 721246
20 D4	Brick Kiln Farm Caravan Park Ashill	01760 441300
20 D4	Pentney Park Caravan Site Kings Lynn	01760 337479
20 D5	The Covert Caravan Club Site Thetford	01342 336732
21 E3	Fakenham Racecourse Caravan & Camping Park Fakenham	01328 862388
21 E3	The Old Brick Kilns Caravan & Camping Park Fakenham	01328 878305
21 E5	Applewood Caravan & Camping Park Banham	01953 888370
21 E5	Dower House Touring Park Norwich	01953 717314
21 F2	Beeston Regis Caravan Park West Runton, Nr. Sheringham	01263 823614
21 F2	Forest Park Caravan Site Cromer	01263 513290
21 F2	Incleboro Fields Cromer	01263 837419
21 F2	Seacroft Cromer	01263 514938
21 F2	West Runton Camping & Caravanning Club Site Cromer	01263 837544
21 F3	Deers Glade Caravan and Camping Park Cromer	01263 768633
21 F3	Two Mills Touring Park North Walsham	01692 405829
21 F3	Woodland Leisure Park Cromer	01263 579208
21 F4	Norfolk Showground Norwich	01603 742708
21 F5	Little Lakeland Caravan Park Harleston	01986 788646
21 F5	Waveney Valley Lakes Wortwell	01986 788333
21 G3	Golden Beach Holiday Centre Norwich	01692 598269
21 G3	Rainbows End Chalet Park Norwich	01692 650491
21 G3	Red House Chalet & C P Bacton	01692 650815
21 G4	Broadlands Great Yarmouth	01692 630357
21 G4	Burgh Castle Marina Great Yarmouth	01493 780331
21 G4	Rose Farm Touring Park Great Yarmouth	01493 780896
21 H4	California Cliffs Holiday Park Great Yarmouth	08716 649716
21 H4	Eastern Beach Caravan Park Great Yarmouth	01493 720367
21 H4	Great Yarmouth Great Yarmouth	01493 855223
21 H4	Great Yarmouth Caravan Club Site Great Yarmouth	01342 336732
21 H4	Hopton Holiday Village Great Yarmouth	01502 730143
21 H5	Beach Farm Residential & Holiday Park Lowestoft	01502 572794
21 H5	Heathland Beach Caravan Park Lowestoft	01502 740337
21 H5	Kessingland Camping & Caravanning Club Site Lowestoft	01502 742040
21 H5	Pakefield Caravan Park Lowestoft	01502 561136
21 H5	White House Beach Lowestoft	01502 740278
22 A5	Golden Sands Holiday Park Rhyl	01745 331888
22 A5	Lido Beach Holiday Park Prestatyn	01745 855626

Pg	Ref	Caravan site name	Town name	Telephone No.
22	A5	Lyons Robin Hood Holiday Park	Rhyl	01745 342265
22	A5	New Pines Caravan Park	Rhyl	0800 717 707
22	A5	Pen Y Ffrith Caravan Park	Prestatyn	01745 854397
22	A6	Bron-Y-Wendon Touring Caravan Park Colwyn Bay		01492 512903
22	A6	Caer Mynydd Park	Denbigh	01745 550302
22	A6	Gaingc View Holiday Park	Abergele	01745 342957
22	A6	Hunters Hamlet Touring Caravan Park	Abergele	01745 832237
22	A6	Penisar Mynydd Caravan Park	St. Asaph	01745 582227
22	A6	Ty Mawr Holiday Park	Abergele	08716 649785
22	A6	Winkups Caravan Park	Abergele	01745 353936
22	B1	Butterflowers Holiday Homes	Millom	01229 772880
22	B1	South End Caravan Park	Barrow In Furness	01229 472823
22	B5	Park Lane Holiday Homes & Country Club	Wirral	01516 332321
22	B5	Presthaven Sands Holiday Park	Prestatyn	0871 231 0888
22	B5	Silver Birch Caravan Park	Holywell	01745 853749
22	B5	Talacre Beach Caravan Park	Holywell	0800 717 707
22	B5	Tree Tops Caravan Park	Nr. Holywell	01745 560279
22	B5	Wirral Country Park	Wirral	01516 485228
22	B5	Wirral Country Park Caravan Club Site	Wirral	01516 485228
22	C1	Holgates Caravan Park	Silverdale Carnforth	01524 701508
22	C1	Lakeland Leisure Park	Flookburgh	01539 558556
22	C1	Morecambe Lodge Caravan Park	Carnforth	01524 824361
22	C1	Old Park Wood Caravan Park	Grange Over Sands	01539 558266
22	C1	Regent Leisure Park	Morecambe	01524 413940
22	C1	Westgate Caravan Park	Morecambe	01524 411448
22	C2	Cala Gran Holiday Park	Fleetwood	01253 872555
22	C2	Fold House Holiday Home & Lodge Park Lancaster		01253 790267
22	C2	Kneps Farm Holiday Park	Blackpool	01253 823632
22	C2	Merlewood Country Park	Nr. Blackpool	01995 604975
22	C2	Ocean Edge Leisure Park	Near Morecambe	01524 855657
22	C2	Rawcliffe Hall Country Club & Caravan Pa Preston		01995 670491
22	C2	Smithy Caravan Park	Garstang	01995 606200
22	C2	Willowgrove Leisure Park	Blackpool	01253 811306
22	C2	Windy Harbour Holiday Park	Blackpool	01253 883064
22	C3	Blackpool South	Blackpool	01253 762051
22	C3	Newton Hall Holiday Park	Staining Blackpool	01253 882512
22	C4	Abbey Farm Caravan Park	Ormskirk	01695 572686
22	C4	Hurlston Hall Caravan Park	Ormskirk	01704 841064
22	C4	Riverside Leisure Centre	Southport	01704 228886
22	C4	Shaw Hall Caravan Park	Ormskirk	01704 840298
22	C4	Southport	Southport	01704 565214
22	C4	Willowbank Holiday Home & Touring Park Southport		01704 571566
22	C6	Chester Fairoaks	Chester	01513 551600
22	D1	Castle View Caravan Park	Carnforth	01524 735857
22	D1	Fell End Caravan Park	Near Milnthorpe	01539 562122
22	D1	Low Greenlands Caravan Park	Near Carnforth	01524 781367
22	D1	Parkfoot Holiday Homes	Ingleton	01524 261833
22	D1	Woodclose Park	Kirkby Lonsdale	01524 271597
22	D3	Beacon Fell View Holiday Park	Preston	01772 783233
22	D6	Elm Cottage Touring Park	Winsford	01829 760544
22	D6	Lamb Cottage Caravan Park	Northwich	01606 882302
23	E1	Langcliffe Caravan Park	Settle	01729 822387
23	E2	Clitheroe Camping & Caravanning Club Site Clitheroe		01200 425294
23	E2	Rimington Caravan Park	Clitheroe	01200 445355
23	E2	Three Rivers Park	Clitheroe	01200 423523
23	E2	Twyn Ghyll Caravan Park	Gisburn	01200 445465
23	E4	Burrs Country Park Caravan Club Site	Bury	01617 610489
23	E4	Gelder Wood Country Park	Rochdale	01706 364858
23	F1	Hawkswick Cote Caravan Park	Skipton	01756 770226
23	F1	Wharfedale	Skipton	01756 753340
23	F2	Strid Wood Caravan Club Site	Skipton	01756 710433
23	F3	Lower Clough Foot Caravan Club Site Hebden Bridge		01422 882531
23	F3	Upwood Holiday Park	Haworth	01535 644242
23	F4	Hollingworth Lake Caravan Park	Littleborough	01706 378661
23	F6	Clover Fields Touring Caravan Park	Buxton	01298 787310
23	F6	Grin Low Caravan Club Site	Buxton	01298 777350
23	F6	Lime Tree Park	Buxton	01298 229880
24	A1	Woodhouse Farm C & C Park	Ripon	01765 658309
24	A2	Reynard Crag Holiday Park	Harrogate	01423 772828
24	A2	St Helenas Caravan Park	Leeds	01132 841142
24	A3	Dobrudden Caravan Park	Shipley	01274 581016
24	A5	Laneside Caravan Park	Hope Valley	01433 620215
24	A5	Losehill	Hope Valley	01433 620636
24	A6	Chatsworth Park Caravan Club Site	Bakewell	01246 582226
24	A6	Darwin Forest Country Park	Matlock	01629 732428
24	A6	Greenhills Caravan and Camping Park	Bakewell	01629 813052
24	B1	Boroughbridge Camping & Caravanning Club Site Roecliffe Boroughbridge		01423 322683
24	B1	The Alders Caravan Park	York	01347 838722
24	B2	Glenfield Caravan Park	Leeds	01937 574657
24	B2	Haighfield Park	Leeds	01937 574658
24	B2	Knaresborough	Knaresborough	01423 860196
24	B2	Knaresborough Caravan Club Site Knaresborough		01342 336732
24	B2	Maustin Park Ltd	Wetherby	01132 886234
24	B2	Rudding Holiday Park	Harrogate	01423 870439
24	B4	Nostell Priory Holiday Park	Wakefield	01924 863938
24	B6	Poolsbrook Country Park	Chesterfield	01246 470659
24	B6	Teversal Camping & Caravanning Club Site Sutton in Ashfield		01623 551838
24	C1	Golden Square Caravan & Camping Park Helmsley		01439 788269
24	C1	Goosewood Holiday Park	York	01347 810829
24	C1	Sheriff Hutton Camping & Caravanning Club Site Bracken Hill		01347 878660
24	C1	Slingsby Camping and Caravanning Club Site Slingsby		01653 628335
24	C2	Ashfield Holiday Cottages and Caravan Park York		01904 488631
24	C2	Beechwood Grange Caravan Club Site	York	01904 424637
24	C2	Hollicarrs Holiday Park	York	08009 808070
24	C2	Mount Pleasant Hol Park & Park Home Estate York		01904 707078
24	C2	Naburn Lock Caravan Site	York	01904 728697
24	C2	Rowntree Park Caravan Club Site	York	01904 658997
24	C2	YCP - York Caravan Park	York	01904 424222
24	C2	York Lakeside Lodges	York	01904 702346
24	C2	York Touring Caravan Site	York	01904 499275
24	C3	Cawood Holiday Park	York	01757 268450
24	C3	The Ranch Caravan Park	Selby	01757 638984
24	C6	Clumber Park Caravan Club Site	Worksop	01909 484758
24	C6	The Shannon Caravan & Camping	Ollerton	01623 869002
24	D1	Wolds Way Caravan & Camping Park	Malton	01944 728463
24	D2	Sycamores Touring Caravan Park	York	01759 388838
24	D4	Woodcarr Park	Doncaster	01427 873487
24	D6	Greenacres Caravan & Touring Park	Newark	01777 870264
24	D6	Milestone Caravan Park	Newark	01636 821244
24	D6	Orchard Park Touring Caravan & Camping Park Newark		01777 870228
25	F1	North Bay Leisure Park	Bridlington	01262 673733
25	F1	Reighton Sands Holiday Park	Nr. Filey	01723 890476
25	F1	Thornwick & Sea Farm Holiday Centre & Greenacre West	Bridlington	01262 850369
25	F2	Barmston Beach Holiday Park	Nr. Driffield	08716 649703
25	F2	Dacre Lakeside Park	Driffield	01964 543704
25	F2	Far Grange Caravan Park	Driffield	01262 468010
25	F2	Longbeach Leisure Park	Hornsea	01964 532506
25	F2	Lowcroft Park	Hornsea	01964 535314
25	F2	Skipsea Sands Holiday Park	Driffield	01262 468210
25	F3	Aldbrough Caravan Park	Hull	01964 529292
25	F6	Bainland Country Park	Woodhall Spa	01526 352903
25	F6	Woodhall Spa Camping & Caravanning Club Site Woodhall Spa		01526 352911
25	G3	Golden Sands Holiday Park	Withernsea	01964 614121
25	G3	Patrington Haven Leisure Park	Hull	08002 125530
25	G3	Sand-le-Mere Caravan Park	Hull	01964 670403
25	G3	Withernsea Sands Holiday Park	Withernsea	01964 611161
25	G4	Sandy Beaches Holiday Village Kilnsea Nr. Withernsea		01964 650372
25	G5	Golden Sands Holiday Park	Mablethorpe	01507 477060
25	G5	Grange Farm Leisure Limited	Mablethorpe	01507 472814
25	G5	Holivans	Mablethorpe	01507 473327
25	G5	Mablethorpe Camping & Caravanning Club Site Mablethorpe		01507 472374
25	G5	Sunnydale Holiday Park	Saltfleet	08716 649776

Pg Ref	Caravan site name Town name	Telephone No.
25 G5	**Woodthorpe Hall Leisure Park** Alford	01507 450294
25 H5	**Greenfield Caravan Park** Mablethorpe	01507 441203
25 H5	**Hawthorn Farm** Mablethorpe	01507 441503
25 H5	**Seacroft Holiday Estate Ltd** Mablethorpe	01507 472421
25 H6	**Butlins Skegness** Skegness	01754 762311
25 H6	**Cherry Tree Site** Sutton On Sea	01507 441626
25 H6	**Croft Bank Holiday Park** Skegness	01754 763887
25 H6	**Ingoldale Park** Skegness	01754 872335
25 H6	**Merryfield Caravan Park** Nr. Skegness	01754 872286
25 H6	**North Shore Holiday Centre** Skegness	01754 763815
25 H6	**Skegness Sands Touring Site** Skegness	01754 761484
25 H6	**Skegness Water Leisure Park** Skegness	01754 899400
25 H6	**Walshs Holiday Park** Skegness	01754 764485
26 A2	**Ryan Bay Caravan Park** Stranraer	01776 889458
26 B1	**Bennane Shore Holiday Park & Pebbles Spa** Lendalfoot	01465 891233
26 B1	**Windsor Holiday Park** Girvan	01465 821355
26 B2	**Three Lochs Holiday Park** Newton Stewart	01671 830304
26 B3	**Glenluce Caravan Park** Stranraer	01581 300412
26 B3	**New England Bay** Stranraer	01776 860275
26 B3	**Sands Of Luce Caravan Park** Stranraer	01776 830456
26 C2	**Glentrool Holiday Park** Newton Stewart	01671 840280
26 C3	**Castle Cary Holiday Park** Newton Stewart	01671 820264
26 C3	**Garlieston** Newton Stewart	01988 600636
26 D2	**Loch Ken Holiday Park** Castle Douglas	01644 470282
26 D3	**Anwoth Holiday Park** Castle Douglas	01557 814333
26 D3	**Auchenlarie Holiday Park** Castle Douglas	01557 840251
26 D3	**Cardoness Estate Holiday Park** Castle Douglas	01557 840288
26 D3	**Mossyard Caravan Park** Castle Douglas	01557 840226
26 D3	**Seaward Caravan Park** Kirkcudbright	01557 331079
27 E2	**Beeswing Caravan Park** Kirkgunzeon	01387 760242
27 E2	**Park Of Brandedleys** Dumfries	01387 266700
27 E3	**Castle Point Caravan Park** Dalbeattie	01556 630248
27 F3	**Southerness Holiday Village** By Dumfries	08716 410479
27 F5	**Dockray Meadow Caravan Club Site** Workington	01946 861357
27 F5	**Inglenook Caravan Park** Cockermouth	01946 861240
27 F5	**Seacote Park** St Bees	01946 822777
27 F5	**Tarnside Caravan Park** Beckermet	01946 841308
27 F6	**Ravenglass Camping & Caravanning Club Site** Ravenglass	01229 717250
27 G2	**Cressfield Caravan Park** Ecclefechan	01576 300702
27 G2	**Hoddom Castle Caravan Park** Lockerbie	01576 300251
27 G2	**Queensberry Bay Holiday Park** Annan	01461 700205
27 G3	**Solway Holiday Village** Wigton	01697 331236
27 G3	**Stanwix Park Holiday Centre** Silloth	01697 332666
27 G3	**Tanglewood Caravan Park** Silloth	01697 331253
27 G3	**The Larches Caravan Park** Wigton	01697 371379
27 G4	**Castlerigg Hall C & C Park** Keswick	01768 772437
27 G4	**High Close Holiday Home Park** Keswick	01768 776300
27 G4	**Keswick Camping and Caravanning Club Site** Keswick	01768 772392
27 G5	**Church Stile Farm Campsite** Seascale	01946 726252
27 G5	**Greenhowe Caravan Park** Ambleside	01539 437231
27 G5	**Low Manesty Caravan Club Site** Keswick	01768 777275
27 G6	**Park Coppice Caravan Club Site** Coniston	01539 441555
27 G6	**Silecroft Caravan Park** Wicham	01229 772659
27 H3	**Englethwaite Hall Caravan Club Site** Carlisle	01228 560202
27 H3	**Green View Lodges** Carlisle	01697 476230
27 H3	**Pine Lake Lodges** Carlisle	01697 476230
27 H4	**Burns Farm Caravan and Camp Site** Keswick	01768 779112
27 H4	**Cove Caravan & Camping Park** Penrith	01768 486549
27 H4	**Flusco Wood** Penrith	01768 480020
27 H4	**Hillcroft Park** Penrith	01768 486363
27 H4	**Hutton Moor End Caravan Park** Penrith	01768 779615
27 H4	**Park Foot Caravan & Camping Park** Penrith	01768 486309
27 H4	**Troutbeck Head Caravan Club Site** Penrith	01768 779149
27 H4	**Ullswater Caravan Camping & Marine Park** Ullswater	01768 486666
27 H4	**Woodside Caravan Park** Penrith	01768 483253
27 H5	**Skelwith Fold Caravan Park Ltd** Ambleside	01539 432277
27 H5	**White Cross Bay Leisure Park & Marina** Windermere	01539 443937
27 H6	**Blackbeck Caravan Park** Ulverston	01229 861274
27 H6	**Braithwaite Fold Caravan Club Site** Windermere	01539 442177

Pg Ref	Caravan site name Town name	Telephone No.
27 H6	**Hill of Oaks & Blake Holme Caravan Estate** Windermere	01539 531578
27 H6	**Meathop Fell Caravan Club Site** Grange-over-Sands	01539 532912
27 H6	**Newby Bridge Caravan Park** Newby Bridge	01539 531030
27 H6	**Park Cliffe Caravan & Camping Estate** Windermere	01539 531344
27 H6	**Windermere Camping & Caravanning Club Site** Kendal	01539 821119
28 A1	**Kielder Caravan & Camping Site** Hexham	01434 250291
28 A4	**Low Moor Caravan Park** Penrith	01768 361231
28 A4	**Lowther Holiday Park** Penrith	01768 863631
28 A5	**Westmorland Caravan Park** Penrith	01539 711322
28 A6	**Low Park Wood Caravan Club Site** Kendal	01539 560186
28 A6	**Waters Edge Caravan Park** Nr. Kendal	01539 567708
28 B5	**Augill Beck Caravan Park** Kirkby Stephen	01763 419440
28 B5	**Wild Rose Park** Appleby-in-Westmorland	01768 351077
28 B6	**Brown Moor** Hawes	01969 667338
28 C1	**Nunnykirk Caravan Club Site** Morpeth	01342 336842
28 C3	**Allensford Caravan Park** Consett	01207 505572
28 C4	**Heather View Leisure Park** Weardale	01388 528728
28 C4	**Hetherick Caravan Park** Barnard Castle	01833 631173
28 C4	**The Kingfisher Country Park** Frosterley	01388 527230
28 C5	**Barnard Castle Camping & Caravanning Club Site** Lartington	01833 630228
28 D1	**Cresswell Towers Holiday Park** Near Morpeth	08716 649733
28 D1	**Forget Me Not Holiday Park** Morpeth	01670 788364
28 D3	**Derwent Caravan Park** Rowlands Gill	01207 543383
28 D3	**Finchale Abbey Caravan Park** Durham	01913 866528
28 D5	**Brompton-On-Swale Caravan & Camping Park** Richmond	01748 824629
28 D5	**Hargill House Caravan Club Site** Richmond	01342 336732
28 D5	**Scotch Corner Caravan Park** Richmond	01748 822530
28 D5	**Swaleview Caravan Park** Richmond	01748 823106
28 D6	**Lower Wensleydale Caravan Club Site** Leyburn	01969 623366
29 E2	**Old Hartley** Whitley Bay	01912 370256
29 E3	**Grange Caravan Club Site** Durham	01913 844778
29 E4	**Crimdon Dene Holiday Park** Near Hartlepool	08716 649737
29 E4	**Strawberry Hill Farm Camping & Caravanning Park** Durham	01913 722512
29 E5	**White Water Caravan Club Park** Stockton-on-Tees	01642 634880
29 E6	**Hillside Caravan Park** Thirsk	01845 537349
29 F4	**Hazelgrove Caravan Park** Saltburn By The Sea	01287 622014
29 F5	**Tocketts Mill Caravan Park** Guisborough	01287 610182
29 F6	**Cherry Tree Caravan Park** York	01439 771603
29 G5	**Low Moor Caravan Club Site** Whitby	01947 810505
29 G6	**Spiers House Caravan & Camping Site** Pickering	01751 417591
29 G6	**Vale Of Pickering Caravan Park** Pickering	01723 859280
29 G6	**Wayside Caravan Park** Pickering	01751 472608
29 H5	**Northcliffe and Seaview Holiday Parks** Nr. Whitby	01947 880477
29 H6	**Arosa Caravan And Camping Park** Scarborough	01723 862166
29 H6	**Cayton Bay Holiday Park** Scarborough	08716 649724
29 H6	**Cayton Village Caravan Park Ltd** Scarborough	01723 583171
29 H6	**Flower of May Holiday Park** Scarborough	01723 584311
29 H6	**Jasmine Park** Scarborough	01723 859240
29 H6	**Scalby Close Park** Scarborough	01723 365908
29 H6	**St. Helens Caravan Park** Scarborough	01723 862771
29 H6	**West Ayton** Scarborough	01723 862989
30 C5	**Machrihanish Caravan & Camping Park** Campbeltown	01586 810366
30 D2	**Lochgilphead Caravan Park** Lochgilphead	01546 602003
30 D4	**Point Sands Caravan Park** Tarbert	01583 441263
31 E1	**Argyll Caravan Park** Inveraray	01499 302285
31 E4	**Lochranza C&C Isle of Arran** Isle of Arran	01770 830273
31 F1	**Ardgartan Caravan & Camping Site** Arrochar	01301 702293
31 F2	**Rosneath Castle Caravan Park** Rosneath	01436 831208
31 F6	**Turnberry Holiday Park** Turnberry	01655 331288
31 G2	**Cashel Caravan & Camping Site** Loch Lomond	01360 870234
31 G2	**Loch Lomond Castle Lodges** Loch Lomond	01389 850215
31 G2	**Lomond Woods Holiday Park** Loch Lomond	01389 755000
31 G2	**Luss Camping and Caravanning Club Site** Alexandria	01436 860658
31 G4	**Viewfield Manor Holiday Village** Irvine	01294 850286
31 G5	**Craigie Gardens** Ayr	01292 264909
31 G5	**Sundrum Castle Holiday Park** Ayrshire	08716 412045
31 G6	**Walled Garden Caravan and Camping Park** Ayr	01655 740323

Pg Ref	Caravan site name Town name	Telephone No.
31 H1	**Callander Holiday Park** Callander	01877 330265
31 H1	**Cobleland Caravan & Camping Site** Aberfoyle	01877 382392
31 H1	**Gart Caravan Park** Callander	01877 330002
31 H2	**Balgair Castle Caravan Park** Fintry	01360 860283
31 H3	**Craigendmuir Caravan & Camping Park** Glasgow	01417 794159
32 A1	**Witches Craig Caravan & Camping Park** Stirling	01786 474947
32 A3	**Strathclyde Country Park** Motherwell	01698 402060
32 B2	**Beecraigs Caravan & Camping Site** Linlithgow	01506 844516
32 B3	**Newhouse Caravan & Camping Park** Lanark	01555 870228
32 B4	**Mount View Caravan Park** Abington	01864 502808
32 B5	**Craigielands Country Park** Moffat	01683 300591
32 B5	**Moffat Camping & Caravanning Club Site** Moffat	01683 220436
32 C1	**Dunnikier Caravan Park** Kirkcaldy	01592 267563
32 C1	**Pettycur Bay Holiday Park Ltd** Kinghorn	01592 892200
32 C1	**Sandhills Caravan Park** Kinghorn	01592 890355
32 C2	**Edinburgh** Edinburgh	01313 126874
32 C2	**Linwater Caravan Park** East Calder	01313 333326
32 C2	**Meadowheads Mortonhall Caravan & Camping Park** Edinburgh	01316 641533
32 C2	**Test Park** Edinburgh	02082 675712
32 C5	**Angecroft Park** Selkirk	01750 623550
32 D2	**Lothian Bridge Caravan Park** Dalkeith	01316 636120
33 E1	**Gilsland Caravan Park** North Berwick	01620 892205
33 E1	**Yellowcraig** Dirleton	01620 850217
33 E2	**Meadowheads Belhaven Bay Caravan & Camping Park** Dunbar	01368 865956
33 E3	**Lauder Camping & Caravanning Club Site** Lauder	01578 750697
33 E3	**Thirlestane Castle Caravan & Camping Park** Lauder	01578 718884
33 E4	**Gibson Park** Melrose	01896 822969
33 E4	**Jedburgh Camping and Caravanning Club Site** Jedburgh	01835 863393
33 E4	**Lilliardsedge Holiday Park & Golf Club** Jedburgh	01835 830271
33 F2	**Crosslaw Caravan Park** Coldingham	01890 771316
33 F2	**Pease Bay Holiday Home Park** Cockburnspath	01368 830206
33 F2	**Thurston Manor Holiday Home Park** Dunbar	01368 840643
33 F4	**Springwood Estate** Kelso	01573 224596
33 F5	**Border Forest Caravan Park** Otterburn	01830 520259
33 G2	**Scoutscroft Holiday Centre** Coldingham	01890 771338
33 G3	**Ord House Country Park** Berwick upon Tweed	01289 305288
33 G3	**Seaview Caravan Club Site** Berwick-upon-Tweed	01289 305198
33 G4	**Highburn House Country Holiday Park** Wooler	01668 281344
33 G4	**Riverside Country Park** Wooler	01668 281447
33 G5	**Clennell Hall Riverside Holidfay Park** Rothbury	01669 650341
33 G5	**River Breamish Caravan Club Site** Alnwick	01665 578320
33 H4	**Beadnell Bay Camping & Caravanning Club Site** Chathill	01665 720586
33 H4	**Dunstan Hill Camping & Caravanning Club Site** Alnwick	01665 576310
33 H4	**Meadowheads Waren Caravan & Camping Park** Bamburgh	01668 214366
33 H4	**South Meadows Caravan Park** Belford	01668 213326
33 H5	**Amble Links Holiday Park** Amble	01665 710530
34 D2	**Balmeanach Park** Isle of Mull	01680 300342
35 E1	**Acharacle Resipole Farm Caravan Park** Ardnamurchan	01967 431235
35 E3	**Roseview Caravan Park** Oban	01631 562755
35 E3	**Shieling Holidays** Isle of Mull	01680 812496
35 E3	**Tralee Bay Holiday Park** Oban	01631 720255
35 F1	**Bunree** Fort William	01855 821283
35 F2	**Invercoe Caravan & Camping Park** Glencoe	01855 811210
35 F2	**Oban Camping & Caravanning Club Site** Argyll	01631 720348
36 A3	**Cruachan Farm Caravan & Camping Park** By Killin	01567 820302
36 A3	**Loch Earn Caravan Park** St Fillans	01764 685270
36 A3	**Maragowan** Killin	01567 820245
36 B1	**Blair Castle Caravan Park** Perthshire	01796 481263
36 B2	**Kenmore Caravan Park** Aberfeldy	01887 830226
36 B3	**Braidhaugh Park Ltd** Crieff	01764 652951
36 C1	**Faskally Caravan Park** Pitlochry	01796 472007
36 C2	**Inver Mill Farm Caravan Park** Dunkeld	01350 727477
36 C2	**Milton Of Fonab Caravan Site** Pitlochry	01796 472882
36 C2	**The Erigmore Estate** Dunkeld	01350 727236
36 D2	**Corriefodly Holiday Park** Blairgowrie	01250 876666
36 D2	**Five Roads Caravan Park** Blairgowrie	01828 632255
36 D2	**Nether Craig Caravan Park** Blairgowrie	01575 560204

Pg Ref	Caravan site name Town name	Telephone No.
36 D3	**Scone Palace Camping & Caravanning Club Site** Scone	01738 552308
36 D4	**Balbirnie Park** Glenrothes	01592 759130
37 E2	**Drumshademuir Caravan Park** Forfar	01575 573284
37 E2	**Foresterseat Caravan Park** Forfar	01307 818880
37 E2	**Lochlands Caravan Park** Forfar	01307 463621
37 E4	**Clayton Caravan Park** St. Andrews	01334 870242
37 E4	**Craigtoun Meadows Holiday Park** St Andrews	01334 475959
37 E4	**Leven Beach Holiday Park** Leven	01333 426008
37 F1	**Dovecot Caravan Park** Laurencekirk	01674 840630
37 F2	**Red Lion Holiday Park** Arbroath	01241 872038
37 F3	**Riverview Caravan Park** Monifieth	01382 535471
37 F3	**Tayview Caravan Site** Monifieth	01382 532837
37 F4	**Cairnsmill Caravan Park** St. Andrews	01334 473604
37 F4	**Kilrenny Mill Caravan Park** Anstruther	01333 450314
37 F4	**Sauchope Links Caravan Park** Crail	01333 450460
37 G1	**East Bowstrips Caravan Park** Montrose	01674 850328
38 C6	**Camusdarach Caravan Park** Arisaig	01687 450221
38 D1	**Inverewe Gardens Camping & Caravanning Club Site** Achnasheen	01445 781249
38 D2	**Sands Holiday Centre** Gairloch	01445 712152
39 E2	**Kinlochewe** Achnasheen	01445 760239
39 E4	**Morvich** Kyle	01599 511354
39 F1	**Ardmair Point Caravan & Camping Park** Ullapool	01854 612054
39 F1	**Broomfield Holiday Park** Ullapool	01854 612020
39 F6	**The Gairlochy Holiday Park** Fort William	01397 712711
39 G4	**Cannich Caravan & Camping Park** By Beauly	01456 415364
39 H2	**Black Rock Caravan & Camping Park** Dingwall	01349 830917
39 H3	**Dingwall Camping & Caravanning Club Site** Dingwall	01349 862236
39 H3	**Torvean Caravan Park** Inverness	01463 220582
40 A1	**Dornoch Caravan & Camping Park** Dornoch	01862 810423
40 A1	**Dornoch Firth Caravan Park** Tain Dornoch	01862 892292
40 A1	**Grannies Heilan Hame Holiday Park** Dornoch	08716 412045
40 A3	**Culloden Moor** Inverness	01463 790625
40 A3	**Nairn Camping and Caravanning Club Site** Nairn	01667 455281
40 A3	**Nairn Lochloy Holiday Park** Nairn	08716 412045
40 A3	**Rosemarkie Camping & Caravanning Club Site** Fortrose	01381 621117
40 A4	**Auchnahillin Caravan & Camping Park** Inverness	01463 772286
40 A5	**Speyside Leisure Park** Aviemore	01479 810236
40 B4	**Grantown-On-Spey Caravan Park** Grantown-On-Spey	01479 872474
40 B5	**Glenmore Caravan & Camping Site** Aviemore	01479 861271
40 B5	**Loch Garten Lodges & Caravan Park** Boat of Garten	01479 831769
40 B5	**Osprey Caravan Park** Boat of Garten	01479 831380
40 C3	**Aberlour Gardens Caravan & Camping Park** Aberlour on Spey	01340 871586
40 C3	**Speyside by Craigellachie Camping & Caravanning Club Site** Aberlour	01340 810414
40 C6	**The Invercauld** Ballater	01339 741373
40 D5	**Tarland By Deeside Camping & Caravanning Club Site** Aboyne	01339 881388
41 E2	**Sandend Caravan Park** Portsoy	01261 842660
41 E3	**Huntly Castle Caravan Park** Huntly	01466 794999
41 E6	**Feughside Caravan Park** Banchory	01330 850669
41 E6	**Silver Ladies Caravan Park** Banchory	01330 822800
41 F2	**Myrus Caravan & Holiday Park** Macduff	01261 812845
41 F2	**Wester Bonnyton Farm** Banff	01261 832470
41 F5	**Hillhead Caravan Park** Inverurie	01467 632809
41 F6	**Silverbank** Banchory	01330 822477
43 F5	**Dalchalm** Brora	01408 621479
44 E3	**Laxdale Holiday Park** Isle of Lewis	01851 706966
47 E1	**Ballyness Caravan Park** Bushmills	02820 732393
47 E1	**Silvercliffs Holiday Village** Ballycastle	02820 762550
47 E1	**Tullans Park Caravan Park** Coleraine	02870 342309
47 F3	**Six Mile Water Caravan Park** Antrim	02894 464963
47 F4	**Lakeside View Caravan Park** Annahilt Hillsborough	02892 682098
47 F5	**Cranfield Caravan Park** Kilkeel	02841 762572
47 G3	**Ballyferris Holiday Park** Ballywalter	07801 228814
47 G4	**Delamont Country Park Camping and Caravanning Club** Killyleagh	02844 821833

Forum of Mobility Centres (sidebar)
Shopmobility (sidebar)

Pg	Ref	Town name	Mobility centre name	Telephone No.
9	E3	Aylesford	Dart Driving Assessment & Advice Service	01622 795719
			Cobtree Ward, Preston Ward Hospital, London Road	
47	F3	Belfast	Northern Ireland Mobility Centre	02890 297880
			Disability Action, Portside Bus Pk,	
12	D1	Birmingham	Regional Driving Assessment Centre	01216 278228
			West Heath Hospital, Rednal Road,	
22	A6	Bodelwyddan	North Wales Mobility & Driving Assessment Service	01745 584858
			North Wales Resources Centre, Glan Clwyd Hospital	
12	B6	Bristol	Mobility Service of the Disabled Living Centre	01179 659353
			The Vassall Centre, Gill Avenue, Fishponds	
11	H6	Cardiff	South Wales Mobility & Driving Assessment Service	02920 555130
			Rookwood Hospital, Fairwater Road, Llandaff	
14	B6	Carshalton	Queen Elizabeth's Foundation Mobility Centre	02087 701151
			Damson Way, Fountain Drive	
13	H6	Crowthorne	Mobility Advice & Vehicle Information Service (MAVIS)	01344 661000
			Crowthorne Bus East, Old Wokingham Road	
19	E3	Derby	Derby DrivAbility Centre	01332 371929
			Kingsway Hospital, Kingsway,	
32	C2	Edinburgh	Scottish Driving Assessment Service	01315 379192
			Astley Ainslie Hospital, Grange Loan,	
24	A3	Leeds	William Merritt Disabled Living Centre & Mobility Service	01133 055288
			St. Mary's Hospital, Green Hill Road, Armley	
13	G4	Oxford	Oxford Driving Assessment Service	01865 227600
			Oxford Centre for Enablement, Headington,	
20	D5	Thetford	Kilverstone Mobility Assessment Centre	01842 753029
			2 Napier Place	
3	G4	Truro	Cornwall Mobility Centre	01872 254920
			Tehidy House, Royal Cornwall Hospital	
14	B4	Welwyn Garden City	Hertfordshire Action on Disability Mobility Centre	01707 324581
			The Woodside Centre, The Commons	
22	D4	Wigan	Wrightington Mobility Centre	01257 256409
			Wrightington Hospital, Hall Lane, Appley Bridge	

Shopmobility ♿

Pg	Ref	Town name	Shopmobility name	Telephone No.
11	H4	Abergavenny	Abergavenny Shopmobility	0800 2983656
			One Stop Shop, Town Hall	
16	C6	Aberystwyth	Ceredigion Mobile Shopmobility	01239 811150
			The Portacabin, Bath Street Car Park	
23	E3	Accrington	Accrington Shopmobility	01254 388388
			45 - 47 Whalley Road	
19	E2	Alfreton	Alfreton Shopmobility	01773 835199
			Alfreton House, High Street	
23	E5	Altrincham	Trafford Access Grp	01619 291714
			Trafford Shopmobility & Access Group, Regent Road Car Park	
7	F2	Andover	Andover Shopmobility	01264 352000
			Bus Station, West Street	
9	F3	Ashford	Ashford Shopmobility	01233 650063
			Vicarage Lane Car Park, Vicarage Lane	
23	F5	Ashton-under-Lyne	Ashton-under-Lyne Shopmobility	0161 3399500
			Old Cross Street	
5	G4	Axminster	Axminster Shopmobility	01297 34684
			Launch Pad, Leacombe	
13	H4	Aylesbury	Aylesbury Shopmobility	01296 336725
			Civic Centre Car Park, Exchange Street	
31	G5	Ayr	Ayr Shopmobility	01292 618086
			33 Carrick Street	
47	E2	Ballymena	Ballymena Ltd	02825 638822
			The Tower Centre, Wellington Street	
47	G3	Bangor	Bangor Shopmobility	02891 456586
			The Arcade, 55-59 High Street	
14	C5	Barking	Barking & Dagenham Shopmobility	020 8252 5340
			51 Ripple Road	
24	B4	Barnsley	Barnsley Shopmobility	01226 786006
			3 Shambles Street	
4	D2	Barnstaple	North Devon Shopmobility	01271 328866
			Albert Lane	
22	B1	Barrow in Furness	Furness Shopmobility	01229 434039
			Oldham Street Car Park, School Street	
15	E5	Basildon	Basildon Shopmobility	01268 533644
			Eastgate Shopping Centre, 7/8 Eastgate Business Centre	
7	G2	Basingstoke	Basingstoke Shopmobility	01256 476066
			Church Street	
12	C6	Bath	Bath and North East Somerset Shopmobility	01225 481744
			7-9 Lower Borough Wall	
14	A2	Bedford	Bedford Shopmobility	01234 348000
			1 The Howard Centre, Horne Lane	
47	F3	Belfast	Belfast Shopmobility	02890 808090
			2 Queen Street	
14	C6	Bexley Heath	Bexley Heath Shopmobility	020 8301 5237
			The Car Park (BHS End), The Broadway	
22	C5	Birkenhead	Birkenhead Shopmobility	0151 6476162
			5 St John Street	
18	C5	Birmingham	Birmingham Shopmobility	0121 2368980
			Snow Hill Railway Station, 7 Colmore Row	
18	C5	Birmingham	Birmingham Shopmobility	0121 6162942
			Level 2, Centre Car Park	
22	D3	Blackburn and Darwen	Baddag Shopmobility	01254 262309
			Blackburn Market, Ainsworth Street	
22	C3	Blackpool	Blackpool (South Shore) Shopmobility	01253 349427
			300 Lytham Road, Blackpool (South Shore)	
22	C3	Blackpool	South Shore Shopmobility	01253 349427
			300 Lytham Road, South Shore	
8	A6	Bognor Regis	Bognor Regis Shopmobility	01243 830077
			Old Fire Station, Town Hall	
23	E4	Bolton	Bolton Shopmobility	01204 392946
			The Archways, Le Mans Cresent	
20	B2	Boston	Boston Shopmobility	01205 315936
			Boston Community Transport, The Len Medlock Centre	
7	E5	Bournemouth	Boscombe Shopmobility	01202 399700
			Sovereign Centre, Sovereign Centre	
7	E5	Bournemouth	Bournemouth Shopmobility	01202 598295
			Ground Level Car Park, Castlepoint	
13	H6	Bracknell	Bracknell Shopmobility	01344 861316
			2 Crossway	
24	A3	Bradford	The Oastler Centre	01274 754076
11	G6	Bridgend	Bridgend Shopmobility	01656 667992
			Level F Rhiw Car Park, Bridgend Borough County Council	
5	G2	Bridgwater	Bridgwater Shopmobility	01278 434254
			52 Clare Street	
18	C5	Brierly Hill	Merry Hill Shopmobility	01384 487911
			Merry Hill	
8	C5	Brighton	Brighton & Hove Shopmobility	01273 323239
			Grenville Street	
12	B6	Bristol	Bristol Broadmead Shopmobility	01179 226342
			The Galleries, 26 Castle Gallery	
5	F6	Brixham	Brixham Shopmobility	01803 521771
			C/o Barclays Bank, Central Car Park	
15	H6	Broadstairs	Broadstairs Shopmobility	01843 871444
			Mobility Store, Westwood Cross Shopping Centre	
14	C6	Bromley	Bromley Shopmobility	020 8313 0031
			The Glades Car Park, High Street	
12	D1	Bromsgrove	Bromsgrove Shopmobility	01527 837736
			Churchfields Multi-Storey Car Park, Churchfields	
18	D3	Burton Upon Trent	Burton Upon Trent Shopmobility	01283 515191
			Unit 35a, Octagon Shopping Centre	
23	E4	Bury	Bury Shopmobility	0161 7649966
			34 Minden Parade	
15	E1	Bury St Edmunds	Bury St Edmunds Shopmobility	01284 757175
			Tourist Information Centre, 6 Angel Hill	
12	A5	Caldicot	Caldicot Shopmobility	01291 430230
			Jubilee Way Car Park, Jubilee Way	
14	C2	Cambridge	Cambridge Shopmobility	01223 457452
			Park Street Car Park, Park Street	
14	C2	Cambridge	Cambridge Shopmobility	01223 461858
			Level 4, East Car Park	
9	G3	Canterbury	Canterbury Shopmobility	01227 459889
			14 Gravel Walk	

Pg Ref	Town name	Shopmobility name	Telephone No.
11 H6	**Cardiff**	**Cardiff Shopmobility** Oxford Arcade Car Park, David Street	02920 399355
27 H3	**Carlisle**	**Carlisle Shopmobility** Level 2 - The Lanes Car Park, Lowther Street	01228 625950
47 F3	**Carrickfergus**	**Carrickfergus Shopmobility** 10c High Street	02893 368415
15 E6	**Chatham**	**Chatham (Medway)** The Brook Multi Storey Car Park , Solomans Road	01634 830555
15 E4	**Chelmsford**	**Chelmsford** Market Road Public Convenience, Market Road	01245 250467
15 E4	**Chelmsford**	**Meadows Shopping Centre** 45-47 High Street	01245 357097
12 D3	**Cheltenham**	**Cheltenham Shopmobility** Level 1, Beechwood Shopping Centre	01242 255333
22 C6	**Chester**	**Chester Shopmobility** Dial House Shopmobility Service, Frodsham Street Car Park	01244 312626
24 B6	**Chesterfield**	**Chesterfield and District Shopmobility** Ground Floor Multi Storey Car Park, New Beetwell St.	01246 559331
7 H4	**Chichester**	**Chichester Shopmobility** East Pallant Car Park	07932 802778
22 D4	**Chorley**	**Chorley & South Ribble Shopmobility** Flat Iron Car Park, Union Street	01257 260888
7 E5	**Christchurch**	**Christchurch Mobile Shopmobility** c/o Poole Shopmobility, Wheels for Freedom, Pioneer Car Park (rear)	01202 661770
15 G4	**Clacton-on-Sea**	**Clacton & Tendring Shopmobility** 114 Pier Avenue	01255 435566
32 A2	**Coatbridge**	**Coatbridge (North Lanarkshire) Shopmobility** Exchange Place	01236 605795
15 F3	**Colchester**	**Colchester Shopmobility** 15 Queen Street	01206 505256
16 D2	**Conwy**	**Colwyn Bay Shopmobility** Conwy Community Transport, 44 Sea View Road	01492 533822
13 F1	**Coventry**	**Coventry Shopmobility** Barracks Car Park, Upper Precinct	02476 832020
8 B4	**Crawley**	**Crawley Shopmobility** County Mall, Station Way	01293 522852
18 B2	**Crewe**	**Crewe Shopmobility** Victoria Car Park, Adjacent to Asda, Victoria Street	01270 580031
14 C6	**Croydon**	**Croydon Shopmobility** Whitgift Car Park, Wellesley Road	020 8688 7336
11 H5	**Cwmbran**	**Cwmbran (Torfaen) Shopmobility** 32 Gwent Square (opposite Library)	01633 874686
28 D5	**Darlington**	**Darlington Association on Disability** 20-22 Horsemarket Darlington	01325 489999
13 G1	**Daventry**	**Daventry Shopmobility** New Street	01327 312555
19 E3	**Derby**	**Derby Shopmobility** Eagle Centre Car Park, Moreledge	01332 200320
46 C2	**Derry**	**Foyle Shopmobility** Foyleside Shopping Centre, Orchard Street	02871 368623
5 F4	**Devon**	**Exeter Shopmobility** Deck F - King William Street Car Park, King William Street	01392 494001
24 A3	**Dewsbury**	**Dewsbury Shopmobility** Kirklees Metropolitan Council, Social Services Info Point	01924 325070
24 C4	**Doncaster**	**Doncaster Shopmobility** South Mall Frenchgate Centre, St Sepulchre Gate	01302 361966
6 B5	**Dorchester**	**Dorchester Mobile Shopmobility** c/o Poole Shopmobility, Charles Street	01202 661770
37 E3	**Dundee**	**Dundee Shopmobility** Overgate Centre	01382 228525
28 D3	**Durham**	**Durham Shopmobility** Level 1 Car Park, Prince Bishop`s Shopping Centre	01913 868556
8 D6	**Eastbourne**	**Eastbourne Shopmobility** Arndale Centre, Terminus Road	01323 439585
7 F4	**Eastleigh**	**Eastleigh Shopmobility** Swan Centre, Wells Place	02380 902402
32 C2	**Edinburgh**	**Leith (Lothian) Shopmobility** Level 3 - Red Car Park, Ocean Terminal, Ocean Drive	01315 558888
32 C2	**Edinburgh (West)**	**Edinburgh West (Lothian) Shopmobility** Unit 42D, The Gyle Shopping Centre	01313 171460
40 C2	**Elgin**	**Moray Shopmobility** 55 High Street	01343 552528
20 C5	**Ely**	**Ely Shopmobility** Ely Museum, The Old Gaol	01353 666655
14 C5	**Enfield**	**Enfield Shopmobility** 10 Little Park Gardens	020 8366 8081
14 B6	**Epsom and Ewel**	**Epsom and Ewel Shopmobility** Ashley Centre Car Park, Ashley Avenue	01372 727086
12 D2	**Evesham**	**Riverside Shopmobility** Top Level, Multi Storey Car Park	01386 49230
32 A2	**Falkirk**	**Central Shopmobility (Falkirk)** Level 4 Car Park, Callendar Square Shopping Centre	01324 630500
3 G5	**Falmouth**	**Falmouth Shopmobility** c/o Marks and Spencer, 44 Market Street	01326 313553
7 G4	**Fareham**	**Fareham Shopmobility** Multi-Storey Car Park , Osborne Road	01329 282929
9 G4	**Folkestone**	**Satellite Scheme of Poole Shopmobility** 7 Town Walk	01303 226500
35 G1	**Fort William**	**Lochaber Shopmobility** Port-a-Cabin, Travel Centre	01397 700051
28 D2	**Gateshead**	**Gateshead (Metrocentre)** Metrocentre Shopping Centre	0191 4605299
28 D2	**Gateshead**	**Gateshead Shopmobility** Gateshead Shopping Centre	0191 4779888
31 H3	**Glasgow**	**Braehead Shopmobility** Kingsinch Road	01418 854630
31 H4	**Glasgow**	**East Kilbride Shopmobility** Centre West	01355 571300
23 F5	**Glossop**	**Glossop and High Peak Shopmobility** 2 Chapel Street	01457 861635
12 C4	**Gloucester**	**Gloucester Shopmobility** 1 Hampden Way	01452 302871
24 D3	**Goole**	**Coalition Shopmobility** The Courtyard, Boothferry Road	01405 837113
7 G5	**Gosport**	**Gosport Shopmobility** Gosport Shopmobility, Bus Station, South Street	02392 502692
14 D6	**Grays**	**Thurrock Shopmobility** Lakeside Shopping Mall, West Thurrock Way	01708 869933
14 D6	**Greenhithe**	**Bluewater Shopmobility** Lower Thames Walk, Bluewater Shopping Centre	01322 427427
8 A3	**Guildford**	**Guildford Shopmobility** Level 3 - Bedford Road Car Park	01483 453993
32 A3	**Hamilton**	**Hamilton Shopmobility** First Floor Car Park, Newcross Centre	01698 459955
14 C4	**Harlow**	**Harlow Shopmobility** Post Office Road	01279 419196
24 B2	**Harrogate**	**Harrogate Shopmobility** Level 10, East Parade, Victoria Car Park	01423 556778
14 B5	**Harrow**	**Harrow Shopmobility** 37 St Georges Centre, St Ann`s Road	020 8427 1200
29 F4	**Hartlepool**	**Hartlepool Shopmobility** Middleton Grange Shopping Centre	01429 861777
9 E5	**Hastings**	**Hastings Shopmobility** Priory Meadows Shopping Centre , Queens Road	01424 447847
14 B4	**Hatfield**	**Hatfield Shopmobility** The rear of The Bill Salmon Centre, 88 Town Centre	01707 262731
7 H4	**Havant**	**Havant Shopmobility** 47 Market Parade	02392 455444
14 D2	**Haverhill**	**Haverhill Shopmobility** Borough Offices, Lower Downs Slade	01440 858051
14 A4	**Hemel Hempstead**	**Hemel Hempstead Shopmobility** Level A Blue Car Park, Marlowes Centre	01442 259259
12 B2	**Hereford**	**Hereford Shopmobility** Maylord Orchards Car Park, Blueschool Street	01432 342166
15 G6	**Herne Bay**	**Herne Bay Shopmobility** Beach House, Beach Street	01227 372487
13 H5	**High Wycombe**	**High Wycombe Shopmobility** Level 2 - Newland Car Park, Eden	01494 472277
19 E5	**Hinckley**	**Hinckley Shopmobility** Hinckley Shopmobility 2nd Level Car Park, The Britannia Centre	01455 633920
14 B3	**Hitchin**	**Hitchin Shopmobility** Waitrose Supermarket, Bedford Road	01462 423399
5 G3	**Honiton**	**Honiton Shopmobility** 29-31 New Street	01404 46529
8 B4	**Horsham**	**Horsham Shopmobility** Level 2, Swan Walk Car Park	01403 249015
14 B6	**Hounslow**	**Hounslow Shopmobility** Blenheim Centre, Prince Regent Road	020 8570 3343
24 A4	**Huddersfield**	**Huddersfield (Kingsgate) Shopmobility** Level 1 Car Park, Kingsgate Shopping Centre	01484 559006
24 A4	**Huddersfield**	**Huddersfield Shopmobility** Gateway to Care, Shopmobility and Equipment	01484 416666

Shopmobility

Pg	Ref	Town name Shopmobility name	Telephone No.

25 E3 **Hull** Kingston Upon Hull — 01482 225686
Level 2 - Princes Quay Shopping Centre Car Park

14 C5 **Ilford** Redbridge Shopmobility — 020 8478 6864
Exchange Car Park, The Exchange Mall

19 E2 **Ilkeston** Ilkeston Shopmobility — 01159 324956
Shopmobility Centre, High Street (near museum)

31 F3 **Inverclyde** Inverclyde Shopmobility — 01475 732600
10 Clyde Square, Greenock

39 H3 **Inverness** Highland Shopmobility — 01463 717624
Falcon Gallery, Car Park Level 2

15 G2 **Ipswich** Ipswich Shopmobility — 01473 222225
Buttermarket Shopping Centre, Buttermarket Shopping Centre

26 C6 **Isle of Man** CIRCA Shopmobility — 01624 613713
Chester Street Car Par, Douglas

5 H6 **Jersey** St Helier Shopmobility — 01534 739672
Lower Ground Floor, Sand Street Car Park

28 A6 **Kendal** Kendal & South Lakes Shopmobility — 01539 740933
Level 3, Westmoreland Shopping Centre Car Park

13 H1 **Kettering** Kettering Shopmobility — 01536 412886
Wadcroft Car Park, Wadcroft Car Park

14 B6 **Kingston upon Thames** Kingston Upon Thames Shopmobility — 020 8547 1255
Eden Walk Car Park, Eden Walk Car Park

32 C1 **Kirkcaldy** Fife Shopmobility — 01592 583248
Mercat Centre Car Park, Tolbooth Street

8 B3 **Leatherhead** Leatherhead Shopmobility — 01372 362400
Level 2, Swan Centre

12 C3 **Ledbury** Individual Living Mobility Scheme — 01531 636001
St. Katherines Car Park

24 A2 **Leeds** Otley Shopmobility — 01943 466335
Civic Centre, Cross Green, Otley

24 A3 **Leeds** Leeds (White Rose) Shopmobility — 01132 773636
White Rose Shopping Centre, Dewsbury Road

24 B3 **Leeds** Leeds Shopmobility — 01132 460125
Unit 92, Merrion Centre

19 F4 **Leicester** Leicester Shopmobility — 01162 532596
Shires Shopping Centre, Level 2 Car Park, High Street

22 D5 **Leigh** Leigh (Wigan) Shopmobility — 01942 777985
Leigh Market Hall, Spinning Gate Shopping Centre

12 A2 **Leominster** Leominster Shopmobility — 01568 616755
6 Morris Mews

14 C6 **Lewisham** Lewisham Shopmobility — 020 8297 2735
29 Molesworth Street

18 D4 **Lichfield** Lichfield Shopmobility — 01543 308999
Multi Storey Car Park, Castle Dyke

25 E6 **Lincoln** Lincoln Shopmobility — 01522 514477
Lincoln Area Dial-a-Ride, The Bus Station, Melville Street

47 F4 **Lisburn** Lisburn Shopmobility — 02892 677557
Lisburn Shopmobility, Sprucefield Centre,

8 A5 **Littlehampton** Littlehampton Shopmobility — 01903 733004
1-5 St Martins Lane

22 C5 **Liverpool** Liverpool Shopmobility — 01517 070877
St John's Centre, 131 St George's Way

32 B2 **Livingston** Livingston (Lothian) Shopmobility — 01506 442744
Unit 95, Almondvale Shopping Centre

14 B5 **London** Brent Cross Shopping Centre — 020 8457 4070
Brent Cross

14 B5 **London** Camden Shopmobility — 020 7482 5503
29a Pratt Street, London Camden

14 B5 **London** Kensington and Chelsea Shopmobility — 020 8960 8774
Out and About, Westway Community Transport, Acklam Road

14 B6 **London** Wandsworth Shopmobility — 020 8875 9585
45 Garratt Lane, Wandsworth

14 C5 **London** Waltham Forest Shopmobility — 020 8520 3366
Selborne Walk Shopping Centre, 45 Selborne Walk

19 E3 **Long Eaton** Long Eaton Shopmobility — 01159 316058
New Street

19 F4 **Loughborough** Loughborough Shopmobility — 01509 634706
Loughborough Town Hall, Market Place

21 H5 **Lowestoft** Lowestoft Shopmobility — 01502 588857
Lowestoft Station, Denmark Road

14 A3 **Luton** Luton Shopmobility — 01582 738936
Level 3 Market Car Park, Arndale Centre

23 F6 **Macclesfield** Macclesfield Shopmobility — 01625 613111
Great King Street, Churchill Way

47 E3 **Magherafelt** Magherafelt Shopmobility — 02879 300414
Meadowlane Shopping Centre, Money More Road

13 H5 **Maidenhead** Maidenhead Shopmobility — 01628 543038
Nicholsons Car Park, The Broadway

9 E3 **Maidstone** Maidstone Shopmobility — 01622 692110
Chequers Centre Management Office, Pads Hill

23 E5 **Manchester** Manchester (Trafford Centre) Shopmobility
Scootamart Ltd, Peel Avenue — 01617 478046

23 E5 **Manchester** Manchester (Wythenshawe) Shopmobility
Manchester Community Transport Ltd, — 01614 373600
The Forum Centre, Poundswick Lane

23 E5 **Manchester** Manchester Shopmobility — 01618 394060
L18 New Arkwright Way, Arndale Centre

24 C6 **Mansfield** Mansfield Shopmobility — 01623 655222
Walkden Street Car Park, (over Tesco Supermarket), Walkden Street

19 G5 **Market Harborough** Market Harborough Shopmobility
HDC Offices, Adam & Eve Street — 01858 410864

13 H5 **Marlow** Marlow Shopmobility — 01628 405218
Court Garden, Pound Lane

19 G4 **Melton Mowbray** Melton Shopmobility — 01664 480677
Tourist Information Centre, 7 King Street

11 G4 **Merthyr Tydfil** Merthyr Tydfil Shopmobility — 01685 373237
St Tydfil Square

29 E4 **Middlesbrough** Middlesbrough Shopmobility — 01642 254545
1st Floor Car Park, Hillstreet

32 A3 **Motherwell** Motherwell (North Lanarkshire) Shopmobility
89 Merry Street — 01698 303199

11 F5 **Neath** Neath Port Talbot Shopmobility — 01639 637372
High Street Car Park

23 E3 **Nelson** Nelson Shopmobility — 01282 692502
Marsden Resource Centre , Rigby Street

13 F6 **Newbury** Newbury Shopmobility — 01635 523854
1 Bolton Place, 1 Bolton Place

29 E2 **Newcastle** South Shields Shopmobility — 01914 546286
35 Mile End Road, South Shields

12 A5 **Newport** Newport Shopmobility — 01633 673845
193 Upper Dock Street

47 E5 **Newry** Newry Shopmobility — 02830 256062
Buttercrane Shopping Centre, Buttercrane Quay

5 E5 **Newton Abbot** Newton Abbot Shopmobility — 01626 335775
Multi Storey Car Park, Sherborne Road

47 G3 **Newtownards** Ards Shopmobility — 02891 814952
19 Court Street

13 H1 **Northampton** Northampton Ability Northants — 01604 233714
Greyfriars Car Park, Greyfriars

22 D6 **Northwich** Northwich Vale Royal Disability Services
The Info Centre, 1 The Arcade — 01606 353525

21 F4 **Norwich** Norwich Shopmobility — 01603 753350
Car Park Level 1, Chapelfield

21 F4 **Norwich** Norwich Shopmobility — 01603 766430
2 Castle Mall

19 F2 **Nottingham** Arnold Shopmobility — 01159 661331
Croft Road Car Park, Arnold

19 F3 **Nottingham** Beeston Shopmobility — 01159 173788
Ground Floor, Multi storey Car Park, Styring Street

19 F3 **Nottingham** Notts Broad Marsh Shopmobility — 01159 153888
St Nicholas Centre, Stanford Street

19 F3 **Nottingham** West Bridgford Shopmobility — 01159 815451
Bridgford Road Car Park (next to public library), West Bridgford

24 D5 **Nottingham** Retford Shopmobility — 01777 705432
Chancery Lane Car Park, Retford

19 E5 **Nuneaton** Nuneaton & Bedworth Shopmobility — 02476 325908
Ropewalk Multi Storey Car Park, Coton Road

35 E3 **Oban** Oban Shopmobility — 01631 567150
Station Car Park

23 F4 **Oldham** Oldham Promobility — 01616 330040
St Marys Way

46 C3 **Omagh** Omagh Shopmobility — 02882 240772
Omagh Volunteer Bureau, 2 Drumragh Avenue

22 C4 **Ormskirk** West Lancashire (Ormskirk) Shopmobility
Two Saints Place, Park Road — 01695 570055

14 C6 **Orpington** Orpington Shopmobility — 01689 833796
241 High Street

17 F4 **Oswestry** Oswestry Shopmobility — 01691 656882
Oswestry Community Action Qube Queens Building, Oswald Road

13 G4 **Oxford** Oxford Shopmobility — 01865 248737
Level 1A - Westgate Multi-storey Car Park, Norfolk Street

13 G4 **Oxford** Templars Square Shopping Centre — 01865 748867
129 Pound Way Cowley

Pg Ref	Town name	Shopmobility name	Telephone No.
13 G3	**Oxon**	**Bicester Shopmobility**	01869 320132
		Crown Walk, Bicester	
5 E5	**Paignton**	**Paignton Shopmobility**	01803 521771
		Victoria Car Park, Garfield Road	
31 G3	**Paisley**	**Paisley and District**	01418 890441
		The Paisley Centre Multi-Storey Car Park, Storie Street	
13 F1	**Park Street**	**Leamington Spa Shopmobility**	01926 470450
		Leamington Spa Shopmobility Level 4, Royal Priors Car Park	
28 A4	**Penrith**	**Eden Shopmobility**	01768 895438
		The Resource Centre, The Resource Centre	
3 E5	**Penzance**	**Penzance Shopmobility**	01736 351792
		The Light and Life Centre, Wharfside Shopping Centre, Market Jew Street	
36 D3	**Perth**	**Perth and Kinross Shopmobility**	01738 783960
		Canal Street Multi-Storey Car Park, Canal Street	
20 A5	**Peterborough**	**Peterborough Council for Voluntary Service**	
		Level 11 - Queensgate Centre Car Park	01733 313133
41 G3	**Peterhead**	**Peterhead Shopmobility**	07748 532242
		Car Park, Maiden Street	
7 H3	**Petersfield**	**Petersfield Shopmobility**	01730 710474
		SDADP, Central Car Park, Park Road	
36 C2	**Pitlochry**	**Highland Perthshire Shopmobility**	01796 473866
		Atholl Leisure Centre, Atholl Leisure Centre, West Moulin Road	
4 C6	**Plymouth**	**Plymouth Shopmobility**	01752 600 633
		Mayflower East Car Park, Mayflower Street	
6 D5	**Poole**	**Poole Shopmobility**	01202 661770
		Level B Multi Storey Car Park, Kingland Cresent	
11 F5	**Port Talbot**	**Port Talbot Shopmobility**	01639 637372
		Aberafan Shopping Centre	
7 G4	**Portsmouth**	**Portsmouth Shopmobility**	02392 816973
		56 Arundel Street	
22 D3	**Preston**	**Preston (The Mobility Centre)**	01772 204667
		28 Friargate	
13 H6	**Reading**	**The Oracle Shopmobility**	01189 659008
		The Management Suite, The Oracle Shopping Centre	
29 F4	**Redcar**	**Redcar Shopmobility**	01642 498894
		2 Pybus Place , The Esplanade	
12 D1	**Redditch**	**Redditch Shopmobility**	01527 63271
		Car Park 3, Kingfisher Centre	
8 B3	**Redhill**	**Redhill Shopmobility**	01737 772718
		The Belfry Shopping Centre	
22 A5	**Rhyl**	**Rhyl Shopmobility**	01745 350665
		155 High Street	
23 E4	**Rochdale**	**Rochdale Borough Shopmobility**	01706 925986
		Unit 3, Bus Station Concourse	
14 D5	**Romford**	**Havering (Liberty) Shopmobility**	01708 765764
		South Mall, The Liberty Shopping Centre	
14 D5	**Romford**	**Havering (The Brewery) Shopmobility**	01708 722570
		The Brewery	
22 D5	**Runcorn**	**Halton Lea (Runcorn) Shopmobility**	01928 717445
		Halton Disability Services , 102 River Walk Halton Lea	
7 E3	**Salisbury**	**Salisbury Shopmobility**	01722 328068
		3B Priory Square, The Maltings	
18 C5	**Sandwell**	**Sandwell Shopmobility**	0121 5531943
		Ground Floor Multi Storey Car Park, Sandwell Shopping Centre	
29 H6	**Scarborough**	**Scarborough Shopmobility**	01723 369910
		5 Somerset Terrace	
24 B5	**Sheffield**	**West Hill Lane car Park**	01142 812278
		Eldon Street, Off West Street	
24 B5	**Sheffield**	**Meadowhall Shopmobility**	0845 6006800
		Management Suite	
17 G5	**Shrewsbury**	**Shrewsbury Shopmobility**	01743 236900
		The Raven Meadows Multi Storey Car Park, Raven Meadows	
22 C4	**Skelmersdale**	**West Lancashire (Skelmersdale) Shopmobility**	
		Concourse Shopping Centre	01695 570055
14 A6	**Slough**	**Slough Shopmobility**	01753 691133
		Alpha Street North	
13 E1	**Solihull**	**Solihull Shopmobility**	0121 7040380
		19 Drury Lane	
7 F4	**Southampton**	**Southampton (West Quay) Shopmobility**	
		Podium Car Park Level 2, West Quay Shopping Centre	02380 636100
7 F4	**Southampton**	**Southampton Shopmobility**	02380 631263
		7 Castle Way	
22 C4	**Southport**	**Southport Link**	01704 546654
		Tulketh Street	
14 B4	**St Albans**	**St Albans Shopmobility**	01727 819339
		Drover's Way Car Park, off Catherine Street	
22 D5	**St Helens**	**St Helens Shopmobility**	01744 613388
		Chalon Way Multi Storey Car Park, Chalon Way Multi Storey Car Park	
18 C3	**Stafford**	**Stafford Shopmobility**	01785 619456
		Broad Street	
14 A6	**Staines**	**Staines Shopmobility**	01784 459416
		Two Rivers Retail Park, Mustard Hill Road	
14 B3	**Stevenage**	**Stevenage Shopmobility**	01438 350300
		15 Queensway	
32 A1	**Stirling**	**Central Shopmobility (Stirling)**	01786 449606
		Bus Station, 19 Goosecroft Road	
23 E5	**Stockport**	**Stockport Shopmobility**	01616 661100
		Level 2 Merseyway Car Park	
29 E5	**Stockton on Tees**	**Stockton on Tees Shopmobility**	01642 605676
		3-5 Bridge Road	
18 B2	**Stoke on Trent**	**Stoke on Trent Shopmobility**	01782 233333
		Potteries Shopping Centre Car Park, Hanley	
15 F2	**Stowmarket**	**Stow Mobility**	01449 616234
		Crowe Street	
13 E2	**Stratford upon Avon**	**Stratford Shopmobility**	01789 414534
		Level 2 Bridge Foot Multi Storey Car Park	
29 E3	**Sunderland**	**Sunderland Shopmobility**	0808 1414266
		101 The Bridges Shopping Centre, Upper Market Square	
14 B6	**Surrey**	**Sutton Shopmobility**	020 87700691
		3rd Floor St Nicholas Centre, St Nicholas Way	
18 D5	**Sutton Coldfield**	**Sutton Coldfield Shopmobility**	0121 3551112
		Gracechurch Shopping Centre, 210A Parade	
18 D4	**Swadlincote**	**Swadlincote Shopmobility**	01283 210770
		10 West Street	
11 E5	**Swansea**	**Swansea Shopmobility**	01792 461785
		Unit 12 St David's Shopping Centre	
13 E5	**Swindon**	**Swindon Shopmobility**	01793 512621
		Wyvern Multi-storey Car Park, Islington Street	
18 D4	**Tamworth**	**Tamworth Shopmobility**	01827 709392
		Ankerside Shopping Centre	
5 G2	**Taunton**	**Taunton Shopmobility**	01823 327900
		Old Market Shoppers Car Park, Paul Street	
5 F5	**Teignmouth**	**Teignmouth Shopmobility**	01626 777775
		Quay Road Car Park, Quay Road	
12 D3	**Tewkesbury**	**Tewkesbury Event Mobility (Mobile Unit)**	
		8 Bayliss Road, Kemerton	01368 725391
5 F3	**Tiverton**	**Tiverton (Mid Devon) Shopmobility**	01884 242099
		Phoenix Lane Multi Storey Car Park	
5 F5	**Torquay**	**Torquay Shopmobility**	01803 380982
		1 Lymington Road	
8 D4	**Tunbridge Wells**	**Tunbridge Wells Shopmobility**	01892 544355
		125-A Royal Victoria Place	
14 A5	**Uxbridge**	**Hillingdon Shopmobility**	01895 271510
		Car Park Level 2, The Chimes Shopping Centre, High Street	
24 B3	**Wakefield**	**Wakefield Shopmobility**	01924 787788
		Ridings Shopping Centre	
22 C5	**Wallasey**	**Wirral Shopmobility**	01516 701600
		Liscard Crescent	
28 D2	**Wallsend**	**North Tyneside Shopmobility**	01912 635029
		Wallsend Peoples Centre, 10 Frank Street	
18 C5	**Walsall**	**Walsall Shop Mobility**	01922 860653
		71 Hillary Street	
6 D5	**Wareham**	**LifeWheels Mobility Centre**	01929 552623
		St Johns Hill	
6 C2	**Warminster**	**Warminster Shopmobility**	01985 217438
		CAB Building, Central Car Park	
22 D5	**Warrington**	**Warrington (Birchwood)**	01925 822411
		Birchwood Shopping Centre, 49 Dewhurst Road	
22 D5	**Warrington**	**Warrington (South)**	01925 231941
		Golden Square Shopping Centre, Legh Street	
14 B5	**Wealdstone**	**Wealdstone Shopmobility**	020 8427 1200
		3 Peel House, Gladstone Way	
13 H1	**Wellingborough**	**Wellingborough Shopmobility**	01933 228844
		1 Orient Way	
14 B4	**Welwyn Garden Centre**	**Welwyn Hatfield (Howard Centre) Shopmobility**	01707 336688
		The Howard Centre	
14 B4	**Welwyn/Hatfield**	**Welwyn Hatfield (Galleria) Shopmobility**	
		The Galleria Shopping Centre, Comet Way	01707 278301
6 B6	**Weymouth**	**Weymouth Mobile Shopmobility**	01202 661770
		c/o Poole Shopmobility, Park Street car park, off Commercial Street	

Pg Ref	Town name	Shopmobility name	Telephone No.
22 D4	**Wigan** Wigan Shopmobility Mesnes Terrace Car Park, Mesnes Terrace		01942 776070
6 D4	**Wimborne** Wimborne Mobile Shopmobility c/o Poole Shopmobility, Allenview car park, opposite the Fire Station		01202 661770
7 F3	**Winchester** Winchester Shopmobility Upper Parking, The Brooks Shopping Centre		01962 842626
14 A6	**Windsor** Windsor Shopmobility Peascod Place, off Bachelors Acre		01753 622330
22 D6	**Winsford** Vale Royal Disability Services (Winsford Shopmobility) The Dingle Centre, High Street		01606 557550
8 A3	**Woking** Woking Shopmobility Level 1 The Peacocks Centre, Victoria Way		01483 776612
13 H6	**Wokingham** Wokingham Town Mobility Volunteer Centre , The Old Social Club, Elms Road		01189 770332

Pg Ref	Town name	Shopmobility name	Telephone No.
18 C5	**Wolverhampton** Wolverhampton Shopmobility 12 Cleveland Street		01902 556021
14 C5	**Wood Green** Wood Green Shopmobility 197 High Road		020 8881 5402
12 C2	**Worcester** Worcester Shopmobility Crowngate Centre		01905 610523
24 C6	**Worksop** Bassetlaw Shopmobility Priory Centre		01909 479070
8 B5	**Worthing** Worthing Shopmobility 12-14 Liverpool Gardens		01903 820980
17 G3	**Wrexham** Wrexham Shopmobility Wrexham Bus Station		01978 312390
24 C2	**York** York Shopmobility Level 2 Piccadilly Car Park, The Coppergate Centre, Piccadilly		01904 679222

Wheelchair accessible boats ⚓

Wheelyboat Trust is a registered charity dedicated to providing disabled people with the opportunity and freedom to enjoy waters large and small all over the UK. Their role is to help and encourage venues open to the public to acquire Wheelyboats for their disabled visitors and to help groups and organisations acquire Wheelyboats for their own use. Wheelyboats make the water accessible via the roll-on, roll-off bow ramp and the level deck provides access to every corner of the boat including the helm.

Wheelyboat Trust   www.wheelyboats.org   info@wheelyboats.org   01798 342222   North Lodge, Burton Park, Petworth, West Sussex GU28 0JT

Pg Ref	Town name	Wheelyboat name
31 G3	Alexandria	Carman Trout Fishery
18 D2	Ashbourne	Carsington Water
17 E4	Bala	Maes y Clawdd
47 F3	Ballyclare	Tildarg Fishery
47 F4	Banbridge	Corbet Lough
33 F3	Berwick-upon-Tweed	River Tweed
36 D2	Blairgowrie	Fingask Loch
21 G4	Bradwell	Fritton Lake & Country Park
25 E4	Brigg	Elsham Hall Country Park
5 F2	Brompton Regis	Wimbleball Reservoir
36 C2	Butterstone	Butterstone Loch
19 G5	Caldecott	Eyebrook Reservoir
32 A2	Caldercruix	Hillend Reservoir
36 A4	Callander	Invertrossachs Estate
27 H3	Carlisle	The Tranquil Otter
17 E3	Cerrigydrudion	Llyn Brenig
24 B6	Chesterfield	Press Manor Fishery
12 B6	Chew Magna	Blagdon Lake
12 B6	Chew Stoke	Chew Stoke
32 B1	Clackmannan	Gartmorn Country Park Alloa
4 B5	Commonmoor	Siblyback lake
23 E6	Congleton	Westlow Mere
39 G3	Dingwall	Loch Achonachie
12 D1	Droitwich	Upton Warren Sailing Lake
47 E4	Dungannon	Parklake Fishery
36 C2	Dunkeld	Butterstone Loch
43 G2	Dunnet	St John's Loch
8 D5	Eastbourne	Arlington Reservoir
17 G4	Ellesmere	Ellesmere, The Mere
5 F4	Exeter Canal	Exeter MS Society
10 B3	Haverfordwest	Llys-y-Fran Reservoir
27 H6	Hawkeshead	Esthwaite Water
21 G4	Hemsby	Eels Foot Inn, Rollesby Broad
28 C2	Hexham	Hallington Reservoirs
16 B1	Holyhead	Llyn Alaw
4 D1	Kentisbury	Wistlandpound Resvr
28 A1	Kielder Water	Leaplish Waterside Park
28 B1	Kielder Water	Kielder Water
24 B1	Knaresborough	Farmire Fishery
8 D4	Lamberhurst	Bewl Water
11 E2	Lampeter	Teglan Fishery (River Aeron)
11 E2	Lampeter	Celtic Lakes Resort
32 B3	Lanark	Newmill Trout Fisheries
4 C4	Launceston	Roadford Reservoir Okehampton
13 E4	Lechlade	Bushyleaze Trout Fishery

Pg Ref	Town name	Wheelyboat name
24 B2	Leeds	Harewood House Lake
19 E4	Leicester	Thornton Reservoir
29 F5	Lingdale	Lockwood Beck
32 B2	Linlithgow	Linlithgow Loch
46 C5	Lisbellaw	Lisbellaw
16 B2	Llangefni	Llyn Cefni
12 A5	Llantrisant	Wentwood Reservoir
32 C1	Lochore	Lochore Meadows Country Park
42 D6	Lochs Migdale & Shin	Kyle of Sutherland
15 E4	Maldon	Chigboro Fisheries
25 E5	Market Rasen	Toft Newton Reservoir
18 D5	Meriden	Packington Trout Fisheries
28 C1	Morpeth	Fontburn Reservoir
13 H1	Northampton	Pitsford Water
19 H4	Oakham	Rutland Water
18 B4	Pattingham	Pattingham
16 C3	Penygroes	Llyn Nantlle
14 B1	Perry	Grafham Water
12 A5	Pontypool	Llandegfedd Reservoir
31 H1	Port of Menteith	Lake of Menteith
38 B3	Portree	Storr Lochs
38 D2	Portree	Lochs Leathan & Fada
13 G1	Ravensthorpe	Ravensthorpe Reservoir
14 B6	Richmond Park	PHAB Holly Lodge
24 A1	Ripon	Bellflask Fishery
9 E5	Sedlescombe	Powdermill Reservoir
8 C3	Sevenoaks	Bough Beech Reservoir
23 E2	Slaidburn	Stocks Reservoir
15 E5	South Hanningfield	Hanningfield Reservoir
13 E5	Swindon	Coate Water
16 D4	Trawsfynydd	Llyn Trawsfynydd
16 D5	Tywyn	Tal-y-llyn
24 B4	Walton	Walton Hall Trout Fishery
14 C4	Ware	Rib Valley Lake
6 D5	Wareham	River Frome
32 B3	West Calder	Cobbinshaw Loch
18 A3	Whitchurch	Dearnford Lake
18 D3	Willington	Willington Trout Fishery
5 F2	Wiveliscombe	Clatworthy Reservoir
9 E3	Yalding	Maidstone Ex-Services AC
6 B4	Yeovil	Sutton Bingham Reservoir